Korean Americans and Their Religions

Korean Americans and Their Religions

Pilgrims and Missionaries from a Different Shore

Edited by
Ho-Youn Kwon,
Kwang Chung Kim, and
R. Stephen Warner

The Pennsylvania State University Press
University Park, Pennsylvania

Library of Congress Cataloging-in-Publication Data

Korean Americans and their religions : pilgrims and missionaries from a different shore/
edited by Ho-Youn Kwon, Kwang Chung Kim, and R. Stephen Warner.
    p.   cm.
    Includes bibliographical references and index.
    ISBN 0-271-02072-5 (cloth : alk. paper)
    ISBN 0-271-02073-3 (pbk. : alk. paper)
    1. Korean Americans—Religion. 2. Korean Americans—Ethnic identity. 3. United
States—Church history—20th century. 4. United States—Religion—20th century.
    I. Kwon, Ho Youn. II. Kim, Kwang Chung, 1937– III. Warner, R. Stephen.

BL2525.K67 2001
200'.89'957073—dc21

00-037452

Chapter 3 appeared in *Amerasia Journal* 22, no. 1 (1996): 149–59. © UCLA Asian American
Studies Center. An earlier version of Chapter 7 appeared in *Emerging Generations of Korean
Americans,* edited by Ho-Youn Kwon and Shin Kim (Kyung Hee University, 1993). An earlier
version of Chapter 12 appeared in *Pacific World,* Journal of the Institute for Buddhist Studies
(1988).

Contents

Acknowledgments   vii

Part I   **Introduction**   I

   1   Korean American Religion in
         International Perspective   3
         Kwang Chung Kim, R. Stephen Warner, and Ho-Youn Kwon

   2   The Korean Immigrant Church as Case and Model   25
         R. Stephen Warner

Part II **Religious Experiences of Korean
           Immigrant Christians**   53

   3   Pilgrimage and Home in the Wilderness of Marginality:
         Symbols and Context in Asian American Theology   55
         Sang Hyun Lee

   4   Ethnic Roles of Korean Immigrant Churches in the
         United States   71
         Kwang Chung Kim and Shin Kim

   5   Religion as a Variable in Mental Health:
         A Case for Korean Americans   95
         Tong-He Koh

Part III **Generational Transition of
           Korean American Churches**   113

   6   A Theological Reflection on the Cultural Tensions
         Between First-Century Hebraic and Hellenistic
         Jewish Christians and Between Twentieth-Century
         First- and Second-Generation Korean Americans   115
         Robert D. Goette and Mae Pyen Hong

7   The Transformation of a First-Generation Church
into a Bilingual Second-Generation Church   125
Robert D. Goette

8   Ethnic Identity Formation and Participation
in Immigrant Churches: Second-Generation
Korean American Experiences   141
Peter T. Cha

9   Beyond "Strictness" to Distinctiveness:
Generational Transition in Korean
Protestant Churches   157
Karen J. Chai

10   Being Korean, Being Christian:
Particularism and Universalism in a
Second-Generation Congregation   181
Antony W. Alumkal

11   The Intersection of Religion, Race, Gender,
and Ethnicity in the Identity Formation of
Korean American Evangelical Women   193
Soyoung Park

Part IV   **Buddhisms in North America**   209

12   The Growth of Korean Buddhism in the
United States with Special Reference to
Southern California   211
Eui-Young Yu

13   Turning the Wheel of Dharma in the West:
Korean Sŏn Buddhism in North America   227
Samu Sunim (Kim, Sam-Woo)

14   Won Buddhism in the United States   259
Bok In Kim

15   Intra-Ethnic Religious Diversity:
Korean Buddhists and Protestants in
Greater Boston   273
Karen J. Chai

Notes on Contributors   295

Index   299

Acknowledgments

MOST OF THE CHAPTERS in this volume were originally presented at the Symposium on Korean Americans: Religion and Society, sponsored by the Center for Korean Studies of North Park University and held in Chicago on October 11–12, 1996. We are indebted to Dr. David Horner, president of North Park University, and to the board of advisors of the Center for Korean Studies for making the symposium possible. We are grateful to Ms. Ann-Helen Anderson, the center's administrative assistant, for her invaluable help in processing manuscripts and to Mr. Song-gu Kwon for assistance with computer programs. Our work as editors was facilitated by our respective academic homes and, in Warner's case, by a fellowship from the Institute for the Humanities at the University of Illinois at Chicago. Several publishers have graciously granted permission for us to reuse and revise materials originally appearing elsewhere; acknowledgments will be found on the copyright page, but we want to record our gratitude here. We are especially appreciative of our wives' indulgence when we disappeared for long business lunches in the welcoming precincts of Chicago's Ariana restaurant.

HYK, KCK, RSW
December 27, 1999

Part I

INTRODUCTION

1

Korean American Religion in International Perspective

Kwang Chung Kim, R. Stephen Warner, and Ho-Youn Kwon

IN THE NEW MILLENNIUM, it will be increasingly difficult for an American to tell what "a Christian" or "a Buddhist" looks like. Christians and Buddhists come in all colors. Race, ethnicity, and religion are no longer hard-linked to one another—if they ever were. Moreover, places of worship decreasingly fit old cultural molds: a small-town Protestant church—red brick walls, high-pitched roof, and white steeple—may be packed with Asians, and those who sit for meditation at a Buddhist temple today are quite likely to be white Americans. By the same token, it is harder to say what Americans believe or, to the dismay of many immigrant parents of American-born young people, what Mexican, Indian, Chinese, or Korean "values" are. These new facts are aspects of what has been called the transnational reality of our times. The nearly one million Korean American Christians who live in the United States today, and the many Korean Buddhist monks who have gathered European American followers as well as serving Korean immigrants, are aspects of that reality.

The interpretations offered in this chapter are diffusely indebted to the insights of Peter Cha, Karen Chai, Henry Finney, Illsoo Kim, Hagen Koo, Sang Hyun Lee, Pyong Gap Min, Paul Numrich, Young Pai, Ronald Takaki, Raymond Williams, and Fenggang Yang, to whom we offer our thanks and our apologies in advance for any misuse of their ideas. We are indebted to Karen J. Chai and Anne Heider for comments on an earlier draft.

Pilgrims and Missionaries from Korea

Religions cross cultural and geographical boundaries through two types of movement: migration and mission. Migrants move from one place to another, carrying their religions along with their baggage; and missionaries propagate religions across oceans, deserts, and mountains, bearing religion as their standard. In the history of the Americas, both processes—migration and mission—were too often violent, as migrants pushed out those who stood in their way and missionaries gained converts through the power of the sword. In the case of Korean religions in America, however, what violence has occurred has been directed against the migrants and missionaries, rather than issuing from them.

To speak of religion moving through migration or mission is to oversimplify in two important respects. First of all, the motives of those who carry religion are often mixed, the missionary spirit increasingly wound up with the urge to settle, and immigrants' new circumstances demanding an intentional religious response. Thus, some missionaries find the mission territory to be especially promising as a place to live as well as to bear witness. Such people come to want the new land to be a place where they belong, and they wind up as immigrants. Correspondingly, those who migrate for secular reasons often find that their religion means more to them in the new land than it did in their homeland; what was carried as cultural baggage becomes in the new home the religious center of existence. Especially among immigrants to the United States, religion often increases in salience after migration (Smith 1978; Williams 1988, 1996; Warner 1993), and some begin to think of themselves as pilgrims in the new land.

Second, both migratory settlers and missionaries' proselytes eventually adjust the imported faith to the new setting. Thus, religions are not simply transplanted from one place to another; they are transformed in the process. An especially wrenching process of change takes place between those who themselves migrated or converted, on the one hand, and their offspring who must come to grips with decisions their forebears made, on the other. They must somehow appropriate to themselves or painfully reject the inherited religion in the new country or the new religion in their home country.

The chapters in this book highlight the experiences of Christian "pilgrims" and Buddhist "missionaries" from Korea and their spiritual heirs, especially the Christian offspring who have tried to meld the Korean, American, and Christian legacies that are their birthright into new cultural forms. The term "pilgrims" is ordinarily applied to those who, like the seventeenth-century Puritan settlers in New England, travel for explicitly religious reasons, to visit a holy place or conduct an errand into a wilderness; hence it may seem inappropriate when applied to those who, like most Korean immigrants, originally came to the United States in search of expanded economic opportunities for themselves and their children. But theologian Sang Hyun Lee, in an influential reflection on the Korean presence in the United States (Chapter 3), sees his people as pilgrims with the calling to make the Christian church more truly universal than it typically is in America and less an idolatrous reflection of an unjust society. Likewise, it may seem equally wrong-headed to call the typically gentle presence of Buddhist monks in the United States an instance of "missionary" activity, but sociologist Henry Finney, himself a European American convert to Zen Buddhism, argues insightfully that America is now mission territory for ancient schools of Asian Buddhism (Finney 1991). Thus it is possible to understand Korean Buddhism in the United States as a long-delayed continuation of the movement that first brought Buddhism from Korea to Japan nearly fifteen hundred years ago. Finally, as Robert Goette and Mae Hong argue (Chapter 6), the heirs of Korean Christian migrants are not passive recipients of a legacy but actors in the drama of a reformed Christianity in American society. (The offspring and progeny of Korean Buddhism in America are still too few in number for analysts of their experiences to have much to say.) This "second generation" holds the Korean American future in their hands.

The three parts of this book that follow the introduction (Part I) concern the religious experiences and institutions of the overwhelmingly Christian immigrant generation from Korea (Part II), their children (Part III), and Buddhists who have come to this country to minister to the Buddhist minority among immigrants and increasingly to European American devotees (Part IV). To set into context the Korean religious presence in America, this chapter outlines the religious situation in Korea and explains the circumstances and consequences of Koreans' bringing their religions to the United States. We shall see that a full understanding requires that we pay attention to the international context of China, Japan, and Russia as well as Korea and the United States (Koo and Yu 1981). Chapter 2 develops implications of the Korean immigrant church experience specifically for the sociology of religion.

The Korean Religious Situation in Brief Retrospect

Of the great world religions, Buddhism was introduced to Korea from China in the fourth century C.E. (and passed from Korea on to Japan in the sixth century), whereas Christianity came to Korea (also originally from China) only in the seventeenth century. Yet by the end of the twentieth century, Buddhism and Christianity had nearly equal shares in the population of Korea (i.e., the Republic of [South] Korea, from which most immigrants come to the United States), Buddhists at 29 percent and Christians at 25 percent. How did this rapid change happen?

Early Korean Buddhism was of the popular and soteriological Pure Land variety, but a more monastic-oriented Buddhism flourished as the established religion of Korea under the Koryo dynasty (918–1392), Buddhist scholarship especially flourishing in the twelfth century. The turning point for Buddhism occurred during the Choson, or Yi, dynasty (1392–1910), which disestablished Buddhism, promoted Confucian learning and influence, and later sought out advantageous relationships with various Christian groups. It was during the Choson dynasty that Korea suffered the devastating Japanese invasion of 1592, from which Korean Buddhism never fully recovered its position of dominance. Confucianism became dominant as an ideology, while a popular form of Buddhism, Minjung teaching, found a home with marginalized classes, and contemplative monks were rusticated. Buddhist leader Samu Sunim gives a brief account in Chapter 13 of three revered monks, whose lives span the seventh to seventeenth centuries, on whose teachings contemporary Korean Buddhism draws.

In the seventeenth century, Korean scholars assigned to Beijing became acquainted with Jesuit missionaries in the Chinese court and brought Roman Catholic learning back to Korea, where it was found attractive for its contribution to scientific knowledge, especially among the neo-Confucian aristocratic classes. But after an initial period of favor, Korean Catholicism was subject to persecution from the late eighteenth to the late nineteenth centuries. The first Korean Catholic martyr was executed in 1791, and official persecutions were mandated in 1801, 1839, and 1866. Thousands of Korean Catholics died for their beliefs before a series of late-nineteenth-century treaties with Western powers guaranteed the safety of missionaries.

Three reasons are usually given for the persecution of Catholics in Korea. First, converts in the period of disfavor were heavily recruited from disempowered, vulnerable classes. Second, an increasingly rigid Confucianism in the Choson dynasty opposed Catholicism as a form of the Western influence it opposed in principle. Third, in the so-called rites controversy, the ancestor worship entailed by Confucianism was, by papal decree, declared incompatible with Catholic religion. This decree, affirmed by Catholic bishops in China, was taken by the Choson dynasty to be a direct and intolerable challenge to Confucian supremacy. As a result of these persecutions, Catholics remained a small and embattled religious group until the twentieth century, when they began to attract adherents once again.

The political situation in Korea was quite different toward the end of the nineteenth century, when Protestantism arrived. Feeling threatened by the growing power of Japan, Russia, and other powers, the Choson dynasty was politically weak and nearing its end. As a strategy to cope with this delicate situation and wanting to balance off one power against another, the Korean government entered into a formal treaty with the United States in 1882, opening its doors to Americans. In 1883 two Protestant missionaries, Horace G. Underwood, a Presbyterian, and Henry G. Appenzeller, a Methodist, arrived; and they and other American, Canadian, and Australian missionaries began a program of building churches, schools, and hospitals. They translated the Bible into the more accessible *hangul* script, which had been disdained in favor of classical Chinese writing by the Confucian literati, and thus they laid foundations for mass literacy and the modern Korean educational system. Many Koreans were favorably impressed with the missionaries' activities and came to think of Protestant Christianity as a positive, modernizing force.

Modernization had an earlier start in Japan, and Japan became the dominant power in the region with its successes in wars against China in 1894–95 and Russia in 1904–5. Japanese troops marched across Korea to confront Russian forces in Manchuria but were not withdrawn after the war, and Japan declared Korea a protectorate in 1905, annexing Korea outright and ending the Choson dynasty in 1910. Japanese rule in Korea, which continued through World War II, was notably harsh.

Between 1883 and 1945, the Christian message spread widely across Korea in the wake of the defeat of the Choson dynasty and the partiality of the Japanese rulers toward Shintoism and their own forms of Confucianism and Buddhism. American Protestant missionaries took sides with the Korean independence movement against Japanese colonialism. Far from being perceived as it was in much of Asia as an adjunct of Western imperialism, Christianity was thus viewed by many Koreans as a force for national liberation and progressive modernization.

After the war, with Japan defeated and China gravely weakened, Korea was partitioned between Russian and American spheres of influence at the 38th parallel. When the two halves of Korea declared themselves republics, the Christian presence in the south was augmented by Christian refugees from the officially atheistic north. The intervention of the United States against the invasion from the north in 1950 strengthened the image of

Western values and religion in the southern republic, creating a still more receptive climate for Christian conversion in the wake of the war's extreme devastation. But at the same time, the strengthened ties to the United States linked South Korea to the world capitalist system. Korea's forced export-oriented modernization of the 1960s was a response, creating more social dislocation to which many people sought religious answers, thus increasing the rate of conversion.

Indigenous pre-Christian and even pre-Buddhist forms of religion remain as undercurrents in Korean culture, but far from preventing the spread of Christianity, they may have aided it (see Kwon 1995). Shamanism, the belief in access to the deities through the ministration of human mediums, remains a widespread practice (both in Korea and among Korean Americans) that Christianity officially shuns. But its image of a spirit-filled world seems to add to the appeal of pentecostal or "full gospel" streams of Christianity. Confucianism, delegitimated as a political ideology by its association with invaders from both north and south, remains a powerful influence in family relations, especially the norm of filial piety. But the conservative Protestantism that is so widespread in Korea (and, as we shall see in Chapter 4, in Korean American churches) also teaches the sanctity of children's obligations to parents. Moreover, Confucianism's basically hierarchical social model facilitated conversions of whole families when the family head decided on Christianity. Thus, within the short space of a century, Korea became one of the most Christianized of Asian nations and the only one with a Protestant plurality within the Christian sector.

Political, Economic, and Religious Factors in Korean Migration to the United States

From the outset, the story of Korean migration to the United States has partaken of this complex international pattern. Koreans first came to Hawaii in 1903 to work in the sugar plantations. Sugar cultivation is labor intensive, and the American planters "systematically developed an ethnically diverse labor force as a mechanism of control" (Takaki 1998, 25), beginning with native Hawaiian laborers, then Chinese, then Portuguese, then in the 1890s, Japanese. When Hawaii was annexed to the United States in 1898, Chinese could no longer be imported (because the U.S. 1882 Chinese Exclusion Act applied in the new territory), and the planters feared they would become too dependent on a largely Japanese labor force. So in 1903, they turned to Korea as a source of labor. But importation of laborers from Korea was short-lived: in 1905 the Korean government, newly under Japanese suzerainty, prohibited further emigration to Hawaii, to curb both competition of Korean laborers with Japanese in Hawaii and Korean independence activities in the United States.

Numbering some 7,000, the early Korean migrants to Hawaii were not destitute. They were disproportionately urban, 70 percent were literate, and 40 percent were Christian. Many of them were mobilized for the journey by Protestant missionaries, and they left Korea expecting greater opportunities than they perceived at home. When they reached Hawaii, many experienced a sense of liberation from Japanese domination. In stark contrast to early Chinese immigrants, who were virtually all male, one out of ten Korean immigrants was female; and after the cut-off of immigration in 1905, an additional 1,100 women came as picture brides before 1924. Thus by 1920, 21 percent of the adult Korean population in the United States, including some 1,700 who had remigrated to the mainland, were women. Even though the age difference between husbands and their picture brides was often twenty years, and many marriages must have been unhappy, the presence of families promoted the development of churches.[1]

From very early on, the Christian church was a center of Korean American activity, both for religion and for independence-oriented politics. By 1905 there were seven plantation-based Korean Christian chapels in Hawaii, with funding from the Korean immigrants, the Protestant denominations, and the planters. On the mainland, the Korean Methodist Church of San Francisco held its first service in October 1905, and the Korean Presbyterian Church was established in Los Angeles a year later. Within ten years, there were twelve Korean churches in California, in coastal cities and such central valley towns as Dinuba, where Koreans found agricultural work (Takaki 1998, 279). A few of these churches persist today.

Korea's position on the Asian front line of the U.S. policy of containment of communism contributed to the second (1951–64) and third (post-1965) waves of Korean immigration. The second wave, set off by the Korean War, consisted primarily of "GI brides," wives of U.S. servicemen (numbering 6,423) and orphaned adoptees (5,348) (Hurh and Kim 1988). Along with a few refugees and some professionals, including students who "adjusted" their status to that of permanent residents, the largely dependent population of the second wave did not provide fertile ground for the development of ethnic churches. Indeed, they might well have "melted away" into the

---

1. To judge from the experience of the American frontier, single men make poor soil for church planting; see Finke and Stark 1992, 33–35.

American population had it not been for unanticipated effects of the immigration law of 1965, which, because of continuing social dislocations in Korea, hugely augmented their numbers and their significance as a cultural vanguard. (A number of today's most prominent Korean American intellectuals, including Won Moo Hurh and Sang Hyun Lee, came to the United States in this second wave.)

The third wave of Korean immigration was impelled by the program of forced modernization under the dictatorial regime of General (later President) Park Chung Hee (1961–79) and facilitated by the 1965 change in U.S. immigration law. Park's "guided capitalism" turned South Korea away from its traditional role as agricultural producer for the peninsula toward export-oriented industrialization and greater dependency on the world capitalist system (Deyo 1987; Koo 1987). The regime favored elite strata of the Korean population at the expense of lower and even middle strata. *Chaebol* (business conglomerates under the control of a single holding company) received tax advantages and monopoly privileges from the government in return for their financial contributions and political support. Members of the military elite were similarly favored. Thus, the "economic miracle" of successful industrialization brought impoverishment of the rural population, weakening of indigenous smaller scale enterprises, career frustration for white-collar workers, polarization between rich and poor, prohibition of labor organizing, violations of civil rights, and widespread social dislocation (K. D. Kim 1976). Conditions were ripe for mass exodus of those with the means to emigrate, and the emigrants thus turned out to be disproportionately middle-class Christians, many of them recently arrived from the communist north (I. Kim 1981, 1987).

Because of immigration law reform, the United States, previously not notably hospitable to Asian migrants, received over three-quarters of a million migrants from Korea between 1965 and 1995. Asian exclusion laws dating from the nineteenth century and European-biased immigration quotas established in the wake of World War I became increasing embarrassments to the United States during the ideological competition of the Cold War, so the immigration law reform of 1965 substituted occupational preference ("brain drain") and family reunification provisions. The family reunification provisions were intended to facilitate immigration of Europeans, who had the most relatives in the United States, but immigration from Europe unexpectedly fell in the 1970s and that from Asia increased sixfold (Warner 1998). For Koreans, the family reunification provision at first benefited those thousands who had come in the second wave, especially wives of servicemen and the former students and professional workers who had become permanent residents. In addition to 13,000 healthcare workers who came under occupational preference provisions between 1966 and 1979 (I. Kim 1987), these reunited families became the nucleus of the nearly exponential increase of Korean migration in the 1970s. By the 1980s, when the third wave was in full swing, more than 30,000 Koreans per year were admitted as permanent residents. Because the immigrants needed resources for the journey, and because some were admitted as skilled healthcare professionals (physicians, nurses, and pharmacists), emigration favored the middle class and the already mobile. Because the Korean middle class tends to be disproportionately Christian, so also were the emigrants; half of those leaving Korea for the United States in the post-1965 period were Christian at the point of embarkation (Hurh and Kim 1990).

Korean immigration to the United States dropped sharply in the 1990s, from an average of 35,000 per year in the late 1980s to fewer than 15,000 per year in the mid-1990s (see Table 1.1).[2] Several factors seem to be involved in this decline. The socioeconomic position of the Korean middle class improved with the eventual replacement of the Park dictatorship and its successor regimes with democratic rule in 1993, and stories of the difficulties of immigrant life in America discouraged many potential emigrants. In retrospect, it may appear that mass migration from Korea to the United States will have been a one-generation phenomenon, with significant consequences for the migrants and their progeny that the chapters in this book explore.

Due to the rapid growth of immigration in the 1970s and 1980s, followed by the sharp decline in the 1990s, the current population of Korean Americans in major urban areas is now clearly distinguished into two generations: immigrants and their children. The 1990 U.S. Census reported that there were about 800,000 Koreans in the United States, only 28 percent of them American-born, and most of those, in turn, children of Korean immigrants. More than 600,000 of the 1990 population were foreign-born. Of these immigrants, about 267,000 came to the United States during the 1970s, and about 339,000 in the 1980s. In 1990 only a small proportion (6.9%) of the Korean-born were of college age (between 18 and 22) and one-quarter (28%) were young adults (between 23 and 35). Most of the Korean-born were immigrant adults (age 36 or older). About 15 percent of the American-born were of college age, and another 15 percent of them were young adults. Very few (6.3%) among the American-born were 36 years old or older; most were children.

---

2. At the same time, it must be pointed out that the proportion of adjusters has grown substantially, from about one-sixth to one-third of new permanent residents.

Table 1.1. Number of Koreans admitted to the United States as legal immigrants by status: 1970–1996

Year of entry	New arrivals	Status adjusters
70	9314	2079
71	14297	4049
72	18876	5513
73	22930	4961
74	28028	4658
75	28362	2364
76	30803	1881
77	28437	2480
78	25830	3458
79	26646	2502
80	29387	2933
81	28819	3844
82	27861	3863
83	29019	4320
84	28828	4214
85	30532	4721
86	30745	5031
87	32135	3714
88	31071	3632
89	28248	5974
90	25966	6335
91	18351	8167
92	14062	5297
93	12375	5651
94	10661	5350
95	9397	6650
96	9479	8706

The Korean American Generation Gap

A high proportion of Korean immigrants came to the United States as adults, a majority when they were between 20 and 40 years of age (Barringer, Gardner, and Levin 1993; Hurh and Kim 1988). Their age at immigration suggests that they were already well socialized into the Korean way of life at the time of emigration, bringing considerable Korean sociocultural resources with them to the United States. As they struggle in American society with the resources they brought with them, their adjustment pattern differs both from that of their peers in Korea and from that of native-born Americans. Their new lifestyle in the United States is a joint product of two sets of factors: the sociocultural resources brought from Korea and the sociocultural system in the United States.

Since most Korean immigrants came to the United States through kinship-based chain migration, they generally have relatives in the area of their current settlement. They typically develop a personal network of family members, kin, and friends, but a network limited to small circles of other Korean immigrants. Because many Korean immigrants came to the United States with college degrees and urban white-collar occupational experience in Korea, their current occupations are diverse, ranging from professional occupations and self-employment in small businesses to low-skilled service or manual occupations (Barringer, Gardner, and Levin 1993). Nonetheless, many could not successfully transfer their credentials to the U.S. labor market, and the great majority have experienced downward mobility as a consequence of immigration, holding marginalized jobs or working long hours as self-employed small shopkeepers (Hurh and Kim 1988; Min 1988). Their marginal occupations, limited social networks, and related sociopsychological problems are factors that push them to seek meaning in their lives through religion (Hurh and Kim 1990).

By contrast, most of the immigrants' children have been Americanized from early in life and speak English as their native tongue. Their career prospects are far brighter than those of their parents. In their elementary school years, the children's Americanization is accompanied by a typically strong desire to be part of the white dominant group and a belief that such assimilation is possible. During their high school years, however, many young Korean Americans gradually realize that they are not part of the white dominant group, and they come to recognize the significance of their Korean ethnic heritage. (Seminary professor and minister Peter Cha analyzes the psychocultural development of Korean American youth in Chapter 8; see also Min and Kim 1999.) A complex interplay of two sociocultural systems, the Korean ethnic heritage and the American way of life, shapes their way of life. Unlike their parents, however, their effort to develop their own identity and lifestyle is more powerfully influenced by their early and current Americanization experience.

The above discussion suggests that Korean immigrants and their children have developed different lifestyles in the United States. As immigrants utilize the sociocultural resources of Korea in their adjustment in the United States, their lifestyle includes dominant Korean elements, however modified they may be in the United States. On the other hand, as children combine the Korean heritage with their American way of life, their lifestyles are likely to be heavily influenced by American elements. Furthermore, the nature of the relationship between immigrant parents and their children increases social distance between the two generations. Korean parents strongly press their children toward academic performance and socioeconomic achievement, often applying this pressure in an authoritarian manner. This kind of intergenerational atmosphere goes against children's desire for autonomy and independence. Thus, as children get older and experience more freedom, they tend to avoid their parents for counseling with their personal problems and to turn to their friends instead (Pai, Pemberton, and Burton 1987).

Generation, Gender, and Race in the Crucible of Korean American Congregations

Because Korean Americans of the two generations are so different in their life experiences, each generation has different church-related needs. The church is an important venue for immigrants' negotiating of their adjustment to America; conversely, many young adults want their own churches independent of those of their parents' generation.

For all their variety, the churches established by the first generation tend to have one thing in common: their male-centered and hierarchical power structure. As Kwang Chung Kim and Shin Kim demonstrate in Chapter 4, Korean immigrant congregations are systematically patriarchal. Senior pastors are almost invariably men, and men dominate the ranks of even associate pastors and youth leaders. Many churches have no women elders, and when women do have the formal status of elder, they are often only symbolic figures without real authority. Church women are expected to serve in such areas as the Sunday school, the choir, and the kitchen. Few churches face up to the issue of this systematic gender inequality.

The immigrant church seems designed to serve the needs of men. As immigrants struggle for settlement in a new country, they face numerous obstacles and often feel discouraged. Korean immigrant men are often disappointed with their occupational status in the United States, and their churches typically meet the needs engendered by this situation. In the church, men's struggles are given religious meaning, and church offices serve as an alternative source of recognition.

By contrast, the needs of first-generation women tend to go unmet. Although women do a disproportionate share of the day-to-day work of congregational life, Ai Ra Kim (1996) and Jung Ha Kim (1997) show that they receive formal recognition only to the extent that they exceed men in the concomitants of "elder" status: education as well as age. Since immigrant

Korean American women often live and labor in socially isolating circumstances, Sunday in church offers them a precious opportunity to meet with
their peers. But their culturally imposed responsibilities as self-denying
givers of service to others, a holdover from Confucian norms, do not cease
when they enter the precincts of the Christian church; instead, they increase.
Thus, for first-generation women the church is a source of frustration as
much as support.

Nonetheless, because the Korean immigrant church tends to be socially
inclusive, with members from different pre- and post-immigration backgrounds, members' social circles are broadened by their participation in
church. As we have seen, half of all Korean immigrants were Christian upon
leaving Korea, but so important is the church for immigrants' needs that half
of the remainder eventually become Christian church members as they settle in the United States. The result is that three-fourths of first-generation
Korean Americans are members of Christian churches, the great majority of
them highly active members (Hurh and Kim 1990). As clinical psychologist
Tong-He Koh observes in Chapter 5, religion has therapeutic value whether
or not that is recognized by pastors and clinicians, and the religious beliefs
of Korean immigrants in need of counseling must be taken into account for
counseling to be successful.

Among Korean American Christians, the American-born second generation and the transitional generation of those who were born in Korea but
came of age in America—the so-called 1.5 generation—so far seem eager
to maintain their Christian identity but less sure that they want to do so
in the context of their parents' churches. In working out a modus vivendi
between their religious lives and those of the parental generation, the
churches of Korean American young adults have taken two different forms of
development. The first is to cultivate increasingly autonomous units within
first-generation churches. Pastor and consultant Robert Goette (Chapter 7)
predicts, partly from the parallel record of Japanese and Chinese Christian
churches in the United States, that second-generation Korean American
Bible-study groups and English-language worship groups will eventually grow
into regular churches. Today's second-generation churches are generally
smaller in size and resources than immigrant churches and receive considerable financial and moral support from them. But a few, including the one
chronicled by sociologist Karen Chai (Chapter 9), are now as big as or bigger than their parent immigrant churches. A second form of young Korean
American church development is to begin as independent churches without affiliation with immigrant churches. Many such churches are currently
struggling to survive, but some are well established and active in various

parts of the United States. They may well represent a wave of the future. Second-generation Korean American Christians also meet in weekday fellowship groups, especially on college campuses, as chronicled by Antony Alumkal and Soyoung Park in Chapters 10 and 11.

Second-generation congregations, whether churches or fellowships, are typically less patriarchal than those of the first generations. Confucian ethics are less binding, and the career aspirations of American-born or -raised men are less subject to the devaluation of old-country credentials than are those of their fathers. Yet even among the second generation, as Park demonstrates in Chapter 11, the issue of gender equality emerges as a sensitive issue, the young men still unready to give up vestiges of their patriarchal legacy and the young women trying to carve out a space to express their own identity amidst the racial discrimination they experience in American society and the gender discrimination they experience from first- (and second-) generation Korean American men. We can expect that there will be greater variety among second-generation congregations than among Korean immigrant congregations in the extent of gender equality.

But the systemic issue that all Korean American second-generation Christian congregations must face that immigrant churches could neglect is the question of their distinctive ethnic composition: Why it is that, as English-speaking Christians, they meet separately. This is the particular focus of sociologist Alumkal (Chapter 10), but it is not far from the surface of all the chapters in Part III. Using English as their primary language, such groups are in principle open to the participation of non-Korean Americans; most Korean American English-language ministries in fact have some non-Korean members. As time goes by, their ethnic composition is likely to be an important issue, raising the question of their raison d'être, which may be in part to provide a refuge against racialization processes in American society (Park 2000).

Racial differentiation is an issue in American society that Korean immigrants, second-generation Korean Americans, and the authors of these chapters experience and conceptualize in different ways, at different times, for different purposes—sometimes as "race," sometimes as "ethnicity." In Korea, the differences between Koreans and Japanese and between Koreans and Chinese are deep-seated and pervasive, but in America, as an aspect of what Omi and Winant (1994) call the system of American "racial formation," Koreans tend to be lumped together with other east Asians as a single racial group. Peter Cha presents an account of the dawning racial consciousness of American-raised young Koreans in Chapter 8, where the early childhood idea that they are "white" like their Caucasian neighbors cedes in adolescence to a conviction of essential physical, or "racial," difference. Yet, as these young people grow up to pursue their own careers and to think of raising their own families, the growing differences between themselves and their parents, who are immigrants, and between themselves and their American peers, whose parents were not immigrants, regain importance, and these differences are experienced as cultural or "ethnic."

Scholars too emphasize one or the other factor. Those focusing particularly on immigration and generational transition often look to the experiences of earlier immigrant groups for analytical models, as do Goette (Chapter 7) and Chai (Chapter 9). Others, notably Alumkal (Chapter 10) and Park (Chapter 11), are skeptical that models based on the experience of the dominantly European immigrants of a century ago can be usefully applied to the case of Koreans and other racial minority groups today, given the overwhelmingly non-European background of today's immigrant streams. Yet some of the assimilationist models of ethnic church development (e.g., Mullins 1987) are, in fact, based on the earlier experiences of Asian Americans, specifically Japanese in Canada. Given the arbitrariness and historical flexibility of racial formation in the United States, we hesitate to predict whether Koreans will forever be racially marginalized in this country or whether they may ultimately be included within some ever-broadening, if still invidiously identified, racial majority.

For now, even when the young people develop congregations separate from those of their elders, they are linked across the generations. First, most American-born Koreans have inherited their Christian identity from their parents' churches. Second, they also generally accept "Korean American" as their primary racial/ethnic identity, although some simultaneously identify as "Asian American" or some other type of American (Kim, Moon, and Song 1999). Although, as Chai (Chapter 9) and Park (Chapter 11) show, somewhat different meanings are attached to these identities, Christianity and their common racial/ethnic identification are features that Korean Americans of the two generations share.

Immigrant churches currently constitute the dominant form of social organization in the Korean American community in major metropolitan areas, but the sharp recent decline in new immigration from Korea suggests that first-generation churches will inevitably shrink. Thus, the churches and fellowships now being built by the Korean American second generation may emerge as the primary Korean ethnic churches in the future. As young Korean American churches grow, they may be in a position to support some of the declining immigrant churches. In this way, the roles of churches of the two generations of Korean Americans are likely to be reversed in the future.

Korean Buddhism and Won Buddhism in America

As we have seen, Christianity and Buddhism are the major world religions in Korea, claiming respectively 25 percent and 29 percent of the population. In the U.S. immigrant context, however, Korean Christians greatly outnumber Korean Buddhists, by a factor of ten or twenty to one. (Such estimates are at best approximate, as Karen Chai indicates in Chapter 15.) Because Korean immigrants tend to come from the Korean urban middle class where Christians are concentrated, Korean immigrants include a large proportion of those who were already Christian before emigration from Korea (Hurh and Kim 1990). Thus, Christian churches proliferate in Korean immigrant communities in the United States, while Buddhism is greatly underrepresented. Yet even 5 percent of the one million Korean Americans (a reasonable estimate for the proportion who are Buddhist) represents some 50,000 persons, a significant constituency. Moreover, Korean Buddhism has attracted white American participants. As a result, already in 1988, as sociologist Eui-Young Yu shows in Chapter 12, Korean Buddhism had become a distinct presence in the United States. Won Buddhism, another religion from Korea, is a recently developed syncretic combination of Buddhist, Protestant, and culturally Korean elements. Though Won Buddhism is a relatively new (founded in 1924) and small religion in Korea, its adherents, particularly Korean American members, are highly dedicated to their religious mission.

The situation of these two religions in the United States is quite different from that of Korean American Christian churches. Since the United States is a predominantly Christian country, Korean immigrant churches feel little need to support missionary activities to American people. Instead, at the early stage of their development, many immigrant churches received various kinds of support from American churches, becoming themselves an object for the mission-minded activities of American Christians. From an American point of view, such churches are decidedly "ethnic." In contrast, both Buddhism and Won Buddhism face a missionary task as well as the pastoral one of tending to their ethnic constituents. One of the primary missions of Buddhist temples is to teach American people about their religion as well as to convert Americans.[3] Samu Sunim, in Chapter 13, chronicles the work of three missionaries who have brought Buddhism from Korea to America in the period since World War II, teaching their mostly white American disciples Korean styles of Buddhist meditation and thought. That Samu Sunim

3. See Yang and Ebaugh 2000 for a parallel analysis drawn from the Chinese experience in the United States.

himself could be added to this list of missionaries is clear from the wider net Yu casts in Chapter 12. Such teachers represent potential religious alternatives for Americans, leaders of "new religions" in American eyes. Both Buddhisms feature universalistic teachings that could potentially appeal to audiences outside their ethnic roots, but both also face competition from other forms of Buddhism that are increasingly available in American metropolitan areas. The activities of Korean Buddhism and Won Buddhism include, therefore, both religious care of their Korean followers and sending their religious message to Americans. The ways they combine these more particularistic and universalistic orientations is a topic worthy of study.

According to the research of Paul Numrich (1996), Buddhist temples in the United States frequently minister to two different groups—one made up of immigrants (or members of an ethnic group) and the other made up of converts (usually white Americans). The two groups seldom mix, which leads Numrich to call them "parallel congregations." Just this pattern is observed by Karen Chai (Chapter 15) in her study of Boh Won Sa temple. A different pattern for the spread of an eastern religion to American is that of ISKCON, the International Society for Krishna Consciousness or "Hare Krishna" movement. ISKCON came to the United States in the 1960s as a missionary offshoot of Hinduism, flourishing for a while with white American converts to a "new religion." Only later did ISKCON temples serve the first vanguard of Indian Hindu immigrants to the United States, before they had the wherewithal to build their own "ethnic" temples. In Chapter 14, Bok-In Kim ponders lessons of the ISKCON experience for the Won Buddhist community in the United States of which she is a minister.

The Genesis of This Book

The world of Korean American religion is big, busy, and growing. Yet little is known about it outside of Korean American Christian and Buddhist circles, and even there what is known is only dimly understood. To fill this gap in knowledge, to bring those who knew one part of the picture together with others who knew a different part, a conference on the religious experiences of Korean Americans was organized by Ho-Youn Kwon, director of the Center for Korean Studies of North Park University, and held in Chicago October 11–12, 1996. Invited were scholars from the disciplines of sociology, psychology, economics, geography, theology, and missiology; lay persons and clergy from Christian and Buddhist communities; those who themselves had immigrated from Korea, whose parents and even grandparents had come from Korea, or who were friends but not members of the Korean American community; senior scholars as well as graduate students working on dissertations; men and women. They brought their disciplinary expertise, their cross-national and cross-ethnic comparative perspectives, their first-hand knowledge of the working of churches and temples, and their cultural backgrounds to bear on questions concerning the dynamics and prospects of Korean American religion. Their presentations ranged from formal reports on social-scientific research, through reflections on the Korean immigrant experience in the light of Scriptures and theology, to accounts of the way their personal experiences shed light on little-understood corners of Korean American religious life. They brought new information, new thinking, and new frameworks to bear on the understanding of Korean Americans and their religions.

We affirm the conference organizers' conviction that a variety of contributions was needed for such a pioneering exploration of these emergent phenomena. It was especially important to hear the perspectives of both practitioners and scholars and, given the importance of religion in the Korean American community, of both theologians and social scientists. As participants in, or close observers of, the particular world they study, that of Korean immigrants, the contributors have access to discussions carried out informally, often sotto voce, in that community—among church members and college students, between men and women, between parents and children, from one clergyman to another—but little documented. Making such informal, contextual, and often emotionally loaded knowledge available for the dispassionate analysis of the conference—and, through this book, now of a wider public—represented a real contribution to learning.

The first drafts of most of the chapters in this book (Chapters 3, 4, 5, 6, 8, 9, 13, and 14) were originally prepared for the North Park conference.[4] Kwang Chung Kim was one of the presenters, and subsequent to the conference, he and Kwon asked R. Stephen Warner, whose work on immigrant religion they were acquainted with, to join them in editing the conference papers into a book. The three editors decided which of the conference papers would be most appropriate and worked with the authors on needed revisions. Most of the original conference papers have been revised since 1996, some extensively. For example, Kim and Kim's discussion of characteristics of first-generation churches in Chapter 4 has been informed by

---

4. Briefer versions of Chapter 3, originally the inaugural address of Sang Hyun Lee as Professor of Systematic Theology at Princeton Theological Seminary, appeared prior to the conference in *Amerasia Journal* as well as in the *Princeton Seminary Bulletin*. An earlier draft of Chapter 10 was prepared for, but not presented at, the 1996 North Park conference.

brand-new survey data. Chai's analysis of a second-generation congregation in Chapter 9 has been updated with a new epilogue.

The editors also sought out additional chapters to fill gaps in the coverage. We asked Robert Goette to update for this volume his analysis of linguistic and generational transition in Korean American churches, widely cited from a previous North Park University conference volume (Kwon and Kim 1993); his revision appears as Chapter 7. Warner, who served on Soyoung Park's dissertation committee, asked Dr. Park to summarize for this book the results of her research on the importance of the factors of race and gender in the religious lives of Korean American women; her contribution appears as Chapter 11. We asked Eui-Young Yu for permission to reprint his path-breaking but obscurely published 1988 article on Korean Buddhism in America as Chapter 12, and he has added some new material for this book. Knowing of Karen Chai's dissertation research on Korean Christians and Buddhists, we commissioned Chapter 15 especially for this book. Chapter 2 consists of a paper Warner presented at a 1990 conference on the Korean Immigrant Church, plus a new treatment of the issues written for this book.

There remain two gaps of which we are aware, one more obvious, the other more consequential. There is no coverage of either the Unification Church in America or of Korean American Catholics. Rev. Sun Myung Moon's Unification Church is a religion imported from Korea and is well known, indeed notorious, to Americans. Formally organized in South Korea in 1954, the Unification Church is deeply rooted in Rev. Moon's interpretation of the Christian Bible and Korean culture and history (Chryssides 1991). From its inception it has been an active but embattled presence in South Korea, with a limited number of followers. Brought to the United States in the early 1960s, the Unification Church succeeded in converting enough American young people to become the target of coercive and controversial "deprogramming" efforts (Bromley and Shupe 1979) on the part of their aggrieved kinsfolk. Nevertheless, the Unification Church has been all but invisible in the Korean American community, its activities not appearing in the religion section of Korean ethnic newspapers. In our estimation, the Korean American community views the Unification Church more as an aspect of American religious pluralism than as a significant factor in Korean American religious life.

More to be regretted is the lack of coverage of Korean American Catholics, who constitute one-quarter of Christians in Korea and probably a slightly smaller proportion in the United States. The conference that was the genesis of this book and the additional chapters included to augment the coverage drew upon the work of scholars in the field known to one or more of us, but we were aware of very little research on this important aspect of the Korean American religious experience. Chai's ongoing dissertation research (Chai 2000) is a rare exception (see also Mortell 1991). We can only hazard a few preliminary generalizations and hypotheses. Because of their linguistic homogeneity, it has been relatively easier for Korean American Catholics than for Filipinos, who are linguistically divided, to organize ethnic congregations in the United States. Thus Korean American parishes, many of them dedicated to St. Andrew Kim, martyr of the nineteenth-century persecution of Catholics in Korea, dot the U.S. landscape. Chai (2000) reports that in 1999 there were 117 local Korean Catholic congregations in the United States, some organized formally as ethnic parishes, but most as "communities" or "centers" within mixed-ethnic parishes. As do U.S. Catholics generally, Korean American Catholics suffer a shortage of vocations to the priesthood, so the majority of the priests serving these groups are on rotation from Korean dioceses (Chai 2000, chap. 4; Mortell 1991, 222), which would likely exacerbate the culturally determined religious generation gap between immigrants and their children. In Hurh and Kim's 1986 survey of Chicago-area Korean Americans, 20.2 percent of those who had been church members in Korea were Catholic, but only 13.6 percent of those who were church members in the United States were (Hurh and Kim 1990, 24), which might indicate that Catholics hold their own numerically after immigration but, unlike the Protestant churches, do not significantly recruit new followers from among those formerly unchurched. To fill this gap within a small but growing literature that is itself a research frontier, the study of Korean American Catholics should have high priority.

The present chapter, providing background knowledge on Korean American religion, was written for this book to explain to readers the intellectual context in which the conference was held and the presentations prepared. As participants in, and/or scholars of, the Korean American religious experience, most of the presenters at the 1996 conference were aware, in outline if not detail, of the facts recounted here (although they would not necessarily endorse our interpretations): the trajectory of Korean history; the relevance of Japan and China and later of Russia and the United States to that history; the Buddhist, Confucian, and shamanistic religious background and present Christian growth in Korea; the circumstances of the post-1965 Korean emigration in the contemporaneous authoritarian rule in Korea; the increasingly apparent Korean American generation gap; and the invention by Korean American young people of the "1.5 generation" label for those of their number who are fully bicultural, a label that has since been extended to bicultural members of other immigrant groups.

Most of the conference presentations and subsequent chapters address questions about the dynamics and prospects of Korean religion in America that the editors (all of whom are sociologists) recognize as classically socio-logical, even when the authors come from other disciplines: How does the immigrant and racial minority experience shape Korean religion in Amer-ica? How do their religions help or hinder Korean Americans in coping with the new society? What kinds of religious institutions are the immigrants building? How do those institutions respond to their circumstances as immi-grants? What are some of the problems and strengths of these institutions? Do they mean different things to the men and to the women who belong to them? To the first and second generation? Will they survive the transition to second-generation predominance? How do they attempt to balance their appeal to the home-country culture and to American culture? To what extent will they cease being "Korean" as they become "American"?

It is in the nature of religion to put such sociological issues into the con-text of theological questions—What is the meaning of the Korean presence in America? What is the significance of the fact that Koreans raised in America wish to break out of their ethnic (or racial) enclaves?—and two of the chapters to follow, those that lead off Parts II and III of the book, are explicitly theological. It is our hope that these reflections will help readers better appreciate the historical and human significance of the stories these chapters tell.

References

Barringer, Herbert, Robert W. Gardner, and Michael J. Levin. 1993. *Asians and Pacific Islanders in the United States*. New York: Russell Sage Foundation.

Bromley, David G., and Anson D. Shupe Jr. 1979. *"Moonies" in America: Cult, Church and Crusade*. Beverly Hills, Calif.: Sage.

Chai, Karen. 2000. "Protestant-Catholic-Buddhist: Korean Americans and Religious Adap-tation in Greater Boston." Ph.D. diss., Harvard University, Department of Sociology.

Chryssides, George D. 1991. *The Advent of Sun Myung Moon: The Origins, Beliefs and Practices of the Unification Church*. New York: St. Martin's Press.

Deyo, F. C., ed. 1987. *The Political Economy of the New Asian Industrialism*. Ithaca: Cornell Univer-sity Press.

Finke, Roger, and Rodney Stark. 1992. *The Churching of America, 1776–1990: Winners and Losers in Our Religious Economy*. New Brunswick: Rutgers University Press.

Finney, Henry C. 1991. "American Zen's 'Japan Connection': A Critical Case Study of Zen Bud-dhism's Diffusion to the West." *Sociological Analysis* 52 (Winter): 379–96.

Hurh, Won Moo, and Kwang Chung Kim. 1988. *Uprooting and Adjustment: A Sociological Study of Korean Immigrants' Mental Health*. Final report to NIMH. Macomb: Department of Sociology and Anthropology, Western Illinois University.

———. 1990. "Religious Participation of Korean Immigrants in the United States." *Journal of the Sci-entific Study of Religion* 29 (1): 19–34.

Kim, Ai Ra. 1996. *Women Struggling for a New Life: The Role of Religion in the Passage from Korea to America*. Albany: State University of New York Press.

Kim, Illsoo. 1981. *New Urban Immigrants: The Korean Community in New York*. Princeton: Princeton University Press.

———. 1987. "Korea and East Asia: Preemigra-tion Factors and U.S. Immigration Policy." In

Pacific Bridges, ed. J. T. Fawcett and B .V. Carino, 327–45. Staten Island, N.Y.: Center for Migration Studies.

Kim, Jung Ha. 1997. Bridge-Makers and Cross-Bearers: Korean-American Women and the Church. Atlanta: Scholars Press.

Kim, Kwang Chung, Ailee Moon, and Young In Song. 1999. "Young Korean Americans' Learning of Being Ethnic Christians: Their Experience at the Church of Their Parents." Department of Sociology, Western Illinois University.

Kim, Kyong Dong. 1976. "Political Factors in the Formation of the Entrepreneurial Elite in South Korea," Asian Survey 16:465–77.

Koo, Hagen. 1987. "The Interplay of State, Social Class, and World System in East Asian Development: The Cases of South Korea and Taiwan." In The Political Economy of the New Asian Industrialism, ed. F. C. Deyo, 165–81. Ithaca: Cornell University Press.

Koo, Hagen, and Eui-Young Yu. 1981. Korean Immigrants to the U.S. Honolulu, Hawaii: East-West Center.

Kwon, Ho-Youn, ed. 1995. Korean Cultural Roots: Religion and Social Thoughts. Chicago: North Park College and Theological Seminary.

Kwon, Ho-Youn, and Shin Kim, eds. 1993. The Emerging Generation of Korean-Americans. Seoul: Kyung Hee University Press.

Min, Pyong Gap. 1988. Ethnic Business Enterprise: Korean Small Business in Atlanta. Staten Island, N.Y: Center for Migration Studies.

Min, Pyong Gap, and Rose Kim. 1999. Struggle for Ethnic Identity: Narratives by Asian American Professionals. Walnut Creek, Calif.: Altamira Press.

Mortell, Anthony. 1991. "The Korean Catholic Community in the U.S.: Present Status and Future Prospects." In The Korean-American Community: Present and Future, ed. Tae-Hwan Kwak and Seong Hyong Lee, 211–30. Seoul: Kyungnam University Press.

Mullins, Mark R. 1987. "The Life-Cycle of Ethnic Churches in Sociological Perspective." Japanese Journal of Religious Studies 14 (4): 321–34.

Numrich, Paul. 1996. Old Wisdom in the New World: Americanization in Two Theravada Buddhist Temples. Knoxville: University of Tennessee Press.

Omi, Michael, and Howard Winant. 1994. Racial Formation in the United States from the 1960s to the 1990s. Second edition. New York: Routledge.

Pai, Young, Deloras Pemberton, and Geri Burton. 1987. Coping Skills for Korean-American Youth: A Study in Direct Communication Skills. Research monograph. Kansas City: School of Education, University of Missouri, Kansas City.

Park, Soyoung. 2000. "The Religious/Racial/Ethnic Identity of Korean-American Evangelical College Students: Christian or Korean." Ph.D. diss. Drew University.

Smith, Timothy. 1978. "Religion and Ethnicity in America," American Historical Review 83:1155–85.

Takaki, Ronald. 1998. Strangers from a Different Shore: A History of Asian Americans. Revised edition. Boston: Little Brown.

U.S. Department of Justice. 1970–97. Statistical Yearbooks of the Immigration and Naturalization Service. Washington, D.C.: U.S. Government Printing Office.

Warner, R. Stephen. 1993. "Work in Progress Toward a New Paradigm for the Sociological Study of Religion in the United States," American Journal of Sociology 98 (March): 1044–93.

——. 1998. "Immigration and Religious Communities in the United States." In Gatherings in Diaspora: Religious Communities and the New Immigration, 3–34. Philadelphia: Temple University Press.

Williams, Raymond Brady. 1988. Religions of Immigrants from India and Pakistan: New Threads in the American Tapestry. Cambridge (U.K.): Cambridge University Press.

——. 1996. Christian Pluralism in the United States: The Indian Immigrant Experience. Cambridge (U.K.): Cambridge University Press.

Yang, Fenggang, and Helen Rose Ebaugh. 2000. "Religion and Ethnicity Among New Immigrants: The Impact of Majority/Minority Status in Home and Host Countries." Journal for the Scientific Study of Religion (forthcoming).

2

The Korean Immigrant Church
as Case and Model

R. Stephen Warner

WITHIN THE LAST GENERATION, the American religious world has changed dramatically, with more diversity than ever before. The one million Korean Americans gathered into over three thousand of their own churches is emblematic of the drama and the diversity. Korean Americans are so well organized religiously and so reflective about their religious experience in the United States that they offer the student of American religion an ideal opportunity to explore the parameters of recent change. Most of the authors in this book have their roots in the Korean American community, but it is my conviction that those outside this community have much to learn from the Korean American experience about themselves and their own communities. Such is the presupposition of this chapter.

The chapter is presented in two sections, originally written about a decade apart. Section I is a previously unpublished but widely distributed and cited (Chai 1998, Chong 1998, Kwon et al. 1997) paper originally written for a conference in 1990, where I was one of three European American scholars invited to reflect on the Korean immigrant church from the perspective of the history and sociology of American religion.[1] I have added

1. The others were the late Timothy L. Smith of Johns Hopkins University and John F. Wilson of Princeton University.

footnotes where it seemed necessary to explain a context or to correct a misimpression, but otherwise the first section is the text that was presented at that conference. Section II was written for this book, and it draws in part on the other chapters herein but particularly reflects my general experience in the study of immigrant religion during the 1990s (Warner 1993a, 1993b, 1994, 1997a, 1997b, 1998a, 1998b, 1999; Warner and Wittner 1998). Both sections present lessons for the Korean American religious experience from American religious history and sociology and, increasingly as the chapter proceeds, state what the Korean American experience teaches America.

The Korean Immigrant Church in Comparative Perspective (1990)[2]

Perhaps because my studies of immigrant religion have been heavily influenced by reports of the Korean experience,[3] I am inclined to see many continuities between that experience and those of other groups that have come to the United States in the past century and a half. But further study has brought to light some potentially significant differences between Koreans and other groups.

Parallels Between Korean and Other Immigrant Religious Expressions

The salience of religion to a society of immigrants is the keystone of Will Herberg's theory of American religion, propounded a generation ago with the history of such groups as Norwegian Lutherans, Polish Catholics, and Ashkenazic Jews in mind:

> Of the immigrant who came to this country it was expected that, sooner or later, either in his own person or through his children, he would give up

2. Paper delivered on February 17, 1990, at the colloquium "The Korean Immigrant Church: A Comparative Perspective," convened by Professor Sang Hyun Lee at Princeton Theological Seminary. The text of the original colloquium paper is presented here with only the following alterations: (1) omission of some introductory and concluding remarks specific to the occasion, (2) copyediting and correction of typographical errors, (3) updating and correction of references to literature that was at the time in draft or in press, and (4) addition of some footnotes, including this one, the original having contained none.

3. The 1990 paper was based in part on observations made in four Korean houses of worship and conversations and interviews with about a dozen Korean American informants. But the paper especially acknowledges the pioneering contributions of Won Moo Hurh and Kwang Chung Kim and of Sang Hyun Lee. Preprints of Hurh and Kim's article on Korean-American religious participation (1990) and Lee's chapter on Korean American Presbyterians (1991) had been circulated in advance to participants. Professor Hurh was another of the invited guests, and I had been previously acquainted and edified by conversations with Professors Kim and Lee.

virtually everything he had brought with him from the "old country"—his language, his nationality, his manner of life—and would adopt the ways of his new home. Within broad limits, however, his becoming an American did not involve his abandoning the old religion in favor of some American substitute. Quite the contrary, not only was he expected to retain his old religion, as he was not expected to retain his old language or nationality, but such was the shape of America that it was largely in and through his religion that he, or rather his children and grandchildren, found an identifiable place in American life. (Herberg 1960, 27–28)

Following the Handlin-Herberg theory[4] of the salience of religion for immigrants to America, the same theory that has informed Hurh and Kim's studies as well as my own, Yvonne Haddad and Adair Lummis (1987) expect that immigrant Muslims will become more actively religious here than they were at home. Their surveys of three concentrations of Muslim population in the United States—East Coast, upstate New York, and Midwest—lend support to the theory. I have just begun to look at the experience of immigrant Buddhists in the United States, and I know of no quantitative surveys comparing old-country religious participation with that in this country. Yet the proliferation of Buddhist Centers (Morreale 1988), particularly of the southeast Asian Theravada tradition, bespeaks an attempt to preserve cultural identity in a new environment.[5]

The recent work by Raymond Williams (1988), based primarily on data from Chicago and Houston, on the religious expressions of immigrants from India and Pakistan—Hindus, Muslims, Sikhs, Jains, Zoroastrians, Christians, and Jews—sounds a similar note:

Immigrants are religious—by all counts more religious than they were before they left home—because religion is one of the important identity markers that helps them preserve individual self-awareness and cohesion in a group.... In the United States, religion is the social category with clearest meaning and acceptance in the host society, so the emphasis on religious affiliation and identity is one of the strategies that allows the immigrant to maintain self-identity while simultaneously acquiring community acceptance. (Williams 1988, 11)

Parmatma Saran's study of Hindus on the East Coast shows similar results:

---

4. The allusion is to Oscar Handlin's *The Uprooted* (1951), heavily cited by Herberg.
5. On immigrant Buddhists, see now the work of Paul David Numrich (1996).

"There is a greater religious consciousness and a need to practice some religious rituals" in the United States (1985, 43). Professors Kim and Hurh (1988) argue in their "additive" model that religion can serve as a means by which immigrants can simultaneously maintain their ethnic identity and enjoy the fruits of Americanization.

So I was not surprised to hear from Hurh and Kim (1990, 25) that "a high proportion of [Korean] non-Christians joined Korean ethnic churches after immigrating to the United States." Nor did it occasion surprise when I read in Sang Hyun Lee's paper (1991, 320–21) that many immigrant Korean Presbyterians have joined independent congregations and that some have aligned themselves with a new denomination, the Korean Presbyterian Church in America (KPCA). I have visited one of those KPCA churches and can testify that it is flourishing. Moreover, I learned just two weeks ago that a group of over one hundred Korean Methodist congregations in the United States are discussing the establishment of a Korean American association, to be called the World Methodist Conference, outside the structures of the United Methodist Church. (The likelihood of this kind of development might have been predicted on the basis of the "urgent issues" analyzed ten years ago by Chan-Hie Kim [1979, 1980].) These immigrant Presbyterian and Methodist congregations seem to want a looser, more congregational polity that allows them to control their own property and pastor recruitment, and a more evangelical theology than what the American denominations provide. They appear to be less than enthusiastic about the opportunities for women to which the Presbyterian Church USA and United Methodist Church are committed. Like northern blacks before the Civil War, they are sensitive to slights on the part of the white American denominations, but they also may want a more diffuse autonomy, a space that they can call their own both now and in the future (Herberg 1960, 112–14; cf. Morris 1984; Evans and Boyte 1986).

Presbyterians specifically are notoriously prone to contention and schism, but it seems to me that American conditions in general contribute a sense of entitlement to the religiously discontented. Lay and local control are American norms. Just last month the Korean United Presbyterian Church of Los Angeles won a lawsuit against the Presbytery of the Pacific over the ownership of its property (J. H. Lee 1989, 1990).

Raymond Williams puts it this way. "The influence [of the American environment and immigrant religion] is reciprocal; new religious affiliations brought by immigrants to the United States affect the identity of the immigrant community and its surrounding society, while, at the same time, the move to the new setting transforms the religious tradition itself. It is the intensity of this reciprocal relationship that leads to the increased participation in religious affairs by many of the new immigrants" (Williams 1988, 13–14).

For example, many parishes of the officially episcopal Roman Catholic Church were established in the United States through lay initiative. Jay Dolan observes, "The post-Vatican II era has rightly been called the age of the emerging laity, but history reminds us quite clearly that, even in the brief past of Catholic America, lay people at one time had a major responsibility for the growth and development of the local church" (Dolan 1985, 192; see also Smith 1971).

The same is reportedly true of the Greek Orthodox church, in theory one of the most episcopal of all Christian religious traditions, but in early practice congregational:

> Each church community was a democracy unto itself. It was governed by a board of trustees or directors, many of whose members were small independent businessmen, marked by that commanding proprietary air so often found in the self-made man. Authority was vested in these laymen; and many a clergyman discovered, much to his astonishment, that if democracy was diverting or rewarding for his parishioners, it was not exactly so for him. Despite the shortage of qualified priests, laymen remained in unquestioned control of church administration. (Saloutos 1964, 129)

I suspect that an inchoate sense of lay entitlement and a yearning for congregational autonomy stand behind the massive conversions of Hispanic Americans, many of them recent immigrants, from Roman Catholicism to various forms of evangelical Protestantism. There is just beginning to be a literature on this issue, much of it journalistic, but it is clear that the Roman Catholic Church cannot take the loyalty of Hispanics for granted. Although they tend to score high on measures of personal piety, Hispanics are not notably attached to the church as an institution (Weyl 1988; Gallup 1988), and Spanish pentecostal missions are mushrooming in U.S. cities. Forty-three percent of U.S. Hispanics report that they have been invited to join someone else's church (Gallup 1988), and perhaps one-fourth them have joined[6] Protestant churches (Weyl 1988, 215; Smith and Chandler 1989; Suro 1989;

---

6. That one-fourth of U.S. Hispanics/Latinos are Protestant is probably an overstatement, based on oversampling those of longest residence in the United States and most fluent in English. But the estimate is not absurd. What must be corrected in this sentence is the implication that Protestantism among Hispanics/Latinos can only stem from a U.S.-based conversion. In fact, many Hispanic/Latino immigrants, especially Puerto Ricans, bring Protestantism with them.

Casuso and Hirsley 1990). Hispanic Protestant churches, many independent, some in Hispanic denominations, some attached to Anglo denominations, offer respected roles for lay leaders, training in biblical literacy, leverage for women against the culture of "machismo," refuge and discipline for youth in violent urban neighborhoods, and an intimate enclave for Spanish speakers in Anglophone society (see Montoya 1987).[7]

Korean Christians seem to be recapitulating the immigrant American experience in many ways, yet there are aspects in which the Korean religious experience seems different.

Differences in the Korean Religious Experience

Every group is unique, and I cannot begin to discuss the particularities of Korean religious history itself. Yet when we look at the information provided by Hurh, Kim, Lee, and others, a few patterns distinctive to the Korean immigrant church stand out.

1. The 70 percent of U.S. Koreans who are church members, and the absolute majority who attend church weekly (Hurh and Kim 1990), represent extraordinarily high proportions. Lee (1990, 318–19) has given some reasons for this. Here are some others from Light and Bonacich (1988): (a) Migration is selective. Proportionately more Christian than non-Christian Koreans come to the United States (291). (b) Immigrants to the United States are heavily recruited from college-educated Seoul residents (288–89). (c) This is due, in part, to the prevalence of northern Koreans (from Pyongyang), who tend to be Christian, in the south, who then provide a pool for emigration (287, 289). (d) Christians in Korea are modernizers, people who are interested in improving their conditions (292). To these factors we should add the fact that the Korean immigrant church rises on the momentum of a pattern of mass evangelization that has been going on in Korea for less than a century. Few Korean Christians are in a position to take their religious identity for granted as shrouded in the mists of time.

2. Korean immigrants, and perforce church members, are highly educated, although their educational credentials may not be accepted in the United States. For this reason among others, Koreans are disproportionately likely to be entrepreneurs or self-employed in the United States (Light 1985, Light and Bonacich 1988).[8] They are not the "huddled masses."

7. For a far more nuanced statement than that of Montoya, see now León 1998; see also Brusco 1995.
8. See also Min 1996.

3. Koreans, like other "Dutch door"[9] immigrants, enjoy relative affluence and have more resources to build their own institutions. Their children may feel less need than was true in past generations to escape the ethnic community in order to enjoy the American dream of plenty. On the other hand, as a more stringent U.S. economy makes occupational preference immigrations less available over time and as chain migrations increase the proportion of immigrants coming in response to family reunification preferences, the average relative affluence of the Korean American (and other Asian American) communities can be expected to decline (K. C. Kim 1988; Williams 1988, 19).

4. Although, as Professor Lee emphasizes (1991, 318; see also Hurh and Kim 1990, 30), Korean immigrant churches are internally socially inclusive, Korean Americans are, as a group, ethnically homogeneous, speaking the same language and sharing many of the same traditions. In this regard, they differ mightily from the Germans who came here during the nineteenth century and the Asian Indians arriving today, whose common identity is forged, or developed by "transmutation," in the United States (Williams 1988, 9–36; Herberg 1960; Smith 1978; Morawska 1990; Yancey et al. 1976).

5. Like Filipinos and Asian Indians, Koreans in the United States are very largely a first-generation group. This factor contributes to the ethnic homogeneity of Korean immigrant churches.[10] Whatever patterns of partial assimilation might have been developing in the Korean immigrant churches that were first planted in Hawaii at the turn of the century have been utterly overwhelmed by the massive post-1965 immigration, with the result that there are few English-speaking Korean congregations to serve as models for those who are called to minister to the emerging second generation. In this respect, the Korean Christian experience has parallels to that of the Jews in the United States near the end of the nineteenth century. In 1820 there were perhaps 5,000 Jews in the United States. Between 1820 and 1870, they were joined by some 200,000 to

9. I cannot remember where I first encountered this wonderfully allusive metaphor used in the literature on the new immigration: a "Dutch door," filling a full-length door frame, has two independently swinging parts, top and bottom. The top is often left open, especially in times of good weather, but the bottom is usually closed. The immigration policy put in place by the 1965 law welcomed those with educational attainments and occupational skills needed in the United States but not those at the bottom of the social structure, the "huddled masses."

10. Yang's study (1998) of a Chinese Protestant church in an East Coast metropolitan area provides a striking contrast of internal diversity within an Asian ethnic congregation, the members differing greatly in immigration cohort, country of origin, and first language. One factor in this greater heterogeneity is that Chinese immigration to the United States has a longer and more incremental history than that of Koreans, with each new cohort having been absorbed into preexisting congregations.

400,000 Jews, mostly "Germans," who began to settle on a program of Reform Judaism. But then 2.5 million more came, mostly from Russia, between 1870 and 1924. According to Herberg (1960), "The promise of [Jewish] unity along American Reform lines … was altogether shattered by the flood of East European orthodox immigrants that began in the 1880s" (176). "The sudden mass deluge of east European Jews completely upset the settled pattern of American Judaism that had begun to emerge in the third quarter of the nineteenth century" (178).

6. Hurh and Kim (1990, 25) report that those who join the church after immigration are less likely to be regular participants than those who brought their Christian affiliation with them. Many observers comment that the Korean immigrant church functions in part as a sociocultural center, and these data are consistent with that interpretation. Yet it is a common pattern for converts to a church to be more active, not less active than those who grew up in it: "Across the religious spectrum, it appears that recruits are a source of on-going institutional vitality" (Roof and McKinney 1987, 178). Do the Hurh and Kim data bespeak a slackness in evangelistic zeal on the part of the churches, a willingness to settle for mere numerical growth rather than enthusiastic converts?

7. Although most U.S. Korean churches are small (J. H. Lee 1990, 320; C-H. Kim 1980, 10–11), a number of them, both here and in Korea, are astoundingly large (Dart 1989, 1990). Is Korean spirituality more likely to be satisfied through very large organizations, particularly as compared to Hispanics? Is Korean congregational religion more associational (*gesellschaftlich*) than communal (*gemeinschaftlich*)?[11] If so, it would accord with an observation Max Weber made about the similar associational character of American Protestantism at the beginning of the twentieth century (Weber 1985, 10–11).

8. While most immigrants speak Korean at home, particularly with their spouses, over three-fourths use English always or often in the workplace (Hurh and Kim 1988, 88; Kim and Hurh 1988, 22). Based on my observations, the necessity for workplace English does not extend to Protestant pastors. Does the church provide a special refuge for the use of the Korean language, a place to reap investment in cultural capital that residence in the United States makes obsolete for most immigrants, such that

11. Participants at the Princeton conference convinced me that, insofar as this conjecture implies a preferred Korean American social "style" or "taste" for *Gesellschaft,* it is unwarranted. Even the largest Korean American churches are typically broken down into "cell groups" that address participants' emotional (or *gemeinschaftlich*) as well as social network (or *gesellschaftlich*) needs (Kwon et al. 1997).

many ministers are less likely to be bilingual than the laypersons in their congregations?

9. Some religious groups—Greek Orthodox, Japanese-Canadian Buddhists, Roman Catholics in general, and Hispanics in particular—have suffered a shortage of available clergy leadership (Saloutos 1964; Mullins 1988; Hoge 1987; Smith and Chandler 1989; Burns 1994; Horgan 1975). From many accounts in the literature (C. H. Kim 1980; Shin and Park 1988; etc.) and from my informants, this is not true of Korean Americans, who seem to enjoy a surplus of pastor candidates. Young men, and increasingly young women, in Korea and the United States aspire to clergy careers, and their numbers in this country compensate for student deficits at seminaries due to declining numbers of aspirants from other backgrounds. Proprietary seminaries enroll students with no guarantee that they will be brought under the care of a denominational structure. Older men retired from secular careers think of capitalizing on much-earlier Korean seminary training. One result may be the propensity for schism in Korean immigrant churches, their consequent small average size (Shin and Park 1988), and the distrust directed toward potentially qualified pastoral candidates that, I have heard, mars the harmony of some Korean churches. Yet an abundance of ambitious would-be pastors is a factor by no means unique to Korean Americans. Nathan Hatch emphasizes that such a condition—an open market for religious entrepreneurs—fueled the Second Great Awakening and thus shaped the fundamental norms of religion in America, by which "ordinary folk came to distrust leaders of genius and talent and to defend the right of common people to shape their own faith and submit to leaders of their own choosing" (Hatch 1989, 14).

Some Problems Facing a Church for the Second Generation

I will now examine some implications of the foregoing items for the future of the church, insofar as the future rests with second and later generations. Let me begin with a cautionary tale provided by Mark Mullins (1988).

Mullins studied the half-century-old Buddhist Churches of Canada (BCC), a denomination with 18 congregations and 3,185 members. Japanese immigrants to Canada were predominantly Buddhist, coming from a variety of sects and schools. According to Mullins, "After their arrival in Canada, however, it was the Nishi Honganji, one of the two Jodo Shinshu (True Pure Land) schools, which responded to their religious needs.... As a result, it has been the True Pure Land Buddhism which has been most effectively established among the Japanese of Canada" (1988, 218–19). Most congregations are located in British Columbia and Alberta, with outposts in Manitoba, Toronto (a large congregation of 800 members), Hamilton, and Montreal. It is difficult for these congregations to foster clerical leadership from within, and they get most of their priests from Japan. But the Japanese priests regard their stay in Canada as a sojourn and intend to finish their careers in Japan. They are thus not well prepared to minister to English-speaking youth, or to do the kind of home visiting that lay Nisei (second-generation) leaders, influenced by Canadian Protestant models, expect. A very few of their priests have been Caucasian. Only a quarter have been Nisei. It was up to lay Nisei leaders to organize Sunday schools for Sansei (third-generation) youth.

The Canadian-born (Nisei and Sansei) membership of the churches is upwardly mobile and tends to lack ethnic consciousness. Intermarriage rates among Sansei range from 50 percent in the rural west to 94 percent in Montreal. Japanese Canadians do not, by and large, marry other Japanese Canadians. And many Sansei seem to be uninterested in a religion that seems so centered on death (Mullins 1988, 226–27). Thus, if congregations persist in being ethnic enclaves, their days are numbered to the life spans of the Issei (first-generation) and a few unassimilated Nisei, and the smaller of them must soon die. First-generation immigration will be sufficient to support such ethnic churches only in very large port-of-entry cities like Vancouver and Toronto.

Yet the only congregation that is actively trying to alleviate its ethnic particularity is the newly formed (1971) church in Calgary, which was established for Sansei, not Issei. The board has four Nisei, four Sansei, and two Caucasians. Its primary language was English from the outset. Its founding priest was a bilingual Japanese Canadian who went to Japan for training but remained Canadian in outlook. He played down death-oriented rituals. The church welcomes other ethnic groups and has a few Chinese and Thai members. But most BCC congregations, oriented to the religious needs of the Issei, resist such accommodation, and only the Calgary church seems to be moving in a nonethnic direction. The dilemma is that churches set up to meet the needs of the first generation are thereby rendered less fit to meet the needs of an assimilating community. So when assimilation is rapid, ethnic churches face the imperative of adjustment or organizational death.[12]

12. It should be emphasized that one empirical presupposition of Mullins's (1988) analysis is the single massive cohort pattern of immigration characteristic of Japanese in Canada (see also Mullins 1987). In retrospect, given the post-1990 decline in the rate of immigration from Korea, that pattern may eventually pertain to Korean Americans as well as Japanese Canadians. Fenggang Yang (1998) shows that it does not pertain to Chinese in America.

Among second-generation Korean Americans at least, acculturation does seem to be rapid. A year ago when I visited the Princeton Korean Presbyterian Church as the guest of Interim Pastor Lee,[13] two brief sentences in English were all I heard in the midst of the two-and-a-quarter-hour service. One was uttered during the period of announcements at the end of the service, when Pastor Lee spoke directly to me to say that he had just introduced me to the congregation. The other came at the end of a violin duet played as the offertory by two young schoolchildren, when Lee addressed them in English to say "Thank you." After the service, I spoke with a Korean American Princeton University student, a Presbyterian in good standing from Pennsylvania, and his friends. I asked them what the sermon topic had been and learned that they had only been able to follow the "gist" of the sermon, which turned out to be very little. Their English was, of course, fluent.[14]

The same pattern obtains at a Thai Buddhist temple in Chicago, Wat Dhammaram, which serves as a cultural center for Chicago's Thai community but was also the site of last fall's American Buddhist Congress convocation (1989). An American Buddhist monk, William K. Bartels, issued this warning to his hosts in the booklet handed out to registrants:

> Unless we develop Buddhism within an understanding of American culture, there is a good chance that 2nd or 3rd generation immigrants will tend to leave Buddhism.... Consider this example: At Wat Dhammaram ... almost everything is done in Thai. Yet the youth are slowly evolving from past Thai identities. At a recent ceremony focusing on children I was sitting next to the children. While every speaker spoke in Thai, all the children talked among themselves in English.... These Thai youth are growing up in American culture.[15]

I harp on this matter of language proficiency in the second generation because it stands out in the findings of Young Pai[16] and his colleagues from their nationwide survey of some five hundred Korean American Presbyterian youth conducted five years ago. When asked whether they would attend a Korean church as adults, many of these young people expressed doubt that they would, and the proportion of doubters increased markedly with school grade (Pai et al. 1987, 52, 85, 156 #57). Wanting to have an adult part in any church was something that seriously mattered for only a small minority

13. Sang Hyun Lee was acting pastor of the church in 1989.
14. I draw upon these experiences in the Princeton church in two articles (Warner 1997a and 1997b).
15. See also Rahula 1987.
16. Pai was another of the participants at the 1990 Princeton colloquium.

of Korean American youth (168 #120). These young people, in other words, were not strongly attached to the church, and a near-majority (48%) gave their lack of fluency in Korean as their reason (72). (When the next survey of the extent of assimilation among Korean Americans is done, I hope that people of the second generation are queried and that their proficiency in Korean is measured as much as their proficiency in English.)

The young Korean church people do not seem to have lost their faith to secularization, for the conviction that God will punish sins also increased with grade level (33), and having God at the center of their lives was the most important life goal for fully 34 percent of them, topped only by having a happy family life and doing well in school (63, 166 #109). Moreover, they seem readily to embrace a "Korean" identity (73). In a nutshell, these Korean American youth seemed to be positive about God, religion, and their ethnic heritage, but negative about the church (63). My conjecture is that behind this pattern is the cultural strangeness to acculturated youth of the institutional church, an alienation indexed by the language problem but probably not confined to it (34).

I offer this anecdote: On a recent visit to the English-language congregation of the large Young Nak Presbyterian Church of Los Angeles, I observed that the congregation was young, much younger than I, and dressed much less formally than the older, Korean-language congregation that had just filed out of the same sanctuary. There was a guest preacher that day who was fluent in English (I assume second generation, or 1.5). He began his sermon with this request to the congregation: "There are two things I'd like you to do that I never see in a Korean church. One is to smile. [There was laughter.] The other is to greet your neighbor [which everyone did]." I think that man had a good idea, to loosen up the service in the direction of what I call the "nascent" style of religious expression (Warner 1988, 37–49), an idea possibly motivated by a conviction that the somber and hierarchical style of worship in so many Korean Protestant churches was oppressive to these young adult worshipers of Korean parentage. Whether the first generation's religious manners are perceived by their offspring as "Korean" or as a precipitate of Victorian missionary culture, I imagined that he thought they were regarded by the young congregation as alien.

To "loosen things up" is a project easier recommended than accomplished, and one that is not without its own drawbacks. I suppose that the formal and dignified worship of Korean immigrant churches, their elaborate governance structure, and the deference to age and authority that they enjoin all provide some of the gratification found in them by many first-generation members. In the words of Professor Sang Hyun Lee, "It is precisely the Korean immigrants' deprivation of the fulfillment of their social roles in the larger American society that makes the holding of church offices (elders, deacons) so important to them. The same factor is behind so much of the intrachurch conflict that arises regarding the election of officers" (1991, 319). Professors Hurh and Kim report that fully 23 percent of the church affiliates in their sample hold staff positions—minister, elder, deacon, exhorter—in their churches (1990, 25) and that the mental health of men is correlated with holding a church position (1990, 27–28). "The Korean ethnic church seems to play an important role in satisfying the needs for social status, prestige, power, and recognition within the immigrant community. These needs would be particularly strong for those male immigrants who are expected to 'succeed' in the new country but cannot penetrate into the mainstream of the dominant group's social structure" (1990, 31). If this is true, then the formal character of the Korean immigrant church is no mere "survival" of "old country" ways.

Yet the second generation needs a place too if the church is to maintain their loyalty. Young Pai and his colleagues call for regional and national denominationally sponsored programs to meet the needs of youth (1987, 53–55), and the Young Nak church seems to be fostering the development of an autonomous, local, second-generation congregation. Here is what one young adult says about his experience of their English-language congregation (from the September 1989 newsletter):

> I realized that a niche existed for me in the future of Young Nak Church. Young Nak was my spiritual home, the place where I first came to know God; but after my graduation from the college group, I felt somewhat displaced. It was difficult for me to find spiritual feeding and fellowship because of my limited Korean speaking ability and comprehension. But through this ministry, I really feel that God has made a place for me and my other English speaking brothers and sisters. And for this I am thankful and give God much praise.

Like the first generation, this man also receives gratification from the structure of his church life, but his orientation seems to be more horizontal, more oriented to fraternal feeling than vertical prestige.[17]

Along with Kim and Hurh (1988), Sang Hyun Lee (1987, 114–15), and Pai (1987), I recognize the advisability, indeed the inevitability in the long run, of biculturalism. Korean American Christians must not take refuge

---

17. See Olson 1989 and 1993 for a related theory of American church life.

solely in ethnicity. Yet their accommodation to America should not come at the cost of their associational and spiritual vitality. I do not presume to know what aspects of the Korean immigrant religious experience will in the future best combine an outreach directed to American conditions with a distinct morale-giving identity.

The Korean Immigrant Church in the Perspective of a Decade (2000)

What I said in 1990 ended with a series of questions and speculations on the future of the Korean immigrant church that were particularly addressed to the Korean American church leaders Dr. Lee had brought together for the Princeton conference. By adding a few footnotes to the 1990 paper for this publication, I have attempted to correct my misimpressions of a decade ago and update items of information then available to me. But so much has happened in the world of Korean American religion and new immigrant religion generally that a new treatment is demanded, which is the burden of Section II of this chapter.

During the 1990s new knowledge has become available and new facts have emerged. Because of the rapid development of scholarship, we can now draw on a significant body of recent work on the Korean American church (e.g., Min 1992; Y.-I. Kim 1994; K. C. Kim and S. Kim 1995; A. R. Kim 1996; Kwon et al. 1997; Chai 1998; Chong 1998; as well as the studies in this volume). Indeed, Korean Americans have been at the forefront of new immigrant groups in coming to scholarly grips with their own religious experience. Other new immigrant religious communities have also gained attention, although to a lesser degree on the part of their own members (see, e.g., Numrich 1996; Eck 1997; Zhou and Bankston 1998; Warner and Wittner 1998; Díaz-Stevens and Stevens-Arroyo 1998),[18] and this knowledge can be used both to put the Korean American experience into new perspective and to suggest extrapolations from it.

Much has also changed in the Korean American social world in the 1990s that must be taken into account, especially three interrelated developments: a slowing in the rate of immigration and consequent aging of the first-generation population as an increasingly distinct cohort; the growth and increasing visibility of an acculturated, English-dominant, second generation; and the consequent increasing awareness of internal differentiation in the

---

18. See also Christiano 1991; Kivisto 1992; Leong 1996; Yoo 1996; Warner 1998b.

Korean American community, especially on grounds of gender and generation. In retrospect, it appears that 1990 was the end of an era for Korean Americans, the last year that annual immigration exceeded 30,000 (Min 1996, 29), when it had become clear that middle-class aspirations were probably better served by staying in Korea than by coming to the United States.

The updated treatment in this section highlights internal differentiation in the immigrant world, but it begins with a consideration of a logically prior issue—the contexts of migration from the home society and reception in the host society—and proceeds to two issues more directly connected to religious institutions—structural adaptations and negotiation of identities[19]—before returning to the same issue that brought Section I to a close: the implications of the emergence of the second generation.

Emigration and Immigration: Contexts of Sending and Reception

Migrants leave one particular place for another particular place, and the characteristics of those places interact in shaping the immigrant community (Smith 1971). Due to violence and persecution in their home countries, for example, many Mayan Indians in Los Angeles are refugees, and their living arrangements in the United States reflect their male-predominant sex ratio, skewed toward the men who were able to leave and earn money to support families in the remote highlands of Guatemala (Wellmeier 1998). To cite another example, Christian women in the Indian state of Kerala have long taken up nursing as a career available to them as educated persons but undesirable as a form of "pollution" to their Hindu neighbors. The 1965 immigration law opened the United States to such women, who later brought their dependent husbands and children to these shores, the men to find what satisfaction they could in the affairs of the Indian immigrant church (Williams 1996; George 1998).

Korean immigrants to the United States, as we saw in Section I, tend disproportionately to come from already Christianized segments of the home-country population, and they are on the average more highly educated and more likely to have professional occupational credentials than the American host population they join. However, they are less likely than other highly educated and skilled immigrants from Asia—especially those from the former Anglo-American colonies of the Philippines and India—to be fluent in English, and therefore they confront all-but-insurmountable barriers to

---

19. These issues are elaborated in a different order in Warner 1998a, 14–27, and in Warner and Wittner 1998, passim.

continuing their professional careers in the United States (Min 1996, 3–4). Many first-generation male Korean immigrants, therefore, are "downwardly mobile" small-scale entrepreneurs, and official positions in church serve their need for recognition (Kwon et al. 1997, 252–53). In all these cases, to understand the group in the United States, one must pay attention to "where they came from."

Both the Korean American experience and the scholars who have studied it have greatly aided our understanding of the religion-migration nexus. Scholars such as Hurh and Kim (1990) begin with the fact that information on religious affiliation and participation in the United States is not available from government sources, whether the Immigration and Naturalization Service or the U.S. Census Bureau. Thus, unlike studies of immigrants' occupational and educational attainment or marital and family status, studies of immigrant religion cannot rely on official U.S. statistics even for such a basic question as How many Korean Americans are Buddhist? (Warner 1998b).

One expedient has been to assume that the profile of the immigrant population in America replicates that of the sending countries, as has been done, for example, to estimate the number of Muslims in the United States. The assumption of this estimating procedure is that migration is random with respect to religion. When a country is religiously homogeneous, as Japan for example tends to be, little harm is done by this procedure. But when the society is religiously diverse, with major groupings of very different faiths— which is true of India, Vietnam, and Korea, to name three Asian societies— multiplying the immigrant population from a given country by the proportion each religious group enjoys in that country is sure to produce misleading results, likely overestimating, in these three cases, the number of Hindus and Buddhists among immigrants.

With the Korean American population so palpably Christian, and Korea itself still being perceived in Western eyes as significantly Buddhist, the assumption of randomness of immigration is popularly implausible as well as factually incorrect. We owe to scholars like Hurh and Kim (1988) the rigorous estimation of the actual religious profile of the Korean American population, including the finding that emigrants from Korea are not at all random with respect to the sending country population but are, as argued in Section I above, a highly selective sample. This recognition has provided a breakthrough for the understanding of the religious communities of other immigrant groups (Warner 1998a, 13), for example, non-Hindus from India (George 1998) and non-Muslims from Iran (Feher 1998).

One of the most disturbing aspects of intercontinental migration is the experience of racism. A participant at the 1990 Princeton conference, a Korean American graduate student who grew up as a member of a "racial minority" in southern California, recalls the thrill of his first trip to Korea when, emerging from the subway into crowded downtown Seoul, he realized that "everyone looks like me!" Koreans and other immigrants encounter the United States as a racialized society (Tseng and Yoo 1998), which is not to say that Americans as individuals are any more (or less) racist than people in other societies. It is to say that how a group stands with respect to "whiteness" has defined how Americans treat one another, from the white/African and white/Indian axes that have organized life from the Atlantic westward for hundreds of years, to the white/Asian axis that has moved eastward from the Pacific for the last century. As one of the later-arriving East Asian groups, Koreans encountered preexisting stereotypes of Chinese and Japanese and are often confused with them under the general category of "Orientals." One potential response in the United States, in politics as well as religion, is the development of "pan-Asian" solidarities.

Unlike African-origin people arriving in the United States today from the Caribbean or from Africa, Koreans and other East Asians do not risk being assigned to the lowest rung on the social ladder, which is still reserved for African Americans.[20] Instead, Korean Americans who are inner-city merchants are likely to encounter hostility from those lower in the social structure (Min 1996), and their children are likely to encounter envy and an eventual "glass ceiling" in their attempts at upwardly mobile professional careers. The religious involvements of Afro-Caribbeans in the United States are in part calibrated on the need to distinguish their group from an African American "proximal host" (Warner 1998a, 18–19; McAlister 1998, 146–49; Hepner 1998, 211–12), and to that extent they navigate in a three-dimensional racial space defined by dominant whites, subordinate African Americans, and their own Caribbean-origin color consciousness (McAlister 1998). The situation of Korean and other Asian Americans differs insofar as they are held up as a "model minority" by those who use them to practice "wedge-issue" racial politics but turn their backs on them when they are subject to racial violence (Omi and Winant 1994, 152–59). For the foreseeable future, they will continue to need their churches as a refuge against lack of racial acceptance by the host society (Chai 1998, 323; Chong 1998; Park 2000; Cha, and Park, this volume) as well as a staging ground for attempts to overcome racism (Tseng and Yoo 1998).

---

20. The situation of South Asians may be significantly different in this regard; see Kurien 1998.

Internal Differentiation

The first priority for the immigrant community, and for those who would understand them, is to come to grips with the new intercultural situation: being newcomers in a strange new land, or being members of the receiving society confronted with new and strange neighbors. In these projects of settlement and comprehension, what is most noticeable at first is the difference between the immigrants (in our case Koreans) and the hosts, and each party to this encounter tends to see both the other and itself as solidary groupings. In many cases they are just that, as concerns for self are subordinated to concerns for family and group loyalty. Thus many immigrant Koreans—wives as well as husbands, children as well as parents—put in long, weary hours together so as to make a success of the family business. And many—too many—Americans lump together the newcomers as unwelcome aliens or, worse yet, opportunistic exploiters.

With time, I expect the urgency of intergroup difference to diminish and the salience of intragroup difference to increase. Widowhood, divorce, and delayed marriage increase the ranks of adult women on their own. (In some cases, adult women have come to the United States on their own; see George 1998.) College-educated young people leave home, at least temporarily, and, with their native-speaker English skills, have career opportunities available to them that were denied their parents, who in the case of Koreans may, like the Jewish proletariat of an earlier generation, turn out in retrospect to be a single generation of shopkeepers. Young people from other communities, discouraged by discrimination on the part of the dominant culture, may align themselves with alienated youth cultures and disdain the naïveté of the new immigrants following them by less than a generation (Zhou and Bankston 1998, 185–215). Relationships, even intermarriages, with non-co-nationals grow, with resulting racialized "black," "Latino," pan-Asian, and Eurasian identities (Rumbaut 1994).

Both because of such social dynamics and because of the influence of socialist and feminist scholarship in general and second-generation scholars in particular, studies are proliferating that treat not only the presumably primordial solidarities of "race" and "ethnicity," but also the differentiating factors of social class and, especially for Korean Americans, gender and generation. These are among the reasons that recent studies of Korean American religion include those focusing on Korean American women (e.g., A. R. Kim 1996; J. H. Kim 1996; Park, this volume) and the second generation (e.g., Chai 1998; Chong 1998; Alumkal, Cha, Chai, Goette and Hong, Goette, and Park, this volume). Both concerns query the influence of home-country and host-country values and structures on women and young people.

Those pondering the situation of Korean American women, for example, point out that Christianity upgraded the status of women relative to the Confucian heritage; yet they also document the many ways in which the Christian church continues to oppress and silence women. Ai Ra Kim (1996), for example, says that both Confucianism and Christianity accord a separate and largely subordinate sphere to women, who are expected to sacrifice themselves in favor of the community. Christianity indeed broadens that community from the home to the outside world, but this, Kim argues, has largely meant not only an expansion of the scope of women's obligatory self-sacrifice from husband to children and beyond them to the world of the church, but also a deeper internalization of those obligations (1996, 54–55, 111, 114, 119). In this sense, it is not clear to Kim that Christianity is healthier for women than was Confucianism.

Similarly, Kelly Chong (1998) points out that churched second-generation Korean Americans typically think of their religious commitment as the result of a born-again experience they have come by on their own, and thereby a factor that might be expected to conduce to their feelings of autonomy and individualism. Yet the very conservative Christian ideology they have embraced serves as a powerful reinforcer of traditional Confucian filial piety. Chong quotes a Bible study instructor's admonition "To obey God and to have Him in you is to obey your parents!" (1998, 276).

The attention to generational differences is not confined to the experience of second (and later) generations. The growth of generational distinctiveness is seen in the chapter by Kwang Chung Kim and Shin Kim in this volume, where the profile and perspectives of the large and still only middle-aged first generation are articulated. These first-generation priorities will determine much of the shape of the Korean American church for many years to come.

Such attention to gender and generation as factors in the Korean American religious experience as well as within other immigrant communities (e.g., George 1998; Wittner 1998, 376–77; Orsi 1996) has informed the studies of identity negotiation that I discuss below.

Institutional Adaptations

It is a thesis of this chapter that the Korean immigrant church serves as a model for other immigrant religious communities. For example, reflection on the Korean experience as reported in Section I above was central to an influential postulation in sociology of religion, my own concept of "de-facto congregationalism" (Warner 1993a, 1066–67; Warner 1994, 73–82). Through this concept, I maintain that the center of energy and authority across religious communities in the United States is increasingly to be found at the level of the local gathered community, as opposed to residing in centralized hierarchies, and that local religious communities in the United States— regardless of specific lineage—tend to approximate the look of American Protestant (and Jewish) congregations. As pointed out in Section I, many Korean American congregations are independent (i.e., formally congregational in polity), while others have joined in new and independent denominations or may threaten to do so in defiance of their formal denominational affiliations. Another way of putting this is that we gain far more information by knowing that a church is Korean than by knowing that it is Presbyterian or Methodist.

"De-facto congregationalism" does not mean that each local Korean American congregation is sui generis. To the contrary, typical patterns pertain to Korean American congregations across denominational traditions and across regions in the United States. Korean American congregations are overwhelmingly conservative (or "evangelical") in their theology. They tend to be multifunctional, with programs and structures meeting significant instrumental, social, and psychological needs as well as religious ones (Min 1992). Indeed, the observation by Eui-Young Yu in Chapter 12 that the Kwan Um Sa temple has developed social programs similar to those of Protestant congregations, combined with my own visit to that temple, influenced the development of my conceptualization of de-facto congregationalism (Warner 1994, 81).

Korean Protestant congregations tend to be prone to schism and are therefore typically small (Shin and Park 1988; Kim and Kim, this volume). They contain elaborate governance structures, offering many official but volunteer positions for lay members, especially men (Hurh and Kim 1990; J. H. Lee 1991; Kwon et al. 1997). They have English-language Sunday schools, often taught by European American seminary students, for the young people (Chai 1998). Larger churches with geographically dispersed memberships feature cell groups to provide greater intimacy and to facilitate delivery of services (Kwon et al. 1997). And, reflecting a significant pattern of change since 1990, many now have English-language ministries for second-generation adults (Goette, Chapter 7, this volume; Chai 1998; Chong 1998), which may have stemmed the outward flow that Pai and his colleagues (1987) would have predicted, as seen in Section I.

In some of these respects, the Korean immigrant church models phenomena to be observed across other new immigrant religious communities. For example, competition for church status among men deprived of significant occupational status by the immigration process has been cited as one cause of schism in a very different religious tradition, that of Indian Orthodox Christians (George 1998). The availability and willingness of evangelical European American seminary students to serve as Sunday school teachers for English-dominant youth (Steensland 1995; Chai 1998; Yang 1998) may be a factor in the apparently increasing religious conservatism of second-generation Asian American Protestants in general. Just as Koreans seem to be among those most resistant to liberalization in the mainline U.S. Presbyterian and Methodist denominations, the religious conservatism of other new immigrants may be reversing the increasing liberalization of other American denominations, specifically the Seventh Day Adventist Church (Hernández 1995; Lawson 1998).

Another aspect of the Korean American experience has broader applicability, that of being what we might call "reverse missionaries," those who bring an intense form of religion back to the country from which they were originally evangelized. In a sense, the grand sweep of Christianity westward from its point of origin in the Levant and that of Buddhism eastward from India have been completed by their crossing the Pacific (see Fields 1992; Lin 1996). The spread of Krishna Consciousness and Won Buddhism compared below by Bok-In Kim (Chapter 14) can be seen as similar missionary efforts. This missionary process, the capacity of the great world religions to cross cultural borders, is extended even as its direction is reversed by the movement of Korean Christians to America and American Zen Buddhists to Japan (Finney 1991). Such reverse missionaries promise to purify their newly embraced religion of cultural accretions they can easily trace to the society from which the religion came to them. The theology of pilgrimage developed below by Sang Hyun Lee (Chapter 3) is one contribution to understanding how these movements facilitate a continuing critique of any religion's cultural captivity. Lee's concluding recommendation that Americans Christians, regardless of their race, embrace their own marginality to American culture, is one that I think resonates with contemporary American religious sensibility (Warner 1999).

Negotiation of Identities

Studies of the Korean American religious experience both illuminate and are illuminated by the increasing scholarly focus on a fourth issue, the "negotiation of identities" among new immigrant groups. Despite Will Herberg's view that immigrants and their offspring retain their "old religion," he knew that identities undergo significant change in the United States, even short of conversion to another faith. Herberg called the process one of "transmutation." We now speak of "negotiation" of identity (Kurien 1998; Feher 1998).

It was pointed out in Section I that the proportion of Korean immigrants who affiliate with churches is very high. Religion, specifically Christianity, is extraordinarily significant for Koreans in the United States. Likewise, religious identities, whether Hindu, Jain, Sikh, Muslim, or Christian, seem to be highly significant for Indians in the United States. By contrast, other groups, for example, Japanese and Palestinians, seem more likely to adhere to national identities. But national identification is clearly at least an option for Koreans and Indians in the United States, and college campuses feature Korean and Indian Student Associations as well as Bible Fellowships and Muslim prayer centers, which compete with one another for the loyalties of the second generation (Chai 1998). Confucianism offers an identity for Asian Americans who wish to uphold respect for nurturing relationships (D. K. Kim 1996).

Within a Protestant context, intergenerational contention over the meaning of the Christian identity is rife in the Korean American community. Does being Christian mean being more Korean? As Kelly Chong (1998) poses the question, is it the case for Korean American youth that to obey God means to obey one's parents? Or, is it the case, as Karen Chai (1998) and Alumkal (this volume) imply, that Korean American young people see their Christian commitment as allowing them to challenge their parents' demands that they find suitable Korean, but not necessarily Christian, mates? To judge from the chapters in Part III below, Korean American youth readily distinguish between the "cultural" demands to which they are subjected, often by their elders, and the presumably profounder "Christian" (or religious) calling they affirm. And here again, Korean American youth are at the forefront of second-generation struggles over identity, especially on gender issues (see, e.g., Yep et al. 1998; Martel and Warner 1998).

A developmental approach, as taken Peter Cha in Chapter 8, promises to help integrate otherwise disparate findings on identity. Is there evidence that Korean American youth wish to escape the identification with Asia to which they are ascribed by white American peers? Are Korean American youth eager, for this reason, to join a "silent exodus" from their parents' churches? Or do most proudly claim an Asian as well as a Christian identity? The answers may hinge as much on the age and year of school when these questions are addressed to them as on variation in the social contexts in which they live (regions of Korean concentration like the New Jersey of Alumkal's study in contrast to those of thinly distributed Korean population like Chai's Boston).

The Korean American experience, and reflection by scholars on it, has clearly been path-breaking with respect to moving the question of assimilation, specifically Americanization, beyond the false either/or polarization it had assumed in the 1960s and 70s: either the melting pot homogenizes all identities, or difference persists. Early on, Kim and Hurh (1988, 1993) proposed that the moves toward Americanization that Korean Americans were clearly undergoing were not necessarily at the expense of their Korean identity, and they proposed the concept of "adhesive assimilation" and later "syncretic assimilation" to comprehend this both/and pattern. Later studies (Y.-I. Kim 1994; Yang 1999; Bankston and Zhou 1995, 1996) have abundantly confirmed this model for Korean, Chinese, and Vietnamese Christians in the United States. In these studies, identification with, and participation in, Christian churches both strengthens Asian-origin ethnic identity and facilitates successful adaptation to American society.

In this respect, studies of Korean American religion can contribute to the basic reconceptualization of assimilation theory now under development by such scholars as Alejandro Portes (1994), Rubén Rumbaut (1994), Mary Waters (Mittelberg and Waters 1992), and Min Zhou (Zhou and Bankston 1998). Central to this new theorizing is the twin recognition that (1) the host society is not monolithic but contains multiple, unequal, and racialized "segments" or "proximal hosts" to which immigrants may be assigned; and (2) that immigrant groups themselves possess a variety and range of resources that may make partial assimilation to one or another of these segments more likely. Thus, while it may be true that the Christian identity tends to obscure Confucian alternatives for Asian American youth (D. K. Kim 1996, 180–81), it is also true that the evangelical Christianity typically affirmed by those youth critiques some of the same pathologies of American culture that Confucianism disdains (Chong 1998).

The Korean Christian Church and the Second Generation

To conclude this chapter, I return to the issue that concerned me and the church leaders at the Princeton conference nearly a decade ago, the implications of the new knowledge and the new facts chronicled in Section II for the relationship between the Korean immigrant church and the Korean American second generation. It should be clear that the issue is, if anything, more urgent now than then. Many fewer new immigrants are now arriving in America from Korea than in the 1980s, and young people who were then in elementary school are now in college. The church faced a crisis: adapt or lose your youth (Mullins 1987, 1988; Goette, this volume). Yet by now it should also be clear that the issue has been addressed by many churches and first- and second-generation leaders. As one index, English-language worship services are now found in Korean American churches, whether Presbyterian or Methodist, not only in Los Angeles but from coast to coast and regions in between (Chong 1998, Alumkal and Chai this volume).

Not to be confused with the English-language Sunday schools and youth groups out of which some of them evolved, these English-language proto-congregations' services are relatively new—at Los Angeles' Young-Nak church dating only from 1989, and at Karen Chai's suburban Boston church only since 1991. As new as they are, it is clear that second-generation worship has "loosened up" considerably relative to the observations from ten years ago reported in Section I, especially in terms of dress and music. As reported by Alumkal (this volume) and Chai (1998), Korean American English-language worship is likely to feature "Vineyard"-style music—praise choruses projected on an overheard screen accompanied by guitar, electronic keyboard, and drums—instead of traditional hymns accompanied by organ and piano.

As Karen Chai makes clear, such stylistic "loosening," to use my own characterization, does not involve a theological relaxation and may, depending on the denomination of the parent church, involve a greater degree of theological conservatism. Perhaps because so many of their leaders are seminary students at such schools as Gordon Conwell (outside of Boston), Trinity Evangelical (near Chicago) and Talbot and Fuller (in greater Los Angeles), these second-generation churches are distinctly evangelical in theology. Moreover, Chai (1998) and Chong (1998) provide some indications that English-speaking Korean American evangelicalism may have more of a communal flavor and less of an individualistic one than the dominantly white Vineyard churches that tend to be their stylistic model. In this way, they may combine elements of the Korean Confucian heritage with their evangelicalism, and in this respect they have the potential of maintaining the critical marginality toward the host society that Sang Hyun Lee so respects. Yet as Alumkal makes clear, second-generation Korean Americans have more alternatives to church than do their parents, so churches have to compete for their loyalties.

Many of the English-language worship groups currently function as "departments" within a first-generation church under the authority of a deacon or elder. Goette, in Chapter 7, provides a scheme of how we can expect these English-language ministries to evolve, and Goette and Hong (Chapter 6) recommend appropriate responses of first-generation leaders to such evolution. The studies in this volume give some grounds for hope, but a great deal of patience and understanding is still called for on the part of both generations—the first generation to recognize the autonomy of the second, the second to recognize the wisdom of the first—because the generational transition remains fraught with pitfalls.

References

Bankston III, Carl L., and Min Zhou. 1995. "Religious Participation, Ethnic Identification, and Adaptation of Vietnamese Adolescents in an Immigrant Community." *The Sociological Quarterly* 36 (Summer): 523–34.

———. 1996. "The Ethnic Church, Ethnic Identification, and the Social Adjustment of Vietnamese Adolescents." *Review of Religious Research* 38 (September): 18–37.

Brusco, Elizabeth E. 1995. *The Reformation of Machismo: Evangelical Conversion and Gender in Colombia.* Austin: University of Texas Press.

Burns, Jeffrey M. 1994. "¿Qué es esto? The Transformation of St. Peter's Parish, San Francisco, 1913–1990." In *The Congregation in American Life.* Vol. 1, *Portraits of Twelve Religious Communities,* ed. James Lewis and James Wind, 396–463. Chicago: University of Chicago Press.

Casuso, Jorge, and Michael Hirsley. 1990. "Wrestling for Souls." *Chicago Tribune,* January 7–9.

Chai, Karen. 1998. "Competing for the Second Generation: English-language Ministry in a Korean Protestant Church." In *Gatherings in Diaspora: Religious Communities and the New Immigration,* ed. R. S. Warner and J. G. Wittner, 295–331. Philadelphia: Temple University Press.

Chong, Kelly H. 1998. "What It Means to Be Christian: The Role of Religion in the Construction of Ethnic Identity and Boundary Among Second-Generation Korean-Americans." *Sociology of Religion* 58 (Fall): 259–86.

Christiano, Kevin J. 1991. "The Church and the New Immigrants." In *Vatican II and U.S. Catholicism: Twenty-five Years Later,* ed. H. R. Ebaugh, 169–86. Greenwich, Conn.: JAI Press.

Dart, John. 1989. "Church Reflects Growing Korean Activity" [about Young-Nak Church], *Los Angeles Times,* June 10.

———. 1990. "Korean Congregation Planning an L.A. Flair: Drive-In Services" [about Los Angeles Christian Reformed Church], *Los Angeles Times,* January 20.

Díaz-Stevens, Ana-María, and Anthony M. Stevens-Arroyo. 1998. *Recognizing the Latino Resurgence in U.S. Religion: The Emmaus Paradigm.* Boulder, Colo.: Westview Press.

Dolan, Jay P. 1985. *The American Catholic Experience: A History from Colonial Times to the Present.* Garden City, N.Y.: Doubleday.

Eck, Diana. 1997. *On Common Ground: World Religions in America.* New York: Columbia University Press.

Evans, Sara M., and Harry C. Boyte. 1986. *Free Spaces: The Sources of Democratic Change in America.* New York: Harper and Row.

Feher, Shoshanah. 1998. "From the Rivers of Babylon to the Valleys of Los Angeles: The Exodus and Adaptation of Iranian Jews." In *Gatherings in Diaspora,* ed. R. S. Warner and J. G. Wittner 1998, 71–94. Philadelphia: Temple University Press.

Fields, Rick. 1992. *How the Swans Came to the Lake: A Narrative History of Buddhism in America,* Third edition. Boston: Shambhala.

Finney, Henry C. 1991. "American Zen's 'Japan Connection': A Critical Case Study of Zen Buddhism's Diffusion to the West." *Sociological Analysis* 52 (Winter): 379–96.

Gallup. 1988. *The Unchurched American: Ten Years Later.* Princeton: Princeton Religious Research Center.

George, Sheba. 1998. "Caroling With the Keralites: The Negotiation of Gendered Space in an Indian Immigrant Church." In *Gatherings in Diaspora,* ed. R. S. Warner and J. G. Wittner, 265–94. Philadelphia: Temple University Press.

Haddad, Yvonne Yazbeck, and Adair T. Lummis. 1987. *Islamic Values in the United States: A Comparative Study.* New York: Oxford University Press.

Handlin, Oscar. 1951. *The Uprooted: The Epic Story of the Great Migrations that Made the American People.* Boston: Little, Brown.

Hatch, Nathan O. 1989. *The Democratization of American Christianity.* New Haven: Yale University Press.

Hepner, Randal L. 1998. "The House That Rasta Built: Church-Building and Fundamentalism Among New York Rastafarians." In *Gatherings in Diaspora*, ed. R. S. Warner and J. G. Wittner 1998, 197–234. Philadelphia: Temple University Press.

Herberg, Will. 1960. *Protestant, Catholic, Jew: An Essay in American Religious Sociology*. Second edition. Garden City, N.Y.: Doubleday.

Hernández, Edwin. 1995. "The Browning of Adventism," *Spectrum* 25 (December): 29–50.

Hoge, Dean. 1987. *The Future of Catholic Leadership: Responses to the Priest Shortage*. Kansas City, Mo.: Sheed and Ward.

Horgan, Paul. 1975. *Lamy of Santa Fe: His Life and Times*. New York: Farrar, Straus, and Giroux.

Hurh, Won Moo, and Kwang Chung Kim. 1984. *Korean Immigrants in America*. Madison, N.J.: Fairleigh Dickinson University Press.

———. 1988. *Uprooting and Adjustment: A Sociological Study of Korean Immigrants' Mental Health*. Final report to NIMH. Macomb, Ill.: Department of Sociology and Anthropology, Western Illinois University.

———. 1990. "Religious Participation of Korean Immigrants in the United States." *Journal for the Scientific Study of Religion* 29 (March): 19–34.

Kim, Ai Ra. 1996. *Women Struggling for a New Life: The Role of Religion in the Cultural Passage from Korea to America*. Albany: State University of New York Press.

Kim, Chan-Hie. 1979. *A Statistical Survey of Korean Churches in Southern California*. Claremont, Calif.: Claremont School of Theology, Center for Asian-American Ministries.

———. 1980. *Some Urgent Issues Involved with Korean-American Ministries Within the United Methodist Church Structure*. Claremont, Calif.: Claremont School of Theology, Center for Asian-American Ministries.

Kim, David Kyuman. 1996. "The Promise of Religion for Asian American Conceptions of the Self." *Amerasia Journal* 22 (Spring): 177–81, 193–94.

Kim, Illsoo 1981. *New Urban Immigrants: The Korean Community in New York*. Princeton: Princeton University Press.

Kim, Jung Ha. 1996. "The Labor of Compassion: Voices of 'Churched' Korean American Women." *Amerasia Journal* 22 (Spring): 93–105.

Kim, Kwang Chung. 1988. "Korean Immigration to the United States, 1904–1984." Paper presented at colloquium on recent Asian immigration, University of Illinois at Chicago.

Kim, Kwang Chung, and Won Moo Hurh. 1988. "Two Dimensions of Korean Immigrants' Sociocultural Adaptation: Americanization and Ethnic Attachment." Paper presented at annual meeting of the American Sociological Association, Atlanta.

———. 1993. "Beyond Assimilation and Pluralism: Syncretic Sociocultural Adaptation of Korean Immigrants." *Ethnic and Racial Studies* 16 (October): 696–713.

Kim, Young-Il. 1994. "The Correlation Between Religiosity and Assimilation of First Generation Korean Immigrants in the Chicago Metropolitan Region." Ph.D. diss., Department of Sociology and Anthropology, Loyola University of Chicago.

Kivisto, Peter A. 1992. "Religion and the New Immigrants." In *A Future for Religion? New Paradigms for Social Analysis*, ed. William H. Swatos Jr., 92–107. Newbury Park, Calif.: Sage.

Kurien, Prema. 1998. "Becoming American by Becoming Hindu: Indian Americans Take Their Place at the Multicultural Table." In *Gatherings in Diaspora*, ed. R. S. Warner and J. G. Wittner, 37–70. Philadelphia: Temple University Press.

Kwon, Victoria Hyonchu, Helen Rose Ebaugh, and Jacqueline Hagan. 1997. "The Structure and Functions of Cell Group Ministry in a Korean Christian Church." *Journal for the Scientific Study of Religion* 36 (June): 247–56.

Lawson, Ronald. 1998. "When Immigrants Take Over: The Impact of Immigrant Growth on American Seventh Day Adventism's Trajectory from Sect to Denomination." *Journal for the Scientific Study of Religion* 38 (March): 83–102.

Lee, John H. 1989. "Koreans Sue Presbytery, Allege Bias, Deceit, Theft." *Los Angeles Times*, February 5, part 2, pp. 1–2.

———. 1990. "Judge Rules Korean Church, Not Presbytery, Owns Property." *Los Angeles Times*, January 11.

Lee, Sang Hyun. 1987. "Called to Be Pilgrims: Toward an Asian-American Theology from the Korean Immigrant Perspective." In *Korean American Ministry: A Resourcebook*, ed. S. H. Lee, 90–120. Princeton: Princeton Theological Seminary.

———. 1991. "Korean American Presbyterians: A Need for Ethnic Particularity and the Challenge of Christian Pilgrimage." In *The Diversity of Discipleship: The Presbyterians and Twentieth-Century Christian Witness*, ed. Milton J. Coalter, John M. Mulder, and Louis B. Weeks, 312–30, 400–402. Louisville, Ky.: Westminster/John Knox.

León, Luis. 1998. "Born Again in East L.A.: The Congregation as Border Space." In *Gatherings in Diaspora*, ed. R. S. Warner and J. G. Wittner, 163–96. Philadelphia: Temple University Press.

Leong, Russell. 1996. "Racial Spirits: Between Bullets, Barbed Wire, and Belief." *Amerasia Journal* 22 (Spring): vii–xi.

Light, Ivan. 1985. "Immigrant Entrepreneurs in America: Koreans in Los Angeles." In *Clamor at the Gates: The New American Immigration*, ed. Nathan Glazer, 161–78. San Francisco: Institute for Contemporary Studies.

Light, Ivan, and Edna Bonacich. 1988. *Immigrant Entrepreneurs: Koreans in Los Angeles, 1965–1982*. Berkeley and Los Angeles: University of California Press.

Lin, Irene. 1996. "Journey to the Far West: Chinese Buddhism in America." *Amerasia Journal* 22 (Spring): 106–32.

Martel, Elise, and R. Stephen Warner. 1998. "Catholicism Is to Islam as Velcro Is to Teflon: Religion and Ethnic Culture Among Second Generation Latina and Muslim Women College Students." Paper presented at annual meetings of the Midwest Sociological Society, Kansas City.

McAlister, Elizabeth. 1998. "The Madonna of 115th Street Revisited: Vodou and Haitian Catholicism in the Age of Transnationalism." In *Gatherings in Diaspora*, ed. R. S. Warner and J. G. Wittner, 123–60. Philadelphia: Temple University Press.

Min, Pyong Gap. 1992. "The Structure and Social Functions of Korean Immigrant Churches in the United States." *International Migration Review* 26 (4): 1370–94.

———. 1996. *Caught in the Middle: Korean Communities in New York and Los Angeles*. Berkeley: University of California Press.

Mittelberg, David, and Mary C. Waters. 1992. "The Process of Ethnogenesis Among Haitian and Israeli Immigrants in the United States." *Ethnic and Racial Studies* 15 (July): 412–35.

Montoya, Alex D. 1987. *Hispanic Ministry in North America*. Grand Rapids, Mich.: Zondervan.

Morris, Aldon D. 1984. *The Origins of the Civil Rights Movement: Black Communities Organizing for Change*. New York: Free Press.

Morawska, Ewa. 1990. "The Sociology and Historiography of Immigration." In *Immigration Reconsidered: History, Sociology, and Politics,* ed. Virginia Yans-McLaughlin, 187–238. New York: Oxford University Press.

Morreale, Don, ed. 1988. *Buddhist America: Centers, Retreats, Practices*. Santa Fe, N.M.: John Muir Publications.

Mullins, Mark R. 1987. "The Life-Cycle of Ethnic Churches in Sociological Perspective." *Japanese Journal of Religious Studies* 14 (4): 321–34.

———. 1988. "The Organizational Dilemmas of Ethnic Churches: A Case Study of Japanese Buddhism in Canada." *Sociological Analysis* 49 (Fall): 217–33.

Numrich, Paul David. 1996. *Old Wisdom in the New World: Americanization in Two Immigrant Theravada Buddhist Temples*. Knoxville: University of Tennessee Press.

Olson, Daniel V. A. 1989. "Church Friendships: Boon or Barrier to Church Growth?" *Journal for the Scientific Study of Religion* 28 (December): 432–47.

———. 1993. "Fellowship Ties and the Transmission of Religious Identity." In *Beyond Establishment: Protestant Identity in a Post-Protestant Age*, ed. Jackson W. Carroll and W. Clark Roof. Louisville, Ky.: Westminster / John Knox.

Omi, Michael, and Howard Winant. 1994. *Racial Formation in the United States from the 1960s to the 1990s*. Second edition. New York: Routledge.

Pai, Young. 1987. "A Case for Biculturalism." In *Korean American Ministry: A Resourcebook*, ed. S. H. Lee, 246–63. Princeton: Princeton Theological Seminary.

Pai, Young, Deloras Pemberton, and John Worley. 1987. "Findings on Korean-American Early Adolescents and Adolescents." Kansas City: University of Missouri School of Education.

Portes, Alejandro, ed. 1994. "Special Issue: The New Second Generation." *International Migration Review* 28 (Winter).

Rahula, Yogavacara. 1987. "Buddhism in the West." *Dharma Voice: Bulletin of the College of Buddhist Studies* 1 (April): 15.

Roof, Wade Clark, and William McKinney. 1987. *American Mainline Religion: Its Changing Shape and Future*. New Brunswick: Rutgers University Press.

Rumbaut, Rubén G. 1994. "The Crucible Within: Ethnic Identity, Self-Esteem, and Segmented Assimilation Among Children of Immigrants." *International Migration Review* 28 (4): 748–94.

Saloutos, Theodore. 1964. *The Greeks in the United States*. Cambridge: Harvard University Press.

Saran, Parmatma. 1985. *The Asian Indian Experience in the United States*. Cambridge, Mass.: Schenkman.

Shin, Eui Hang, and Hyung Park. 1988. "An Analysis of Causes of Schisms in Ethnic Churches: The Case of Korean-American Churches." *Sociological Analysis* 49 (Fall): 234–48.

Smith, Lynn, and Russell Chandler. 1989. "Catholics, Evangelical Christians Battle for Latino Souls." *Los Angeles Times*, December 2.

Smith, Timothy L. 1971. "Lay Initiative in the Religious Life of American Immigrants." In *Anonymous Americans*, ed. Tamara K. Hareven, 214–49. Englewood Cliffs, N.J.: Prentice-Hall.

———. 1978. "Religion and Ethnicity in America." *American Historical Review* 83 (December): 1155–85.

Steensland, Brian. 1995. "Ethnic Community in Flux: The Social Transformation of a Japanese American Church." Master's thesis, Department of Sociology, University of Illinois at Chicago.

Suro, Robert. 1989. "Switch by Hispanic Catholics Changes Face of U.S. Religion." *New York Times*, May 14, pp. 1, 22.

Tseng, Timothy, and David Yoo. 1998. "The Changing Face of America." *Sojourners* 27 (March-April): 26–29.

Warner, R. Stephen. 1988. *New Wine in Old Wineskins: Evangelicals and Liberals in a Small-Town Church*. Berkeley and Los Angeles: University of California Press.

———. 1993a. "Work in Progress Toward a New Paradigm for the Sociological Study of Religion in the United States." *American Journal of Sociology* 98 (March): 1044–93.

———. 1993b. "Pentecostal Immigrants and the Making of the Sun Belt" [review essay on *Rising in the West* by Dan Morgan], *Christian Century* 110 (August 25): 819–22.

———. 1994. "The Place of the Congregation in the American Religious Configuration." In *The Congregation in American Life*, ed. James Lewis and James Wind, 2:54–99. Chicago: University of Chicago Press.

———. 1997a. "Observations About Liturgical Catechesis: Clueing in the Visitor," *Proceedings of the North American Academy of Liturgy*, Chicago, January 4–7, pp. 30–34.

———. 1997b. "Religion, Boundaries, and Bridges: The 1996 Paul Hanly Furfey Lecture," *Sociology of Religion* 58 (Fall): 217–38.

———. 1998a. "Introduction: Immigration and Religious Communities in the United States." In *Gatherings in Diaspora*, ed. R. S. Warner and J. G. Wittner, 3–34. Philadelphia: Temple University Press.

———. 1998b. "Approaching Religious Diversity: Barriers, Byways, and Beginnings." 1997 Presidential Address to the Association for the Sociology of Religion. *Sociology of Religion* 59 (Fall): 193–215.

———. 1999. "Changes in the Civic Role of Religion." In *Diversity and Its Discontents: Cultural Conflict and Common Ground in Contemporary American Society*, ed. Jeffrey C. Alexander and Neil J. Smelser, 229–43. Princeton: Princeton University Press.

Warner, R. Stephen, and Judith G. Wittner, eds. 1998. *Gatherings in Diaspora: Religious Communities and the New Immigration*. Philadelphia: Temple University Press.

Weber, Max. 1985. "'Churches' and 'Sects' in North America: An Ecclesiastical Sociopolitical Sketch." *Sociological Theory* 3 (Spring): 7–13.

Wellmeier, Nancy J. 1998. "Santa Eulalia's People in Exile: Maya Religion, Culture, and Identity in Los Angeles." In *Gatherings in Diaspora*, ed. R. S. Warner and J. G. Wittner, 97–122. Philadelphia: Temple University Press.

Weyl, Thomas. 1988. *Hispanic U.S.A.: Breaking the Melting Pot*. New York: Harper and Row.

Williams, Raymond Brady. 1988. *Religions of Immigrants from India and Pakistan: New Threads in the American Tapestry*. Cambridge: Cambridge University Press.

———. 1996. *Christian Pluralism in the United States: The Indian Immigrant Experience*. Cambridge (U.K.): Cambridge University Press.

Wittner, Judith G. 1998. "A Reader Among Fieldworkers." In *Gatherings in Diaspora*, ed. R. S. Warner and J. G. Wittner, 365–83. Philadelphia: Temple University Press.

Yancey, William L., Eugene P. Ericksen, and Richard Juliani. 1976. "Emergent Ethnicity: A Review and Reformulation." *American Sociological Review* 41 (June): 391–403.

Yang, Fenggang. 1998. "Tenacious Unity in a Contentious Community: Cultural and Religious Dynamics in a Chinese Protestant Church." In *Gatherings in Diaspora*, ed. R. S. Warner and J. G. Wittner, 333–61. Philadelphia: Temple University Press.

———. 1999. *Chinese Christians in America: Conversion, Assimilation, and Adhesive Identities*. University Park: Pennsylvania State University Press.

Yep, Jeanette, Peter Cha, Susan Cho Van Riesen, Greg Jao, and Paul Tokunaga. 1998. *Following Jesus Without Dishonoring Your Parents: Asian American Discipleship*. Downers Grove, Ill.: InterVarsity Press.

Yoo, David. 1996. "For Those Who Have Eyes to See: Religious Sightings in Asian America." *Amerasia Journal* 22 (Spring): xiii–xxii.

Yu, Eui-Young. 1983. "Korean Communities in America: Past, Present, and Future." *Amerasia Journal* 10 (Fall/Winter): 23–52.

Zhou, Min, and Carl L. Bankston III. 1998. *Growing Up American: How Vietnamese Children Adapt to Life in the United States*. New York: Russell Sage Foundation.

Part II

RELIGIOUS EXPERIENCES
OF KOREAN IMMIGRANT
CHRISTIANS

3

Pilgrimage and Home in the Wilderness of Marginality

Symbols and Context in Asian American Theology

Sang Hyun Lee

THERE WAS NO PARTICULAR problem with my life in this country when I thought of myself as a foreign student from Korea. All I had to do was study hard and get good grades. But when I began teaching in a small town in the Midwest with the prospect of living my entire life here, something disturbing began to emerge in my consciousness. However long I stayed in this country, I seemed to remain a stranger, an alien. And this condition of being a stranger appeared to have two dimensions: the experience of being in between two worlds, the Korean and the American, belonging to both in some ways, but not wholly belonging to either; and the sense that I as a non-white person might never be fully accepted by the majority of the dominant group in this country.

It is not that there are no experiences of a positive nature for Asian immigrants. Acts of human kindness expressed across racial ethnic lines, the warmth of sunny days, and other ordinary blessings of life abound in this land. However, the pervasive and relentless reality of the cold glances and gestures of disdain and rejection from the American public at large sadly clouds over the positive experiences and finally gets an Asian person to admit in the depth of his or her soul: "I don't belong here. I am a stranger!"

This predicament of marginality is vividly expressed in a poem by Joann Miyamoto, an American-born Japanese American. Here is an excerpt:

When I was young
Kids used to ask me
what are you?
I'd tell them what my mom told me
I'm an American
chin chin Chinaman
You are a Jap!
Flashing hot inside
I'd go home
my mom would say
don't worry
he that walks alone
walks faster

people kept asking me
what are you?
And I would always answer
I'm an American
they'd say
no, what nationality

but there was always
someone asking me
what are you?
Now I answer
I'm an Asian
and they say
why do you want to separate yourselves
now I say
I'm Japanese
and they say
don't you know this is the greatest country in the world
now I say in America
I'm part of the third world people
and they say
if you don't like it here
why don't you go back.[1]

1. Quoted from *Roots: An Asian American Reader,* ed. Amy Tachiki, Eddie Wong, and Franklin Odo (Los Angeles: UCLA Asian American Studies Center, 1971), 98–99.

A 12-year-old Korean American girl summed it up this way in an oratorical contest in Los Angeles: "In this country I feel like a stranger. If I returned to Korea, I would be a stranger there, too. But then who am I? I hope someday I will know the answer to this question."[2]

It is with people like Joann Miyamoto and that 12-year-old Korean American girl—that is, in the context of marginality—that the Asian American church is called upon to live out its Christian faith.[3] And the Asian American church has been asking for some time now: How do we as Christians live in this bewildering predicament of in-betweenness and in face of the painful alienation in the American society? What is the Christian meaning of living one's whole life as a stranger?

What I propose to do in this chapter is mainly twofold: first, I want to give some specificity to the term "marginality" as used in reference to the Asian American experience; and second, I will look at two historic Christian symbols—pilgrimage and home—and show how these symbols are given particular expressions by the Asian American context and also how these symbols continue to challenge, widen, and correct the life and work of Asian American Christians.

Marginality as Forced Liminality: The Context of Asian American Theology

The classic discussion of marginality by sociologists Robert E. Park and Everett Stonequist in the 1940s already recognized the existence of two elements in marginality: in-betweenness and nonacceptance by the dominant group. A marginal person, according to Stonequist, "is poised in psychological uncertainty between two (or more) social worlds; reflecting in his soul the discords and harmonies, repulsions and attractions of these worlds, one of which is often 'dominant' over the other." Such a person, furthermore, "emulates and strives to be accepted by a group of which he is not yet, or is only peripherally a member."[4]

One of the many criticisms of Stonequist's work by subsequent researchers has been that he did not emphasize sufficiently the factor of exclusion by

2. *Hankuk Ilbo* (Korea Times), February 28, 1979.

3. The term "Asian American" is used as a shorthand term for convenience. People such as the Pacific Islanders should not be excluded from the meaning of that term.

4. Everett V. Stonequist, *The Marginal Man: A Study in Personality and Culture Conflict* (New York: Russell and Russell, 1937), 8; see also Charles Marden and Gladys Meyer, *Minorities in American Society* (New York: Van Nostrand Reinhold, 1968), 44–45.

the dominant group in the marginalization of minority people. It has been pointed out, for example, that marginality results from a hierarchical relationship of groups in which "a resistance is offered by members of the non-marginal and dominate group, to his [the marginal person's] entry into the group and the enjoyment of its privileges." It is due to the dominant group's resistance, in other words, that "the individual in a marginal position possesses characteristics (those gained from the process of acculturation) which would 'ordinarily' give him a higher status, but which do not."[5] The "resistance" by the dominant group as at least one of the causes of a nonwhite person's marginality, however, was already present in Stonequist's discussion. And the value of Stonequist's analysis is that he clearly saw the presence of both in-betweenness and nonacceptance by the dominant group as components of the marginality experience.

Some anthropologists, on the other hand, use the term *marginality* to refer primarily to the experience of "in-betweenness." It was the Dutch anthropologist Arnold van Gennep who spoke about the transitional period in a rite of passage as marked by "margin" or *limen* ('threshold' in Latin). The anthropologist Victor Turner further developed the idea of *liminality* in his many influential studies of the changes in traditional societies. Turner analyzed the liminal period of in-betweenness as a transitional condition of being out of the usual structure in people's lives—a creative condition in which an experience of communities can occur.[6]

Liminality, or in-betweenness, is clearly an essential part of the Asian American experience. Asian Americans are caught between two worlds. But their liminality exists in the context of nonacceptance by the dominant group.[7] Their liminality is made permanent by the barrier of the dominant group's nonacceptance. In such a situation the creativity of liminality cannot flourish, nor can any fruits of the in-between experience be brought back productively into structure. Such liminality, then, is a frustrated and suppressed liminality, and the people caught in it are deprived of completing the process of human becoming. By the term *marginality*, then, we mean a

5. See H. F. Dickie-Clark, *The Marginal Situation: A Sociological Study of a Coloured Group* (London: Routledge and Kegan Paul, 1966), 24; E. C. Hughes and H. M. Hughes, *Where People Meet: Racial and Ethnic Frontiers* (Glencoe, Ill.: Free Press, 1952), 190.

6. See Victor Turner, *The Ritual Process: Structure and Anti-Structure* (Ithaca: Cornell University Press, 1969), 94–203.

7. The Asian immigrants' in-between liminality and their strangerhood caused by the American society's nonacceptance are two of the major themes that run throughout Ronald Takaki's masterful narrative of Asian Americans' history. See his *Strangers from a Different Shore: A History of Asian Americans* (New York: Penguin Books, 1989).

For an interesting attempt to reinterpret the meaning of the Asian American experience of marginality from the perspective of the Asian worldview, see Jung Young Lee, "Marginality: A Multi-Ethnic Approach to Theology from an Asian-American Perspective," *Asian Journal of Theology* 7 (2) (1993): 244–53.

forced and permanent liminality—an in-betweenness that is suppressed, frustrated, and unfulfilled by barriers that are not in one's own control. This definition of marginality, I believe, enables us to recognize a potential creativity of liminality in the Asian American experience without ignoring the negative factor of racism in the American society.

Our discussion thus far also enables us to point to an important difference between the experience of white European immigrants and that of nonwhite immigrants such as Asian Americans. The experience of an immigrant from Europe can usually be explained in terms of the so-called straight-line theory of assimilation. That person will arrive and then experience a period of in-betweenness. With an increasing acculturation, "structural assimilation" will follow since a European immigrant would not experience nonacceptance. That person will become "one of us" to the dominant group in America.[8]

But the straight-line assimilation theory does not apply to nonwhite immigrants. A Korean immigrant, for example, may speak beautiful English and have a name like Peter, Nancy, or Michael. But when that person walks down Main Street, he or she is still a stranger, a new arrival.[9]

I have been in this country for over thirty-eight years. When I am away from campus, people still ask me, "Where are you from?" I answer, of course, "Princeton, New Jersey." But they ask again: "No, no, where are you from?" "Princeton, New Jersey" is hardly ever sufficient in my case. Small reminders like this occur for Asian Americans day after day, week after week, year after year, and decade after decade. And eventually you get it. You get that they don't think you belong here. Race sticks for Asian Americans as it does for other nonwhite persons in this country. They are indeed "strangers from a different shore" as the Asian American historian Ron Takaki puts it.[10]

Asian Americans, however, do not all feel a sense of marginality to the same degree. The rule is that the more they adopt mainstream white America as their reference group and want to belong to it, the more they will be conscious personally of what mainstream white America thinks of them— namely, of their marginality.[11] We shall return to this point.

8. See Harry H. L. Kitano and Roger Daniels, *Asian Americans: Emerging Minorities* (Englewood Cliffs, N.J.: Prentice-Hall, 1988), 1–9.

9. Won Moo Hurh, "Comparative Study of Korean Immigrants in the United States: A Typology," *Koreans in America*, ed. Byong-suh Kim et al. (Memphis, Tenn.: Association of Korean Christian Scholars in North America, 1977), 95.

10. Takaki, *Strangers from a Different Shore*.

11. See Alan C. Kerckhoff and Thomas C. McCormick, "Marginal Status and Marginal Personality," *Social Forces* 34 (October 1977): 50; Won Moo Hurh and Kwang Chung Kim, *Korean Immigrants in America: A Structural Analysis of Ethnic Confinement and Adhesive Adaptation* (Rutherford: Fairleigh Dickinson University Press, 1984), 138–55.

To summarize what I have been saying thus far: all processes of change have three stages—ending, transition period, and reaggregation or return to structure.[12] Asian Americans are a people who left a world and are going through transition. They now need to be realigned, restabilized in a social structure. They are allowed in—but only to the edges of this society. Asian Americans, in short, are trapped in the wilderness of in-betweenness and need a structure to return to.

Historic Christian Symbols and the Asian American Context

What are the important faith responses, both in word and deed, of the Asian American churches to their marginality? I will deal with this question by lifting up two symbols—pilgrimage and home—that are important in the Asian American church and by discussing their particular meaning in the Asian American context.

My discussion assumes two principles. First, the living Christian symbols exist not in abstraction but in concrete contexts, and new contexts can bring out certain fresh meanings of symbols that may not have been sufficiently recognized before. And second, the historic Christian symbols are not just reappropriated and reinterpreted, but they continue to critique, challenge, and deepen the Christian church's faith responses.

I am reminded here of the image of water as it is used by Taoism as in Tao Te Ching.[13] The ultimate reality, this book says, is like the water that makes its way down a stream. Water yields to, and is shaped by, the contours of the stream bed, by the stones and rocks it encounters. But the water that yields also has a shaping power. In the long run, the stream and everything in it is reshaped by the gentle force of the water. The historic Christian symbols live on by yielding to the ever new contexts, but in a most fundamental way those symbols reshape and mold the life and work of Christians in their particular contexts.

12. For a discussion of the change process, see, for example, William Bridges, *Transitions: Making Sense of Life's Changes* (Reading, Mass.: Addison-Wesley, 1980.)

13. I owe this reference to Tao Te Ching to Bishop Roy I. Sano, "A Theology of Struggle from an Asian American Perspective," *Branches* (Journal of the Pacific and Asian Center for Theologies and Strategies), Fall/Winter, 1990, 8.

Pilgrimage in the Wilderness of Marginality

The image of the Christian believer as a pilgrim who does not absolutize any one place or idea but is always ready to leave the present situation toward a God-promised goal has been important for the Asian American church.[14] The way Abraham obeyed and left home when he was called, "not knowing where he was to go," and the way he and his family sojourned in the wilderness as "strangers and exiles," seeking the true "homeland," "a better country," "the city whose builder and maker is God"—these images from the New Testament Letter to the Hebrews have been deeply meaningful to many Asian American Christians.

Most Asian immigrants, of course, do not come to America consciously thinking of themselves as pilgrims. They usually come here for very mundane reasons—for a better education, for a better financial future, and the like. And these dreams are fulfilled for some of them—sometimes beyond their expectations. The Christian pilgrimage, however, emerges as a compelling image as Asian immigrants invariably face their uprootedness that results from emigration. They come to America scarcely prepared for the consequences of leaving home. In addition, as a nonwhite people they encounter the cold glances of disdain from the American public. So after a number of years in this country, a crisis of sorts develops. In the secret places of their minds, Asian immigrants ask themselves: Did we make a mistake? Is there any meaningfulness in living as strangers? Most of them dare not voice these questions too loudly because surrounding them in the living room are their own deeply Americanized children for whom home is nowhere but in America. Studies have shown a strong tendency on the part of most Asian immigrants to shrink away from the cold winds of marginality and to cling

---

14. The meaning of the pilgrimage symbol I am adopting follows closely that of J. B. Soucek, "Pilgrims and Sojourners: An Essay in Biblical Theology," *Communio Viatorum I* (1958): 3–17. I have also found helpful Richard R. Niebuhr's observation: "Pilgrims are persons in motion—passing through territories not their own—seeking something we might call completion, or perhaps the clarity will do as well, a goal to which only the spirit's compass points the way" ("Pilgrims and Pioneers," *Parabola* 9, no. 3 [1984]: 7).

Definitions of the term *pilgrimage* range from strict and narrow to comprehensive and broad. H. B. Partin, for example, finds four essential elements in pilgrimages: separation, journey to a sacred place, a fixed purpose, and a hardship ("The Muslim Pilgrimage: Journey to the Center," Ph.D. diss, University of Chicago, 1967; quoted in William G. Johnsson, "The Pilgrimage Motif in the Book of Hebrews," *Journal of Biblical Literature* 97 [1978]: 244). Another anthropologist, Alan Morinis, however, offers a much broader definition. The term *pilgrimage,* according to Morinis, "can be put to use wherever journeying and some embodiment of an ideal intersect" ("Introduction: The Territory of the Anthropology of Pilgrimage," in *Sacred Journeys: The Anthropology of Pilgrimage* [Westport, Conn.: Greenwood Press, 1992], 3). For a recent discussion of the metaphor of pilgrimage with a different application from mine, see Margaret Miles, "Pilgrimage as Metaphor in a Nuclear Age," *Theology Today* 45 (July 1988): 166–79.

to the cozy comforts of their ethnic enclaves at the risk of bringing about a dangerous isolation from the larger American society.[15]

It is in this context of having problems of leaving home and really arriving in America that the image of the Abrahamic obedience to God's call has been invoked in the Asian American church. The challenge is to see the Asian immigrants' de facto uprootedness as an opportunity to embark on a sacred pilgrimage to some God-promised goal, and therefore to believe that life as strangers and exiles can be meaningful. One of the hymns written by a Korean immigrant pastor has the following first stanza: "Obeying when he was called, / leaving home by faith, / Abraham made an altar wherever he wandered. / We are all Abraham; / let us learn of his faith; / through our faithfulness to God, / may God's own purpose fulfill."[16]

We must pause here, however, and ask whether or not the above appropriation of the pilgrimage symbol has a sufficient regard for the particular context of Asian Americans. I myself have written and preached about the Asian immigrants' Christian calling to be pilgrims, but I have now for some time been growing a bit suspicious as to whether such talk goes far enough in taking account of the full import of Asian Americans' marginality.[17] For Asian immigrants, to enter America or to make it their reference group is asking for trouble—namely, to become consciously aware of their marginality. Therefore, it is not adequate to call upon Asian immigrant Christians to become pilgrims and to enter into the American society as if their doing so would be the same as it would be for white European immigrants.

What then is the particular meaning of the Asian Americans' pilgrimage into America? Why should they be asked to do something that is bound to bring them trouble? Beyond and above the secular goal of "making it in America" by getting a piece of the so-called American Dream, what is the Christian reason why Asian Americans should at least once in a while leave the comforts of their ethnic enclaves and mix with the majority people in America at the risk of becoming marginalized?

15. See Hurh and Kim, *Korean Immigrants in America,* 84–86, 146–49.

16. Byung-sup Bahn, *Jil-Geu-Reut-Gat-Un-Na-Eh-Ge-Do* (Even for me an earthen vessel) (Seoul, Korea: Yang-Suh-Kak, 1988), 97.

17. For one of my earliest attempts relate the pilgrimage symbol to marginality, see "Called to Be Pilgrims: Toward a Theology Within the Korean American Context," in *The Korean Immigrant in America,* ed. Byong-suh Kim and Sang Hyun Lee (Montclair, N.J.: Association of Korean Christian Scholars in North America, 1980), 37–74.

I have benefited from numerous other theological reflections by Asian American scholars. In addition to those already mentioned, see, for example: Roy I. Sano, *From Every Nation Without Number: Racial and Ethnic Diversity in United Methodism* (Nashville, Tenn.: Abingdon, 1982); Wesley S. Woo, "Theological Themes," in *Asian Pacific American Youth Ministry* (Valley Forge, Pa.: Judson Press, 1988), 11–22; Ha Tai Kim, *Tai-Pyong-Yang-Geun-Neu-Kanaan-Tang* (The land of Canaan across the Pacific) (Pasadena, Calif.: Korean Church of the Pacific, 1979).

In thinking about this question, a passage from H. Richard Niebuhr's *The Meaning of Revelation* continues to have for me a hauntingly irresistible quality. Niebuhr writes: "He [Christ] is the man through whom the whole human history becomes our history. Now there is nothing that is alien to us. All of the wanderings of all peoples and all the sins of men in all places become parts of our past through him. . . . Through Christ we become immigrants into the empire of God which extends over all the world and learn to remember the history of that empire, that is of men in all times and places, as our history."[18] Speaking from his radical monotheism perspective, Niebuhr regards all parts of the world and all aspects of human history as the realm of God's activity and thus sacred though finite. It is a responsibility of a faithful Christian, then, to make a pilgrimage to every part of history and to every place of the world and to include them in his and her remembering.

But what does it mean to make every part of human history our own for Asian Americans in America? I would like to suggest here that to get at the specific implications for Asian Americans of what Niebuhr is saying here we need to pay a more direct attention to the Asian American Christians' own experiences of making pilgrimage into America.[19]

The racial uprising of 1992 in South Central Los Angeles, I believe, is particularly instructive. The initial reaction of the Korean immigrants in Koreatown was one of surprise: How could this happen in America? They asked. These Korean immigrants were mostly living in ethnic self-confinement and had not really entered the American society. What happened to them on April 29 can be said to be a coerced entrance into the American realities: a painful lesson in their own and other minority groups' marginality in the American society. What resulted was awareness, in other words.

Awareness then led to sympathy and solidarity. The first- and the younger second-generation Korean Americans suddenly forgot all of their generational conflicts and joined together in relief work and marched together in a peace demonstration. A Korean American young woman told me that the pain she felt at the sight of other Koreans' suffering told her that she was a Korean after all. Korean American and African American churches and church leaders came together in various ways to worship, to share each others' experiences, and to discuss the ways of helping each other in their common struggle for justice and human dignity. Being consciously at the margin of

18. H. Richard Niebuhr, *The Meaning of Revelation* (New York: Macmillan, 1962), 116.

19. Darryl M. Trimiew, working out of his African American context, also critiques and learns from H. Richard Niebuhr's thought. See his *Voices of the Silenced: The Responsible Self in a Marginalized Community* (Cleveland, Ohio: Pilgrim Press, 1993).

the society gave them the capacity to become aware of others at the margin; this capacity was also a capacity for solidarity. To put it in Victor Turner's language, having become aware of their alienation from the American society and thus in a sense freed from the dominant social structure, Korean immigrants became consciously liminal and thus open to communities' experience.[20] Whatever else it may mean for Asian Americans to become pilgrims, it does mean to become self-conscious strangers and thereby to become capable of solidarity with other strangers.

All this suggests that creative and redemptive events occur at the in-between and often despised margins of this world. Margins can be creative centers, in other words. Is it any accident, then, that we find the following words in the Letter to the Hebrews? "So Jesus also suffered outside the gate in order to sanctify the people through his own blood. Therefore let us go forth to him outside the camp and bear the abuse he endured. For here we have no lasting city, but we seek the city which is to come" (13:12–14, RSV). In this passage, pilgrimage theme and redemption theme come together. "Outside the camp" is where Jesus began his redemptive project.[21] And it is the pilgrims who know that "here we have no lasting city" and are willing to follow Christ to the margins that participate in Jesus project. And these pilgrims are not alone: they have Jesus as "the pioneer and perfecter of their faith." In other words, something more than sheer human courage is going on here. There is behind all this an intentionality of God's own self, God's own journey, and God's own project.

God's Household for the Strangers in the Margin

To be pilgrims and self-conscious strangers at the margins, then, can lead to an experience of community and solidarity. But one cannot stay in such ecstatic moments indefinitely. Asian American pilgrims, as all mortal humans,

20. A series of insightful analyses of the tragic events of 1992 in Los Angeles appeared in a Korean American journal, *The Christian Herald,* in the spring of 1994. See, for example, Chan-Hie Kim, "The April 29 Event from the Biblical Perspective and Koreans in America I and II," *Christian Herald,* April 8, 1994, 20–22, and April 15, 14–17; Sung-do Park, "The April 29 Event and the Emergence of New Life II," *Christian Herald,* May 6, 1994, 21–25.

21. See Helmut Koester, "'Outside the Camp': Hebrews 13:9–14," *Harvard Theological Review* 55 (1962): 299–315; William G. Johnson, "The Pilgrimage Motif in the Book of Hebrews," *Journal of Biblical Literature* 97, no. 2 (1978): 239–51. For an important study of the Letter to the Hebrews by an Asian American theologian, see Roy I. Sano, *Outside the Gate: A Study of The Letter to the Hebrews* (Cincinnati, Ohio: United Methodist Church, 1982). For an instructive essay on the themes of home and the Christ "outside the camp," see Charles C. West, "Where Is Our Home and Who Is Welcome in It?" *Presbyterian Outlook,* June 10, 1985, 14–15.

need a hospitable structure for belonging. They need a home. And as many people know, in the Asian American community it is the ethnic church that has played a greater role in meeting this need for belonging than any other institution. The church is the home, or at least a home away from home, for many Asian immigrants and their succeeding generations.[22]

It is interesting to note at this point that according to the biblical scholar John H. Elliott, the "home for the homeless" is precisely the way 1 Peter in the New Testament conceives of the essential nature of the church as the eschatological community itself. According to Elliott, the Good News offered by 1 Peter to the socially marginalized Christians in Asian Minor was "not an ephemeral 'heaven is our home' form of consolation but the new home and social family to which Christians can belong here and now . . . a supportive circle of brothers and sisters." And "status here is not gained through blood ties nor by meeting social prerequisites; it is available to all classes and races of mankind as a divine gift."[23] They remain despised strangers in society; but in the household of God, everything has changed. They are "the elect of God." "But you are a chosen race, a royal priesthood, a holy nation, God's own people. . . . Once you were no people but now you are God's people; once you had not received mercy but now you have received mercy" (1 Peter 2:9–10).

What the symbol "household of God" or "home for the homeless" stands for receives a powerful expression in the Asian American church, which is one place in America where Chinese Americans, Japanese Americans, or Korean Americans feel like they are somebody. As Asian Americans come together in their ethnic churches, sit next to each other, worship together, eat together, and just be together, they experience an inversion of status, turning upside down the way they are viewed in the society outside.

In this way, the church as the household of God takes an ethnically particular form in the Asian American context. But the Asianness of the Asian American church is nothing to apologize about; ethnicity, in this case, can be an instrument of the church's redemptive function. When Asian Americans are marginalized and made homeless because of their ethnicity, how can

---

22. In the case of Korean immigrants, for example, almost 70 percent are affiliated with Korean immigrant churches, and about 85 percent of them attend church regularly. See Hurh and Kim, *Korean Immigrants in America,* 129–69.

23. John H. Elliott, *A Home for the Homeless: A Sociological Exegesis of 1 Peter—Its Situation and Strategy* (Philadelphia: Fortress Press, 1981), 127, 130–31, 199. Elliott draws a sharp distinction between the "heavenly home" "beyond time and history" of the Letter to the Hebrews and the "household of God," which is "a place of belonging" here and now, of 1 Peter (see 129–32, 224–27). Even if we suppose that this distinction is correct, it would seem that we would need both the transcendent dimension of the ultimate realization of God's kingdom in the Letter to the Hebrews and the this-worldly embodiment of the kingdom in 1 Peter.

a church be a home to them if it did not affirm and celebrate the dignity of their particular ethnicity? As the Japanese American theologian Roy Sano puts it, liberation *through* ethnicity and not *from* ethnicity has to be an essential function of the Asian American church.[24] The symbol "household of God," then, has to be contextualized in this way in the Asian American context of marginality.

For the second and later generations, their particularity as Asian Americans takes the form of an in-between ethnicity, a hyphenated synthesis that is neither just Asian nor just American. The first-generation immigrants also experience an in-betweenness, but their rootedness in their homelands and the strong first-generation church provide them with much comfort. But the later generations often feel alienated both from their parents' first-generation church and community and from the American society. In other words, neither the Asian nor the American community quite accepts them for what they are.

The Asian American church as a household of God must become a place where the second- and later-generation people are accepted as they are—neither just as Asian nor just as American but as a new synthesis of the two with an integrity all of its own.[25] In the Asian world, they are often criticized for not being Asian enough; while in the American society, they are looked down upon for not being American enough. In the household of God, they should not have to be enough anything—except to be what they are and to have faith in Christ. The in-between colors have names, as one Korean American woman put it. She said: "I thank God for making the rainbow, the rainbow with beautiful primary colors and lots of in-between colors. When we mix red and yellow, we have orange. . . . Yet orange is not red, orange is not yellow. Orange is another color with its own name and its own color. I am the 'in-between.' In-between colors have names, too."[26]

Another way to look at the particularity of Asian American ethnicity is to point to its fundamentally dynamic and open character. The Asian American identity and ethnicity is not an eternally fixed reality; it is in the making. And the making of this something new requires the creative energies inherent in the in-between, liminal condition of Asian Americans. One of the essential

24. Roy I. Sano, "Ministry for a Liberating Ethnicity: The Biblical and Theological Foundations for Ethnic Ministries," in *The Theologies of Asian American and Pacific Peoples: A Reader,* comp. Roy I. Sano (Berkeley, Calif.: Asian Center for Theology and Strategies, Pacific School of Religion, 1976), 291.

25. See Won Moo Hurh, "Toward a New Community and Identity: The Korean-American Ethnicity," in *The Korean Immigrant in America,* ed. Kim and Lee, 1–25.

26. Soomee Kim Hwang, "In-between Colors Have Names Too," *Pacific and Asian American Christian Education Newsletter* 7 (March 1992): 1; quoted from Fumitaka Matsuoka, "Out of Silence: Emerging Themes of Asian-American Churches," unpublished manuscript, 108.

tasks of the Asian American church, then, would be to free up the creativity of the in-between people by affirming them for what they are. The household of God, in other words, has to be a place where Asian Americans can dream dreams. Gaston Bachelard has noted that home is a place "that protects the dreamer, allows one to dream in peace."[27]

The Asian American church, then, must affirm all the particularities of Asian Americans in their new emerging ethnicity. But to be a true embodiment of the household of God, the Asian American church also has the challenge to become ever more inclusive—both internally and externally. The one area where most Asian American churches have a long way to go in becoming a true embodiment of the household of God has to do with the place of women. Asian American women are marginalized not only in American society but also within the Asian American community itself. Much of the economic success of many Asian immigrants is due to the inordinate amount of labor provided by women at business places. But women do not enjoy the same status and privileges as men either at home or in the church.[28]

What Asian American women, especially the first generation, are up against is the whole Confucian metaphysics with its conception of household in which women exist primarily to serve men.[29] The household metaphor, therefore, is ambiguous for Asian American women. The Asian cultural ideology about women needs to be purged and corrected by the reality of the biblical household of God. And the church as a household needs to be presented as a liberating household in which the usual ideas of women are turned upside down. Liberated from their double marginalization, it should be noted, the creative energies of Asian American women's two-sided in-betweenness or liminality—their liminality as women and their liminality as Asian American—can be set free.[30]

27. Gaston Bachelard, *The Poetics of Space* (Boston: Beacon Press, 1969), 6; quoted from Sharon Daloz Parks, "Home and Pilgrimage: Companion Metaphors for Personal and Social Transformation," *Soundings* 72 (Summer/Fall, 1989): 304.

28. Kwang Chung Kim and Won Moo Hurh, "The Wives of Korean Small Businessmen in the U.S.: Business Involvement and Family Roles," in *Korean American Women: Toward Self-Realization,* ed. Inn Sook Lee (Mansfield, Ohio: Association of Korean Christian Scholars in North America, 1985), 1–41. A good anthology of articles on Asian American women's experiences is *Making Waves: An Anthology of Writings By and About Asian American Women,* ed. Asian Women United of California (Boston: Beacon Press, 1989).

29. See Inn Sook Lee, "Korean American Women and Ethnic Identity," in *Korean American Ministry,* expanded English edition, ed. Sang Hyun Lee and John V. Moore (Louisville, Ky.: Presbyterian Church USA, 1993), 192–214; Soon Man Rhim, "The Status of Women in Traditional Korean Society," in *Korean Women in a Struggle for Humanization,* ed. Harold H. Sunoo and Dong Soo Kim (Memphis, Tenn.: Association of Korean Christian Scholars in North America, 1978), 11–37; Minza Kim Boo, "The Social Reality of the Korean American Women: Toward Crashing with the Confucian Ideology," in *Korean American Women,* ed. Inn Sook Lee, 65–93.

30. For a discussion of women's "experience of nothingness" and its creativity, see, for example, Carol Christ, *Diving Deep and Surfacing: Women Writers on Spiritual Quest* (Boston: Beacon Press, 1980), 9–14.

The symbol of the household of God also challenges the Asian American church to become ever more inclusive in its external relations with other peoples and other churches. To affirm the Asian American ethnicity in all of its particularities, as we saw above, is an essential dimension of the Asian American church as church. However, the ethnic particularity must not be absolutized. Whenever this absolutizing happens, the demonic consequences of the idolatrous ethnocentrism will only be perpetuated again—this time in its Asian American form. The Asian American church, in short, has this most delicate and difficult calling: to affirm its ethnic particularity over against racism, and at the same time to resist the temptation toward self-enclosure and constantly move beyond itself toward others. To be at home in the household of God, in other words, is to be at home in such a way that one does not fear the margins—that is to say, one never ceases to be a pilgrim.

In sum, the two historic symbols of the Christian faith—pilgrimage and home—manifest their original power in new ways when they are appropriated in the Asian American context of marginality. Pilgrimage for marginalized people means the willingness to face up to one's marginality and to join with other strangers in the margins. But it is precisely their pilgrimage or their freedom from the idolatrous centers of the world that prepares them for an experience of the reality of the household of God that God is building for all humankind. Pilgrimage and home, then, necessarily go together. This can only be so because, in the final analysis, pilgrimage and home are connected by a story that is God's own story.

God's Own Story

In conclusion, then, we ask: What is God's own story in which pilgrimage and home have their foundation and unity? What we have been saying in this chapter suggests an answer that we can only mention here without elaboration. God is also a pilgrim who left home. Not that God was not perfect from eternity, but rather that God wanted to repeat God's inner life of loving community now in time and space.[31] But the world did not welcome God. God was not accepted by the idolatrous and absolutized centers of this world and became stranded in the wilderness of marginality. So the marginalized pilgrim God began a project of building the loving community in the

31. The idea of the creation as God's "repetition" of God's inner being comes from Jonathan Edwards. See his "Concerning the End for Which God Created the World," in *Works of Jonathan Edwards*, vol. 8, *Ethical Writings*, ed. Paul Ramsey (New Haven: Yale University Press, 1989), 433.

margins of this world. This project will be a struggle because it is carried out in the margins. But it cannot fail because it is God's own project.

And also, because this project is God's own, it is a project and a story that all God's creation, regardless of their race, are invited to join. To do so, however, means that they first become pilgrims and embrace their own wilderness in their own ways. Asian American theology in the context of marginality, in short, is an invitation for all to meet in the margins as fellow strangers and to stand by each other in solidarity as they join in God's own joyous struggle to build the household of God, where all of God's creation can come and be at home.

4

The Ethnic Roles of Korean Immigrant Churches in the United States

Kwang Chung Kim and Shin Kim

AS A DIRECT CONSEQUENCE of the 1965 abolition of the National Origins Act of 1924, the immigrants coming to the United States after 1965[1] have been highly diversified in terms of race and cultural backgrounds. As Warner observes, "The new immigrants are racially, ethnically, linguistically and religiously more heterogeneous than those of a century ago" (1993, 1061). In spite of this heterogeneity, religion is found to play a prominent role in the daily lives of these post-1965 immigrants (George 1998; Hurh and Kim 1984, 1990; Illsoo Kim 1981; Kivisto 1992; Min 1992; Shin and Park 1988; Warner 1993; Williams, 1988). This chapter is about the religious experience of one of the new immigrant groups. More specifically, it is an attempt to understand the Protestant church experience of Korean first-generation immigrants in the United States.

Racially and culturally, Korean immigrants are clearly distinct from the dominant group in the United States. Nonetheless, a great majority of Korean immigrants share the same religion with native-born Americans—Christian faith. What proportion of Korean immigrants identifies with Christianity?

---

1. These immigrants are dubbed as the "new," "recent," or "post-1965" immigrants. In this article, these three terms are used interchangeably. The bulk of these immigrants are from non-European countries, mostly from Asia and Latin America.

Estimates vary slightly, but between 60 and 65 percent self-identify with Protestantism, and 10 to 15 percent with Roman Catholicism. Regardless of their Protestant or Catholic identity, however, almost all of them are affiliated with Korean ethnic churches. As Hurh and Kim put it, ethnic "church involvement is indeed a way of life" for the vast majority of Korean immigrants (1990, 20). The preponderance of Christians among Korean immigrants is extraordinarily high, especially when two facts are considered: first, despite strong growth in recent years, only about a quarter of the population in Korea are Christians; and second, cultural life in the United States since the 1960s is characterized by religious diversity and tolerance of difference. Thus, the pressure on immigrants to conform to the dominant group's religion (Christianity) has been milder than in previous decades.[2]

Why then is there such high church participation among Korean immigrants? What functions are served for immigrants by Korean ethnic churches? What are the consequences of such an intensive church involvement? Is there a distinctive character of Korean immigrants' church life? These are some of the questions that naturally emerge. By any measure, studies of Korean American church experiences are few. The first two questions nevertheless have spawned a few analytical studies (Hurh and Kim 1984, 1990; I. Kim 1981; Min 1992; Shin and Park 1988). In contrast, the last two questions have not been addressed much at all. This chapter aims to fill this void. Admittedly, these questions are interrelated, so that in order to answer one, we have to refer to the other questions. Still, each of these questions merits a detailed examination on its own.

Before proceeding further, one point of clarification should be made. That is, the history of the post-1965 Korean immigration now extends to more than thirty years, and the children of these immigrants are on the verge of establishing their own churches, independent of their parents' churches. The chapters in Part III of this volume speak about their experience. This chapter is not about the children's church life, but about the immigrant parents' church experience.

Previous studies directed to the first two questions—why so many Korean immigrants are ethnic church affiliates, and what functions the Korean immigrant church performs for individual church members—derive an answer from either of two following facts. First, nearly half of Korean immigrants

2. We do not imply here that immigrants in the past were pressed to conform religiously, and the new immigrants are not especially urged to become Christian. In fact, the United States has been (and still is) a country with a greater religious heterogeneity than most other nations. Relatively speaking, though, non-Western religions have been more tolerated in recent years than in the past. Thus, non-Christian immigrants feel less intimidated to practice the religion they brought with them.

were Christian prior to emigration due to their urban and middle-class back-grounds. Naturally, these pre-emigration Christians are drawn to churches after their immigration. Since the uprooting and rerooting process of immi-gration is potentially a religious experience (Smith 1978; Williams 1988), very few pre-emigration Christians are likely to drop out. Second, Korean immigrants' avenues to satisfy their social needs are severely restricted due to their language limitation and/or racial minority status in America. As a result, even the pre-emigration non-Christians are attracted to ethnic churches after immigration. The first fact refers to the religious motive of joining Korean ethnic churches, whereas the second fact alludes to a social motive. Not surprisingly, sociological studies tend to focus on social motives independent of the religious ones. On the other hand, theological studies emphasize the religious motive and run the risk of dismissing the social ones. It is our contention that these two motives are inherently intertwined. Sep-arating them does not and cannot describe the whole picture. What are the shortcomings of setting them apart?

It is true that a majority of Korean immigrants are from the urban middle class, and urban areas in Korea contain a greater proportion of Christians than rural areas. In short, Korean immigrants' religious background predis-posed them to Christian churches. But only half of Korean immigrants were Christians prior to immigration, while the vast majority are Christians after immigration. Moreover, why do virtually all of them affiliate with ethnic churches from the beginning of, and throughout, their immigrant life? As the length of residence in America extends, even the first-generation immi-grants' English proficiency and familiarity with American system improve. Thus, we might expect ethnic church affiliation to lessen. Yet it does not. As for the social motive explanation, participation in churches demands a lot more energy and resources than nonreligious organizational participation. From a strictly instrumental point of view, then, churches would be less preferred organizations with which to get involved.

Is an ethnic church the only existing and/or the best organization to sat-isfy Korean immigrants' social needs? We doubt it: Koreans do participate actively in organizations other than churches, such as high school and col-lege alumni associations and other voluntary associations. Moreover, if one accepts the gender separation in Korean custom, then churches are not likely to be the most preferred avenue to satisfy their social needs because churches involve both genders. In short, neither the religious motive nor the social motive alone explains sufficiently the extremely high church partici-pation among Korean immigrants.

To analyze church experience among Korean immigrants properly, one must combine these two motives. We therefore contend that the "ethnic" roles of Korean immigrant churches are not a social function devoid of religious function, or vice versa, but rather an amalgamation of the two. With this perspective, this chapter examines the distinctive characteristics of Korean immigrants' church participation. Before proceeding, though, a brief discussion of demographic changes among Korean immigrants in recent years and their implications for ethnic churches will be helpful.

A Brief Sketch of Recent Korean Immigration

The great majority of Korean immigrants came to the United States during the two decades of the 1970s and 1980s. During the peak periods—the second half of the 1980s—more than 34,000 Koreans immigrated to the United States every year. But the number of Korean immigrants began to decline in the very late 1980s, and this decline accelerated in the 1990s. In the second half of the 1990s, the annual number of Korean immigrants was about half as many as during the peak periods of the 1980s (U.S. Dept. of Justice 1970–97). This sustained decline is a distinctly Korean phenomenon when compared to other countries sending significant numbers of immigrants in recent years.

Concurrently, the number of Korean immigrants who permanently returned to Korea (reverse migration) increased. According to a *New York Times* report (August 11, 1995), the number of such reverse migrants ranged each year between 5,000 and 6,000 in the early part of the 1990s. The International Monetary Fund (IMF) crisis in Korea since late 1997 has drastically cut the number of the reverse migrants. But it does not appear to have affected the numbers of either emigrants from Korea or immigrants overall.[3] This pattern is not surprising since paper processing for immigration takes two or three years.

While there are a few unsubstantiated reports in ethnic newspapers of an increase in illegal immigration, the IMF crisis is nonetheless unlikely to increase significantly the number of Korean immigrants in the United States. The reasons are that most South Koreans view the IMF crisis as transitory, and North Korea does not appear likely to open diplomatic relations with

---

3. For aliens, there are two general administrative paths to becoming legal immigrants: First, one applies for an immigrant visa while living abroad and enters the United States with such a visa (new arrivals). Legal permanent residence is granted at the time of entry. Second, non-immigrants already living in the United States apply for adjustment of status to legal permanence residence (status adjusters). When their applications are approved, they are granted legal permanence residence.

United States in the near future.[4] In any case, what could be the cause of this significant decline in immigrants? What does this reduction imply for the demographic composition of Korean immigrants?

Undoubtedly, the single most important cause of the decline is the sustained improvement in living standards in South Korea during the 1980s and 1990s. Moreover, the sector in Korea that benefited most from economic growth is the very sector from which immigrants were most drawn: the urban middle classes. This fact is critical because of its implications for the mentality of Korean immigrants who remain in America. Korean immigrants in the 1970s and 1980s came to America with an expectation that their economic situation would be considerably better than that of their reference group in Korea. When this expectation went sour, the existential questions of immigrant life—the whys, the meaning of their life in a new land—created strong self-doubt among the immigrants. Furthermore, the 1992 Los Angeles disturbance added bewilderment to this mentality of self-doubt.

The decline in the number of immigrants from Korea also changed the demographic composition of Korean immigrants in the United States. First, the median length of residence increased and the proportion of old-timers rose markedly. Second, Korean immigrants on the average got older. Their children are growing up, and the intergenerational connection between Korean immigrant parents and their American-born children is increasingly precarious. In short, on the average, Korean immigrants are disappointed at the turn of events in their immigrant life.

It is not surprising, therefore, that they have turned to religion. Since there are many Korean Protestant churches already organized, they turn to Christianity, and their participation in churches adds gravity and meaning to their lives. Only at Korean churches can immigrants meet many fellow immigrants who have gone through the same kinds of problems in their life in America. This explains why they did not choose American churches. A phrase commonly expressed even among the native-born Korean Americans—"I do not have to explain to fellow immigrants (co-ethnics)"—succinctly states this point. Such unspoken understanding and mutual support are unavailable in American churches. The upshot of this is that the religious role of churches must be rendered *within their ethnic context* to be meaningful for Korean immigrants. At the same time, they have some opportunity

4. In this chapter, Korea refers only to South Korea unless specified otherwise. Korea is a country divided between South and North. North Korea still does not have normal diplomatic relations with the United States; consequently, no legal immigration is allowed from North Korea. There are many family members of Korean Americans living in North Korea. They are likely to immigrate to the United States if diplomatic ties between North Korea and the United States are normalized. Their numbers can potentially be considerable.

to assume public responsibilities in ethnic churches. In other words, the religious role played by Korean ethnic churches is not purely an abstract religious role but is a religious role combined with a social role. It is the "ethnic role" as defined in this chapter.

How is the reduction in immigrants likely to affect Korean immigrant churches? According to a recent report in an ethnic newspaper, *The Korea Central Daily* (Chicago, November 6, 1997), it appears that the total number of churches has slightly decreased initially.[5] The same article reports that at the same time new churches are being continuously organized, creating two tracks: established and new churches. A majority of the current Korean churches were opened in the 1970s and 1980s. With ten or even twenty years of history, many of these churches are organizationally well established. Several churches in major metropolitan areas are today recognized as prominent ethnic organizations in Korean immigrant communities. Some existing small churches have merged as well. Furthermore, many new churches are continuously organized and active alongside these established churches. With the decreasing number of immigrants from Korea and an aging population, many newly organized churches might not survive for long. In any case, the slight decrease in the number of churches obscures the robust and strong undercurrent in church (re)formation in Korean immigrant communities (see *Korea Central Daily,* Chicago, July 6, 2000).[6]

Furthermore, the children of Korean immigrants were generally young in the 1970s and 1980s. Most of the children attended the church of their parents until high school. Most parents' churches provided English-speaking ministry under the leadership of youth leaders or junior pastors. In the 1990s many of the children are college students or young adults, and a growing number of young Korean Americans are organizing their own churches with or without financial support from parents' churches. Even when some sort of formal tie is maintained, this connection is generally ineffectual. In any event, as the number of churches of young Korean Americans gradually expand, there is a growing realization among Korean American church leaders that immigrant churches will continue to exist only within the life span of current immigrants. This foreboding sense of finality is somehow manifested in church leaders' behavior.

5. The precise number is unknown. This article also estimates the overall number of Korean Protestant churches in the United States and in the Chicago area in 1997—171, which is 8 fewer than the previous year.

6. This article reports that the number of churches in the Chicago area has increased to 261 in 2000. About thirty new churches were established in the first six months of 2000.

In short, the decline in immigration affects the mentalities of church members and leaders in the Korean immigrant community. Thus, the church experience of Korean immigrants must be understood within these emigration and immigration contexts. Since the 1990s contexts differ from those in the earlier periods, an analysis of Korean immigrants' church participation must be conducted with data from the 1990s and beyond.

The data for this chapter come from the Presbyterian Panel Study of 1997–99 (PCUSA 1998) and the Racial Ethnic Presbyterian Panel Studies. As a part of an ongoing research project to profile Presbyterians as a people, the Presbyterian Church (USA) reestablished the Presbyterian Panel (PP) in 1996 and established the Racial Ethnic Presbyterian Panel (REPP) for the first time in the same year.[7] The REPP was necessary because all Presbyterian Panels have been predominantly Caucasian. For example, the most recent PP is 98 percent Caucasian, while the immediately previous one (1994–96) was 92 percent Caucasian.[8] Three nonwhite racial ethnic groups are included in the REPP—African Americans, Hispanics, and Koreans. This chapter utilizes the REPP data on African Americans, Hispanics who were born outside of Puerto Rico,[9] and Koreans, as well as nonclergy Caucasians in the PP.

The fact that these panels are restricted to Presbyterians does not necessarily pose a serious problem for the analysis of the religious experience of Korean immigrants. About half of Korean Protestant Christians are Presbyterian (Hurh and Kim 1990; Kim and Kim 1995a). However, for the other ethnic groups, generalizing the panel findings to the respective population group in general could be problematic because Presbyterians are a minority—in some cases, a very tiny minority—in each respective group. Moreover, being a Presbyterian is rather atypical religious status among African Americans and Hispanics. Thus, generalizations in this chapter are made only with Koreans. When comparisons of Korean findings with other ethnic groups are made, they are used to underscore findings on Koreans.

---

7. The United Presbyterian Church in the USA (the northern Presbyterians) began the Panel in 1973. After the merger of northern and southern (Presbyterian Church in the U.S.) branches into the Presbyterian Church (USA) in 1983, the Presbyterian Panel continued. It is reestablished every three years.

It must be noted also that the Presbyterian Panel includes clergy (both parish and specialized clergy), whereas the Racial Ethnic Presbyterian Panel covers only nonclergy. In this chapter, thus, data on members and elders only in the PP are compared with data in the REPP.

8. All figures in this chapter regarding Caucasians are calculated based on the number of nonclergy population in the PP.

9. Those born in Puerto Rico are U.S. citizens legally. Regardless of their legal status, whether they regard themselves as U.S. citizens or as noncitizens (immigrants) is an important factor that affects their church activities. Since it is impossible to discern this from existing academic studies, we excluded those who were born in Puerto Rico from analysis in this chapter.

Are comparisons with other ethnic groups helpful? The answer is a definite yes. Why compare with all three groups of Caucasians, African Americans, and Hispanics? First, Caucasians are the dominant group in the United States and thus can be the common reference group for all other groups (including Koreans). Second, African Americans are an (almost exclusively) native-born and racial/ethnic minority. Koreans are also a racial/ethnic minority, but they are almost exclusively immigrants in the REPP. The Hispanic panel contains a sizeable number of immigrants, particularly when Puerto Ricans are excluded (18% with Puerto Ricans, and 30% without). These similarities are reasons that results from all three non-Korean groups are compared with Koreans. However, it must be emphasized once again that only preliminary (and limited) comparisons are attempted in this chapter. Still, limited comparisons nonetheless shed light on the church experience of Korean immigrants. Hence, the following short perusal of four groups' demographic characteristics is needed.

Demographics of Four Groups Compared

The Research Center of the Presbyterian Church (USA) mailed the first part of questionnaires in the REPP study to 1,900 African Americans, 1,072 Hispanics, and 1,355 Koreans nation-wide in 1997. Return rates were about 50 percent: 1,084 African Americans (57%), 501 Hispanic Americans (47%), and 675 Korean Americans (50%). In November 1996, as a part of the PP study, 2,163 members, 1,759 elders, and 2,530 clergy in PCUSA churches received questionnaires,[10] and 63 percent of members (N = 1,361) and 75 percent of elders (N = 1,316) responded. This panel is 98 percent Caucasian. Since Puerto Rico–born respondents are excluded, we are comparing results from 1,084 African Americans, 279 Hispanics, 2,677 Caucasians, and 675 Koreans.

More female respondents are included among African Americans (70%), Hispanics (62%), and Caucasians (54%). Among Koreans, the gender ratios are more balanced with 49 percent males and 51 percent females responding. Only a small proportion of the respondents (7% of African Americans and Hispanics, 12% Koreans, and 10% of Caucasians) are less than 30 years old. About 60 percent of African Americans, Caucasians, and Hispanics are between the ages of 30 and 64, while 78 percent of Koreans are in this age

10. Since the PP includes clergy, the questionnaire sent to the PP includes numerous occupation-related questions, such as the source of stress and clerical training. As noted, data on clergy population in the PP is not used in this chapter.

range. As a whole, Korean respondents are younger than the others; only 9 percent of Koreans are 65 or older, compared to one-third of African Americans and Caucasians, and 23 percent of Hispanics. A majority of the African Americans (60%) and two-thirds of Hispanics (76%) are currently married. Among Koreans and Caucasians, the proportion of currently married respondents is significantly higher (over 85%). On the other hand, African Americans, Hispanics, and Caucasians are more likely to have experienced divorce than Koreans (23% for African Americans, 21% for Hispanics, and 16% for Caucasians, compared to 7% for Koreans).

While almost all of African Americans (95%) and Caucasians (98%) are native-born, virtually all of Koreans (98%) were born in Korea. Hispanic respondents are split between 70 percent U.S.-born and 30 percent non-natives, mostly born in Latin American countries. As expected for Presbyterians, the samples are rather highly educated: 54 percent of African Americans, 36 percent of Hispanics, and 63 percent of Koreans are college graduates.[11] These rather high proportions of college graduates are reflected in their family incomes. A high proportion of the respondents (57% of African Americans, 45% of Hispanics, 58% of Koreans, and over 70% of Caucasians) report their 1996 (yearly) family income in the excess of $40,000. On the whole, thus, the socioeconomic status of the respondents is higher than that of the general population in their respective groups. Since the respondents in all groups are biased in the same direction, the data appear to be still good for comparative purposes.

What are the characteristics of Korean immigrants' church experiences as revealed in the REPP study? As mentioned before, half of Korean church affiliates in the United States are members of Presbyterian churches (Hurh and Kim 1990; Kim and Kim 1995a). Therefore, findings from the Korean data in the REPP can reveal many aspects of the church-focused activities of Korean church affiliates in the United States in general.

Distinct Characteristics of Korean Immigrants' Church Life

Korean immigrant churches are not neighborhood churches. Half of Koreans, even among those living in large metropolitan areas with many Korean churches in their neighborhood, indicate that their church is located ten miles or more away from their residence. In contrast, half of all other

---

11. Unfortunately, the PP questionnaire does not ask education level of members and elders.

groups—African Americans (51%), Hispanic Americans (48%), and Caucasian (55%)—attend churches within three miles of their homes. Only a small proportion of other groups—African Americans (17%), Hispanics (24%), and Caucasians (10%)—reside ten miles or more away from churches. Koreans are known for their scattered residential pattern; that is, there is no discernable residential concentration of Koreans in any American metropolitan areas. Thus, the lack of neighborhood churches among Koreans comes as no surprise. Moreover, even though it is found only among Koreans in this data set, it is not uniquely Korean in general. Geography does not appear to play a significant role in many other religious and ethnic groups such as Muslims and Hindus. Still, this fact provides one context that is significant to our discussion on Korean immigrants' church life. For instance, if one assumes that the religious motive alone (or religious motive independent of social motive) is the reason for joining Korean immigrant churches, then a question emerges: Why do such a high proportion of Korean immigrants commute a long distance instead of attending immigrant churches closer to their residence?

Another meaningful contextual feature is the size of church membership. Fully half of Korean respondents attend congregations with a membership of 100 or fewer. More than three-fourths (85%) report 300 members or fewer, and only 10 percent attend churches with 500 or more members. The corresponding figures for Caucasian Presbyterians are less than 10 percent for 100 or fewer membership, a little over a quarter for 300 or fewer, and over 40 percent for 500 members or more. Figures for African Americans and Hispanics are not as noticeably disparate from Koreans as those of Caucasians. For example, about one-third of African Americans and 40 percent of Hispanics attend churches of 100 or fewer members, about three-quarters of 300 or fewer, and 23 percent of African American and 16 percent of Hispanics go to churches of 500 or more. Even though the size difference between Koreans and other ethnic groups is not as dramatic as the commuting distance, there is nonetheless a clear difference in the size of churches. In sum, Koreans attend smaller churches than the other groups.

Admittedly, the size of membership itself is not a good proxy for the extent of church establishment in general. In the case of Korean immigrant churches, though, the membership size can be a good representation because there is no duplication of congregation in the panel. That is, only one respondent from any one congregation is included in the panel. Hence, it makes one ponder on the effectiveness of churches in performing social functions.

Given these background features, we will discuss distinctive characteristics of Korean immigrants' church life in terms of the following four points:

(1) stability of membership, (2) in-group and out-group distinction, (3) gender and age composition of elders, and (4) theological orientation and personal beliefs.

Stability of Membership

Most African American, Hispanic, and Caucasian congregations exhibit stable membership. For example, 69 percent of African Americans, 60 percent of Hispanics, and 65 percent of Caucasians have been members of their current congregation for more than ten years. About one-third of them (36% of African Americans, 34% of Hispanics, and 30% of Caucasians) indicate being members of the same congregation for twenty-five years or more. In contrast, almost half of the Koreans have been members of their congregation for six years or less, and close to one-third for less than three years. Only 2 percent have been with their current congregation for twenty-five years or more. Koreans are "new" immigrants, and thus a short tenure with current congregations in isolation is not revealing unless the following facts are juxtaposed: First, 62 percent of them have never belonged to other than Presbyterian religious groups, and their median year of being Presbyterian is twenty-six years. Second, close to half (44%) have lived in the United States for twenty years or more. Third, as mentioned previously, Korean immigrants attend ethnic churches from the beginning of and throughout their immigrant lives, and their inter-area mobility is limited.[12] Fourth, the median age of Korean immigrants is close to 50. As expected, the length of tenure with their current congregation is longer among elders than non-elders. Nevertheless, even among elders, close to 15 percent have been with the current congregation for less than three years. In short, Korean immigrants' membership in their congregation seems subject to rapid turnover.

Furthermore, close to 40 percent indicate that they are "not sure" or that it is "not likely" that they will stay with their current congregation five years from now. These data hint at extreme fluidity of congregational membership. The other racial and ethnic groups display less uncertainty—24 percent of African Americans, 19 percent of Hispanics, and 20 percent of Caucasians indicate such possibility of changing congregations. As "important" or "very important" reasons for their possibly switching congregations, Koreans list the following reasons; (1) moving away from the area, (2) services do not satisfy spiritual needs, (3) too much conflict in the congregation, (4) do not

---

12. Close to a half have lived in only one state in the United States. Three-quarters indicate that they have lived in two or fewer states. These figures are quite comparable to those among Korean immigrants in general.

appreciate the pastor, and (5) don't like the programs it currently offers. When combined with the short tenure with their current congregation, this list provides telltale evidence of the much-suspected yet never-verified "congregation hopping" among Korean immigrants.

In sum, membership of Korean immigrant congregations is rather fluid. That is, Korean immigrants' tenure with a particular ethnic congregation is short, and they are more likely than other groups to switch congregations.

In-Group Commitment and Out-Group Indifference

In spite of their short tenure with their current congregation, Korean respondents participate in church activities very intensely. Four-fifths of Koreans (78%) report they attend their congregation's Sunday worship every week, compared with 34 percent of African Americans, 49 percent of Hispanics, and 28 percent of Caucasians. Also, the proportion of those who regard "attending church regularly" as an essential quality of a good Christian life is higher among Koreans (67%) than other ethnic groups (39% among African Americans, 52% among Hispanics, and 32% of Caucasians). This observation reveals that Korean immigrant church affiliates believe that they have to, and indeed do, attend church every week.

Koreans also spend more time than others at their churches beyond Sunday worship services. More than half of Koreans (54%) spent six hours or more at church activities during the previous month of the survey. Among other ethnic respondents, the figure is about 40 percent: African Americans (36%), Hispanics (39%), and Caucasians (40%). Intensity of participation in church activities is positively correlated with ordination status, especially with elder ordination in all ethnic groups. A small proportion—much smaller than among others—of Koreans have been ordained as elders. Therefore, the contrast between Koreans and others here is much bigger than the numbers at first might signify.

Koreans also give more to their current congregations financially than do other ethnic groups. The majority of Koreans (62%) contributed $2,000 or more in regular giving to their current congregations in the previous year. Only 35 percent of African Americans, 26 percent of Hispanics, and 40 percent of Caucasians report giving that much. Moreover, more than a quarter (27%) of Koreans gave more than $5,000. The corresponding rates are 8 percent for African Americans, 6 percent for Hispanics, and 11 percent for Caucasians. Once again, the amount of regular giving is markedly different depending on whether one has been ordained as an elder or not. Thus

Koreans—fewer of whom are elders—certainly contribute a lot more financially than other ethnic groups to their current congregation.

These findings indicate that Koreans are much more committed to their
current congregations than are other groups. We call this Koreans' strong
in-group commitment. In contrast to their strong commitment to their
current congregations, Korean immigrant Christians participate very little
in activities outside their congregation. The majority of Korean respondents
(70%) indicate that in the month prior to the survey, they did not spend
even one hour to help less fortunate people or to help make their community a better place to live. One-third of African American (33%) and about
40 percent of Hispanics (38%) and Caucasians (42%) belong to this category. Close to 20 percent of Koreans gave no money to nonreligious causes,
while 4 percent of Caucasians, 5 percent of African Americans, and 15 percent of Hispanics report likewise.

The contrast is glaring: The majority of African Americans, Hispanics, and
Caucasians give some volunteer time and financial contributions to improve
the communities outside their churches, whereas Koreans put all their
energy and resources into their current congregations. For Korean immigrant church affiliates, the in-group and out-group partition occurs clearly
at the site of their current congregation. They are intensely committed to
their in-group and genuinely indifferent to their out-groups.

Older Male Domination of Eldership

Being ordained as an elder apparently carries special prestige in Korean
immigrant churches.[13] A relatively small proportion (15%) of Koreans have
been ordained as elders. On the other hand, 47 percent of African Americans, 43 percent of Hispanics, and 65 percent of Caucasians[14] have been
ordained as elders. Being ordained as a deacon, on the other hand, does not
have such an exclusivity: about one-third of Koreans (29%), African Americans (28%), and Caucasians (36%), and about 20 percent of Hispanics, have
been ordained as deacons. Among Koreans, there appears to be a strong
sense of hierarchy—elder is a much higher status position than deacon. One

13. Most Korean immigrant churches that are not affiliated with the Presbyterian Church (USA) still
maintain the tradition of lifetime elders; that is, once ordained, an elder serves on the session until he or
she retires, dies, or leaves the congregation. Korean PCUSA churches do not follow this tradition. In practice, elders in the Korean churches take a mandatory leave of at least one year after serving six years (two
three-year terms) on the session.

14. The figure for Caucasians here is likely an overestimation because the PP oversampled elders
intentionally.

indication in this regard can be found in the fact that no one among Koreans has served as a deacon after having been ordained as an elder. Those who followed this path are not numerous among other groups either. Still, there are some who have served as deacons after serving as elders. Another indication is the fact that the average household income differs by ordination positions. The average elder's family income is highest, and deacons' family income, in turn, is higher than the income of those who have never been ordained as elders or deacons.

Because elder is a higher status position, it is expected that a greater proportion of males will be ordained elders than females. Over 90 percent (92%) of Korean elders are males, whereas only 8 percent are females. Another way to look at this point is that only 2.3 percent of female members in the Korean sample are ordained elders, whereas 28.6 percent of male members are. By contrast, 57 percent of Caucasian, 39 percent of Hispanic, and 30 percent of African American females have been ordained as elders. Among males, 73 percent of Caucasians and over 45 percent of Hispanics and African Americans have been ordained as elders. Thus, even in non-Korean groups, males have a greater probability than females to be ordained as elders. Among Koreans, males literally dominate the eldership in Korean immigrant churches.[15]

Another glimpse of male domination (of eldership) can be found in the fact that over 90 percent of female elders had college education or more, whereas among male elders the figure is 74 percent. In addition, the position of elder in Korean churches is reserved only to older males. Ninety-two percent of elders are found to be 45 years old or older. The youngest age of male elders is 25 years old, while that of female elders is 38 years of age. Median household income is much higher among female elders than male elders. In short, Korean females have to be older, more educated, and richer to be ordained as elders. No such great differences between elders of two genders in terms of age, education, and income are found in other ethnic groups.

What does being an elder mean in Korean immigrant churches? In short, elders are expected to make greater financial contributions to, and to participate more in activities at, their current congregations. As predicted, in 1996 Korean elders made regular offering (on the average) of $3,000 on an individual basis and $5,200 by household. In contrast, deacons' average

15. It is a fact that a majority of Presbyterian churches in Korea prohibited elder ordination of females until 1995. On the other hand, Korean immigrant churches that belong to the Presbyterian Church (USA) have been under constant pressure to have female elders all along. Besides the PCUSA, there are at least two other Presbyterian denominations—the Presbyterian Church of America and the Korean Presbyterian Church in America—with sizeable numbers of Korean immigrant churches.

regular offering was $1,750 per individual and $3,000 per household. Some very cautious estimates indicate that elders gave 13–16 percent of their income to their current churches, while nonelders gave 6–8 percent. In addition to greater financial contributions, elders spend more hours attending events and give more volunteer time at their current congregations. One exception is serving as Sunday school teachers. An extremely low proportion of elders (3%) serves as Sunday school teachers. One plausible explanation for this can be found in the fact than in Korean immigrant churches most Sunday school classes are for children and are conducted in English. Older Korean immigrants have a lower English proficiency, and thus, with such a predominance of older males in eldership, this phenomenon is not odd. In sum, besides Sunday school teaching, elders are expected to invest a lot more pecuniary and nonpecuniary resources into their current congregations. Among other ethnic groups also, elders made a greater financial and nonfinancial contributions than nonelders. Nevertheless, the difference is not so obvious as among Koreans. All in all, being ordained as elder carries connotations of "being elevated to eldership" in Korean immigrant churches. Thus, it enhances one's status in terms of power and prestige at the same time that certain reciprocities in terms of money and time are expected from ordained elders.

Theological Orientation and Personal Beliefs

Slightly less than half of Koreans (44%) self-identify as "conservatives" on theological issues, a third (33%) as "moderates," and about a quarter (23%) as "liberals." For the proportion who label themselves as a liberal, there is no difference among three ethnic groups. But only one-fifth of African Americans (22%) perceive themselves as conservatives, and the majority (53%) consider themselves moderates. Among Hispanics, 47 percent claim to be conservatives, and nearly a half (46%) claim to be moderates. Corresponding figures for Caucasians are 40 percent conservatives, 44 percent moderates, and 16 percent liberals. From these figures, it appears that both Koreans and Hispanics are more conservative on theological issues than African Americans, and fewer Koreans self-identify as moderates than the rest. A word of caution is needed here. The meaning of the term "conservative" could differ among four ethnic groups; thus, the comparison based on the self-identification might not be appropriate.

What does "conservative" connote among Korean immigrant Christians? To probe this question a step further, we created a five-point scale with following questions: "Do you think there is a heaven?" "Do you think there is a hell?" "The Devil (Satan) really exists," "Jesus was born of a virgin," and "Jesus will return to the earth some day." The results are striking: Even though differences among conservatives (95%), moderates (88%), and liberals (70%) exist, 87 percent of all Koreans scored the most conservative score of five.[16] In short, regardless of how they self-identify, Korean immigrant church affiliates are theologically conservative. Moreover, the higher the ordination status in churches, the more conservative one is. That is, the proportion of conservatives is highest among elders, next highest among deacons, and lowest among members.

Another check of their theological orientation is their perspectives on the Bible. None of Koreans and only 1 percent of the other ethnic groups profess to believe that the Bible is an important piece of literature but largely irrelevant to our lives today—the most secular view offered in the survey. One-fourth of Koreans (26%) and Hispanics (24%) take the opposite position of the Bible as the literally inerrant Word of God and a guide for faith and secular matters. About one in ten African Americans and Caucasians take this least secular view. The distribution of Hispanics' perspectives on the Bible is similar to that of Koreans. At the same time, African Americans' views on the Bible are similar to those of Caucasians. Only among Koreans is ordination status significantly tied to views on the Bible; that is, proportionally more elders than deacons, and more deacons than members, take the least secular view. In sum, Korean immigrant church affiliates maintain quite a conservative theological orientation on the whole, and elders are the most conservative.

When Koreans' view on the essential qualities of good Christian life is added to their theological orientation, conservatism among Koreans is basically identical to evangelicalism. Three items dealing with personal relations with God—"studying the Bible regularly," "spending time in prayer," and "attending church regularly"—received more than 60 percent "essential" rating.[17] At the same time, "actively seeking social and economic justice" received the lowest "essential" rating with 19 percent. Even "taking care of those who are sick or needy" garnered only slightly more than 25 percent "essential" rating.

This proclivity toward personal salvation manifests Koreans' view of their fellow Christians' everyday behavior. Half of Korean respondents admire

16. These five questions in the REPP, in our view, are most closely tied to the core beliefs of "conservative" Korean Christians. Since the same assertion cannot be made in other ethnic groups, the same analyses are not conducted for other ethnic groups.

17. The categories are "essential," "very important," "somewhat important," and "not at all important."

those who are satisfied with their lot in life (50%) and live their faith quietly (46%). A much smaller proportion of others—African Americans (27%), Hispanics (28%), and Caucasians (31%)—admire those who are satisfied with their lot in life. "Living faith quietly," again, received a lower rating among non-Koreans than Koreans—22 percent of African Americans, 23 percent of Hispanics, and 36 percent of Caucasians admire such trait.

In addition, Koreans strongly adhere to the sanctity of heterosexual marriage. Heterosexual cohabitation outside of marriage received an 82 percent "highly disapprove" rating among Koreans. Corresponding rates are 48 percent (African Americans), 44 percent (Caucasians), and 60 percent (Hispanics). Homosexual partnership or lifestyle received a 90 percent of "highly disapprove" rating among Korean respondents. Relatively lower proportions of African Americans and Caucasians (about 50%) highly disapprove of an openly gay or lesbian lifestyle even as part of a committed couple.

Discussion

An overall picture of Korean immigrants' life in ethnic churches gradually emerges from the above data. First, the great majority of Korean immigrants attend ethnic churches from the beginning of and throughout their immigrant life in the United States. Second, each congregation is rather small on the average. Third, tenure with a particular congregation is rather short, and Koreans often drive long distances to attend churches. Fourth, Korean immigrant church affiliates are intensely committed to their *current* congregations. They spend many hours and resources participating in activities at their congregation. At the same time, they are quite indifferent to others outside of their current congregation. Even religious activities in other ethnic churches do not attract much of their attention. Fifth, as the male domination of eldership provides a glimpse, Korean immigrant churches operate in the way that is discriminatory toward females and the young. Sixth, Korean immigrant Christians are extremely conservative in their theological orientation and beliefs. For instance, they emphasize personal relations with God and view the Bible as the absolute guide for secular as well as religious matters. They adhere to traditional views on marriage, considering non-traditional sexual relations as evil.

Since about 70 percent of Korean immigrants are found to be affiliated with Korean immigrant churches in the United States (I. Kim 1981; Hurh and Kim 1990; Kim and Kim 1995a), we may return to the following questions: Why are such a high proportion of Korean immigrants affiliated with immigrant churches? What do ethnic churches mean to Korean immigrants in the United States?

As discussed before, one should not separate religious motives and social motives of joining ethnic churches. This is particularly true in the case of Koreans in the 1990s and beyond. As the Korean economy grows and immigration from Korea declines sharply, Korean immigrants in the United States live a life of double jeopardy. The first jeopardy is due to their minority immigrant status and its consequences of hardship, uncertainty, and downward economic mobility. Thus, they need to secure the meaning of their life and various support or services from others in times of personal stress and crisis. In other words, they turn to religion and religious organizations for both religious and social motives. However, this is not necessarily unique to Korean immigrants. Various immigrant groups manage these needs of immigrants in different ways. In the case of Korean immigrants, these needs happen to be handled mostly by immigrant Christian churches. This explanation is appealing; nevertheless, it is insufficient to account for such a continuously high ethnic church affiliation among Korean immigrants.

The second jeopardy Korean immigrants face is unique to Koreans. A great majority of Korean immigrants came to the United States in the 1970s and 1980s when Korea was less developed economically. Thus, at least relative to their reference group in Korea, they were able to maintain psychological satisfaction. In the meantime, the Korean economy grew by leaps and bounds, and friends and relatives of immigrants in Korea displayed much more affluent lifestyles. The military threat from North Korea has been reduced and political democratization in Korea has occurred. Consequently, Korean immigrants' search for the meaning of their lives became much more complex. This quest of theirs surely has a strong religious undertone. Nonetheless, it cannot be answered in any other religious organizations except ones with fellow immigrants. In our view, it extends beyond conducting religious activities in their native tongue and providing opportunities to satisfy social needs of immigrants. This religious quest of Korean immigrants must be conducted within a fellowship of other fellow immigrants. Putting it differently, some Korean immigrants may attend ethnic churches due to social motives, but their social motives have a strong religious undertone, consciously or unconsciously. In short, the religious and social motives are not separable.

Still another question is why Koreans have chosen Christian churches. Among Korean immigrants, Christian churches have several advantages over other religious organizations. First, as mentioned previously, close to a majority of Korean immigrants were Christians prior to immigration. The initial expansion of Christian churches with encouragement from American churches further strengthened their advantage. As Christian churches pro-liferated, churches emerged as the major ethnic organization. Second, as religious organizations churches offer, and members are expected to attend, worship services and other religious activities every Sunday. For other eth-nic organizations, religious or nonreligious, it is difficult to arrange for Korean immigrants to meet as frequently and regularly as churches do. Third, Korean immigrant churches generally state fellowship among mem-bers as one of their explicit goals (a major manifest function) and provide lunch/coffee hours after worship and district/cell meetings. As church members get together, keep close relationships, and perform the church-related responsibilities assigned to them, many opportunities to satisfy their primary and secondary group needs are created. Once again, religious and social roles are combined.

Furthermore, as inclusive organizations, churches in the Korean immi-grant community are one of the few ethnic organizations open to all family members, particularly to both husband and wife. This can work as a double-edged advantage. For example, if both spouses are satisfied with their church, their commitment to that particular congregation is likely to solidify. The opposite is also possible. That is, when both or either husband or wife is dissatisfied with their church, their joint experience would intensify their dissociation from that particular congregation or lead them to get involved in church conflict.

On the whole, the above advantages of Korean immigrant churches draw a great number of Korean immigrants to Christian churches. There is another more subtle advantage of churches over other religious organizations. That is, the Christian population in Korea in the 1970s and 1980s was perceived as the socioeconomically middle or upper-middle classes. Thus, preemi-gration non-Christians might have a status-seeking reason to join churches post-immigration.

How can we reconcile Korean immigrants' short tenure with a particular congregation and their strong commitment to their current congregations? Wouldn't a sense of loyalty (toward a particular congregation) naturally be developed with intense participation and commitment? Thus, Koreans' unusually strong in-group commitment and their short tenure appear to be contradictory. As hinted before, it again can be understood within the frame-work of combined religious and social motives.

Pastors at Korean immigrant churches preach the Bible message every Sunday, and church members are expected to accept the message as the will of God. Church members also are engaged in Bible study or various other religious activities. When they accept the Bible message as an expression of God's will collectively with fellow immigrants, people gain a new and firm perspective to interpret their immigrant life. Their belief thus regulates their daily life outside of churches. In other words, churches' religious roles spill over and incorporate nonreligious roles. In the United States, the daily life of Korean immigrants is generally confined to a small circle of family, kin, and personal friends along with a limited social life at the workplace. Immigrant churches offer them a valuable opportunity to meet many different people and hence to expand their social networks and satisfy both their primary and secondary group needs. Korean immigrants often report that they met many of their current close friends at church (Hurh and Kim 1988). Active involvement in the current congregation thus opens up opportunities to hold positions with public duties even in small congregations. It is true that barriers to entry to mainstream society and occupational frustration drive many Korean immigrants to be actively involved in church activities. Consciously or unconsciously, the compensatory psychology is likely to operate here. Yet their intense involvement in their current congregation is not only a fulfillment of social motives but also an expression of their religious faith. To put it differently, their social motives are inseparably intertwined with religious motives.

This rather long discussion points to the fact that to fulfill their needs Korean immigrants must be strongly committed to their current congregation. Then they not only do not have time or energy to go beyond the boundary of current congregation, but they do not feel the need to do so. A high proportion of Korean immigrants are currently engaged in labor-intensive small businesses or other jobs and find it difficult to manage both their family life and work activities. In addition, as immigrants struggling to settle, Korean immigrants' self-concept may not be secure or strong enough to venture out beyond their congregation. Thus, immigrant churches work as a safe place for immigrant to satisfy their complex needs.

This hold of immigrant churches does have possibly perilous facets. The observed short tenure with a current congregation is one such manifestation. Operation of this facet has three possible sources: First, since ethnic churches involve both wife and husband, the probability of dissatisfaction with the current congregation increases. Second, as immigrants' needs become more complex, churches are more likely to fail to meet their needs. The previously mentioned list of reasons for possible church-switching implies this source. Third, the proliferation of Korean immigrant churches indicates that there are other ethnic congregations to switch to when a particular congregation fails to meet their needs. In sum, Korean immigrants' needs are neither religious nor social alone, but both religious and social. To fulfill these intermeshed needs, they participate at the current congregation intensely. Active involvement brings about a greater possibility of being dissatisfied. With other ethnic congregations to switch to, they stay with a particular congregation for a rather short period of time when they become discontented. Korean immigrants do indeed hop from one congregation to another.

The older male domination of eldership in Korean immigrant churches appears to be a typical case of gender and age discrimination. The sexism and ageism explanations do have a great deal of appeal, yet they leave a few nagging questions unanswered. For instance, why is such discrimination more prevalent in Korean churches than other racial/ethnic churches? Putting it differently, are Korean churches more discriminatory than other racial/ethnic churches? If so, what is the major culprit? Is it the "Korean culture"?

It is true that one of the major Presbyterian denominations in Korea did not approve the female eldership until 1995. Yet Korean PCUSA churches have been under consistent pressure from the denomination to have female elders for years. Thus, it is difficult to accept without question that the preponderance of males among elders has been and is still persisting in Korean immigrant churches because it is a practice brought from Korea. On the other hand, the persistence of the practice may demonstrate its usefulness to Korean immigrant church affiliates. As discussed before, Korean immigrants in the 1990s lead a life of double jeopardy, and ethnic churches provide many opportunities to fulfill the complicated needs of members. It is quite possible that the types and/or intensity of needs differ between males and females because of the traditional gender role expectation immigrants brought from Korea (Hurh and Kim 1988; Kim and Kim 1995b). As discussed below, the complication that the life of double jeopardy creates calls for unambiguously strict religious standards. Korean immigrants' life conditions in the United States also leave very little opportunity to reexamine their gender orientation. It is again the case that the social needs are being combined into the religious needs.

Korean immigrants are rather inward-looking; they seek to fulfill their *own* needs and the needs of their own family members. This inclination is further reinforced and justified by their evangelical religious orientation, which is mainly concerned with individual salvation and personal dialogue with God. This evangelical orientation is basically part of what they brought from Korea (Han 1994). At the same time, their life conditions enhance their evangelical orientation: First, they are generally isolated from the mainstream

American churches and lack stimulating theological ideas that would modify their religious orientation. Second, the evangelical orientation seems to be what they urgently need. In contrast to their daily experience of uncertainty and insecurity, the evangelical orientation gives them absolute belief and strict moral standards. As Yang observes of Chinese church members, Korean immigrant church members find the certainty in evangelical belief attractive and try to maintain a firm hold on it (Yang 1998).

Conclusion

After two decades of increases, the yearly flow of immigrants from Korea began to decline drastically in the early 1990s, and the decline continued throughout the decade. Thus, the median age of immigrants has increased, and the average length of residence in the United States has lengthened. Children of immigrants are growing up and beginning to establish churches of their own, independent of parents. Among the post-1965 immigrant groups, Korean immigrants are known for their high ethnic Christian church participation. During the 1990s, Korean immigrants' ethnic church participation does not appear to have abated.

As mentioned, there are only a handful of academic studies regarding Korean immigrants' church experience. To explain Koreans' high church participation, most studies differentiate the social motive from the religious motive for joining ethnic churches. This chapter also refers to the two motives. Nonetheless, we take the position that the two motives are not separable but are inherently intertwined. As the Korean immigrants' reference group in Korea experiences improving economic and political conditions, the needs of Korean immigrant church affiliates become more complex and enmeshed. Their religious needs take on the conditions of the social needs, and the social needs add the character of religious needs. The ethnic role of Korean immigrant churches as an amalgamation of religious and social roles is to fulfill these complicated needs of immigrants. Without a framework based on this perspective, it is impossible to explain the unabating ethnic church participation among Korean immigrants.

Our discussion in this chapter regarding distinct characteristics of Korean immigrants' church life attempts to fill a void in the literature. While Christianity carries a universal message, each group of Christians practices their faith in a specific way under a specific social context. Korean immigrants demonstrate a specific pattern in their religious activities. In addition to two contextual findings—attending immigrant churches from the beginning of and throughout their immigrant life, and small congregations—we have discussed four specific points: (1) membership instability—a short tenure at a particular congregation, (2) a sharp distinction between in-group and out-group in terms of participation intensity—strong commitment to their current congregation and almost complete indifference to needs outside of their current congregation, (3) gender composition of eldership—almost exclusive older male domination, and (4) extremely evangelical and traditional theological orientation and beliefs. With the data made available to us by the Research Center of the Presbyterian Church (USA), we have compared three other ethnic Presbyterian groups—African Americans, Hispanics, and Caucasians—with Koreans. It must be noted that the comparison made in this chapter is not intended to explain the differences among various ethnic groups, but to put the Korean experience in a broader picture.

What makes the case of Korean immigrants interesting is that in spite of changed immigration and emigration contexts (which could very well diminish their church participation), Korean immigrants in the 1990s and early twenty-first century continue to actively participate in ethnic churches, and their church participation is focused on one particular congregation at a time. The main reason for this is that through their active ethnic roles, Korean immigrant churches effectively handle immigrants' strong and complicated nonreligious needs along with religious needs. That is why a high proportion of Korean immigrants actively participate in ethnic churches in sharp contrast to their lack of concern with the communities outside their churches. On the other hand, the blend of the religious role and nonreligious role is apparently precarious, which explains why many Korean immigrant congregations exhibit fluid membership and remain small.

Another aspect of Korean immigrants' church life is to perpetuate or reinforce some church practices brought from Korea. Unless these practices meet their current needs in the United States, they are not likely to be reinforced or perpetuated. This mechanism of perpetuation *partly* explains Korean church affiliates' general tendency toward an evangelical orientation and male domination of eldership. In sum, distinct features of Korean immigrants' church life are practices brought from Korea modified by their life conditions in the United States. The direction in which the modification occurs is determined by the immigration and emigration contexts of Korean immigration in the 1990s and beyond.

References

George, Sheba. 1998. "Caroling with the Keralites: The Negotiation of Gendered Space in an Indian Immigrant Church." In *Gatherings in Diaspora: Religious Communities and the New Immigration,* ed. R. Stephen Warner and Judith G. Wittner, 265–94. Philadelphia: Temple University Press.

Han, Gil Soo. 1994. *Social Sources of Church Growth: Korean Churches in the Homeland and Overseas.* Lanham, Md.: University Press of America.

Hurh, Won Moo, and Kwang Chung Kim. 1984. *Korean Immigrants in America.* Madison, N.J.: Fairleigh Dickinson University Press.

——.1988. *Uprooting and Adjustment: A Sociological Study of Korean Immigrants' Mental Health.* Final Report submitted to National Institute of Mental Health, U.S. Department of Health and Human Services.

——. 1990. "Religious Participation of Korean Immigrants in the United States." *Journal for the Scientific Study of Religion* 29:19–34.

Kim, Bok-Lim. 1978. *The Asian Americans: Changing Patterns, Changing Needs.* Montclair, N.J.: Association for Korean Christian Scholars in North America.

Kim, Illsoo 1981. *New Urban Immigrants: The Korean Community in New York.* Princeton: Princeton University Press.

Kim, Kwang Chung, and Shin Kim. 1995a. "Korean Immigrant Churches in the United States." In *Yearbook of American and Canadian Churches, 1995,* ed. Kenneth B. Bedell, 6–9. Nashville, Tenn.: Abingdon Press.

——. 1995b. "Family and Work Roles of Korean Immigrants in the United States." In *Resiliency in Ethnic Minority Families: Native and Immigrant American Families,* ed. Hamilton McCubbin, Elizabeth Thompson, Anne Thompson, and Julie Fromer, 223–42. Madison: University of Wisconsin Press.

Kivisto, Peter. 1992. "Religion and the New Immigrants." In *A Future for Religion? Trends in Social Analysis,* ed. William H. Swatos Jr., 92–107. Newbury Park, Calif.: Sage.

Min, Pyong Gap. 1992. "The Structure and Social Functions of Korean Immigrant Churches in the United States," *International Migration Review* 26:1370–92.

——. 1998. "Korean American Families." In *Minority Families in the United States,* ed. Ronald L. Taylor, 198–225. Upper Saddle River, N.J.: Prentice-Hall.

Presbyterian Church (USA). 1998. *The Presbyterian Panel: Listening to Presbyterians, 1997–1999 Background Report.* Louisville, Kentucky.

Shin, Eui Hang, and Hyung Park. 1988. "An Analysis of Causes of Schisms in Ethnic Churches: The Case of Korean-American churches." *Sociological Analysis* 49:234–48.

Smith, Timothy. 1978. "Religion and Ethnicity in America." *American Historical Review* 83:1155–85.

U.S. Department of Justice, 1970–96. *Statistical Yearbook of the Immigration and Naturalization Service.* Washington D.C.: U.S. Government Printing Office.

Warner, R. Stephen. 1988. *New Wine in Old Wineskins: Evangelicals and Liberals in a Small-Town Church.* Los Angeles: University of California Press.

——. 1993. "Work in Progress Toward a New Paradigm for the Sociological Study of Religion in the United States." *American Journal of Sociology* 98:1044–93.

Williams, Raymond Brady. 1988. *Religions of Immigrants from India and Pakistan: New Threads in the American Tapestry.* Cambridge (U.K.): Cambridge University Press.

Wuthnow, Robert. 1989. *The Struggle for America's Soul: Evangelicals, Liberals, and Secularism.* Grand Rapids, Mich.: William B. Eerdmans.

Yang, Fenggang. 1998. "Tenacious Unity in a Contentious Community: Cultural and Religious Dynamics in a Chinese Christian Church." In *Gatherings in Diaspora: Religious Community and the New Immigration,* ed. R. Stephen Warner and Judith G. Wittner, 333–61. Philadelphia: Temple University Press.

5

Religion as a Variable in Mental Health: A Case for Korean Americans

Tong-He Koh

RELIGION, KOREAN CHRISTIAN CHURCHES especially, has played a dominant role in the Korean American community during the past twenty years. Since the 1965 Immigration Act, about 30,000 Koreans have come to the United States each year. It is estimated that over 100,000 Korean individuals are living in the greater Chicago area alone; and there are over 200 Korean Christian churches. According to the Hurh and Kim survey (1988), three-fourths of the Korean American respondents in the Chicago area were found to be affiliated with Korean Christian churches. As the major reasons for their church affiliation, many answers—religious belief, to worship God, for salvation, or to encourage religious faith among children—indicated a deep religious motive. Others mentioned meeting people or fellowship with church members and psychological/emotional support by their congregation. Korean churches thus appear to be a significant cultural institution, providing meaning, affiliation, and support for many Korean Americans.

For Korean Americans, especially for the first generation, sociological variables such as group affiliation and identification may have been a major factor in their attending Korean churches. Many new immigrants who have low English proficiency and acculturation rates may prefer to be associated with Korean-speaking people who share a similar cultural background.

Korean churches also offer a refuge from racism. Many Korean Americans feel more empowered as soon as they enter a Korean church. It presents a communal ritual space in which people can experience their own sense of specialness and power, something they cannot do outside that space in the mainstream society.

Korean churches seem to have a widely recognized function to reach out to people in times of transition and trouble. In turn, many people in distress prefer to seek help from their clergy or religious community rather than from mental health professionals. The main reason for this trend could be easy accessibility to and affordability of the clergy. The concept of mental health is foreign to many Korean Americans, but it is also stigmatizing for them to seek help for their psychological weaknesses. Still another reason may be that many Korean Americans view with suspicion the discipline of psychology, which they consider Eurocentric individualism and thus irrelevant to people coming out of a much more communal orientation. That lack of relevance is a big part of why Korean Americans have not used mental health professionals. It is therefore very crucial for mental health professionals to understand the relationships between religion and mental health and to design psychotherapeutic counseling techniques that are relevant to the Korean American cultural/religious background.

Religion and Mental Health

The empirical literature suggests that religious involvement in many instances influences attitudes and behaviors of people in both the psychological and social arenas (Kosmin and Lachman 1993; Gartner 1986). Elements of religious involvement and affiliation can be understood in terms of their dynamic role in supporting or impeding mental health. It has been shown that a majority of helping professionals believe that people's values and lifestyles have an impact on mental health and emotional functioning and that some values do more to promote mental health than others (Jensen and Bergin 1988).

The culturally encapsulated stereotype that religiously devout people are more emotionally disturbed or less rational and intelligent than less religious people has given way to a more thoughtful, culturally sensitive perspective that affirms the beneficial aspects of theistic and spiritual beliefs and values while acknowledging that some beliefs and practices can be used in harmful and dysfunctional ways (Bergin 1991; Richards 1991; Richards, Smith, and Davis 1989). With this more balanced understanding, the door has been opened to a consideration of how such beliefs, values, and practices can be approached therapeutically to enhance clients' well-being (Bergin 1988a, 1988b, 1991; Bergin and Payne 1991; Payne, Bergin, and Loftus 1992; Richards and Potts 1995).

Allport and Ross (1967) distinguished two orientations in religiosity: intrinsic and extrinsic. Intrinsic individuals internalize their beliefs and live by them with less regard for external consequences. In contrast, extrinsic orientation is more utilitarian. Religion is therefore used to obtain status, security, sociability, and self-justification. Recent and extensive research on this dual dimension of religiosity has shown, with few exceptions, that positive mental health indexes are generally aligned with intrinsic orientation, and extrinsic orientation is paired with less healthy and sometimes pathological or negative correlates (Donahue 1985).

A more recent review by Masters and Bergin (1992) also concluded that intrinsic religiousness is positively related to mental health. But what is it about being intrinsically religious that is beneficial? The authors suggest that at the base of this effect is a sense of purpose and meaning in life. It is also possible that the strength of conviction to these worldviews is equally important.

It is hypothesized that beneficial mental health consequences are an outcome of congruence or behaving in synchrony with one's religious values (Pargament, Steele, and Tyler 1979), whereas acting contrary to personal values results in dissonance, with consequences of guilt, anxiety, despair, or alienation (Mickleburgh 1992).

Pargament (1990) studied people's use of religion to cope with major life stressors ranging from illness to war to the Oklahoma City bombing. In several studies involving hundreds of subjects, Pargament found that people who embrace what could be called the "sinners-in-the-hands-of-an-angry-God" model had poorer mental health outcomes. People who felt angry toward God, believed they were being punished for their sins, or perceived a lack of emotional support from their church typically suffered more distress, anxiety, and depression. In contrast were people who embrace the "loving God" model. These people saw God as a partner who works with them to resolve problems. They viewed difficult situations as opportunities for spiritual growth. And they believed their religious leaders and fellow congregation members gave them the support they needed. Thus, they enjoyed more positive mental health outcomes.

A wide range of research supports Pargament's findings. Kirkpatrick (1993), for instance, used attachment theory as the basis of a study that also concluded that mental health outcomes depend on the way people view their relationship with God. Kirkpatrick discovered that people who viewed God as a warm, caring, and dependable friend were much more likely to have positive outcomes than people who viewed God as a cold, vengeful, and unresponsive deity or who were not sure whether to trust God. People who classified their attachment to God as secure scored much lower on loneliness, depression, and anxiety and much higher on general life satisfaction.

Both psychology and religion offer belief systems, traditions, and rituals. Both focus on issues like guilt, right and wrong, and what it means to be human. And both strive to help people cope with life. The difference is that religion typically puts responsibility in the hands of God, a belief nearly impossible to reconcile with psychology's emphasis on personal responsibility. But discounting religion can have a detrimental effect on treatment, and ignoring religion may not even be possible. The idea of value-neutral psychotherapy has become untenable.

Role of the Psychologist

Psychologists have much to gain from looking beyond their own borders to the broader world around them. When they do, they find that religious beliefs, practices, and institutions are more alive and well than they might have guessed on the basis of their own religious commitments. Furthermore, they find that religion has the capacity to build, sustain, and rebuild human lives, individually and collectively, in many ways. And finally, they discover a number of new opportunities for interaction between psychological and religious communities. One opportunity would be to incorporate methods of religious coping into the process of psychotherapy. Another opportunity is to work with the religious community as partners assisting people in their search for significance. For example, mental health and religious communities have pooled their resources in collaborative attempts to solve problems of homelessness, physical illness, or mental illness (e.g., Cohen, Mowbray, Gillette, and Thompson 1991; Eng and Hatch 1991).

It is not the business of psychologists to stand in judgment of their clients' beliefs and religious convictions (American Psychiatric Association 1990), but it remains a part of their mission as caregivers and healers to recognize and help their clients come to terms with the pathological and maladaptive aspects of their religious commitments and investments. The scientific vantage point enables psychologists to discriminate those aspects of their clients' beliefs that are supportive, mature, reasonable, and psychologically adaptive, as opposed to those aspects that are destructive, misleading, misguided, and needlessly productive of guilt, anxiety, depression, and despair. To the extent that psychologists can approach their religious clients with respect for their needs and struggles with the vicissitudes of human existence and hopes, caregivers can use their therapeutic skills more effectively to enable clients to lead more satisfying and religiously fulfilled lives.

Mental health professionals would be intensely concerned with the quality of their clients' lives, the effectiveness and meaningfulness of their object relations, the degree to which their beliefs contributed to a psychologically mature and responsible capacity to meet the exigencies of their lives and careers, and the way in which they facilitated their adaptation to the challenges and demands of their lives. The hallmark of clients' pathology would be the degree to which their beliefs had destructive and maladaptive influences on their lives and their work. The therapeutic emphasis falls not on the belief system, on its truth or falsity, but on its pathogenicity and the degree to which it reflects the underlying pathogenicity of the client's self-system (Meissner 1986).

Role of the Clergy

It would seem that religious methods of coping with everyday stresses are functionally redundant. After all, numerous groups apart from religious communities care deeply about the well-being of others. Support and care can be gained from many sources other than spiritual and congregational ones. A few investigators have tested whether religious methods of coping add anything above and beyond secular approaches to coping with life stresses. For example, one study of 586 members of mainline Christian churches dealing with serious negative life events found that both religious and nonreligious forms of coping accounted for unique proportions of variance in several measures of adjustment to the events (Pargament et al., 1994). Similar results have been found in studies of high school students making the transition to college (Maton 1989) and college students coping with the stresses of the Persian Gulf War (Pargament et al. 1994). Religion, these results suggest, adds another dimension to the coping process. But what? What's so special about religion anyway?

Part of the unique power of religion may lie in its ability to respond to so many needs in so many different ways. The abstract, symbolic, and mysterious character of most religious traditions may frustrate its adherents at times. However, it is just these qualities that allow religions to bend and flex with changing times, circumstances, and needs. In their writings, social scientists may have underestimated the diversity and flexibility of religious life. For Sigmund Freud, religion offered a shelter from destructive human impulse and a precarious world. For anthropologist Clifford Geerts, religion is largely a system that provides meaning in life. Sociologist Emile Durkheim spoke of religion as a source of social integration.

Important as the versatility of religion is, it is the sacred that makes the religious search for significance so distinctive and so potentially powerful. From the religious perspective, the sacred is a goal in itself, one that cannot be reduced to other psychological or social ends. "It is the ultimate Thou whom the religious person seeks most of all," wrote Johnson (1955, 70). Measures of spiritual motivation have been tied to distinctive attitudes and behavior (Pargament et al. 1994; Welch and Barrish 1982). Although these mechanisms are diverse, they offer a counterpoint to traditional secular approaches to coping. Much of everyday life is taken up with attempts to master big and little problems. Efficacy, agency, and control are guiding principles in coping, particularly in Western culture, which stresses the value of individualism and achievement. Unfortunately, however, not all problems are controllable. Faced with the insurmountable, Western culture has less to say or offer. The language of the sacred—forbearance, mystery, suffering, hope, finitude, surrender, divine purpose, and redemption—and the mechanisms of religion become more relevant here. At the risk of exaggerating, it might be said that Western culture (psychology) helps people gain control of their lives, whereas religion helps people come to grips with the limits of their control.

In fact, several studies have indicated that religious forms of coping are especially helpful to people in uncontrollable, unmanageable, or otherwise difficult situations (Bickel 1992; Maton 1989; Park, Cohen, and Herb 1990; Siegel and Kuykendall 1990). For instance, in a two-year longitudinal study of a community sample, Williams and his colleagues (1991) found that attendance at religious services buffered the effects of increased numbers of undesirable life events on subsequent psychological distrss. Maton (1989) reported that spiritual support was tied to less depression and greater self-esteem among those who had suffered the death of a child. Bickel (1992), working with a sample of Presbyterian church members, found that a collaborative religious coping style buffered the effects of perceived uncontrollable stress on depression; a more self-directed coping style, alternatively, exacerbated these same effects as the perception of uncontrollable stress increased. These studies suggest that the sacred is particularly helpful in the worst of times. Vested with unlimited strengths and compassion, the sacred offers a source of solace, hope, and power when other resources have been exhausted and people must look beyond themselves for help.

Culture and Mental Health

Public and governmental job announcements usually include the statement that a given institution is an "equal opportunity employer." Sometimes such phrases are followed by explanatory statements that no discrimination in hiring will be made on the basis of gender, ethnicity, or culture. These announcements reflect an ideal of nonessential characteristics over which people have little or no control. Even though in our culture religion is seen as a self-chosen aspect of life rather than something with which one is born, it is almost always included in the individual traits to be ignored.

Interestingly enough, while the goal of being bias-free is still the professional ideal, clinicians have come to feel that attending to such issues as gender, race, religion, or culture in the psychotherapeutic task is crucial. "The Ethical Principles of Psychologists and Code of Conduct" of American Psychological Association (1992) mandates that special training, experiences, consultation, or supervision in dimensions of human differences or diversity, including religion, may be required to ensure the competence of the services they render, or else they should make appropriate referral. It appears that what is *proscribed* in employment decisions is *prescribed* in psychotherapy (Jackson 1990). In fact, training in cultural diversity is now required for licensure in several states.

In recent years, there has been a greater recognition and realization of the influence of culture in individual expression of mental distress, in psychiatric diagnosis and treatment, and in the delivery of mental health care community-wide.

DSM-IV (1994), the most recent Diagnostic and Statistical Manual published by the American Psychiatric Association, contains a simple classificatory summary of presumably cross-cultural manifestations of some mental disorders. This marks an initial concerted attempt to portray some of the cultural differences in the manifestations of mental disorders. It indicates that some behaviors that might have been misinterpreted as psychopathological in the past may reflect cultural variations.

Cultural concepts, values, and beliefs shape the way mental symptoms are expressed and how individuals and their families respond to such distresses. Cultural norms dictate when a cluster of symptoms and behaviors are labeled "normal" or "abnormal." Culture also determines the accessibility and acceptability of mental health services. Clearly, effective mental health care cannot be divorced from the cultural context in which the formation and expression of psychic distress occur, the coping strategies of the clients and their families and communities, and the diagnostic and therapeutic activities of the "healers."

Research on the relationship between culture and mental health is proliferating (Marcella and White 1982). The manifestations of mental disorders among Asian Americans might be different from those of non-Asian Americans because, to some extent, sociocultural factors (such as interpersonal styles of relating; philosophical ideas; cultural beliefs, values, and practices; and economic and political circumstances) determine the pattern of personality development and the content of mental disorders. For example, cross-national comparisons by the World Health Organization suggest that, despite core features of depression resembling Western criteria, each culture has its own specific depressive symptoms; for example, depressive disorders are characterized by a preponderance of somatic symptoms rather than sadness in certain cultures.

There has been evidence of interethnic differences among Asian American groups in terms of their psychopathology. A study of Japanese American and Filipino American patients who had the same psychiatric diagnosis demonstrated clear group differences in symptoms: Japanese Americans showed more depression, more withdrawal, more disturbed thinking, and more inhibition; whereas Filipino Americans had more delusions of persecution and more overtly disturbed behavior. Similarly, a factor analysis has shown that Chinese Americans, Japanese Americans, and European Americans differ in which symptoms, complaints, and emotions tend to form syndromes (Marsella et al. 1973).

Accurately diagnosing psychopathology and assessing rates of psychopathology among different racial groups also requires that behaviors be judged in their social context. A therapist who is ignorant or naive about racism in this society might misinterpret discriminatory behaviors experienced by an African American client as paranoia rather than a realistic perception of social injustice, or "healthy paranoia."

A clinician who is unfamiliar with the nuances of an individual's cultural frame of reference may incorrectly judge as psychopathology those normal variations in behavior, belief, or experience that are particular to the individual's culture. Clinicians must have basic knowledge about the ways in which varied cultural backgrounds affect the content and form of the symptom presentation, preferred idioms for describing distress, and information on prevalence.

Although external racial difference has been the dominant theme in writing about differences that should be considered in psychotherapy, a broader understanding of cultural differences should include "internalized values and beliefs," or religion. The importance of religion must be appreciated by mental health professionals since ignoring the crucial interrelationships between religion and healing factors may lead to the planning of treatment strategies that are unsound. So it would be of interest to see how individuals in their unique cultural contexts use religious ritual for psychologically beneficial purposes. But we also have to be aware of how religion and culture may sometimes complicate the healing process. Religion and culture define explanatory models of psychological suffering. It is the existence of a belief system that transforms the simple complaint of some suffering or sickness into a culture-bound illness. The belief system also affects the curative intervention and transforms it into a healing process that is mediated through special and particular elements that can be delineated in the unique religious rituals. Clinical examples of ritually grounded therapeutic experience illustrate how the individuals involved bring their religious beliefs to bear on the emotional trouble and rely on the ritual for psychological sustenance.

There is a considerable literature discussing the period of altered consciousness prescribed for certain social and ceremonial occasions. Possession is an explanation of the observation that people sometimes break out of their world of ordinary social routine into a dissociated or often ecstatic state of having been taken over by some culture-specific other, often a deity, spirit, deceased relative, or historical personage. The actual events that have been considered as instances of possession are of several different kinds. Possession may be the indigenous explanation of a psychotic state, but sometimes "possessed" behavior is simply the playing out of a socially prescribed role. Thus, possession may be used to explain both the behaviors and the experiences that constitute elements of certain culture-bound syndromes, trances, or other altered states that occur as desired and expected parts of a group's rituals or ceremonies.

Ignorance of the cultural beliefs of some Asian Americans can therefore be a source of misdiagnosis. For example, when a Southeast Asian client talks about seeing or talking with deceased relatives, it could reflect a cultural belief in the supernatural rather than a delusion or psychosis (Tung 1985).

In understanding religious clients, it is incumbent upon clinicians to develop at least a rudimentary understanding of religions and their institutional expressions. This familiarity with religious traditions that can be gleaned through a study of comparative religion will need to be complemented by a clinically sophisticated inquiry of the client's unique religiousness. This will necessarily include an understanding of religious commitments within the family of origin; religious education; formative faith experience; present challenges within the context of faith development; and current involvement in a religious congregation, faith community, or spiritual tradition.

As found in the research on intrinsic and extrinsic motivation in religion, it is equally important to understand the internal structure and functions of an individual's religiousness. We are then more inclined to perceive that religion can have a positive as well as a negative effect on mental health. Our charge is to address both sides of the religious question. In other words, the beliefs, practices, values, and affiliations expressed within the structure of a formal religious body or held privately hold the potential to be significant variables in mental health. Psychologists should keep an open mind and be willing to explore religious concerns as an important component of cultural diversity.

Psychotherapy with Clients of Different Religious Backgrounds

Psychotherapy in schools, colleges, counseling agencies, and other settings are confronted in the twenty-first century with a clientele drawn from an increasingly wide range of religious backgrounds. In dealing with clients of different religious backgrounds, psychologists cannot avoid the necessity of knowing something about their clients' belief systems and practices. An awareness of individual and group worldviews can help psychologists develop the skills needed for effectiveness in cross-cultural psychotherapy. In the study of other religions, however, we are confronted with the problem of controlling our own values, biases, stereotypes, and assumptions as we encounter others' worldviews. We cannot do justice to our clients' beliefs if we approach them wearing ideological blinders. A method or approach for studying religions that would minimize the distortion of personal prejudices and presuppositions would be of significant value to psychologists. Such a method or approach should be compatible with traditional counseling values of acknowledging and respecting the client's own beliefs and values.

Of the various approaches to the study of religion, a phenomenological approach, as practiced by many scholars of comparative religion, can best satisfy psychologists' needs to learn about other religions while controlling their own biases and assumptions. The aim of this approach is to view religious ideas, acts, and institutions with due consideration to their "intention," without subscribing to any one philosophical, theological, metaphysical, or psychological theory. Through the use of the phenomenological method, psychotherapists studying the religions of their clients can "see" the religious differences without the coloration of personal, professional, or ideological lenses. Such unbiased, empathic understanding can enable the psychotherapist to communicate better with clients and develop sensitive and effective intervention strategies.

A Case of an Overworked/Depressed Religious Korean American Woman

The theoretical perspective of cognitive therapy on religion suggests that cognitive therapy is a highly flexible therapeutic framework for including a patient's religious faith as an active part of the therapeutic process. Using the framework of cognitive therapy, there appear to be at least four categories of religious cognitive therapy interventions: (1) understanding the influence of cognition on emotion and behavior; (2) monitoring cognitions, including thoughts, beliefs, and assumptions; (3) challenging cognitions; and (4) cognitive restructuring and behavior modification.

A middle-aged female sought therapy because of loneliness, unhappiness, and an extended period of crying. She worked full-time at a dry-cleaning store and took care of her three teenage children and the husband. She often felt that she was not doing as well as expected of a "good woman" and felt hopeless. She had traditional Korean values about female roles in what it means to be a "good woman," and her life had no meaning unless she accomplished this divine assignment given to her by God. The notion that "overworking" behavior was healthy behavior had to be challenged.

A useful tool for this challenging process was the Christian view of community as a reflection of the Trinity, in which there is equal mutuality and equal give-and-take, with equal responsibility. Also, the point was discussed that there is no hierarchy between the three persons of the Trinity. This notion was presented as a challenging schema to her initial view of demanding of herself that she do everything. That overworking (traditional cultural value) was not the only way to achieve the goal given to her by God (religious belief) was discussed. Her realization that it is not a "bad thing" to ask her husband and the children to help out, and that she could still fulfill her "God-given" duties to make them happy and successful, made her everyday life more manageable and happier. This relieved her not only from physical complaints but also from guilty feelings from "not fulfilling God's will." Her depression lessened, and the family life became more productive.

It appears that the effectiveness of cognitive-behavioral therapy can be enhanced if aspects of the client's religious belief system are used to provide not only a motivation for self-examination, but also a challenge to some of the client's dysfunctional schemas. It must be acknowledged, however, that this approach to therapy, as with any therapy approach, is not value-free. In most cases, clients are asked to look at their religious beliefs somewhat differently. In other cases, they are asked to pay attention to aspects of their religious beliefs that had heretofore been ignored, as in the above case.

Some religious individuals, when confronted with new ideas, may go back to their religious authorities for confirmation. For most clients, the disconfirmation of their dysfunctional beliefs is surprisingly supported by the religious authorities. This is especially the case if the therapist has been careful to stay within the client's religious tradition. If the clinician is outside the individual's faith, it would be important to consult with someone from within the client's faith to ensure that one's interpretations support the individual's faith. What is needed is an understanding on the part of the therapist of how a particular client's belief system may be effectively and ethically included in the therapeutic process. In other words, cognitive-behavioral therapy offers a treatment approach that is well suited to the examination and modification of all forms of belief, including religious beliefs, as they affect the mental health of the individual.

A Case of a Religious Korean American Professional Male in a Mid-life Crisis

Psychotherapy with religious persons and spiritual seekers can be a meaningful process when both therapist and client are open to exploring the vital area of human experience "beyond the personal realm." Transpersonal psychotherapy offers the client an opportunity to explore the interior realms of the psyche and discover his or her unique, authentic spirituality in a way that contributes to psychological health and maturity. Transpersonal psychotherapy is an approach to healing and growth that aims at the integration of physical, emotional, mental, and spiritual aspects of well-being. The goals of transpersonal psychotherapy encompass normal healthy functioning but go beyond these to include spiritual issues explored from a psychological perspective.

A transpersonal context in psychotherapy is established by the therapist who values the integration of spirituality in the healing process, regardless of whether the client is formally affiliated with an organized religion or not. This does not mean that the transpersonal therapist is necessarily religious in the traditional sense, rather that he or she is informed about the variety of spiritual issues that may be encountered by religious persons.

Because religion generally provides an individual with a creed, a code of ethics, and a community of like-minded persons who share a particular orientation to life, these cultural and social influences are also taken into account. It affirms the possibility of living in harmony with others and the environment, reducing fear and greed, and developing compassion and sense of meaning and purpose in life, regardless of the particular beliefs that may be espoused.

Mr. K, a 55-year-old Korean American male, sought therapy because he felt empty and apathetic, anxious and depressed. He was a successful businessman and lived a rather comfortable life with a loving wife and two grown sons. He had sent his sons to good colleges, and they had both become successful professionals. After the sons were married and had left home, Mr. K felt empty as he began to reflect on his life.

He came to this country twenty-six years ago after graduating from college in Korea and established an import-export business in Koreatown. Mr. K did not come from a Christian family, but he joined a Korean church when he was married to a Christian wife. The family attended church regularly and enjoyed their fellowship with other Korean Americans who shared the same language and cultural background. He also contributed generously to the church; that gave him a sense of significance in his life as a respected member of the Korean American community. His contact with the mainstream society was very limited, however.

Six months before Mr. K sought therapy, his father died suddenly of a heart attack and a close colleague in his firm was killed unexpectedly in a car accident. Confronted with the "impermanence" of life, it dawned upon him that he was psychologically dying and suffocating under unquestioned ways of living. He was disappointed by his wife's lack of attention and the layers of falseness that he felt at work and at church. Mr. K was struggling between psychic aliveness and psychic death. He said he was creatively stagnant, no longer growing. He said the church did not give him answers to the most important questions in his life: "Who am I?" and "What am I?"

Transpersonal therapy addresses multiple levels of the spectrum of identity—prepersonal, personal, and transpersonal. One of the therapist's tasks was to help Mr. K learn to inquire in as many ways as possible and to become aware of aspects of his subjectivity that have been more or less neglected. Eventually he may freely associate his concerns, readily accessing his deeper thoughts, feelings, memories, imaginings, intuitions, and anything else that goes on in his awareness. This may help him to experience a realm of his psyche that is deeper, more subjective, and less accessible than discursive intellect, yet that remains on this side of the Self as pure unconditioned being and awareness.

When he is fully immersed in his stream of immediate inner experiencing, he is likely to discover his own unique, authentic spirituality. This process gradually brings awareness to the unconscious organizing principles out of which Mr. K constructs his personal identity—the structure of his experiencing, the characteristic ways in which he experiences himself and his world—from a perspective within, rather than outside, his unique frame of reference.

As Mr. K entered his subjective realm and described his concerns, he gradually began to learn that he had the persona of highly achieving to please others, be they parents, teachers, wife, the community, even the minister of the church. These personality traits brought him the recognition he wanted, but others' responses no longer satisfied him. He was giving them what they expected, but he rarely noticed his own thoughts, feelings, and desires.

As he probed even more deeply into his psyche and worked to understand and reexperience his dependency and fear, his experience of desperately needing to be affirmed began to dissolve. His awareness of himself as an individual temporarily disappeared and there followed a spontaneous blossoming of awareness of the real nature of creation, a profound experience of inner freedom. The process of probing can be a precondition for a deeper personal and spiritual exploration. After his spiritual experience, Mr. K began to use his therapy to inquire even more concentratedly into these fundamental questions.

A Case of a Fundamentalist Korean American Woman with Heavenly Visions

A 34-year-old Korean American woman was brought to a local hospital by the police. She was wandering around the street in a daze. She later claimed that she was raped by a "black man." On physical examination, she complained of severe headaches, lower back pain, extreme shakiness, and blackout after the alleged rape. There were no signs of forced penetration or genital trauma, however, and laboratory works of specimens including stains, hair, and so forth all came out negative.

She was then interviewed by a psychologist. The client had apparently, for the past fifteen years, been having "different levels of visionary states" during which she both saw and heard God. Recently she had been receiving religious and political messages from God and believed North Koreans were sent here to harm Korean Americans from South Korea who interfered with North Koreans' supreme mission of unifying the two Koreas. She believed the rapist was sent by this North Korean group through God's will. Her description of these visionary experiences and history was coherent and articulate and was delivered in a matter-of-fact manner with many vivid and startling details.

She was born in Korea. Her father was a fundamentalist Christian minister, and she had been deeply involved in the church from an early age. She completed high school and obtained a job in a U.S. Army Officers' Club near Seoul (capital of South Korea), against her parents' wishes. She later married a GI and came to the United States. She lived with him for ten years and had a daughter, but she left him when she discovered that he had molested their daughter. She has worked sporadically since then. After she left the husband, the client moved to another town with her daughter. She reported that fourteen months before the current admission, she had slept with a stranger in a motel.

An interview with the client while in the hospital also revealed that she held firmly to her religious beliefs, and she claimed that many prophecies she made came true. She produced tape cassettes from various people throughout the country who shared her religious beliefs. In these tapes she was generally praised for her steadfast faith and her gift of prophecy. In some tapes "speaking in tongues" was prominent.

The client was discharged after a week. She refused any follow-up care and told her church members that she was heading West in the hope of continuing her evangelical work. Her daughter remained in the custody of the child welfare department because she allegedly neglected the child.

The central question in this case was whether or not the visions, voices, unusual beliefs, and sexual activities/attacks are symptoms of true psychotic disorder—a disorder in which there is gross impairment in reality testing. By definition, a delusion is a belief that is not ordinarily accepted by other members of the person's culture. This client has a long history of association with fundamentalist religious sects in which such experiences as speaking in tongues and having visions of God are not uncommon. Can this woman's unusual perceptual experiences and strange notions be entirely accounted for by her religious beliefs? It is true that receiving messages from God and instructions to do various things to carry out God's will are common among such groups. However, this client's elaborate notions of an invasion by North Koreans and God's instructions to attack her sexually to prosecute seem well beyond the range of even extreme fundamentalist beliefs. Thus it was doubtful that this client's behavior is merely the reflection of a culture-bound pattern of beliefs and behavior and without psychopathological significance.

If one accepts the authenticity of the delusions and hallucinations in this case, then the following specific diagnostic categories need to be considered: Schizophrenia, Brief Psychotic Disorder, Bipolar Disorder, and Delusional Disorder. There was no evidence of common features of Schizophrenia such as flat affect and disorganized speech. A Delusional Disorder is ruled out by hallucinations lasting more than a few hours. A provisional level of Somatization Disorder diagnosis was made because of characteristic pseudoneurological symptoms (shakiness, blackout spells) and pain symptoms (headache, lower back pain). In view of the long history of disturbed interpersonal relationships, a diagnosis of a Personality Disorder would seem appropriate. The client's history reveals prominent histrionic features and suggestion of significant antisocial traits (neglect of child, sexual misconduct, if not delusional behavior). In the absence of more information, a diagnosis of Personality Disorder Not Otherwise Specified with Histrionic and Antisocial Traits seems appropriate.

The reestablishment of reality contact and the rebuilding of a sense of personal identity and self-worth are the two principal goals to counter the client's estrangement in therapy process. Attainment of these goals rests, first, on the development of trust between client and therapist. Many hours of untiring perseverance are required before she will gain enough faith in her therapist to dare face the world of reality again. The therapist must feel genuine respect for the client. A sincere desire to be of assistance is needed to help carry the therapist through a long, slow, and not-too-promising process of treatment. Should trust and a cognitively clear line of communication be developed, the therapist will have established the foundation for further progress.

Conclusion

Interaction between psychology and religion must rest on a respect for the differences as well as the similarities between the two disciplines. Clergy should not be mistaken for psychologists. And churches should not be mistaken for mental health centers. The missions and values of the two systems are, in important ways, distinctive. However, psychological and religious communities are linked by their commitment to the well-being of those they serve. Clearly, both groups must wrestle with the points of commonality and divergence in their visions of the world before they can work together effectively. But there may be much to gain in this process. It is hoped that psychologists realize that they do not have a monopoly on helpful methods of coping. The same is true of the religious community. By recognizing the strengths and limitations of each tradition, both communities may multiply their own resources and enhance their value to people searching for significance and psychological well-being.

By understanding the unique cultural background of the clients we serve, we will be able to strengthen our resources and enhance our value to people searching for significance and psychological well-being.

References

Allport, G. W., and J. M. Ross. 1967. "Personal Religious Orientation and Prejudice." *Journal of Personality and Social Psychology* 5:432–43.

American Psychiatric Association. 1990. "Guidelines Regarding Possible Conflict Between Psychiatrists' Religious Commitments and Psychiatric Practice." *American Journal of Psychiatry* 147:542.

American Psychological Association. 1992. "Ethical Principles of Psychologists and Code of Conduct." *American Psychologist* 41:1597–611.

Bergin, A. B. 1988a. "Three Contributions of a Spiritual Perspective to Counseling, Psychotherapy, and Behavior Change." *Counseling and Values* 33:21–31.

———. 1988b. "The Spiritual Perspective Is Ecumenical and Eclectic" (rejoinder). *Counseling and Values* 33:57–59.

Bergin, A. E. 1991. Values and Religious Issues in Psychotherapy and Mental Health." *American Psychologist* 46:394–403.

Bergin, A. E., and I. R. Payne. 1991. "Proposed Agenda for a Spiritual Strategy in Personality and Psychotherapy." *Journal of Psychology and Christianity* 10:197–210.

Bickel, C. 1992. "Perceived Stress, Religious Coping Styles, and Depressive Affect." Ph.D. diss., Loyola College, Columbia, Maryland.

Cohen, E., C. T. Mowbray, V. Gillette, and E. Thompson. 1991. "Preventing Homelessness: Religious Organizations and Housing Development." *Prevention in Human Services* 11:169–86.

Donahue, M. J. 1985. "Intrinsic and Extrinsic Religiousness: Review and Metanalysis." *Journal of Personality and Social Psychology* 48 (2): 400–19.

Eng, E., and J. W. Hatch. 1991. "Networking Between Agencies and Black Churches: The Lay Health Advisor Model." *Prevention in Human Services* 11:123–46.

Gartner, J. B. 1986. "Antireligious Prejudice in Admissions to Doctoral Programs in Clinical Psychology. *Professional Psychology: Research and Practice* 17:473–75.

Hurh, W. M., and K. C. Kim. 1988. "Uprooting and Adjustment: A Sociological Study of Korean Immigrants' Mental Health." Report submitted to National Institutes of Mental Health, Department of Human Services.

Jackson, J. S. 1990. "The Therapeutic Equation and Cross-Cultural Psychology." In *Toward Education and Training*, ed. G. Stricker et al., 206–10. Washington, D.C.: American Psychological Association.

Jensen, J. P., and A. E. Bergin. 1988. "Mental Health Values of Professional Therapists: A National Interdisciplinary Survey." *Professional Psychology: Research and Practice* 19:290–97.

Johnson, P. E. 1955. *Psychology of Religion.* Nashville, Tenn.: Abingdon Press.

Kirkpatrick, L. E. 1993. "Fundamentalism, Christian Orthodoxy, and Religious Orientation as Predictors of Discriminatory Attitudes." *Journal for the Scientific Study of Religion* 32:256–68.

Kosmin, B. A., and Lachman, S. P. 1993. *One Nation Under God: Religion in Contemporary American Society.* New York: Crown Trade Paperbacks.

Marsella, A. J., E. Kinzie, and P. Gordon. 1973. "Ethnic Variations in the Expression of Depression." *Journal of Cross-Cultural Psychology* 4:435–58.

Marsella, A. J., and G. M. White, eds. 1982.

Cultural Conceptions of Mental Health and Therapy. Dordrecht: D. Reidel.

Masters, K. S., and A. E. Bergin. 1992. "Religious Orientation and Mental Health." In *Religion and Mental Health,* ed. J. F. Schumaker, 221–32. Oxford (U.K.): Oxford University Press.

Maton, K. I. 1989. "The Stress-buffering Role of Spiritual Support: Cross-sectional and Prospective Investigations." *Journal for the Scientific Study of Religion* 28:310–23.

Meissner, W. W. 1986. *Psychotherapy and the Paranoid Process.* Northvale, N.J.: Aronson.

Mickleburgh, W. E. 1992. "Clarification of Values in Counseling and Psychopathology." *Australian and New Zealand Journal of Psychiatry* 26:391–98.

Pargament, K. I. 1990. "God Help Me: Toward a Theoretical Framework of Coping for the Psychology of Religion." *Research in the Social Scientific Study of Religion* 2:195–224.

Pargament, K. I., K. Ishler, E. Dubow, P. Stark, R. Rouiller, P. Crowe, E. Cullman, M. Albert, and B. J. Royster. 1994. "Methods of Religious Coping with the Gulf War: Cross-sectional and Longitudinal Analyses." *Journal for the Scientific Study of Religion* 33:347–61.

Pargament, K. I., R. E. Steele, and E. B. Tyler. 1979. "Religious Participation, Religious Motivation, and Individual Psychosocial Competence." *Journal for the Scientific Study of Religion* 18:412–19.

Payne, I. R., A. E. Bergin, and P. E. Loftus. 1992. "A Review of Attempts to Integrate Spiritual and Standard Psychotherapy Techniques." *Journal of Psychotherapy Integration* 2:171–92.

Park, C. L., L. C. Cohen, and L. Herb. 1990.

"Intrinsic Religiousness and Religious Coping as Life Stress Moderators for Catholics Versus Protestants. *Journal of Personality and Social Psychology* 59:562–74.

Richards, P. S. 1991. "Religion Devoutness in College Students: Relations with Emotional Adjustment and Psychological Separation from Parents." *Journal of Counseling Psychology* 38:189–96.

Richards, P. S., and R. Potts. 1995. "Using Spiritual Interventions in Psychotherapy: Practices, Successes, Failures, and Ethical Concerns of Mormon Psychotherapists." *Professional Psychology: Research and Practices* 26:163–70.

Richards, P. S., S. A. Smith, and L. F. Davis. 1989. "Healthy and Unhealthy Forms of Religiousness Manifested by Psychotherapy Clients: An Empirical Investigation." *Journal of Research in Personality* 23:506–24.

Siegel, J. M., and D. H. Kuykendall. 1990. "Loss, Widowhood, and Psychological Distress Among the Elderly." *Journal of Consulting and Clinical Psychology* 58:519–24.

Tung, T. M. 1985. "Psychiatric Care for Southeast Asians: How Different Is Different?" *Southeast Asian Mental Health: Treatment, Prevention, Services, Training, and Research.* Washington, D.C.: Department of Health and Human Services.

Welch, M. R., and J. Barrish. 1982. "Bringing Religious Motivation Back In: A Multivariate Analysis of Motivational Predicators of Student Religiosity." *Review of Religious Research* 23:357–69.

Williams, D. R., D. B. Larson, R. E. Budkler, R. C. Heckman, and C. M. Pyle. 1991. "Religion and Psychological Distress in a Community Sample." *Social Science Medicine* 32:1257–62.

Part III

GENERATIONAL
TRANSITION OF
KOREAN AMERICAN
CHURCHES

A Theological Reflection on the Cultural Tensions Between First-Century Hebraic and Hellenistic Jewish Christians and Between Twentieth-Century First- and Second-Generation Korean American Christians

Robert D. Goette and Mae Pyen Hong

UNDERSTANDING TENSIONS BETWEEN GENERATIONS in the contemporary ethnic church has been a difficult challenge for many years. The conflicts have often resulted in bitter divisions, confusion, resentments, and broken relationships in families as well as in the church. Congregations are accustomed to seeking biblical answers to problems, but it is easy for them to assume that the Bible does not address such a contemporary ministry issue as tensions between first- and second-generation Koreans (or any other ethnic group) in the church. This chapter presents a biblical framework for understanding the complex cultural and intergenerational tensions in the ethnic church. It examines the early church in the book of Acts and draws parallels between the tensions between Hebraic and Hellenistic Jewish Christians in the first century and the contemporary tensions between first- and second-generation Koreans in the United States. Although it is not often recognized, Acts documents multicultural experiences. It provides significant insight into the interplay between language, culture, and faith. These insights can have far-reaching implications for contemporary faith and intergenerational relationships.

The goal of this discussion is to promote intergenerational understanding and self-awareness among Korean Americans, not to provide a simplistic formula to resolve these tensions. By understanding present-day tensions in the Korean church in light of biblical narratives, those in ministry can receive direction, purpose, and encouragement while wrestling with difficult cultural issues. Although this discussion is intended to be nonpartisan, each group may draw different conclusions about its role in this context. First-generation leaders will gain a vision for what needs to happen in the development of the next generation—from a cultural and church perspective. The 1.5 and second generations will better understand their roles as bridge-builders, similar to Paul's role in the book of Acts. Despite tensions and frustrations between the groups, the emphasis for all parties is perseverance, conciliation, and mutual effort to work through these tensions together (Romans 15:4–6).

Background

Acts 6:1[1] introduces two different groups of Jewish Christians: the Hebraic (*Hebraios*) and Hellenistic/Grecian Jews (*Hellenistes*). In general, the Hebraic Jews lived in the Palestine area in Judea and Galilee. The Hellenistic/Grecian Jews were those who lived elsewhere in the Roman Empire.

Jerusalem had been the center of Hebrew culture for a thousand years before Christ. Aramaic, which is similar to Hebrew, was the primary language of the Hebraic Jews in the Middle East, including Judea and Galilee. Culture and religion were impossible to separate for the Hebraic Jews. "Being Jewish" was as much about following the religious law as it was about cultural heritage. The written law of the Torah, combined with the oral laws of commentary and interpretation, formed a major portion of the culture of the Hebraic Jews. For instance, the act of male circumcision represented both theological and cultural adherence.

The Hellenistic Jewish Christians, however, had migrated to many different parts of the Roman Empire where languages other than Aramaic were spoken (Acts 2:5, 8–11). They also understood Greek, the lingua franca of the Roman Empire. Consequently, the Hellenistic Jews adopted the cultural influences and perspective of the Greeks. The Hellenistic Jews assimilated quickly into their new host culture and were mostly well respected. Although they quickly established themselves in the new society, they still maintained strong attachments to Jerusalem. They went to Jerusalem to celebrate the

---

1. Because of the claim of the author of Acts to careful historical research (Luke 1:1–4; Acts 1:1) and the many confirmations through archaeological research, the authors of this chapter consider Acts to be a superior primary source for this topic.

Jewish festivals such as Passover and Pentecost. In this respect, they did not drift far from their religious roots. However, living in the Roman Empire allowed the Hellenistic Jews to develop relationships with others outside their own ethnic group. Some God-fearing Gentiles even worshiped with the Hellenistic Jews in their synagogues. Hebraic Jews, however, did not associate with Gentiles. Although ethnically the same, the Hebraic and Hellenistic Jews used different primary languages and adhered to different cultures.

The apostle Paul embodied elements of both Hebraic and Hellenistic Judaism. Paul's birthplace of Tarsus historically was considered the meeting point between East and West (Ramsay 1908, 235). Although Hellenistic by birth (Acts 22:3), he appears to have been speaking Hebrew/Aramaic at home (Philippians 3:5). He was sent to Jerusalem at an early age to study under Gamaliel's tutelage. Paul's hybrid background made him a prime candidate for what Christians think of as God's plan for taking the gospel to the Hellenistic Jews and then to the Gentiles (Acts 9:15; 22:3) (Ramsay 1908, 88).

Analysis of Cultural Tensions Between Hebraic Jews and Hellenistic Jews

The book of Acts represents a history of major adjustments in the Hebraic Jewish mind-set. When Jesus commanded the apostles to go and preach to all nations (Matthew 28:18–20), the command was initially interpreted to refer only to the *Jews* in all the nations.

Because of the different cultural backgrounds between the Hebraic and Hellenistic Jews, language differences created significant tensions within the early church. An important biblical basis for affirming cultural and language differences appears in Acts 2 (*circa* A.D. 30). During Pentecost, when God's gift of the Holy Spirit was manifested through "tongues of fire," the gospel was communicated in the mother tongues of the Hellenistic Jews. This might have resolved the language issue between the Aramaic-speaking Hebraic Jews and the Hellenistic Jews. The Holy Spirit legitimized the native languages of the Hellenistic Jews. The event not only captured the attention of people speaking different languages but also provided a lesson about the role of the vernacular in spiritual matters. God's Spirit brought the gospel to the people in a form that each group could understand. The Hellenistic Jews could not be considered linguistically inferior for not speaking Aramaic.

Acts 6:1–7 (*circa* A.D. 31) illustrates another cultural tension between the Hebraic and Hellenistic Jews of the early church in Jerusalem. The issue involved the treatment of poor widows. Hebraic widows received ministry and care, while Hellenistic widows were neglected. This discrepancy may be attributed to several different factors. The Hebraic Jews may have been in charge of the care of widows and unaware of the needs of the Hellenistic widows visiting Jerusalem from various regions. There may also have been inadequate communication between the two groups. Acts 6:5 describes the resolution of the problem in the appointment of spiritual Hellenistic leaders to oversee the ministry to their own widows.

Acts 10 demonstrates another significant shift in the Hebraic Jewish mindset. God had miraculously called Peter, the leader of the Hebraic Jewish Christians, to Caesarea to preach the gospel to Cornelius—a God-fearing Gentile—and his family. As Peter preached, God gave the gift of the Holy Spirit to the Gentiles, just as he had to the Jews at Pentecost (Acts 10:47). Peter realized that God was affirming his acceptance of the Gentiles even without their adoption of the Jewish law. Upon arriving in Jerusalem, Peter was criticized by other Hebraic Jews for eating and fellowshiping with uncircumcised Gentiles. Peter had to defend his actions and explain how God clearly demonstrated his intent to save the Gentiles, even though they did not follow the Hebraic law (Acts 11:17–18). Through Cornelius's salvation, God illustrated that culture was subordinate to faith.[2]

Despite Peter's realization of God's larger purposes for saving the Gentiles as portrayed in Acts 10, he continued to struggle with the distinction between culture and faith. In a later event described in Galatians 2:11–16, Peter visited the church in Antioch where he ate with the Gentile Christians. However, when Hebraic Jews arrived from Jerusalem, Peter ate separately from the Gentiles. His separation from the Gentiles led other Jewish Christians to follow his "hypocrisy" (Galatians 2:13). Paul chastised Peter sharply for failing to embrace as equal believers in the kingdom those who did not obey the Law. According to Paul, Peter's actions of "forcing the Gentiles to follow Jewish customs" were counter to the doctrine of justification through faith in Christ (Galatians 2:14–16).

The period between Acts 10 and Acts 15 (A.D. 49) was a significant time of growth in ministry to the Gentiles. Despite the previous illustration of God's distinction between cultural adherence to the Jewish law and faith in Acts 10, Acts 15 shows that the theological implications of this principle still were not clearly understood by the Hebraic Jews. After completing his first missionary trip, Paul traveled to Jerusalem. At that time, some of the Hebraic

2. For a more elaborate discussion of the relationship between God and culture, refer to Kraft 1979, 103–15. Kraft summarizes H. Richard Niebuhr's classical categories and suggests the "God-*Above-But-Through*-Culture Position" that both authors of this paper hold.

Jewish Christians in Jerusalem insisted that the Gentiles must be circumcised and obey the law of Moses (Acts 15:5).

However, Paul was teaching that God did not require circumcision (or any other act of the Law) as a prerequisite for, or evidence of, salvation (Romans 3:20–30; Galatians 5:2–6). Paul wrote that the purpose of the Law was to expose the sinfulness of sin and point to faith in Jesus Christ (Romans 7:7–13; Galatians 3:19–25). Paul clearly believed that Jews and Gentiles stood on equal ground as sinners (Romans 3:9) and that God was equally concerned about the salvation of non-Jews and Jews (Romans 3:29–30). He reasoned that because no one could fulfill the Law, faith in Jesus Christ was the only way for anyone to achieve true righteousness. The implication was that if one (Jew or Gentile) could come to faith in Jesus Christ without knowledge of or obedience to the Law, then the Law became unnecessary because its goals were already fulfilled. Consequently, salvation and true spirituality could be achieved outside the realm of Jewish culture (that is, apart from the Law). This revolutionary concept was extremely difficult for the Hebraic Jews to embrace.

Ultimately, at the end of the Council of Jerusalem in A.D. 49, the Hebraic Jewish Christians did not require Gentile adherence to the Law for several reasons. First of all, Peter reminded them how God had demonstrated his acceptance of Cornelius and his Gentile friends and relatives (Acts 15:8–9). Then Peter pointed out that faith in Christ—not a cultural ritual—was the means by which God purified hearts and saved them (Acts 15:9, 11). Rather than being the sole means to an end (faith), they recognized that the Law and Hebraic culture was a burden to which the Hebraic Jewish Christians themselves could not even adhere. Salvation could be achieved outside of the Law.

Nonetheless, the issue remained unresolved regarding Hellenistic Jewish Christians' adherence to the Law, which was still viewed by the Hebraic Jewish Christians as an integral part of the culture. Although the Gentiles could be released from following Jewish culture and still have faith, the Hellenistic Jews were still expected to maintain strict obedience to the Law for cultural purposes if not for spiritual ones. Abandoning the Law was akin to abolishing their ethnic identity.

Because of this, eight years later when Paul was visiting Jerusalem after his third missionary trip, the Hebraic Jewish Christians became angry with Paul for not enforcing the law more rigorously among the Hellenistic Jewish Christians (Acts 21:20–21). They thought he was leading the Hellenistic Jews away from the culture because they made major cultural concessions. The Hellenistic Jewish Christians, however, saw the fulfillment of the law in

Christ. They embraced the same "liberty" or "freedom" from the Law as the Gentiles. They freely adapted to whatever cultural environment they had to in order to more effectively share the gospel (1 Corinthians 9:20–23). In short, Paul defused the tensions while in Jerusalem and exemplified his freedom to adapt to any culture by participating in a traditional Jewish ritual.

The major blow to the Hebraic Jewish Christians allegiance to the Law more than likely occurred in A.D. 70 when the temple was destroyed. No longer could the Hebraic Jewish Christians offer sacrifices and fulfill many other requirements of the Law.

Lessons About Culture and Faith

The tensions between the Hebraic Jewish Christians and the Hellenistic Jewish Christians illustrate the significant role of culture in the practice of faith. Culture is the lens through which spiritual principles are interpreted and put into practice. From a biblical perspective, cultural ideals reveal man's inability to live up to them, which ultimately reveals his need for Jesus Christ. Jesus continuously made the distinction between faith and the Law (John 5:37–47), and taught that the Law always pointed to him.

Paul echoed this distinction between culture and faith. He believed that Christ ultimately fulfilled the law. Consequently, believers in Christ (Jew or Gentile) did not have to fulfill the law to be saved. In addition, his reasoning in 1 Corinthians 9:19–23 demonstrates how culture can be a fluid medium through which to communicate faith. When among Jews, Paul adapted to Jewish culture; when among Gentiles, he adapted to their culture. Culture (that is, the Law) played a subservient role to faith. While Paul maintained an appreciation for his cultural heritage (Romans 9:1–5; Philippians 3:5–6), he shunned ethnocentrism.

Lessons for the First- and Second-Generation Korean Church

Even though the cultural tensions between the Hebraic and Hellenistic Jewish Christians were not resolved during the first generation of the early church, the principles for understanding the distinction between culture and faith provide the biblical framework for the contemporary conflicts in the first- and second-generation Korean American church. The tensions between the Hebraic and Hellenistic Jewish Christians demonstrated a need for a paradigm shift. Rather than viewing the Hellenistic Jewish Christians as deviant from Hebraic culture and faith, the Hebraic Jewish Christians needed to see the Hellenistic Jewish Christians in a completely different light. They had to view them as a separate entity, legitimate in its own culture and language and valid in its own faith, with tremendous potential for being the bridge to other people groups.

In the same way that the Hebraic Jews wanted Hellenistic Jews to follow the Law (an important God-given part of their culture), the first-generation Korean American church often adheres to a strict ethnic culture as an important component of the faith and ethnic identity. As one can observe from the Appendix, the differences between American and Korean cultures are far from superficial, dealing with such fundamental issues as self-identity. Understandably, much of the first generation's tenacity in adhering to its native culture stems from a painful political history that now causes it to resist any implication of cultural loss. But the Korean American church's insistence upon language retention and obedience to cultural rules and expectations must be reconsidered.

The apostle Paul argued that to be truly Jewish is not a matter of cultural adherence (Romans 2:28–29). Of ultimate importance was that one have the same faith as that of Abraham whether or not one adheres to the culture (Romans 4:12, 16). Likewise, for second-generation Korean Americans, if Korean cultural adherence is achieved without the transference of a living faith in Christ Jesus, what is of ultimate importance has been missed. As at Pentecost, second-generation Korean Americans need to hear the gospel in their own "heart" language. Too often U.S.-born Korean Americans have been alienated by the Korean church, which places a premium on cultural transference because they have been unable to meet the expectations of an unfamiliar culture and to identify with a faith expressed through that culture.

Leaders of second-generation ministries, as they insist on contextualizing their ministries to reach the second generation and many other English-speaking people, face the same accusations and tensions that Paul faced from the Hebraic Jews: betrayal of mother culture, compromise of faith, and abandonment of tradition. However, cultural accommodation (although some may call it cultural loss) has allowed the second generation to reach others outside its own people group, which ultimately fulfills God's plan for advancing the kingdom and taking the gospel to all people.

Once the spiritual legacy of faith has been passed on, there is an even higher calling to become multilingual and multicultural. Language and culture not only become a bridge to cross generation gaps within one's own ethnic group, but become bridges to various other language and culture groups

(1 Corinthians 9:20–23). Even if the second generation never achieves the same kind of multiculturalism that Paul achieved, the loose adherence to its mother culture does not necessarily sacrifice its ethnic identity. God will use each first- or second-generation Korean American to fulfill his purposes to reach all ethnic groups (Matthew 28:18–19).

Neither generation can claim sole jurisdiction over God's plan for the Korean ethnic group. As in the early church, God called some Jews to ministry among Jews—for example, Peter—and some to ministry among more diverse people groups—for example, Paul (Galatians 2:7–8). A narrower generational and ethnic calling and a broad, multiethnic calling both must be viewed in the larger context of advancing the gospel. Obeying God's plan for expanding the kingdom—and not a particular culture—must be the ultimate priority of both generations.

As the Hebraic and Hellenistic Jewish Christians struggled through cultural tensions, so first- and second-generation Koreans will continue to experience parallel conflicts. While the early church could not easily resolve the tensions within one generation, the Korean church must learn to apply the biblical principles of culture and faith as it perseveres to build relationships and bridges across generations and to different people groups.

Appendix: Differences Between American and Korean Cultures

	AMERICAN CULTURE (Individual Centered)	KOREAN CULTURE (Relationship Centered)
1. Relationship	**Egalitarianism**	**Hierarchical Relationship**
	1.1: See others as equals.	1.1: See others in hierarchical terms.
	1.2: Informal interpersonal relationship.	1.2: Formal interpersonal relationship.
	1.3: Less complex rules for speech and conduct.	1.3: Very complex rules for speech and conduct.
2. Values	**Individual's Rights**	**Duties and Responsibilities**
	2.1: Premium attached to the individual's rights.	2.1: Emphasis on roles assigned to different hierarchical positions.
	2.2: Self-reliance and self-determination.	2.2: Emphasis on performing appropriate functions.

	AMERICAN CULTURE (Individual Centered)	**KOREAN CULTURE** (Relationship Centered)
3. Attitudes	**Assertiveness and Self-Expression**	**Respect for Authority**
	3.1: Standing up for (demanding) personal rights.	3.1: Emphasis on docility.
	3.2: Expression of personal thoughts and feelings.	3.2: Conformity to assigned roles.
4. Identity	**Personal Ability and Achievement**	**Status (position) in a Group**
	4.1: The individual's competence, achievements, success.	4.1: The individual's position in a group (e.g., family, church corporation, etc.).
	4.2: Development of a person's unique qualities.	4.2: Self-development related to group expectations.
	4.3: Self-initiated activities for personal success.	4.3: Ascriptive motivation (succeeding for the group).
5. Socialization	**Active Involvement**	**Observation and Emulation**
	5.1: Participatory decision making.	5.1: Watch, listen and do.
	5.2: Frequent exchange of ideas and feelings.	5.2: Communication by commands and demands.
6. Thinking Style	**Analytic and Detail Specific**	**Global and Impressionistic**
	6.1: Separating the cognitive from the affective as well the objective from the subjective.	6.1: The cognitive and the affective as well as the objective from the subjective are often combined.
	6.2: Serial exchange among communicants.	6.2: Spontaneous and/or simultaneous exchanges among communicants.
	6.3: Relatively loosely structured teaching learning situations.	6.3: Highly structured teaching learning situations.

Source: Pai, Pemberton, and Worley 1987, 67–68.

References

Kraft, Charles H. 1979. *Christianity in Culture.* Maryknoll, N.Y.: Orbis Books.

Pai, Young; Deloras Pemberton, and John Worley. 1987. *Findings on Korean American Early Adolescents and Adolescents.* Kansas City: University of Missouri School of Education.

Ramsay, William M. 1908. *Cities of St. Paul.* New York: Armstrong.

7

The Transformation of a First-Generation Church into a Bilingual Second-Generation Church

Robert D. Goette

WITH THE RAPIDLY INCREASING number of Korean Americans who prefer to communicate in English,[1] Korean church leaders realize that in order to develop a successful church they need a thriving English ministry. Various models are being developed and copied with little consideration given to the inevitable turbulent transformation process that Korean American churches are experiencing. The Korean American church needs both direction and an understanding of some of the crises it will encounter in order to effectively minister to both the Korean- and English-preference Korean American communities it seeks to target. Failure to carefully navigate the crises has unnecessarily disenfranchised large segments of both communities.

The Context

While the Korean American population is rapidly approaching the official U.S. Census count of one million,[2] Korean churches are continuing to proliferate.

This chapter is a major revision of a chapter published under the same title (Goette 1993).

1. Using 1990 U.S. Census information on language preference, Korean immigration statistics of the 1990s, and Asian American birth rate and death rate estimates, the author has estimated the English-preference Korean American population (5 years old and older) at 27 percent in 1999 and increasing at an average annual rate of 1.2 percent between 2000 and 2010 and 1.0 percent between 2010 and 2020 until 50 percent of the Korean American population prefer English in 2020 (see Goette 1998, 14).

2. Many would argue that this estimate is based on a serious 1990 census undercount.

But because of the diversity of Korean Americans, one should not hastily assume that all Korean Americans are being served adequately by these churches (see Fig. 7.1).[3]

Most Korean churches in the United States target "nuclear" Korean Americans who speak Korean fluently and prefer Korean cultural values over American values. The large number of youth groups and English ministries that have begun in these churches are aimed at "fellow traveler" Korean Americans who are somewhat bilingual but prefer English over Korean, and American cultural values to Korean ones. The two groups that currently need greater attention are the "marginal" and "alienated" groups. "Marginal" Korean Americans usually speak very little Korean and feel uneasy around first-generation[4] Korean immigrants. At the same time, they are not completely comfortable in predominantly European American social settings. Prejudice from both sides due to either language ability or race is the major reason for this sense of marginalization. "Alienated" Korean Americans rarely associate with other Korean Americans outside their own family and feel at ease among European Americans.

As Peter Cha demonstrates in Chapter 8, Figure 7.1 is not a static model. A given individual may move back and forth from one category to another.

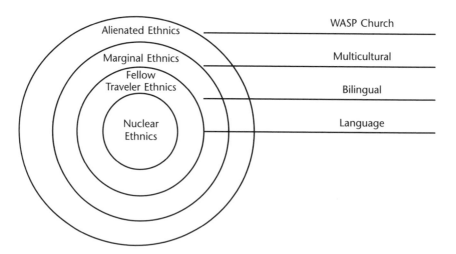

Figure 7.1

3. Other more complex breakdowns of ethnic communities exist (Romo 1993, 72–74), but Wagner's model is adequate for this discussion.

4. The term "first generation" is used loosely in this chapter to designate any Korean American who prefers speaking in Korean and living predominantly according to Korean cultural values. Likewise, the term "second generation" is used to refer to anyone who prefers English and predominantly American cultural values.

The individuals he interviewed migrated between various categories through-out their lives as they sought to more fully understand their ethnic identity. However, if one understands the model's fluid nature, it can adequately fulfill its purpose to illustrate the diversity of the Korean American community.

Almost every church leader would agree that the church should take the gospel to each person in his own heart language and cultural context (Acts 10:34–35; 1 Corinthians 9:19–22). Likewise, the Korean American church would like to minister to the spiritual needs of every family and individual, both recent immigrant as well as native-born. Ideally each individual of every family would be both bilingual and bicultural so that communication would never be a problem. Everyone would also like to see each family worshiping together and respectful and understanding of each other. Reality, however, causes those involved in ministry to creatively develop different methodologies to meet the complex problems and needs of real people who are seldom completely bilingual or bicultural.

Since I was raised in both Korea and the United States and received seminary education in the area of missions both in the United States and in Korea, my perspective is itself bicultural. While studying in Korea, I was challenged to view English-speaking Korean Americans as an emerging new "people group"[5] (Dayton and Fraser 1980, 6–7). To gather data for a paper concerning English-speaking Korean Americans, I traveled to New York City, Washington, D.C., Chicago, Los Angeles, Atlanta, Dallas, Houston, and Seattle. I interviewed Korean pastors, elders, deacons, campus and youth pastors, and young people from a variety of churches affiliated with the Southern Baptist Convention, the Presbyterian Church USA, and the United Methodist Church concerning the status of emerging ministries to English-speaking Korean Americans. Subsequently, I saw the need for existing Korean churches to design programs and adjust church structures to accommodate this new people group. Brand-new churches would also be needed to meet the specific spiritual and sociological needs of this particular group. This has been confirmed repeatedly during my fifteen years of full-time ministry with English-preference Korean Americans in the context of youth groups and new churches connected to first-generation Korean churches and separate from them. As I conversed with Korean American church leaders throughout the United States, I recognized a distinct developmental pattern

---

5. In missions literature, the term *people group* has become widely accepted to designate any group of people with a distinct self-identity because of nationality, language, culture, ethnicity, socioeconomic class, occupation, or geographical location. Even though English-speaking Korean Americans share much in common with their Korean-speaking parents, because of the cultural and language differences they warrant the status of a distinct people group.

occurring in Korean American churches. This pattern did not seem to be significantly different from the experience of fifty- to seventy-five-year-old Japanese and Chinese American churches that I had observed in Chicago. A telephone conversation with Peter Yuen[6] confirmed the validity of this pattern and its similarity with the experiences of other Asian American communities.

The Transformation Process

Just as the immigrant family goes through tremendous changes during the first two or three generations after they have immigrated, so does the immigrant church. Figure 7.2 depicts the transformation process Asian American

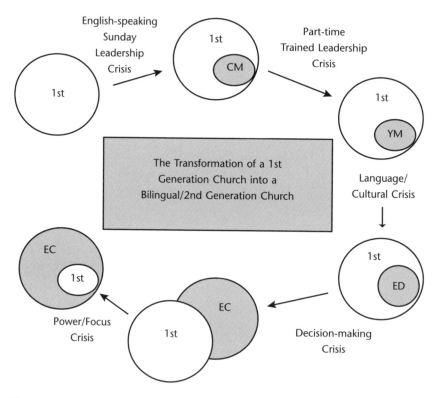

Figure 7.2

6. Peter Yuen is the editor of the American-born Chinese (ABC) quarterly newsletter *About Face*. The primary contributors of articles to the newsletter are veteran ABC pastors with an average of more than thirty years of ministerial experience throughout the United States. My conversation with him occurred in September 1991.

churches have experienced and will continue to go through over a twenty-five to forty-year period (Yuen 1990, 3).

Stage One—In a church of very recent immigrants, as long as both the adults and the children communicate well in the home-country language, the only major problem is the enlistment of willing adults to help with the children. Because new immigrants often work long hours, volunteers may be few.

First Crisis—(English-speaking Sunday Leadership Crisis) A Korean American church composed of recent immigrants soon faces its first crisis when the young children begin having some difficulty speaking Korean and prefer a Sunday school class in English. The search for an adult who speaks English with some proficiency and has the ability and willingness to teach young children at several grade levels is often challenging. There are two common solutions to this crisis. First, until one can be found in the congregation, outside volunteers have been used. A mission-minded adult from a European American church or another larger Korean American church, a college student from a nearby Christian college, or even a mature high school student have often been used to fill this role (Chai 1998, 310). Some churches have wisely used "outside help" not only to teach but also to develop indigenous leadership. A second solution is to gain permission for the Korean church's children to attend the Sunday school of the church from which they are renting facilities. As long as the Korean church has relatively few children, this arrangement temporarily solves the problem.

Stage Two—(Children's Ministry [CM] in English) A common challenge of this particular stage is the burnout and high turnover rate of children's workers. If the workers are neither fluent in Korean nor receiving spiritual encouragement from the Korean congregation or another ministry, burnout can be expected. Cross-cultural mentoring by the pastor, an elder, or a deacon is one possible solution to the problem of burnout.[7] If they cannot provide the necessary mentoring, Sunday school leaders will likely seek out another source of training and spiritual nourishment. Other needs the young teacher(s) have include regular encouragement, a partner, and frequent short breaks from their responsibilities in order for renewal.

Second Crisis—(Part-time Trained Leadership Crisis) When the church's children become junior high and high school students, the church faces the next crisis of needing a leader not only with high English proficiency but also with an understanding of both American and Korean cultural values.[8]

---

7. Resources might include Ogne and Nebel (1995), and Logan and Cole (1995).

8. The reader may find the bibliographical sources by Yep et al. (1998); Goette (1982); Pai, Pemberton, and Worley (1987); Park (1979); and Stewart and Bennett (1991) helpful in understanding the cultural differences between Korean and American cultures.

The leader will encounter both the perceptive questions and the critical attitudes of those often-turbulent adolescent years. At least some theological training and time to assist families through the problems associated with raising adolescents will be required. It is probably more crucial that the part-time youth pastor be able to identify with the language and the culture of the youth than that of the parents even though Korean proficiency is advantageous. Even though hiring a part-time youth pastor is often a tremendous financial burden, the sacrifice helps alleviate some of the sense of alienation the youth feel from the church.

Stage Three—(Youth ministry [YM] in English) During this stage, some critical decisions will be made. Will the young people attend the main worship service and listen to the sermon translated simultaneously, or will there be a separate youth worship service in English? It is hard enough to hold young people's attention when the service is entirely in English and focused on the issues relevant to them, so most churches are opting for a separate service.

Usually a youth group follows one of two ministry patterns. The first is a "church-based," centralized model focusing on the children of church members. The youth group's activities usually happen at the church building and include a worship service, a Sunday school program, a Friday or Saturday evening youth group meeting, and a variety of activities. The second, more decentralized model follows the "parachurch" model in reaching church members' children and their unchurched friends. Besides a worship service at the church building, there are youth group meetings as close to their non-Christian friends as possible. The youth group meetings often occur near a high school or rotate each week from house to house. Usually accountability groups complement the larger youth group meeting so that the young people who are particularly spiritually hungry are discipled more thoroughly. Regardless of which model is used, the Korean congregation will encounter the challenge of helping the youth group feel integrally involved in the church. Typically, Korean churches have not given them many opportunities to participate in the decision-making processes concerning finances, programming, and scheduling.

To help both parents and other leaders within the Korean congregation understand the necessity of allowing the young people greater participation in the decision-making process at church and at home, cross-cultural parenting classes with an emphasis on cross-cultural motivation could be offered. By beginning at this stage to help the first-generation congregation begin grappling with the cross-cultural implications of English ministry, the first generation is allowed several years to make the behavioral and conceptual adjustments that will ensure an environment conducive to an adult English-language congregation later.

Besides supervising the youth program, the youth pastor's responsibilities entail helping young people come to know Christ personally and developing their primary identity in Christ. In addition to their Christian identity, they will better understand and appreciate their Korean American identity when given the freedom to be ethnically Korean without necessarily being fluent in Korean or conforming to every Korean cultural value.[9]

During this stage the pastor of the Korean congregation will shift his focus from Sunday school leadership to cross-culturally mentoring the youth pastor. The youth pastor will in turn supervise and nurture the Sunday school leadership.

The college years are especially critical, but this is the time the church often neglects its youth. The vast majority will leave home to attend college, and there is a good possibility that they will stop attending church, occasionally get involved in a cult/cultic group, and never return to church when they graduate.[10] To ensure a smooth transition from a youth group into a supportive Christian environment, representatives of various reputable campus ministries have been invited to talk with the students about their particular campus organization before the students leave for college.[11]

While the young people are in college, a definite communication and visitation strategy maximizes long-distance ministry. During the four or more years that a college student is away from his or her home church, the church will continue to evolve, so it will not be the same church the student left. To help the college student feel involved in the development of the church, some churches schedule special meetings, retreats, and fellowships for those returning home for extended vacation breaks.

Third Crisis—(Language/Cultural Crisis) After students graduate from college or graduate school, are they expected to return home? In a major metropolitan area almost 50 percent can be expected to return, especially if they have a church family and a community of Christian friends to whom to return. In other places, the percentage will be considerably lower. Will the returning college graduates fill Sunday school leadership positions and

9. See Cha (1996) for a case study of Korean American identity development. American-born Chinese Wayland Wong (1988) and Dona Dong (1987) echo the same concern among Chinese Americans.

10. Chai (1998, 300) quotes two estimates that 90–95 percent of post-college Korean Americans no longer attend church.

11. If Korean American churches are truly serious about raising up new English-speaking church leadership for their churches, there is a desperate need to strategically and aggressively start and support English-speaking Korean American/Asian American campus ministries and churches in all the major collegiate areas of the United States.

fit into the Korean-speaking adult service? Many will not feel spiritually adequate to accept a leadership position, and many will not understand enough
Korean to benefit from attending the Korean-speaking worship service. The
third crisis is a language/cultural crisis because the church will be forced to
relinquish the dream that a significant portion of the second generation will
someday become bilingual and bicultural enough to join the Korean-speaking
service. Seeking to attract the older second generation, a growing number
of churches have begun young adult English worship services separate from
the youth worship services they may have (Eng 1989, 2).

Stage Four—(English Department [ED]) A number of first-generation
churches have entered this stage, developed a young adult English department, and encountered serious problems because they have not given serious consideration to the following:

1. The first generation's long-range vision for the English ministry of their
   church. If the vision differs significantly from the English department's
   vision, divergent paths are inevitable.
2. The conceptual and value changes that need to take place in their perspective to provide the supportive environment in which an English congregation can flourish (Goette 1998, 20–21).
3. The assets and liabilities of sponsoring an English congregation. By having an English ministry, a church is able to attract families with English-
   speaking members, attract and retain the members' children longer, ensure
   the longevity of the church, reach other English-preference people, and
   have an almost steady supply of Sunday school teachers. However, there
   is a considerable cost in having an English ministry. Additional facilities
   are needed. There will be scheduling as well as cross-cultural communication problems. Initially the English ministry members may not be able
   to significantly contribute to the financial support of the ministry. English
   ministry leaders are not readily available. Furthermore, as the English
   ministry develops, it is more difficult to control; and as the constituency
   becomes more diverse ethnically, there is the threat of the English congregation losing its ethnic identity. When a congregation evaluates the
   assets and liabilities of launching an English department, they are better
   prepared to willingly pay the price.
4. The church preferences of English-speaking Korean Americans and their
   perspective concerning the assets and liabilities of being connected to a
   Korean congregation. In a 1994 survey of a random sample of one hundred of the 1,500 Korean American undergraduates attending UCLA,
   those surveyed were asked, "Ten years from now, what kind of a church

would you like to attend?" The results were as shown in Table 7.1. A church that understands that possibly only one-third of the English-speaking Korean American community is interested in either the Korean or English service being offered by the church will seriously consider how to maximize the assets and minimize the liabilities of an English congregation being associated with a Korean-speaking church. Several English ministry pastors have suggested the following assets: (1) financial support, (2) facilities, (3) stability during transitions or difficult times, (4) the children's program is usually in place, (5) family ties can be kept, (6) opportunities to minister to children, (7) some spiritual guidance and wisdom, (8) role models for second generation concerning loyalty to church, respect for ministers, etc., (9) wider prayer base, (10) a Korean-Christian spiritual legacy can more easily be transferred to the next generation. The following liabilities have been suggested by the same pastors as reasons why a larger percentage of pastors as well as laity desire a church separate from the first generation: (1) control by the first generation, (2) it is often assumed that the English congregation will take care of the children and youth of the Korean congregation, (3) multiple meetings in both English and Korean to attend, (4) the decision-making process takes longer because of the need to coordinate decisions with the first-generation congregation, (5) it is hard to gain agenda harmony between the English ministry and the first generation, (6) cross-cultural communication problems, (7) patronizing, paternalistic, or overprotective attitudes often hinder the group's ability to take risks and maximize their potential, (8) it is more difficult to reach beyond one ethnic group, (9) it is harder to reach multiracial families, (10) scheduling problems and the difficulty of getting prime times and facilities, (11) contextualization takes longer, (12) periodic first- and second-generation leadership clashes, and (13) a church split among the first-generation church could be devastating to the English ministry.

5. The developmental stages of an English congregation and appropriate policies that will maximize the assets and minimize the liabilities listed above and promote agenda harmony between the two congregations.

The creation of an adult English department/congregation ushers in the opportunity to truly contextualize ministry for the future generations of English-speaking Korean Americans. It also brings with it all the challenges of a new church. Churches at this stage make a number of stylistic changes so that the new congregation is not a "youth congregation" with an adult facade but a genuinely contextualized adult congregation for adults.

Table 7.1

Church preference	Percentage
Korean-speaking service of a Korean church	2%
English-speaking service of a Korean church	30%
Separate English-speaking Korean church	46%
Asian American or Multiethnic church	7%
Anglo church	4%
None	11%
Total:	100%

Source: Kim 1996, p. 36.

The demands of initiating a new congregation will necessitate a full-time English-speaking associate pastor/church starter almost immediately. A sad reality is that this person is often seen as a threat by the Korean-speaking pastor, especially if the associate pastor is bilingual. Often the English-congregation pastor is better trained, equipped with innovative ideas, more capable of being the link between the two language groups—and an additional burden upon the church's limited finances. He may also be theologically more conservative and less committed to the mainline denomination with which the church is connected.

Where the senior pastor has been overly hesitant in hiring an English-speaking associate pastor, the English-speaking department has worked through the older deacons and elders who value a growing English-speaking department in order to secure the financial support to hire an associate pastor. If the church does not act quickly to meet the needs of this English-speaking portion of their church, the young adults will steadily leave for churches where they will receive the nurture they need (Lee 1996).

Once the associate pastor is hired, the success of the English ministry will be determined not only by his effectiveness but also by his relationship with the senior pastor. Loyalty and trust between the two have proven to be essential to the success of every English ministry.

Fourth Crisis—(Decision-making Crisis) The growing English-speaking department will soon desire a significant part of the decision-making process concerning the church programming, budget planning, leadership selection, and so on. Decision-making is an intimate part of the Americanized Koreans' identity (Goette 1998, 13–14). Until they are able to have a significant, representative voice in the decision-making process of the Korean church, they will feel marginalized. The leadership of some Korean congregations have solved this crisis by encouraging the selection of deacons and elders from the English congregation and regularly soliciting suggestions from their members.

Stage Five—(English Congregation [EC]) The process of learning to work cooperatively will continue during this stage. The tensions may increase as the English-speaking portion of the church increases numerically and influentially. The goal, however, will be parity between the two congregations. Even though it may be difficult culturally for older first-generation members to treat younger English congregation members as equals, this will ensure that the English-speaking portion of the church is not disenfranchised.

Fifth Crisis—(Power/Focus Crisis) In time, under the leadership of good full-time English-speaking leaders, the church will attract many "marginal" Korean Americans as well as other non-Koreans. The English-speaking congregation may outgrow the Korean-speaking portion of the church. Sometime before this happens, the church may find it necessary to have an English-speaking pastor as the senior pastor of the church if the Korean-speaking pastor has not become proficient in English and is uncomfortable with American cultural values. With a larger number of English-speaking people, the focus of the church may shift, touching off a power crisis—the older Korean-speaking leadership attempting to retain a major portion of the decision-making process in a search for personal significance.

Stage Six—During this stage the Korean American church has become a predominantly English-speaking church with a Korean-speaking department. A Korean-speaking pastor is still needed to minister to the Korean-speaking portion of the congregation, which is composed of grandparents, older parents, and more recent immigrants. At this time the church may find it easier to attract "marginal" Korean Americans, other Asian Americans, and even a variety of non-Asians.

This transformation process will probably take twenty-five to forty years for the average church. Some churches, however, will choose not to proceed beyond a certain stage. Others will take the proverbial "two steps forward, one step backward" several times. Some new churches will skip the first few stages and begin at one of the later stages. Quite often there will be English-speaking members who will become impatient and frustrated with the gradual transformation process. After all, individuals acculturate more rapidly than an organization. In contrast, some Korean-speaking members will think the church is changing too quickly. The Korean-speaking will join other Korean-speaking churches and the English-speaking will look elsewhere. There are several attractive options available:

Other Ministries to English-speaking Korean Americans

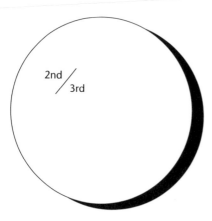

2nd / 3rd

Figure 7.3

1. An English-speaking Korean American Church (Woo 1988, 1–3; see Fig. 7.3)—To immediately reach the "marginal" Korean American or the disgruntled "fellow traveler," a new kind of church has been started. Grace Baptist Church of Glenview, Illinois, is an example of this type of church, which is neither culturally Korean nor American but a unique Korean American blend—attempting to take the best of both cultures as seen in the light of Scripture. This kind of church will be almost entirely English-speaking, composed of second- and third-generation Korean Americans, other Asian Americans, and interracial and interethnic couples. There are several advantages to this kind of church. It can more quickly adapt to the needs of the English-speaking Korean American, attract many more Asian Americans and other English-speaking people, and experiment to develop a church lifestyle that matches Korean Americans in that region of the United States.

There are also considerable challenges. Even though there are plenty of English-speaking Korean American adults in the major metropolitan areas of the United States, there may still not be enough English-speaking adults to financially support this kind of endeavor in some of the smaller cities. Marketing this kind of church to a very specific, scattered, and mobile niche in the urban market can also be formidable. For now, the leadership of this kind of church will be relatively young and inexperienced and will lack the seasoned wisdom and broad-based experience of older members. The Korean-speaking parents and grandparents of the members will not be ministered to in a church like this, but in the next few years how many English-speaking Korean Americans will be living in the same area as their parents or grandparents?

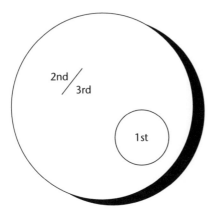

Figure 7.4

2. An English-speaking Korean American Church with a Korean-speaking Department (see Fig. 7.4)—To meet the need for family unity and ministry to the entire family, some English-speaking Korean American churches may start Korean-speaking departments to minister to their Korean-speaking relatives. Even though this church may look similar to stage six of the "transformed" church, its history will be completely different and may not encounter the same problems of the power/focus crisis.

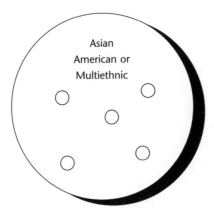

Figure 7.5

3. An Asian American or Multiethnic church (see Fig. 7.5)—Korean Americans who are interracially or interethnically married and those who are especially concerned with evangelizing their co-workers and neighbors may find this kind of church more appealing. It provides a familiar context with other Asian Americans and enough diversity to which to bring people of different ethnic backgrounds. The Evergreen Baptist Churches of Southern California and the New Song Community Church of Irvine, California, would be excellent examples of this type of church.

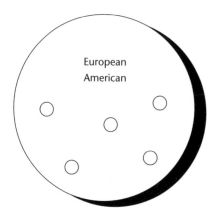

European
American

Figure 7.6

4. A predominantly European American church with a few Korean American individuals (see Fig. 7.6)—"Alienated" Korean Americans feel at ease in a European American church and usually do not feel any need to relate to the other Asian Americans in the church any more than they would to anyone else. If the European American church has an excellent worship service, a good discipleship program, and some ethnic diversity, even "marginal" Korean Americans are attracted to the church in spite of not feeling as comfortable as they might in an English-speaking Korean American church. The main disadvantage is that the Korean American has to act "European American" to really fit into this church.

5. The European American church with various departments (see Fig. 7.7)—To reach greater numbers of "marginal" Korean Americans or other Asian Americans, some European American churches have special English-speaking Asian American fellowships that meet periodically for ethnic fellowship. "Language" departments have also been formed to meet the special needs of those who prefer to worship in Korean, a Chinese dialect,

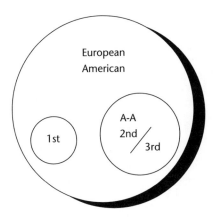

Figure 7.7

Japanese, or some other language. The disadvantage in this situation is that Asian American leaders do emerge as quickly as they would in a predominantly Asian American church.

Because of the complexity of the Korean American community, there are a variety of churches at various stages attempting to minister to Korean Americans in order to equip them to be a blessing to others. No one kind of church is able to reach every Korean American. Each church and ministry is to accomplish the work that God has specially called them to do and to appreciate the work that God is doing through a mosaic of ministries.

Conclusion

The key to a smooth transformation within Korean American churches is the first-generation leadership—pastors, elders, and deacons. By understanding the transformation process, they will be able to anticipate future crises, greet them with less anxiety, and respond to them strategically. They also have the ability to empower the next generation of English-speaking leaders and the opportunity to cross-culturally mentor them. One of the greatest challenges the first-generation leaders face is to follow in Paul's footsteps and make major cultural concessions in order to effectively minister to Americanized Korean Americans (1 Corinthians 9:19–22).

References

Cha, Peter T. 1996. "Ethnic Identity Formation and Participation in Immigrant Churches: Second Generation Korean-American Experiences." Paper presented at the Sixth North Park College Korean Symposium, Chicago, October 12.

Chai, Karen J. 1998. "Competing for the Second Generation: English-Language Ministry at a Korean Protestant Church." In *Gatherings in Diaspora: Religious Communities and the New Immigration*, ed. R. Stephen Warner and Judith G. Wittner, 295–331. Philadelphia: Temple University Press.

Dayton, Edward R., and David A. Fraser. 1980. *Planning Strategies for World Evangelization.* Grand Rapids, Mich.: Wm. B. Eerdmans.

Dong, Donna. 1987. "The American Reality: The Context for ABC Ministry." *About Face* 9 (February): 1–3.

Eng, William. 1989. "Up with English Worship!" *About Face* 11 (November): 1–2.

Fong, Kenneth Uyeda. 1990. *Insights for Growing Asian-American Ministries.* Rosemead, Calif.: EverGrowing Publications.

Goette, Robert D. 1982. "A Biblical Critique of Confucian Status Structure." Unpublished paper, Asian Center for Theological Studies and Mission, Seoul, Korea.

———. 1993. "The Transformation of a First Generation Church into a Bilingual Second Generation Church." In *The Emerging Generation of Korean Americans,* ed. Ho-Youn Kwon and Shim Kim, 237–51. Seoul, Korea: Kyung Hee University Press.

———. 1998. "The Urgency of Contextualized English Ministry Among Korean Americans." Unpublished paper, Southwestern Baptist Theological Seminary, Fort Worth, Texas.

Kim, Sharon P. 1996. "Generational Transition Within Korean Churches." Master's thesis, Sociology Department, University of California at Los Angeles.

Lee, Helen. 1996. "Silent Exodus." *Christianity Today* (August 12): 50–53.

Logan, Robert E., and Neil Cole. 1995. *Raising Leaders for the Harvest.* Alta Loma, Calif.: CRM Publishing.

Ogne, Steven L., and Thomas P. Nebel. 1995. *Empowering Leaders Through Coaching.* Alta Loma, Calif.: CRM Publishing.

Pai, Young, Deloras Pemberton, and John Worley. 1987. *Findings on Korean American Early Adolescents and Adolescents.* Kansas City: University of Missouri School of Education.

Park, Myung-Seok. 1979. *Communication Styles in Two Different Cultures: Korean and American.* Seoul: Han Shin Publishing Company.

Romo, Oscar I. 1993. *American Mosaic: Church Planting in Ethnic America.* Nashville, Tenn.: Broadman Press.

Stewart, Edward C., and Milton J. Bennett. 1991. *American Cultural Patterns: A Cross-Cultural Perspective.* Yarmouth, Maine: Intercultural Press.

Wong, Wayland. 1988. "An ABC Culture." *About Face* 10 (August): 1–3.

Woo, David. 1988 "Should We Have ABC Churches?" *About Face* 10 (May): 1–3.

Yep, Jeanette, Peter Cha, Susan Cho Van Riesen, Greg Jao, and Paul Tokunaga. 1998. *Following Jesus Without Dishonoring Your Parents.* Downers Grove, Ill.: InterVarsity Press.

Yuen, Peter. 1990. "What's Your ABCMI?" *About Face* 12 (August): 1–4.

Ethnic Identity Formation and Participation in Immigrant Churches

Second-Generation Korean American Experiences

Peter T. Cha

DURING THE PAST THREE DECADES, Korean American churches have experienced exponential growth. A conservative estimate indicates that there are more than 3,500 Korean American churches today, approximately one Korean immigrant church for every 300 Korean Americans (Kim and Kim 1995). This remarkable growth, however, is gradually being overshadowed by another significant development in the church—namely, the "silent exodus" of second-generation Korean American young adults from their home churches.

Although it is difficult to ascertain an exact number, several studies have predicted (Pai, Pemberton, and Worley 1987) and observed (Oh 1993; Carvajal 1994) that a majority of second-generation young adults are leaving—and will continue to leave—their ethnic churches. Alarmed, many concerned Korean American church leaders have sought to understand the cause and the nature of this "silent exodus," often speculating on who or what might be responsible for this phenomenon. This chapter will also be concerned with the question of why so many of these young people are leaving their ethnic churches. However, rather than focusing on the church's shortcomings and failures, it will examine some of the broader developmental experiences of second-generation young people. Specifically, we will explore the dialectical relationship between two journeys that many second-generation young people undertake: ethnic identity formation and spiritual identity formation.

Method of the Study

In 1994 and 1996, I conducted a qualitative study by interviewing twelve second-generation Korean American undergraduates who attended a premier private university located in the Midwest. The university, situated in the suburb of a large metropolitan city, successfully attracts highly qualified students from diverse geographical as well as ethnic backgrounds; more than 85 percent of first-year students were in the top 10 percent of their high school graduating class, while up to 30 percent of its students come from various ethnic minority backgrounds. Currently, 18 percent of its 7,000 undergraduates are Asian Americans.

The respondents in this study were recruited by two different methods. In 1994 I announced my research study at an Asian American Christian Fellowship gathering, inviting second-generation Korean Americans who grew up in Korean American immigrant churches to volunteer. Ten Korean American students expressed an interest. Then, in 1996, I obtained a list of six more Korean American students from an Asian American campus minister. I contacted each of the potential respondents to explain the nature of the research project and to learn more about each of their own backgrounds.

Out of the sixteen volunteers, twelve eventually participated as respondents. All of the respondents of this study share the common ethnic background of being second-generation Korean Americans—that is, they were either born in the United States or immigrated to this country before the age three.[1] Furthermore, as self-professed Christians who grew up in Korean American immigrant churches, these respondents share a common spiritual background. For this particular study, I decided not to interview those Korean Americans who no longer identify themselves as Christians, since I am interested in studying the cultural and social dimension of the Korean American church experience, not so much the spiritual or theological ones.

---

1. Strictly speaking, only those who are American-born to parents who were born in Korea should be called "second-generation" Korean Americans (Koh 1994). Those Korean American young people who immigrated to the United States during their late childhood and/or adolescence are generally called "1.5 generation," and they characteristically possess a unique perception of self-identity that is shaped by bilingual and bicultural experiences (Hurh 1993; Koh 1994). Four of the respondents I interviewed immigrated to the United States before the age of three. Since they do not fit the description of 1.5-generation Korean Americans and, more importantly, because they view themselves as second-generation Korean Americans, I will refer to all respondents as second-generation Korean Americans.

While the respondents shared similar ethnic and religious backgrounds, the group nonetheless reflected a good deal of diversity in other ways. There was diversity in gender (seven women and five men); location of their home towns (six were from the Chicago area, while the rest were from the East Coast, the West Coast, and the Southwest); their age (three freshmen, two sophomores, two juniors, and five seniors); and their current church affiliations (five were attending predominantly Caucasian churches, four were in independent second-generation Korean American churches or Asian American churches, and three were attending immigrant churches in the Chicago area).

Given the paucity of research on this topic, I designed my study to be more inductive than deductive, and more hypothesis-generating than hypothesis-testing. Data collection consisted primarily of semistructured, open-ended interviews. Each session began with "grand tour questions" that were broad and general enough to encourage the respondents to share their thoughts and feelings with a sense of freedom and flexibility, thus increasing the possibility of giving "surprising" answers (Werner and Schoepfle 1987). I inquired largely about their experiences growing up as bicultural individuals and about their experiences in the Korean American church.

In addition, interviews were carried out in small groups (four to five respondents in each group) as well as on an individual basis. During the group sessions, on the one hand, my respondents often talked about their "shared" experiences as second-generation Korean Americans and stimulated each other's thoughts and insights. On the other hand, during the individual interview sessions, the respondents focused more on their personal experiences, often openly talking about the various struggles they themselves or their families had encountered. Since I was interested in learning about my respondents' personal experiences as well as the experiences they shared as a cohort group, the use of both small group and individual interviews proved to be an effective approach.

Initially, as a student in the field of sociology of religion, I had as the main aim of my study to identify some of the "manifest" and "latent" functions of the Korean immigrant church and to examine how some of these functions are proving to be dysfunctional, particularly for second-generation young people. However, during the process of this ethnographic study, the focus of the study began to shift in a surprising direction. Although all of the respondents agreed that Korean immigrant churches have many faults and limitations, their stories also began to point to another possible explanation for the "silent exodus" phenomenon.

Before discussing the findings of the research study, a broad caveat is appropriate. Given the relatively small size of the sample, I am not expecting the results and findings of my study to be generalizable to all second-generation Korean American experiences. My hope is that this study would deepen readers' understanding of the respondents' ethnic and spiritual identity-formation experiences and those of young people whose backgrounds and experiences are similar.

Findings of the Study

Although these twelve individuals came from somewhat diverse backgrounds, their experiences and struggles within the developmental periods of their lives—their childhood, adolescence, and young adulthood—bore striking resemblances. That is, during each of these life stages, these second-generation young people responded similarly to their "Koreanness," to their "Americanness," and to the Korean American church. In this section, I want to briefly discuss how my respondents understood their bicultural identity during these periods and how their understanding, in turn, shaped their attitudes toward the Korean American church.

Early Childhood Experiences

Desiring to Fit In / Being Ashamed of Their Koreanness

Most of my respondents identified this period as a period of yearning to be like others—that is, to be like their Caucasian friends—and to distance themselves from Korean "things" or their Koreanness. Many respondents pointed out that when they were in elementary school most of their close friends were Caucasian. In fact, one respondent mentioned that when she was little she saw herself as no different from a "white" person: "Everyone [Korean American children] thinks they are basically white, and I thought . . . I mean I didn't think I was white in the sense, you know, that I was blond and blue-eyed. But I didn't think myself different from anyone else." Another respondent described her childhood attitude in a similar way when she said, "I was a twinkie when I was in elementary school and stuff. And all my Korean friends were twinkies." Some other respondents also used terms such as "banana" or "twinkie" to describe their state of being during this period—that is, they were "white" inside but "yellow" outside.

Because they so desired to be like their American friends during their childhood period, many of my respondents made various efforts to distance themselves from "Korean things," such as their Korean name, food, friends, or even parents, that might have reminded them and their friends that they were different. One person said: "This might sound sort of funny because, in elementary school, whenever there would be a PTA get-together or something like that, I would never tell my parents about it. . . . I always felt weird about my American friends coming over to our house. Just, especially when my parents were home, I always was kind of relieved when my parents were not home."

Another respondent also shared: "I remember that I used to go to school with my little brother, and he would call me *hyung* ['older brother,' in Korean], you know. And people would always make fun of that. So I would tell him, 'Stop! Don't ever call me that at school.' I guess I really wanted to fit into the mainstream of things. I didn't want to be different in any way."

Another respondent joked about being nervous when his American friends, while visiting his home, asked, "Hey, do you have anything to eat?" It is interesting that some of the respondents mentioned that they preferred American food when they were in this age group. In short, many respondents felt rather ashamed of their Korean background, fearing that their American friends might reject them for their Koreanness. One person summed it up succinctly when she said, "When I was a kid, I wished that I wasn't a Korean because all my other friends, besides church friends, were Caucasians."

Early Childhood Experiences in the Korean American Church

Given the above experiences, many of the respondents did not enjoy their Korean American churches during their childhood. A number of them talked about how they resented having to go to church every Sunday; they went simply because their parents forced them to go with them. One person said: "When Sunday comes, automatically church. A part of me was bored, since I went every week. Just because, all my American friends can sleep in late on Sundays and my father, especially, he has to scream, saying, 'Tina yah, uh suh il uh nah! [Tina, hurry up and get up!]' And when I am at church, singing along and doing the usual thing, and I am like, 'Oh, another Sunday has passed. I am looking forward to Monday.'" For many, attending Korean churches on weekends was an inconvenience; but for others it was an intrusion to their American way of life, so they looked forward to Monday, when they could go back to their schools and be with their American friends.

Adolescent Experiences

Recognizing "Differences"

Then, during their adolescent period, my respondents' attitudes toward "Koreanness" and "Americanness" took a drastic turn. To begin with, most of the respondents pointed out that it was during their junior high school and high school years when they began to realize that there was a growing difference between them and their Caucasian friends.

Some respondents pointed out that it was during this time when they and their American friends began to focus on their physical differences. One woman commented, "So I remember in junior high school, people would notice some physical differences, me as an Asian American and them as Caucasian Americans, and I was very insecure up to a certain point." For a male respondent, who was a super athlete during his elementary school years, the experience was a disappointing one in a different way: "I realized that I wasn't gonna grow any more, and I couldn't excel in athletics as I used to." So he began to hang around and play basketball with other Korean American guys and less with his white buddies.

In addition to their recognition of physical differences, many of the respondents also began to realize during their teenage years that their adolescent lifestyle was going to be quite different from that of their American friends, mainly due to the restrictions their parents imposed. One respondent shared:

When I went through high school, I realized that I was having a hard time opening up to my Caucasian friends because they just didn't understand my mentality and the way my parents raised me, just the whole idea—like "going-out" or having fun with your friends or even in the way that they related to their parents, they would just talk back at them or yell at them, have fights with them. These are some things I just couldn't do ... like you have to show them your respect. And it was hard for me to talk to them, you know, "Aren't you going to 'go out'?" And I would say, "Oh, I really can't." And, they ask "Why?" "Well, because my mom wouldn't let me." And they would say, "Well, you are old enough. Can't you do ...?" "Not really." That was kind of hard for me.

Most of the respondents felt that they couldn't do many of the "American teenage things" because their parents were too strict. In addition to the physical differences, these young people began to realize that their lifestyle and value system also differed from those of their American friends. These differences began to increase the distance between them and their American friends. Many of the respondents pointed out that during their high school years they did less and less with their Caucasian friends. They did not think it was racism or prejudice that allowed their friendships to dwindle. Rather they suspect that it was because, as their differences became more significant, the commonalities that once held their friendships together were becoming more precarious.

The Formation of a Korean American Identity and Subculture

While many of my respondents lost nearly all of their American friends during their adolescent years, they also, during this period, gained many new friendships with other second-generation Korean Americans. In fact, some pointed out that the latter development was a significant cause of the former. Furthermore, as they began to mingle more with their Korean American friends, these young people began to think more about their Korean identity.

For many, this shift was a dramatically life-changing one. One respondent said:

> I guess it was kind of like when I got older, when I grasped like my Korean identity, maybe like during my early years in high school ... or even junior high school, when I guess a lot of Korean people just started hanging out and coming to grips with their Koreanness ... and be proud of it ... and take their identity in it. But then again, it was kind of, in a lot of ways, kind of narrow though. Because people just shut themselves [in] ... people just living in the Korean world. Like Korean friends, Korean parties on weekends, Korean church.... Even me, because I got sucked into the Korean world, I stopped doing many things. I stopped my high school sports after my freshman year because I wanted to spend more time with my Korean friends. And, I guess, a lot of my friendships with, you know, my non-Korean friends, kind of died out as the result. I pretty much lost all my good friendships with them [non-Korean friends] by my sophomore year in high school.

It is fascinating to note that as these young Korean Americans hung out with each other, they not only formed their Korean American identity or strengthened it but also seemed to create their own unique subculture. One respondent noted: "There are all these Korean Americans in the New York–New Jersey area, and they have their own social subculture. You know, they dress differently, they listen to different music, they talk differently, they drive their distinct kinds of cars. For instance, they were all wearing black baggy pants and with white button tops ..." When this respondent talked about this newly emerging Korean American subculture at the group interview session, four other respondents all nodded and laughed. Even though they all came from different regions in the country, they were all able to understand and agree with his description of this newly emerging subculture.

Finally, it was also interesting to note that there is significant peer pressure on second-generation Korean Americans to participate in Korean American social groups and its subculture. One respondent observed: "In the Korean American world, if you are not a part of it, you will be labeled as a twinkie, and there was harsh animosity against people who were called twinkies. And, it's like, 'Oh, you are ashamed of being a Korean ... that's why you don't have many Korean friends and you hang out with white people ... you are ashamed of your culture.'" So these same young people who behaved like "twinkies" and in fact wanted to be like their white friends during their childhood, were later desperately trying to take off their "twinkie" identity, often going to the other extreme of owning ethnocentric sentiments, such as "Koreans are the best."

Adolescent Experiences in the Korean American Church

Given the above experience, I was not surprised to find that for all of my respondents, their youth group experiences in the Korean American church were very positive. For many of them, the Korean American church provided an ideal setting where they could hang out with their Korean American friends. To begin with, as one respondent pointed out, Korean American parents trust their church; they allow their children to stay out later if these young people are at church functions. Another respondent used the phrase "supporting network" to describe her youth group experiences. As young people facing similar problems and challenges came together, they were willing to share their feelings and pains with one another and to support each other.

In this context of a supportive community, respondents experienced many different kinds of growth during their adolescent years. One respondent, very grateful for his youth group experience in his home church, summarized his experience in the following way: "I was a real shy guy. I was intensely shy all throughout my whole life until my sophomore year in high school, and that's when I moved to a larger Korean American church. It had a larger youth group, and there was a greater sample of people to relate to. And for me, I really grew a lot socially during those years.... Because, I really felt like I had a strong peer group there, good support, very strong support. And I feel like I really found my identity there within the group."

However, more than a sense of personal identity, their youth group experience also seems to have played a central role in the development of their ethnic identity and ethnic pride. Pointing out that it was her immigrant church, not her immigrant family experience, that fostered this sense of ethnic pride, one respondent commented: "And, thinking about this, I don't know why this is so, but even in high school, being with my family did not make me happy about being a Korean American. I didn't like the fact that we are a Korean family in America. But then, being with my church friends made me feel like it was OK that I was a Korean. So it was constant fluctuation between the Korean pride and then the Korean shame." If the Korean American church was a source of nuisance and irritation for my respondents during their childhood years, it became an indispensable source of personal growth, comfort, and support during their adolescent years.

Young Adulthood Experiences

One way to describe the experiences of these respondents during their childhood and adolescent years is to think of them as a pendulum swinging from one extreme to another. Looking back, many respondents expressed some regrets about their narrow preoccupation with their Korean identity and their Korean friendships. For them, the stage they are at now, their young adulthood, is the period during which they feel a need to find a good balance.

A Desire to Break Out of Stifling Conformity

One Asian proverb says, "A nail that sticks out gets hammered." In other words, in an Asian communal life one does not want to "stick out"; one wants to be like others. Apparently, this ethos is strongly prevalent in second-generation Korean American group life. One respondent shared:

> I have been noticing that when we get together as a group of Korean Americans, in my experience, we do have a tendency to become like each other. I remember, in my high school youth group, if somebody got into basketball, then everyone did it. And then... whoever did take a step to do something, we all followed. We were very communal in that sense, which is good. But there is no sense of growth. There is a strong sense of intimacy, but it's like a static intimacy. It's like you are not moving anywhere.

Another respondent was even more critical about this aspect of the Korean American subculture. While commenting on why she decided to leave the Korean American church, she said:

The Korean American church produces the same people. There is no uniqueness about the people that the church is bringing out. They all talk the same,
they pray the same ... no individual uniqueness. I think a part of my reaction to that was, "Maybe I won't go to a Korean church, so I won't be the
same as everybody else." You know, I want to be the unique individual that
God created and a part of setting myself apart is going to a non-Asian-
dominated Christian fellowship on this campus and to an American church.

Another type of conformity that a number of respondents were concerned about was Korean American young people's very narrow definition
of what success is. For instance, for Korean American young people, a number of vocations are considered prestigious. In this context, when an individual chooses another vocation, no matter how talented he or she might
be, that person will not be treated with respect. While talking about why
one young adult left her church recently, a respondent shared the following
story that illustrates this point:

One of the founders of our church ... got up at church one day and said,
"Oh, I am so proud of our church because we have so many professionals
in our midst. Jane is going to be a doctor, Jenny is going to be a doctor. Joe
is a dentist. So and so is in dental school, so and so is in finance, and so and
so is in architecture." But this woman's name was left out because she was
a teacher. Basically, she is 28 but she is completely floating. I mean she has
been to Korea as an English teacher. She has a degree in teaching, and right
now, she is in school again, getting a Master's in piano. So, she wasn't mentioned in spite of her vast education. She was hurt by this experience, and
she left.

Another respondent, while talking about a similar experience she had observed, made the following impassioned comments: "God made each of us
different, and each person has a different role in this life. Not everyone
should be doctors, not every one should be lawyers, for that matter mechan-
ics or hairdressers. I mean everyone has a different role. We got to work
on this."

In short, many respondents are weary of the pressure of conformity that
suppresses their individuality in their Korean American community life.
When the communal pressure to conform begins to interfere with their personal growth and freedom, when this pressure brings unjustifiable pain and
grief to them and to their friends, many of these young people are beginning to view it as an expression of oppression, not of unity.

A Desire to Break Out of Ethnic Insulation

Many respondents also agreed that they need to be more intentional about breaking out of their ethnic "ghetto" experiences. They all recognized that their Korean American friends understood them better and could provide them with much support and encouragement. However, many respondents felt that comfort was a luxury one cannot afford if it stunts one's personal growth.

One respondent, an economics major looking for a job in the business world, made the following comments:

One of the regrets I have is not being more culturally open, not making friends with Caucasians, not making friends with Indians and stuff like that. I feel I have a social handicap because I find myself really hard to associate with white American culture. Which I feel might hurt me in the long run because of the fact that when I go out into the working world, that all I am going to be surrounded with ... the working culture ... is primarily, you know, American white culture. So, surrounding myself with Koreans was more like a luxury or something like that, in a sense. But these days, I realize the importance of the flip-side.

Another respondent, who came to a similar conclusion, made a number of intentional efforts to surround himself with non-Korean friends. He also began to attend an American church and a Christian fellowship group on campus that did not have many Korean Americans in it. From this experience, he discovered that he came to know himself better by being in the midst of people who are not like him. He said, "If you surround yourself with different people, you can see yourself in contrast."

Young Adult Experiences in the Korean American Church

In the past, I was often baffled by one thing: why are so many Korean American young people, who thoroughly enjoyed their Korean Immigrant church youth group experiences, now expressing many complaints, if not leaving the church altogether? When we look at the developmental experiences of my respondents, we can see one possible answer to that question. It is clear that many Korean American young people are leaving their Korean American churches because they are at a life stage where they want to grow and be challenged in a different way. One respondent who had been attending an American church during the past four years put it this way: "For myself, I guess I consider myself as one who left [the Korean American church], at least during the past four years, I kind of wanted a new 'wineskin' in a sense. Just kind of ... I felt like I had a grasp of what the Korean church had to offer. I just wanted a new direction, wanted to see what else was available."

To be sure, during the interview sessions, many respondents in fact did mention a number of shortcomings and weaknesses of the Korean American church, aspects such as rigid hierarchicalism, authoritarianism, closed-mindedness, shame-producing legalism, and hypocrisy. At the same time, these respondents also pointed out that even though they had some frustrations with their churches, many were wanting to leave simply because they wanted new and different kinds of church experiences, because they wanted to go beyond the Korean American church experience. One respondent put it this way: "I think one thing I see is that a lot of people, including myself, couldn't necessarily have so many negative experiences in the Korean American church as much as they just wanted to experience something new. Especially with a new page in your life being in college or whatever or graduating from college, you want something new and fresh. So it might not be that they had some big negative experiences ... in some cases."

Discussion

In this section, I want to focus on the following two themes that have emerged in the study: (1) the process of ethnic identity formation taken by this group of second-generation Korean American undergraduates and (2) the strong link that exists between their attitudes toward their ethnic identity and toward their ethnic church involvements.

In the past, Asian American scholars and pastors who are interested in the topic of Asian American ethnic identity have used two particular theoretical models. The first model distinguishes four forms of ethnic identity among Asian Americans—"traditionalists," "assimilationists," "bicultural," and "marginal" (S. Sue and D. W. Sue 1971). A similar classification of Asian Americans has been proposed and popularized by Kitano and Daniels (1988). This model eventually became quite familiar to those who are in Asian American ministry (Fong 1991; Kim 1996). Although such a classification of ethnic identity does serve some purpose as a heuristic device, some have pointed out that the model is imprecise, simplistic, and stereotypical (Uba 1994).

The experiences of the respondents of this study also seem to point to the limitation of this model, particularly the static and rigid nature of its four categories. Although all of my respondents see themselves as bicultural individuals at this point in their life stage, these same individuals also acknowledge that they were strong "traditionalists" and "assimilationists" at different stages of their lives. Their experiences, then, demonstrate that Asian Americans are not permanently stationed in one particular classification of ethnic identity.

The other theoretical model that has been receiving much attention from those who are interested in Korean American / Asian American ethnic identity is the Minority Identity Development (MID) model developed by Atkinson, Morten, and Sue (1989). Although the model was developed to provide a perspective on the development of identity among members of all minority groups, many Korean American scholars (Pai, Pemberton, and Worley 1987; Koh 1993; Kim 1996) identified the usefulness of this model in analyzing and interpreting second-generation Korean American experiences.

According to the MID theory, members of minorities in the United States—including Asian Americans—go through a process in which they seek to understand themselves, their minority culture, the dominant culture, and the relationship between these two cultures. The MID model, which consists of five developmental stages, can be succinctly summarized as follows:

The conformity stage—characterized by the preference for dominant cultural values over one's own, feelings of racial self-hatred, and negative beliefs about one's own culture;

The dissonance stage—characterized by cultural confusion and conflict, and by the challenging of the accepted values of the conformity stage;

The resistance and immersion stage—characterized by an active rejection of the dominant society and culture and by a complete endorsement of one's own culture and community;

The introspection stage—characterized by the conflict between the loyalty and responsibility to one's own group and personal autonomy, and by questioning the absolute rejection of the dominant culture, and;

The integrative and awareness stage—characterized by the objective examination of the cultural values of one's own group and of the dominant group, and by the attainment of a more integrated bicultural orientation that is more realistic and workable.

Although my research study was not carried out to validate or prove any hypothesis or theory, the findings of the study seem to provide broad empirical support for the MID model. Even from a very casual glance, one can observe a noticeable parallel between the pendulum-swing stages that my respondents have gone through and the five stages outlined by the MID theory. Most of my respondents' early childhood experiences fit the description of the *conformity stage*; their adolescent experiences, the *dissonance stage,* and the *resistance and immersion stage*; and their young adulthood experiences, the *introspection stage* and the final stage of the *integrative and awareness stage*.

The above suggestions and findings of the study are further supported by a number of recent studies that examined the development of ethnic identity among ethnic minority children, adolescents, and young adults. Some studies suggest that preschool and early elementary-school-age children cannot yet grasp the meaning of their ethnicity, leading them to view their ethnicity as something that can be changed and to deny that they belong to their ethnic group (Gay 1985; Aboud 1984). However, as they enter adolescence, many of these minority students begin to feel the need to affirm their ethnic identity (Phinney and Chavira 1992) and make intentional efforts to learn more about their own ethnicity and culture (Phinney 1993). A recently published book that compiled narratives on ethnic identity written by first, 1.5, and second-generation Asian Americans also notes that many native-born Asian Americans, when they were very young, considered themselves Americans; however, as they grew older, they intentionally embraced their ethnic identity and heritage (Min and Kim 1999).

It needs to be pointed out, however, that not every respondent's experiences neatly fit into the five-stage sequence of the MID model. In fact, in proposing the MID model, Atkinson, Morten, and Sue (1989) also acknowledged that the boundaries between the stages are fluid, that one does not always proceed through all the stages, and that one may "revert" to earlier stages. This seems to be especially the case with two of my respondents who grew up in very multiethnic and predominantly nonwhite neighborhoods and schools. In both cases, for instance, they did not seem to have experienced *the conformity stage* and *the dissonance stage* in a significant way. It seems, then, that the strong similarity found among the respondents' experiences may be partly, if not largely, due to the fact that most of them grew up in predominantly white neighborhoods in large metropolitan areas and that they came from similar socioeconomic backgrounds, namely middle and upper-middle classes.

Further studies are needed, then, to answer a few related questions. If some second-generation Korean Americans grew up in "Koreatown," or in predominantly African American neighborhoods (or in other minority neighborhoods), or in small towns and cities that do not have Korean American communities, would their ethnic identity formation experiences be different from those of my respondents? If there is a large though not predominant

population of Korean Americans in the neighborhood, does that make a difference in the stages these young people go through?

In addition to the process of ethnic identity formation, the findings of this
study also point to the strong link that exists between the respondents' attitudes toward their "Koreanness"/ "Americanness" and their attitudes toward
the Korean American church. On the one hand, understanding this connection can offer us some insights about the phenomenon of the "silent exodus"
of second-generation young people from their churches. For instance, as a
pastor and a campus minister who worked with second-generation Korean
American young people during the past fourteen years, I was often baffled
to see that many of the young people who left the church were also the
ones who particularly enjoyed their youth group experiences in the church
and were quite committed to the group throughout their adolescent years.
Perhaps one possible explanation for this dramatic change in their attitudes
toward their immigrant churches might be that while the strong ethnic-
oriented—and in some cases, very ethnocentric—ministry of these immigrant churches may have appealed to these young people when they were
journeying through the *resistance and immersion stage,* this same characteristic
of the church has repelled them when they were going through the *introspection stage* and the *integrative and awareness stage*. In short, those aspects of
the church ministry that are quite functional for second-generation young
people who are in one stage of their ethnic identity journey might prove to
be somewhat dysfunctional for those who are in another stage of the process.

Understanding this connection between the ethnic and religious identity
formations, then, might suggest some ways in which the Korean American
church can serve its second-generation young people with more sensitivity
and effectiveness. For instance, for many young adults who are going through
the *introspection stage* or the *integrative/awareness stage,* a ministry with a bicultural orientation, which appreciates certain aspects of the Korean culture as
well as that of the dominant culture, might be more appealing than one that
demands a blind loyalty to the Korean culture and its value system. Furthermore, the findings of this study and the MID theory both suggest that if the
Korean American church were to provide an affirming setting in which these
young people can cultivate their bicultural identities, it needs to overcome
not only its ethnocentric mind-set but also its culture of conformity/shame
that silently suppresses individuality in its community life.

Many social psychologists agree that the surrounding culture and society
play a critical role in an individual's identity formation process. A healthy
identity formation requires an affirming surrounding that encourages exploration (Erikson 1950) and that provides a deeply caring, relational support

system (Gilligan 1982). Sadly, for many second-generation young people with whom I have worked, neither the mainstream culture/society nor their Korean families have provided that nurturing environment in which they could construct a healthy identity as a bicultural person and as a uniquely created child of God. Given this situation, the Korean American church has a vital role to play in the lives of many second-generation young people. It must strive to provide a safe and affirming setting in which these young people can work on their identities and life plans, for only then will the church be able to develop its corporate identity as a multigenerational institution that can serve emerging generations of Korean Americans.

References

Aboud, Frances. 1984. "Social and Cognitive Bases of Ethnic Identity Consistency." *Journal of Genetic Psychology* 145 (2): 217–30.

Atkinson, D., G. Morten, and D. Sue. 1989. *Counseling American Minorities: A Cross-Cultural Perspective*. Dubuque, Iowa: W. C. Brown.

Carvajal, Doreen. 1994. "Trying to Halt the 'Silent Exodus.'" *Los Angeles Times,* May 9, A1.

Erikson, E. 1950. *Childhood and Society*. New York: W.W. Norton.

Gay, Geneva. 1985. "Implications of Selected Models of Ethnic Identity Development for Educators." *Journal of Negro Education* 54 (1): 43–55.

Gilligan, C. 1982. *In a Different Voice: Psychological Theory and Women's Development*. Cambridge: Harvard University Press.

Fong, K. 1991. *Insights for Growing Asian-American Ministries*. Rosemead, Calif.: EverGrowing Publications.

Hurh, Won Moo. 1993. "The 1.5 Generation: A Cornerstone of the Korean-American Ethnic Community." In *The Emerging Generation of Korean-Americans,* ed. Ho-Youn Kown and Shin Kim. Seoul, Korea: Kyung Hee University Press.

Kim, G. 1996. "Asian North American Youth: A Ministry of Self-Identity." In *People on the Way: Asian North Americans Discovering Christ, Culture, and Community,* ed. D. Ng. Valley Forge, Pa.: Judson Press.

Kim, Kwang Chung, and Shin Kim. 1995. "Korean Immigrant Churches in the U.S." In *Yearbook of American Canadian Churches 1995,* ed. Kenneth Bedell. Nashville, Tenn.: Abingdon Press.

Kitano, H., and R. Daniels. 1988. *Asian Americans: Emerging Minorities*. Englewood Cliffs, N.J.: Prentice-Hall.

Koh, T. H. 1993. "Ethnic Identity: The Impact of Two Cultures on the Psychological Development of Korean-American Adolescents." In *The Emerging Generation of Korean-Americans,* ed. H. Y. Kwon and S. Kim. Seoul, Korea: Kyung Hee University Press.

———. 1994. "Ethnic Identity in First, 1.5, and Second Generation Korean-Americans: An Exploratory Study." In *Korean Americans: Conflict and Harmony,* ed. Ho-Youn Kwon. Chicago: Covenant Publications.

Min, Pyoung Gap, and Rose Kim, eds. 1999. *Struggle for Ethnic Identity: Narratives by Asian American Professionals*. Walnut Creek, Calif.: Alta Mira Press.

Oh, S. 1993. *Christian Korean American Alliance Survey Result, 1992–1993*. Bellflower, Calif.: Christian Korean American Alliance.

Pai, Y., D. Pemberton, and J. Worley. 1987. *Findings on Korean-American Early Adolescents*. Kansas City: University of Missouri, School of Education.

Phinney, Jean. 1993. "A Three-Stage Model of Ethnic Identity Development in Adolescence." In *Ethnic Identity: Formation and Transmission Among Hispanics and Other Minorities,* ed. Martha Bernal and George Knight. Albany: State University of New York Press.

Phinney, Jean, and V. Chavira. 1992. "Ethnic Identity and Self-Esteem: An Exploratory Longitudinal Study." *Journal of Adolescence* 15:271–81.

Sue, S., and D. W. Sue. 1971. "Chinese American Personality and Mental Health." *Amerasia Journal* 1:36–49.

Uba, L. 1994. *Asian Americans: Personality Patterns, Identity, and Mental Health*. New York: Guilford Press.

Werner, Oswald, and Mark Schoepfle. 1987. *Systematic Fieldwork*, vols. 1 and 2. Newbury Park, Calif.: Sage.

Beyond "Strictness" to Distinctiveness

Generational Transition in Korean Protestant Churches

Karen J. Chai

SCHOLARS HAVE ESTABLISHED THAT the ethnic church has historically been the most important social institution for Korean immigrants in the United States (Hurh and Kim 1990; Min 1992; Kim and Yu 1996). Hurh and Kim's (1990) finding that over 75 percent of the Korean immigrant community is affiliated with a Korean Christian church attests to the important functions—political, social, economic, and spiritual—that the church performs in the Korean community. Although figures for second-generation participation are not based on scientific data collection procedures, it has been observed that while younger Korean Americans tend to accompany their parents to church while growing up, many of them do not attend church once they leave for college. For example, Chong (1998) cites estimates from Chicago Korean church leaders that second-generation ethnic church participation up to the age of 17 is about 65 to 70 percent, but the rate declines during at least the initial years of college. Likewise, a study of New York City Korean Americans found that only 5 percent of second-generation Korean Americans remain in the church after college.[1]

---

1. From an interview with Dr. Stephen Linton, research associate at the Center for Korean Research, Columbia University, New York, January 3, 1997. During his ten years as a Christian educator, Linton traced the religious participation of 200 young Korean Americans.

As Cha notes in Chapter 8 of this volume, there is even a sense of alarm among church leaders at how many second-generation Korean Americans are leaving the church. In an earlier paper, Cha (1994) estimates that 90 percent of post-college Korean Americans are no longer attending church. He states that while many second-generation Korean Americans desire an affirmation of their heritage, they see traditional Korean churches as ineffective in addressing their real needs. Similarly, Song (1994) and Lee (1996) point toward evidence of a "silent exodus" of a whole generation of Korean Americans. It is an "exodus" because the number of second-generation Korean Americans exiting is "staggering." It is "silent" because their exit is often unnoticed or not given serious attention within Korean churches.

Although the rate of second-generation participation in the Korean church is lower than that of the first generation, more recent evidence suggests that the drop in attendance may not be as dramatic as is suggested by church leaders. In his 1998 study of second-generation Korean Americans in New York City, Dae Young Kim found that 65 percent still identify themselves as either Protestant or Catholic. Of those who belong to a church, 61 percent attend a Korean church.[2] These findings may reflect the effect of large English ministries targeting the second generation that have sprung up in the past decade (Chai 1998; Chong 1998; D. K. Kim 1993; Cha in this volume; Alumkal in this volume). There is variation among different congregations, but many of these ministries can be seen as successful and strong, considering the amount of money members contribute, the time they spend on church-related activities, and the importance they attach to their identity as Christians. Thus, it seems that for those second-generation Korean Americans who do choose to participate, the ethnic church is a very important aspect of their lives. What theoretical perspectives help us to understand the success of some of these churches in appealing to the second generation?

In this chapter I will briefly assess the contributions of two theories in explaining religious strength at the level of congregations and of social movements. Although these theories can be helpful in understanding the success or decline of churches and religious movements over time, they do not specifically address how these mechanisms may be different for ethnic churches. I will then develop a new theory and apply it to a case study of how one particular Korean ethnic church—Paxton Korean Church (PKC)[3]—

---

2. Survey respondents were between 25 and 35 years of age. The complete results of Dae Young Kim's 1998 New York Second Generation Survey are discussed in his doctoral dissertation (see Kim 1998).

3. Although the study took place in the Boston metropolitan area, all names of persons and specific places have been changed.

managed to establish a successful ministry for second-generation Korean Americans in the Boston metropolitan area.

Paxton Korean Church's second-generation[4] ministry has grown in membership at a rate of nearly 25 percent per year for the past eight years. Having surpassed the first generation in membership size, the English ministry has its own worship services, Bible studies, community outreach programs, campus fellowships, and prayer meetings. Each summer, several members travel abroad as short-term missionaries through agencies such as Campus Crusade for Christ, InterVarsity, Youth With a Mission, and Navigators. PKC's English ministry has also organized its own missions trips, sending members to work with Korean missionaries in Southeast Asia and Central America for periods of a few weeks to one year. Over the course of ten years, a 30-member group of young adults has evolved into a new 250-member "de facto congregation" (Warner 1993, 1994) within the PKC structure. The English ministry has attracted the next generation, implementing innovative changes while maintaining a "distinctiveness" made possible through three key factors: association with evangelical Christianity, an affirmation of Korean ethnic identity, and a sense of second-generation autonomy and ownership of the English ministry.

My findings are based on data obtained through (1) more than thirty interviews with current members, former members, and nonmembers of PKC; (2) over ten years as a member, four of those years as a participant observer; (3) site visits to other Christian and non-Christian religious congregations around the country to check for geographical variation; (4) literature review; and (5) review of church archives.[5] Interviews and participant observations were conducted in both English and Korean, depending on the interviewee's English ability and the activities being observed. The interviews ranged in length from thirty minutes to two hours and occurred in homes, restaurants, or the church, according to the preferences and availability of interviewees.

---

4. It is important to note that some of the members of PKC's English ministry are 1.5-generation Korean Americans. According to the definition employed by Kim and Yu (1996), 1.5 generation refers to those who came to the United States before completing high school. There are some differences between the 1.5- and second-generation members, most notably in terms of age and Korean language ability. The older members of the English ministry (ages 30 to 40) are mostly 1.5 generation. The younger members (college students) are mostly second generation. Because a discussion of in-group differences is beyond the scope of this chapter, I will group 1.5- and second-generation members of PKC's English ministry together under "second-generation members" for the purposes of this chapter. Because the 1.5-generation members that I interviewed were raised in the United States from an early age, their views with respect to the issues I address are similar to those of the second generation.

5. For more about my ethnographic research methods, see Chai (1998, 296, 324).

Introduction to Paxton Korean Church

Located in the affluent Boston suburb of Paxton, Massachusetts, Paxton Korean Church was founded in 1974 by Reverend Kim and a small group of Korean immigrants.[6] Unlike most pastors in the denomination, Korean and non-Korean alike, Reverend Kim has managed to maintain his position as senior pastor of the church, withstanding a number of attempts by both denominational leaders and some dissatisfied church members to have him transferred to other congregations.

The largest Korean Protestant church in New England, PKC holds two services each Sunday in its Paxton location: a 200-member Korean Worship Service (KWS) at 11:30 A.M. and a 250-member English Worship Service (EWS) at 1:45 P.M. In addition, both services run simultaneous Sunday school programs for a total of 150 children. An important contributor to the denomination's funds, PKC's Korean-speaking ministry operates on an annual budget of about $470,000, and the English-speaking ministry operates on a separate annual budget of $217,000. The Korean-speaking congregation recruits foreign students from Korea as well as first-generation immigrants, but most of PKC's growth has been in the English-speaking ministry.

PKC currently shares ownership of its Paxton facilities with the predominantly white Community Church of Paxton. Although the Community Church of Paxton and PKC had begun with a landlord-tenant relationship, the two churches negotiated an agreement for joint ownership in 1988. According to the agreement, PKC was to finance building renovations, and the two churches would subsequently form a third organization—a joint corporation—whose board members would come from both congregations. This joint corporation now owns and maintains the Paxton church facilities. Through the arrangement, the dwindling membership of the Community Church of Paxton was relieved of financial hardship, and PKC members secured ownership of excellent facilities in a convenient location.

The English ministry at PKC was begun in the early 1980s, centered around the Friday night Bible study. Members would gather at 7:30 on Friday evenings for a series of activities that included singing, small-group studies, and refreshments. Because most of the original members of this Young Adults Group (YAG) had been born in Korea or were foreign students from Korea, they were also comfortable speaking some Korean in their Bible study groups and singing gospel songs in Korean. YAG members conducted

6. For a more detailed description of Paxton Korean Church, see Chai (1998, 302–6).

most of their Bible studies in English, but they still attended the Korean-language Sunday worship service.

By 1991, however, most of the incoming college students had been born in the United States and spoke very little Korean. The Friday night songs now came from American evangelical music ministries such as the Vineyard Christian Fellowship and Hosanna Integrity Music, not from the Korean gospel tradition. Because these newer YAG members lacked Korean-language ability, they could not participate meaningfully in the Korean worship services.[7] Some Friday night Bible study participants therefore chose to attend services at other churches on Sundays.

PKC's first generation had attempted to address the increasing language barrier by introducing a simultaneous translation system during their Korean Worship Service. Although it technically enabled English speakers to understand much of the service, the awkward system still could not ensure an edifying worship experience and was gradually discarded. As other Korean churches in the area began planning their own English worship services, it became apparent that PKC would need to address the issue or face the risk of losing members and potential members to the other churches.

Despite the recognized need for an English-language worship service at PKC, there was neither a pastor capable of leading the service nor the adequate funds designated to hire one. In 1989, however, four PKC Young Adults Group men left their promising careers and, one by one, enrolled in nearby Gordon-Conwell Theological Seminary to pursue the ministry. Soon these seminarians approached leaders of PKC and Community Church of Paxton with plans for an English-language worship service for the second generation and their friends.

Before their plans were approved, these seminarians and leaders were required to justify the establishment of a new worship service, even without an ordained pastor. The pastor of Community Church of Paxton did not understand why they wanted to hold a separate service when an English service—one in need of new members—was already being offered by his church at 9:30 A.M. in the same building. The Young Adult leaders argued that language was not the only issue; second-generation Korean Americans desired ethnic fellowship and a service designed to help them overcome the challenges and conflicts that are unique to their experience. In other

---

7. At the same time, with the improvement of the Korean economy, increasing numbers of young Korean students were coming to the Boston area. As the YAG became more decidedly English-speaking, the Korean speakers began their own program in 1990 to cater specifically to the needs of the students from Korea. Members of the Korean-speaking Young Adults Group attend the Korean Worship Service on Sundays but hold their own Friday night Bible studies, fellowship events, and retreats. They are now completely segregated from the English-speaking young adults with no joint activities between the two groups.

words, they wanted their own space, an opportunity to express and explore their own unique identity as Korean Americans, as Christians, and as a group of young adults. They were not ready to be assimilated into mainline white Protestant culture, fearing a loss of their sense of ethnic solidarity, a squelching of their evangelical zeal, and a diminishing of their most powerful appeal—Korean ethnic fellowship.

Their goal was finally realized on September 15, 1991, with PKC's first English Worship Service, held at 1:30 P.M. with 120 people in attendance. Although each of the three remaining seminarians at PKC had felt unable to lead by himself, they joined forces to preside over services and deliver the sermons in rotation. Today, the PKC's English ministry has two full-time pastors[8] and two seminarian interns, and the English ministry is moving toward establishing itself as an independent church, not merely a department of PKC. The head English ministry pastor has developed a church development model—"church alongside a church"—that allows the Korean and English ministries to share facilities and some resources but with complete autonomy in financial matters as well as in staffing decisions. While these provisions have been approved by first-generation leaders on paper, there have been some tensions between the Korean and English ministry leaders concerning exactly how changes are to be implemented. The autonomy granted to the English ministry is essentially an internal agreement that rests precariously on personal respect and trust between the pastors and leaders of the two congregations. Differences between the two congregations need to be addressed delicately, since the denomination still regards both congregations within PKC as one church under Reverend Kim.

There is a remarkable difference between the worship styles of the first and second generations at PKC. While the first generation's Korean Worship Service follows a traditional Protestant liturgy with organ-accompanied hymns, the English Worship Service features a five-piece band, including drums and electric guitar. It follows a distinctly new-style evangelical format and draws from contemporary gospel music. The pastor sometimes shows clips from famous movies such as *Forrest Gump* and *Chariots of Fire* to illustrate his sermons. PKC's second-generation ministry has been successful because the second generation had the resources to establish a sense of ownership that enables the group to simultaneously be welcoming to new members and firm in maintaining distinctiveness and multiple boundaries with respect to the outside.

8. Although neither of these two pastors is ordained, the head pastor has applied for a license as a local preacher by the denomination, and the other is currently undergoing the ordination process.

Is "Strictness" the Key?

By all accounts, PKC's English Worship Service has flourished in its first eight years, maintaining a large membership even in the face of the "silent exodus" and a membership decline in the denomination as a whole. According to one theory (Kelley 1972; Finke and Stark 1992; Iannaccone 1994), churches flourish when they are "strict," maintaining a sectarian tension with the surrounding culture and making no concessions to it. The perspective implies two dimensions of "strictness." The first is strictness as a static cultural conservatism, a resistance to accommodating changes in the surrounding culture or in members' lifestyles. The second dimension of strictness involves the high demands that weed out "free riders," ensuring that all members have a high level of commitment.

In the sense of cultural conservatism, strictness at a Korean immigrant church would involve the costs and stigmas that result from continued maintenance of Korean cultural elements in the practice of Christianity. It would require adherence to a more formal style of worship and an emphasis on close affiliation with the Korean ethnic community, especially in friendship networks and mate selection. Because strictness at an immigrant church would prevent children from adopting the values and lifestyles of American society, this perspective implies that resistance to assimilation would maintain church strength. Although strictness in the sense of weeding out free riders can increase overall levels of commitment, it alone is insufficient in attracting and retaining members of the 1.5 and second generation in the ethnic church. In this chapter, I argue that if those wishing to minister to second-generation Korean American young adults were to apply "strictness" theory, they would follow the lead of first-generation congregations and maintain distance from American society, preserving a strict Korean cultural orientation and resisting American influences. The result, however, would be that Korean church leaders would find their churches emptied of second-generation Korean Americans.

At the same time, Korean American identity is still important, as demonstrated by the fact that PKC's second-generation members had no interest in joining the Community Church of Paxton when they wanted to worship in English. It is clear that PKC's English ministry and other successful ministries to second-generation Korean Americans are different from the churches of the wider American society. The success of PKC's English Worship Service and similar ministries, however, was not the result of "strictness"; rather, its success can be better understood in terms of *distinctiveness*.

Smith (1998) offers a theory of church strength that extends beyond congregations and denominations to religious movements that cut across these organizational boundaries. This study of the strength of evangelicals in the midst of pluralism and constant threats adds a new dimension to what affects church strength. Smith's "subcultural identity" theory of religious strength states: "In a pluralistic society, those religious groups will be relatively stronger which better possess and employ the cultural tools needed to create both clear distinction from and significant engagement and tension with other relevant out groups, short of becoming genuinely counter cultural" (118–19). This theory goes beyond "strictness" in an attempt to explain other dimensions of strength by arguing that the evangelical movement's vitality is not a product of its protected isolation from pluralistic modernity but a product its vigorous engagement with that pluralistic modernity.

Although the "subcultural identity" theory offers a viable alternative approach, it does not consider the interaction between religious identity and ethnic identity. The boundaries that Smith discusses are primarily with respect to religious identity, but I have found that ethnic churches such as PKC must protect a number of additional boundaries. PKC's English ministry sets itself apart through multiple boundaries, creating a distinctive cultural space that is important in the lives of its members and different from the boundaries of other evangelical groups. In the rest of this chapter, I will discuss how PKC has defended its boundaries and successfully adapted to challenges in its environment by enhancing its *distinctiveness*.

Adaptation at PKC

In the face of assimilating forces such as the American educational system, a Korean church cannot expect young people who grew up in the United States to feel comfortable with the overt emphasis on Korean culture and ethnic exclusivity. However, PKC leaders have managed to package the Korean ethnic church as a church that offers the second generation the best of both worlds: a trendy new-style evangelical orientation and plenty of fellow Korean Americans who share the same experiences. While the main draw is still the Koreanness of the group, the evangelical openness to non-Koreans decreases their feelings of conflict about ethnic exclusivity. The fact that 10 percent of current English ministry members are non-Korean demonstrates that the openness has worked to a degree. The fact that two-thirds of the non-Korean PKC members are Asian American suggests an emergent Asian American pan-ethnicity along religious lines.

Ironically, Korean American ethnic solidarity and a cohesive religious community have been built up by deemphasizing Koreanness. In some respects, PKC English ministry members see themselves as a group of evangelical Christians, and the Korean fellowship that they experience is secondary. The fact that the ministries catering to the second-generation Korean Americans are following a more evangelical branch of Christianity is very significant, for evangelicalism itself is a strong contemporary social movement in the United States (Smith 1998; Shibley 1996).[9] At the same time, the success of this approach has fostered a large degree of networking and intermarriage among like-minded second-generation Korean Americans, changing the outward form but nonetheless preserving the importance of the ethnic church among Korean Americans. In the case of PKC, it was precisely the lack of strict adherence to the existing standards that enabled EWS leaders to "do their own thing," thereby helping to maintain this very kind of Korean orientation in the second generation through the church.

Although their needs went beyond that of language, the language barrier between generations has facilitated the success of PKC's second-generation congregation. Language is a dividing force between generations, but it also gave the second generation an opportunity to break away and create its own worship service, all within the same church. Without the language barrier, the second generation would have been left with the choice of attending a less relevant Korean-language worship service, joining another church, or dropping out altogether.

Instead of a strictness that resists accommodation to and engagement with the surrounding environment, PKC's English ministry has altered its form at the surface, putting a new-style evangelical face on the church and strengthening its doctrinal core. At the same time that it draws members for what the church *is*, it maintains strength by maintaining a degree of tension and boundaries with respect to what the church *is not*. The four primary groups with which the English ministry at PKC maintains this tension are: (1) the first generation, or the parents of the English ministry members; (2) non-Christians; (3) non-Koreans; and (4) non-churchgoing second-generation Korean Americans.

In the previous sections, I have discussed some of the ways in which PKC leaders have changed the ministry format and style in response to changes in the environment and community. In the next section, I will describe some of the programs they have created. I will then discuss the tensions with

9. In this chapter I use the term *evangelicalism* broadly to refer to a movement in Protestant Christianity that spans denominations. Evangelicals stress belief in personal conversion and salvation by faith, the authority of the Bible, and evangelism. For a detailed account of American evangelicalism, see Smith et al. (1998).

respect to the four out-groups and consider how the process of accommodation and maintaining tension has created the distinctiveness that makes the ministry strong. I will also examine how "strictness" in the sense of enhancing commitment and raising barriers to entry can also function to reinforce commitment to the English ministry.

Accommodation and Engagement

PKC's English ministry leaders have adapted to the changing desires and needs of their target group, developing a series of programs and activities that embed members in a Korean Christian social network and community, building up and maintaining a common culture. First and foremost are the programs that establish an evangelical Christian identity. These programs capitalize on the appeal of a community that is reminiscent of their high school youth group experiences and yet is more sophisticated. A considerable amount of resources is spent on maintaining the "praise team," the band that leads the congregation twice a week in thirty minutes of pop gospel music. This effort is well worth the investment, for the praise time is consistently ranked as the favorite part of the PKC English Worship Service in church surveys. As previously mentioned, even sermons contain references to popular movies and magazines, further supporting the pop-culture appeal to this younger generation in their search of a brand of ethnic and religious identity that distinguishes it from the first generation and from white mainline Protestants.

Retreats are another important church-sponsored program because of the intense spirituality and emotion coupled with "hang out" time. At retreats, members engage in emotional times of intense prayer and personal sharing, thereby building group solidarity. Prayer meetings also foster immediate intimacy as members come together and present their requests to God. At retreats and at prayer meetings, members share some of their innermost secrets in the spirit of confession and develop a sense of close-knit community.

The annual events sponsored by the ministry also provide PKC members with the opportunity to celebrate the community as well as the individual characters within the community. For example, "Welcome Night," held each fall in honor of prospective members, consists of a Korean meal, games, singing, a sermon, and skits by representatives from different campuses. This night offers members an opportunity to come together and plan how they want to represent the community to outsiders. Skits often contain elements of pop culture—such as rap music and popular films—as well as hidden jokes poking fun at various members. It is a surreal experience to sit in the traditional New England mainline church sanctuary and hear non-Christian rap music blaring from the speakers as a backdrop to a skit.

In the process of planning the evening and the skits, members identify the unique aspects of the church. While the event is meant to introduce the church to potential members, it also serves a secondary function as a "pep rally" for current members to prepare for the coming school year. A similar reinforcement is made through "Thank You Night," which takes place in May of every year. This event honors members who are leaving the Boston area with special skits, songs, and prayers. Not only does it celebrate the contributions of individual members, but it also enables those who are to remain to come together and rebuild the community.

Finally, special ministries within the church bring together members with similar interests or talents. These ministries are oriented toward both the congregation and the outside world. They include the homeless ministry and sandwich outreach, which provide food to the homeless in Boston, as well as summer missions teams whose members travel as a church team overseas. Furthermore, there are cell groups that meet weekly in members' homes, a drama team that writes and performs thought-provoking skits for church events and special services, a praise team, and a welcoming committee, among others. An African American member even formed a step team at PKC, bringing elements of Afro-American culture into the Korean ethnic church. These ministries create smaller like-minded communities within the larger PKC church community and enable members to incorporate elements of the surrounding culture into the church.

Complementing these programs are a wide range of secondary "fellowship" activities, including small-group dinners, campus prayer meetings, and picnics, as well as a number of informal gatherings where members go out to dinner together, watch movies, and play card games—opportunities for members to share experiences and ultimately develop a sense of group solidarity and belonging. Not surprisingly, those who become friends with the most committed members usually become very committed themselves. Those who do not attend Friday night Bible study or any of the outside activities are welcomed but stay at the margins. PKC's English ministry is seeker-sensitive to the degree that it is open to the noncommitted. Once someone joins, they see that the full benefits of membership can be had only with more time and energy devoted to church-related activities. Therefore, distinctiveness is what brings them and what keeps them at the church, but high demands can be used later to bolster commitment among leaders and active members. Nevertheless, these demands are established by the second generation on their own terms, not imposed by the first generation.

Distinction and Tension

Second Generation vs. First Generation

Despite the numerous ways in which the ministry has accommodated changes, four important tensions are still maintained to some degree, preserving the distinctiveness of the group to members and nonmembers alike. The first group that the EWS members distinguish themselves from is the first generation, more specifically, their parents. Jean Bacon (1996) notes that second-generation Indian Americans establish their identity not with respect to Indian and American society but in contrast to the first generation. I have found that Korean Americans are also concerned with differentiating themselves from their parents. The second generation grew up seeing parents go to church and participating in church activities; however, they also witnessed church conflicts and subsequent schisms that did not appear so "Christian" to them. They also felt parental pressure to attend prestigious colleges and pursue high-paying occupations in order to elevate their family status. This seemingly hypocritical behavior led some second-generation Korean Americans to formulate their own ideals about how Christianity should be.

There are important reasons why these two groups are different from each other. First, while immigrant parents may seek out other Koreans because of their lack of familiarity with American society, members of the second generation are fluent in English and are familiar with American culture. A culture gap exists between the two groups based on their experiences growing up in different societies. Second, there are obvious age-based differences between the generations. The ministry needs of a group of people primarily in their twenties differ from those of a group in their forties and fifties. Third, in many cases the generations have had very separate religious education and experiences. Because most Korean immigrant church members were ill-equipped to implement a Christian education curriculum in English, the churches sometimes recruited local non-Korean seminarians, college students, or "mission-minded" adults (Goette 1993, 241) to teach the children. In other cases, parents enrolled their children in the "Sunday school of the Caucasian church from which they [were] renting their facilities"

(Goette 1993, 241) or sent their children to Bible programs at local evangelical churches.

The seminarians tended to be evangelical in their teachings and introduced excited youth to guitar-accompanied contemporary gospel songs. Non-Korean evangelical churches also introduced the children to their own brand of American Christianity and provided youth with Christian role models who, unlike many of the parents, were fluent in English. Therefore, most second-generation children did not grow up worshiping with their parents. Even if a family attended a Korean church together, religious experiences were difficult for the different generations to discuss. This system set the stage for the second generation's questioning of their parents' faith, as well as the first generation's concern that their children had become "too religious" in some cases. While some parents are pleased with the ethnic and spiritual fellowship available to their children at PKC, some interviewees reported that their parents object to the amount of time they spend on church-related activities.

It is important to note that, except in a handful of cases, PKC's English ministry members are not the children of PKC's Korean ministry members. Because the members of the English ministry started attending PKC as students or professionals, the first-generation members see them as adults and grant them freedom as adults. This freedom has been crucial to the success of the English ministry. Those English ministry members whose parents attend PKC's Korean service have also served as informal liaisons and disseminators of information, reporting "inside" accounts of what the respective congregation members "really think" about various issues.

Whereas Korean immigrants have worked hard to build up their ethnic churches from scratch, the second generation has had the benefit of their parents' and PKC's financial security. PKC's first-generation leaders have always had to meet payment deadlines and build up church rosters to provide stability for the younger generation. The second-generation leaders, however, emphasize missions and service. For example, one college student remarks that the first generation is more "fervent" and faithful in activities such as prayer. At the same time, he criticizes the first-generation leaders for emphasizing numbers: "The leaders like you to bring friends to church just to have the church grow in size." In turn, the first-generation members sometimes remark that the second generation has been "spoiled" by not having had to worry about the bottom line, subscribing to a naive and unrealistic belief that they are somehow more genuine Christians, striving for higher principles than their parents or members of PKC's Korean ministry.

Christian vs. Non-Christian

As an evangelical Christian ministry, PKC's English ministry also embodies the distinction made between the secular and the Christian, the "unsaved" and the "saved" who "have a relationship with Jesus Christ." As it is with other evangelicals, the notion of being "born again" is key in the second-generation conception of Christianity at PKC. More than demonstrating loyalty and commitment to the church, it is important that one have experienced a personal encounter with God.

Evidence of PKC English ministry's evangelical orientation can be found in its strong connection to the evangelical Gordon-Conwell Theological Seminary. As the main source of seminarian leaders for PKC's English ministry, Gordon-Conwell has a significant impact on the ministry. Not only does it draw the seminarians to the Boston area in the first place, but it also initiates them into a larger evangelical network, equipping them with a theology and worldview that they can then transmit in their ministries in the ethnic churches. The process of formal seminary education helps to incorporate these ethnic Korean churches into the evangelical community through their leaders, decreasing the gap between Korean ethnic churches and the wider American evangelical movement. Although the Korean-speaking congregation is also rooted in the evangelical tradition that is prevalent in Korea (Chung 1996), its direct affiliation and interaction with its more liberal mainline denomination means that it is less affiliated with the American evangelical movement. For example, the Korean ministry has often hired seminarians from the more liberal Harvard Divinity School and the Boston University School of Theology. Its services generally fit the mainline mold in terms of liturgy and organizational form, while the English Worship Service has been insulated because the denomination sees it essentially as a youth ministry within PKC. As the English Worship Service has grown in size and visibility, it must prepare to interact with denomination leaders directly, and time will tell if a satisfactory fit can be found within the denomination.

PKC's English ministry also has ties to evangelical parachurch organizations such as Campus Crusade for Christ and InterVarsity, which began to actively recruit Asian Americans on college campuses in the 1970s (Busto 1996). As stated earlier, many PKC members have participated in summer missions training programs through these parachurch organizations. Furthermore, the parachurch efforts resulted in a strong network of campus-based Asian American and Korean Christian Fellowships. Although these parachurch organizations can compete with PKC and other churches for members on some campuses, they also provide a space for networking among Christians that enables members to spread the word about PKC to their college peers. Even the potential competition with the parachurch groups has been helpful to PKC in that it has helped motivate PKC to alter and expand its ministries in order to compete effectively. One example can be found in the fact that PKC began to sponsor more campus-based activities, appointing campus representatives and holding prayer meetings and gatherings during the week.

Another evangelical network from which PKC English ministry leaders draw is a monthly prayer breakfast for pastors of ministries to second-generation Asian Americans in the Boston area. This group is evangelical, most of the clergy having attended Gordon-Conwell. It also includes campus staff members of InterVarsity branches at local Boston schools. This network of leaders began coordinating joint Asian American Christian activities in recent years, such as an annual Easter "Sonrise" worship service, a summer missions trip to Asia, and a fundraising effort for North Korean famine relief. While maintaining an Asian American orientation, the group crosses ethnic lines, since two of the churches represented are Chinese American, and the parachurch groups are Asian American. This is evidence of an emerging pan-Asian American evangelicalism, pointing to the importance of a common racial identity.

Because evangelicalism creates a new identity through a "born again" conversion, Busto (1996) acknowledges that the relationship between ethnicity and faith is unclear. While the relationship may be confusing for members of Asian American evangelical communities, for nonbelievers, evangelical Christianity may be seen as a "threat to ethnic identity and a move towards an unwelcome form of assimilation" (Busto 1996, 139).

Korean vs. Non-Korean

If the second-generation Korean American Christians are so insistent on being true to their evangelical beliefs and maintaining a distinction with respect to the first generation, there are plenty of evangelical churches that they could attend in the Boston area. In fact, there are a number of Korean Americans who do attend those multiethnic (but predominantly white) churches. It is interesting to note, however, that those multiethnic ministries often have clusters of Korean or Asian American members who form close-knit subgroups within the church. Thus, ethnic as well as race-based fellowship seems to be an important component of the religious experience for the second generation, whether at a predominantly Korean church or within a larger multiethnic church.

Although some second-generation PKC members express ambivalence about their social motives for attending the church, the most consistently cited reason for membership is the opportunity to be with people who share their cultural background. At PKC members form close relationships with others who have been shaped by the same Korean and American cultural forces. The second generation finds that the Korean ethnic church can meet a deeper sense of spirituality because they need not explain to their friends why they face so much parental pressure to study hard, to marry another Korean, to succeed. Church is the place where they find their all-consuming identity as Koreans, as Americans, and as Christians. Thus, despite PKC's openness and embracing of non-Koreans on the surface, members greatly value the interaction with other Korean Americans.

There have been conflicting findings as to whether the ethnic church facilitates the supplanting of Korean identity in favor of an evangelical Christian identity, or whether the church perpetuates Korean values and traits among the second generation. For example, David Kyuman Kim's (1993) study of second-generation Korean American Christians in Boston concludes that "Korean American Christians are becoming grounded, particularly those who have taken on an Evangelical form of faith, in religion that replaces a core 'Korean' identity" (41). Kelly Chong (1998), however, finds in her study of Chicago-area Korean American Christians a strong sense of ethnic identity and exclusivity among second-generation churchgoers. She argues that this reflects "defensive ethnicity" due to their "perceived 'marginal' status within American society as a non-white minority group" (262). Thus, Christianity can be used by different groups as the primary identity, superseding the conflict between Korean and American. It can also be used as a backdrop against which Korean ideals and values are perpetuated in the name of Christianity. Alumkal's chapter in this volume (Chapter 10) predicts that Korean American churches will shift between the polarities of ethnic particularism and Christian universalism over time with changing circumstances. These two phenomena, however, can coexist; I have found evidence of both at PKC.

For example, the tension between things Korean and American can be seen in members' somewhat unrealistic desire to characterize their church as a new-style evangelical church that happens to have many Korean members. Christianity is the key identifying factor; in fact, there is no mention of "Korean" on the English Worship Service bulletins or on the English ministry pastor's outgoing voice-mail message. In his study of Asian American involvement in parachurch groups, Busto (1996, 138) found a similar phenomenon among evangelical fellowships that identify themselves as Asian American and target Asian and Asian American students for outreach and membership. At the same time that they appeal to potential members on the basis of racial identity, these fellowships also affirm "a non-race-specific evangelical identity" (138).

Although there are several very active members at PKC who are neither of Korean nor Asian descent, the overwhelming majority of members are indeed Korean American. These members bring with them the beliefs and assumptions that they grew up with and subtly reinforce values and principles that can be seen as Korean. One example from PKC's English ministry can be found in the assumptions about who should be preparing the communal meals for special church events. Until two years ago, the women of the Korean ministry at PKC prepared the meals for both the Korean and English ministries on special holidays and church celebrations. As the English ministry sought autonomy, however, it was proposed that English ministry members should take responsibility for their own meal preparations and refreshments. As a result, the women of the Couples Group within the English ministry were asked to prepare the special meals. While most College Group and Young Adults Group members saw this as a natural request, a woman in the Couples Group expressed her displeasure to me: "I don't see why everyone should expect *us* to do the cooking. If anything, we are the busiest members of the church, with our own families, and especially with our children. *We* are the ones who need a break from cooking the most." While this expectation for married women to cook is not unique to Korean culture, it is a reflection and perpetuation of the examples and values that the second-generation Korean Americans grew up with and regarded as "normal" in their ethnic churches.

Another attitude and expectation that PKC members have internalized is the importance of education. College education for the second generation is taken for granted among PKC members. One is either in the college group or the post-college group, with no room for someone who is above college age but did not attend college. Furthermore, these solidly middle-class members attend well-known institutions in the Boston area and are quite ambitious. Occasionally, there will be a visitor who did not attend college or who attends a community college. Many awkward moments follow, as member after member greets the visitor with, "What school do you go to?" or "What do you do?" These well-intentioned questions serve to reinforce the awareness that those who are not college-educated and middle class are outside the accepted norms of PKC's English ministry. They also convey the subtle status hierarchies that are established according to the school one attends and the occupation one pursues. Nevertheless, Korean culture is by no means alone in emphasizing educational attainment, and these assumptions are also a reflection of members' class background. It is interesting to note that members of the Korean ministry have much more variation in education and occupation levels, since some immigrants have less than a high school education and others have doctorates. This disparity, however, reflects the high degree of stratification within Korean society, and it may explain why first-generation immigrants place a great deal of importance on their children's education.

Churchgoing Korean Americans vs. Secular Korean Americans

In addition to the three distinctions that second-generation Korean American Christians make with respect to other groups, they make a finer distinction with respect to their own generational cohort—nonevangelical or "secular" second-generation Korean Americans. For example, evangelical zeal and exclusivity on the part of some second-generation Korean American churches have fostered a degree of tension with the secular Korean Students Associations (KSA) on most campuses. Churchgoers tend to regard the KSAs as self-serving social organizations whose primary purpose is to hold intercollegiate dance parties. In turn, KSA members sometimes view churchgoers as self-righteous and narrow-minded in their pursuit of "holiness" while ignoring important social issues pertaining to the Korean community.

A PKC woman admits, "I culturally associate spirituality with certain behaviors, and there is a stigma attached to KSA people [as opposed to] church people." She believes that the evils of smoking, drinking, and dancing, which were instilled by Protestant missionaries to Korea, have been passed down from immigrants to their children. A Catholic Korean American college student has observed divisions between KSA members and the evangelical Christian Korean Americans who are part of the campus Asian American Christian Fellowship (ACF): "The Koreans who go to KSA meetings and the Koreans who go to ACF meetings, they usually do not get along with each other. Most of the time because the KSA is very infamous for drinking. . . . They [members of the KSA and ACF] don't say, 'Hi, how are you doing?' When they go to class, they never study together. They form their own cliques and their own groups. They're like, 'Him and I, we just don't get along because we think very differently.'" Because he is Christian but not evangelical, this Catholic college student can relate to both groups and often finds himself in a mediating role.

With respect to the church-KSA tension, a Gordon-Conwell seminarian serving at one of PKC's "rival" churches declares: "The number one problem

for Korean American college students is the KSA. It is the single most detri-
ment[al] [organization].... They [church and KSA] are fundamentally incompatible, because the KSA and the church have different goals. One is to
glorify Korean culture, and the other is to glorify God ... the KSA provides
an alternative for Korean American college students instead of joining a
Korean church." Thus, the polarization of evangelical Christianity and the
KSA have created a dilemma among Korean American students on many
campuses, with both groups competing for unwavering commitment. As an
additional complication, Korean American evangelicals regard their fellow
Korean Americans, including KSA members, as prime targets of evangelism.
Not only does this offend some KSA members, but it also offends those who
practice other religions such as Buddhism. I explore the boundary between
Korean American Christians and Buddhists in Chapter 15 of this volume.

The zeal of PKC members can alienate non-Protestants who feel as though
they are being looked down upon for not being "saved." Another Catholic
Korean American notes his feelings about Korean American Protestants:
"I felt like the Protestants were saying, If you're not one of us, then you're
going to hell.... I felt sometimes that Protestants believe so strongly in their
faith that they were ready to reject anyone that didn't [believe]." He adds that
he sees the Korean Catholic church as being more tolerant, more patient,
and more willing to educate and perhaps less demanding in terms of costs
and stigmas.

A Korean American woman who did not grow up attending a church
expresses disdain for the second-generation Korean American evangelicals
on her campus:

> I thought these people were a bunch of religious automatons ... this kind
> of group mentality was just absolutely insane, and it made me really kind
> of annoyed. It's hard to discern whether it was my distaste for religion,
> which I certainly had, or whether it was my distaste for the insular, Korean,
> group mentality. Maybe it's the conflation of the two.... They [Korean
> Christians] made me feel guilty as if you weren't doing your duty as a
> Korean person if you didn't join.... No one defines your ethnic identity
> through some religious affiliation. Come on. Religion, if anything, is a com-
> pletely individual experience, and it's experience that is contingent upon
> individual faith. There's no group consensus.

This woman has few Korean American friends, and she has only dated white
men. Despite the efforts of PKC and other English ministries to distinguish
itself from the negative aspects of Korean American society, she sees the

ethnic church—even the English ministries—as the embodiment of those negative traits. As a college student she also made an active decision not to join the KSA or the Asian American Association, saying that "organizations like these ... make more divisive lines as opposed to creating some degree of racial parity." For someone like her, particular weaknesses at PKC's English ministry are not necessarily keeping her away. She is against the idea of ethnic organizations in principle and would most likely find them distasteful and counterproductive in any form.

These four tensions—with the first generation, nonevangelicals, non-Koreans, and non-churchgoing second-generation Korean Americans—combined with the positive benefits of PKC membership, serve to unite members of PKC's English ministry with a common purpose and to maintain distinctiveness from other groups.[10]

Conclusion: The Need for Distinctiveness

The case of the Korean ethnic church illustrates the need to expand the variables of analysis beyond "strictness" based on social-class stratification and "subcultural identity" (Smith 1998), which ignores the added complexity of ethnic identity. From my analysis of PKC, I propose that the key to church success is a *distinctiveness* that corresponds to stratification based not only on social class but also on ethnic identity. Furthermore, it must be recognized that the forms of mobility achieved over generations are not only vertical (upward), but also horizontal (immigration and assimilation).

Shibley's (1996) study of a Midwest Vineyard church supports my argument that strictness in terms of cultural conservatism is not necessarily the key to success. While conservative Protestants have relied on strictness, what makes new-style evangelicals distinct is "not their strictness with regard to contemporary culture but rather their increasing tolerance of it" (109). He finds that the mechanism for commitment is the meeting of individual needs and argues that social strength is a "necessary but not sufficient condition for growth" (136). In a pluralistic society, strong churches will not continue to grow if their strictness moves them too far from the cultural norms that surround their institutions.

---

10. Although cultural distinctiveness has been an important factor in accounting for the success of PKC's English ministry, it is important to note the crucial role of other types of factors in its success. For an assessment of the several key resources—such as a large supply of second-generation Korean American seminarians to serve as leaders—that have enabled PKC to adapt successfully to environmental changes and attract the second generation, see Chai (1998, 317–19).

Thus, continued growth in established evangelical denominations depends on the "cultural fit" between its constituents and the beliefs and practices it promotes. If strictness requires cultural conservatism and the unwillingness to adapt to changes in society, strict churches will not necessarily retain the next generation. Rather, the church must possess a *distinctiveness* that offers services and rewards to its members while maintaining an identity that sets it apart from others. A high level of demand is a consequence of the strength of the ministry, not a cause. A by-product of church strength may in fact be a high level of commitment, but high levels of commitment can also be indicators of church weakness. As Ammerman (1997a) finds in her study of over twenty churches around the country: "If commitment is measured in terms of regular attendance and giving high percentages of their personal incomes, the members of declining congregations are, on average, the most committed. They are giving sacrificially, knowing that with only small numbers everyone's dollars count" (327). Since members of churches in crisis know their crucial role in saving their church, they give everything they can to keep the church going. In contrast to the high-demand/high-commitment model, Ammerman (1997b) notes that healthy congregations only need to impose high demands on enough people to sufficiently sustain themselves. The vast majority of people, in fact, live with a good deal less than total commitment.

In the case of PKC, it is more useful to state that in order to grow and survive, the organization must maintain boundaries through distinctiveness, and this distinctiveness then sets it apart from competitors in its particular niche. This can take the form of conservatism, or it can mean that a church departs from tradition through adopting casual dress, contemporary gospel songs, and a socially progressive doctrine. Once a church designs programs that appeal to certain segments of the population, it draws members through those programs. Members develop close ties with other members and become dependent on the Christian social networks. In order to maintain the multiple boundaries of membership, the church does require sacrifice in terms of time and behavior from its committed members. The strict codes for leaders, however, can lead other members to feel relieved from observing the code themselves.

While the first generation is forced to choose the ethnic church, the second generation chooses it not because they have no other options but because it is a safe space where ethnicity and spirituality merge into one. Fueled by successive waves of continued immigration, the Korean ethnic church may very well continue to survive in the United States. If the first generation wishes to ensure survival through the descendants of current members, however, there must be a successful generational transition in power and in cultural orientation. The first generation must give the second generation the space and support to develop its own vision for ministry, while the second generation must nurture leaders from its own ranks. Survival over generations is not a matter of maintaining sectarian strictness in the churches, but it is a matter of reacting creatively and swiftly to environmental changes with sufficient resources.

On one level, PKC's English worship service is a new-style evangelical church embracing all ethnic groups. It is culturally current, incorporating the newest technology, pop culture, and marketing techniques to attract and retain members. On another level, it is a very Korean church, with most of its members drawn by the promise of ethnic fellowship. Members also reinforce Korean cultural elements in their church activity, such as gender roles and emphasis on educational attainment. PKC's English ministry leaders go to great lengths to open their services to all "seekers," yet they demand much from committed members. PKC is to its members many different things, and the fact that it maintains its strength in the midst of these paradoxes and tensions attests to the complexity and the resilience of religion among second-generation Korean Americans. The elements that distinguish PKC from other churches all communicate the message "This is not your parents' church; this is not your white neighbor's church; this is *your* church."

Epilogue

September 13, 1998, marked another milestone in the history of PKC as the English Worship Service planted another English service in an urban setting. Called "New Hope Church," the service takes place at 9:30 A.M. on Sunday mornings at a borrowed hall located just steps away from a convenient subway stop in downtown Boston. While it expects to draw many Asian Americans to the service, the stated intention of the English ministry pastor is to reach the "unchurched and previously churched members of Generation X." To that effect, thousands of dollars were spent on hiring the services of a direct-mail company to send out invitational postcards to both Asians and non-Asians in the area. It is too early to judge the long-term prospects of this new outreach ministry, but the response so far has been mixed.

On April 30, 1999, Pastor Lim, head of the English ministry, submitted his letter of resignation to the council and to Senior Pastor Kim of Paxton Korean Church. He stepped down from heading PKC's English ministry over a conflict regarding the autonomy status of the English ministry. Although the English ministry's autonomy had been approved on paper, leaders of the Korean ministry continued to insist on final approval by Reverend Kim for financial matters. This was seen as a setback to the freedom of the English ministry to pursue its own vision. It is unclear whether lay leaders and members of PKC's English ministry will stay at PKC and not pursue autonomy, or if they will seek other options outside of PKC.

Thus, PKC is in the process of facing yet another challenge in dealing with the second generation. This can be seen as an example of the second generation feeling that they need to pursue their evangelical Christian goals apart from the constraints imposed by the first generation. It can also be seen, however, as a series of events that show that the second generation is no more successful than the first at avoiding schisms.

References

Ammerman, Nancy. 1997a. *Congregation and Community*. New Brunswick: Rutgers University Press.

———. 1997b. "Organized Religion in a Voluntaristic Society." *Sociology of Religion* 58 (3): 203–16.

Bacon, Jean. 1996. *Life Lines: Community, Family, and Assimilation Among Asian Indian Immigrants*. New York: Oxford University Press.

Busto, Rudy. 1996. "The Gospel According to the Model Minority? Hazarding an Interpretation of Asian American Evangelical College Students." *Amerasia Journal* 22 (1): 133–47.

Cha, Peter. 1994. "Toward a Vision for Second Generation Korean American Ministry." Paper presented at Katalyst, Sandy Cove, Maryland, August.

Chai, Karen. 1998. "Competing for the Second Generation: English-Language Ministry at a Korean Protestant Church." In *Gatherings in Diaspora: Religious Communities and the New Immigration*, ed. R. Stephen Warner and Judith Wittner, 295–331. Philadelphia: Temple University Press.

Chong, Kelly H. 1998. "What It Means to Be Christian: The Role of Religion in the Construction of Ethnic Identity and Boundary Among Second-Generation Korean Americans." *Sociology of Religion* 59 (Fall): 259–86.

Chung, Chai-Sik. 1996. "Global Theology for the Common Good: Lessons from Two Centuries of Korean Christianity." *International Review of Missions* 85, no. 339:523–38.

Finke, Roger, and Rodney Stark. 1992. *The Churching of America, 1776–1990: Winners and Losers in Our Religious Economy*. New Brunswick: Rutgers University Press.

Hurh, Won Moo, and Kwang Chung Kim. 1990. "Religious Participation of Korean Immigrants in the U.S." *Journal for the Scientific Study of Religion* 29 (March): 19–34.

Iannaccone, Lawrence. 1994. "Why Strict Churches Are Strong." *American Journal of Sociology* 99 (March): 1180–11.

Kelley, Dean M. [1972] 1986. *Why Conservative Churches Are Growing: A Study in the Sociology of Religion*. Macon: Mercer University Press.

Kim, Dae Young. 1998. "1998 New York Second Generation Korean American Survey." Data for unpublished doctoral dissertation, Department of Sociology, City University of New York.

Kim, David Kyuman. 1993. "Becoming: Korean Americans, Faith, and Identity—Observations on an Emerging Culture." Master's thesis, Harvard Divinity School.

Kim, Elaine, and Eui-Young Yu. 1996. *East to America: Korean American Life Stories*. New York: New Press.

Lee, Helen. 1996. "Silent Exodus." *Christianity Today*, August 12, 51–52.

Min, Pyong Gap. 1992. "The Structure and Social Functions of Korean Immigrant Churches in the U.S." *International Migration Review* 26 (4): 1370–94.

Shibley, Mark. 1996. *Resurgent Evangelicalism in the United States: Mapping Cultural Change Since 1970*. Columbia: University of South Carolina Press.

Smith, Christian. 1998. *American Evangelicalism: Embattled and Thriving*. Chicago and London: University of Chicago Press.

Song, Minho. 1994. "Towards the Successful

Movement of the English-speaking Ministry Within the Korean Immigrant Church." Paper presented at Katalyst, Sandy Cove, Maryland, August.

Stark, Rodney, and William Sims Bainbridge. 1985. *The Future of Religion: Secularization, Revival, and Cult Formation.* Berkeley and Los Angeles: University of California Press.

Warner, R. Stephen. 1993. "Work in Progress Toward a New Paradigm for the Sociological Study of Religion in the United States." *American Journal of Sociology* 98 (March): 1044–93.

———. 1994. "The Place of the Congregation in the Contemporary American Religious Configuration." In *American Congregations,* ed. James P. Wind and James W. Lewis, 2:54–99. Chicago: University of Chicago Press.

10

Being Korean, Being Christian

Particularism and Universalism in a Second-Generation Congregation

Antony W. Alumkal

ETHNIC-SPECIFIC CHRISTIAN CHURCHES in the United States have long faced a dilemma: to what extent should they identify with their specific ethnic group, and to what extent should they identify with a Christian community that transcends ethnic boundaries? For example, Lincoln and Mamiya (1990, 12) observe that the historic black churches "reflected the dialectic tension between the universalism of the Christian message and the particularism of their past racial history as institutions emerging out of the racism of white Christianity and the larger society." They argue that there is no synthesis or ultimate resolution to this and other dialectic tensions[1] in the black churches. Rather, churches shift between polarities in historic time.

Raymond Williams (1988) makes similar observations in his study of the religious communities of Indian and Pakistani immigrants in the United States. Williams outlines four ideal typical trajectories of adaptation for religious communities. On one end of the continuum are "ethnic" religious groups that stress a union of religious devotion and regional-linguistic identity. On the other end of the continuum are "ecumenical" groups that claim

---

1. Lincoln and Mamiya (1990) list a total of six such dialectic tensions, including "priestly and prophetic functions," "other-worldly versus this-worldly," "the communal and the privatistic," "charismatic versus bureaucratic," and "resistance versus accommodation."

to transcend regional and linguistic boundaries.[2] Williams argues that these ideal types are rarely found in pure form. In particular, he argues that "the ecumenical is always in tension with the national and the ethnic, as most religious groups appeal to some form of universalism" (279).

It is useful to apply Lincoln and Mamiya's categories of "particularism" and "universalism" in the analysis of the Korean American church. For the immigrant generation, the churches are clearly closer to the particularistic pole. Studies of the Korean American immigrant church emphasize the centrality of churches in the organization of Korean community life and their role in preserving Korean culture for immigrants (I. Kim 1981; Hurh and Kim 1984, 1990). The strong cultural emphasis of these churches is understandable in light of Korean immigrants' high levels of ethnic attachment and low levels of assimilation, the latter resulting partially from language barriers and occupational segregation (Min 1995).

We find a much different situation among the growing number of ministries to the Korean American second generation. In contrast to many of their parents, second-generation Korean Americans generally face no language barrier in relating to members of the larger society. They are also more likely to have strong social ties with people from other ethnic groups. And their ministries, especially those in college campus settings, are becoming increasingly influenced by an American evangelical subculture that often downplays the significance of ethnic boundaries (Busto 1996). Yet as racial minorities, Korean Americans continue to find themselves marginalized by American society. Many second-generation Korean American Christians desire to be in fellowship with others who share their experience as racial minorities as well as their distinct upbringing in the Korean American church. All of this suggests that for second-generation Korean American Christians, negotiating between particularism and universalism can be considerably more difficult than it is for their parents.

This chapter presents a case study of a second-generation[3] congregation in a Korean American church. I examine the various ways in which religious and ethnic identity and the relationship between the two are understood by members of the congregation. I pay specific attention to how members negotiate between particularistic and universalistic impulses in their religious life.

2. The other two ideal typical trajectories are "national" groups that combine religious devotion with identification with the nation of India or Pakistan, and "sectarian" groups characterized by allegiance to a particular hierarchy.

3. I use the term "second generation" to refer to all Korean Americans who were born in the United States and/or who spent significant portions of their childhood there. This includes the so-called 1.5 generation.

Religious and Ethnic Identity in the Second-Generation Church

While there are a number of studies on the religious life of immigrant-generation Korean Americans, only a few studies so far have looked at the second generation. At least two of these have addressed the issue of the relationship between religious and ethnic identity. David Kim (1993) examines second-generation ministries in two Boston-area Korean American churches. He argues that members of the churches adopt a core identity as a "Christian" that takes precedence over both "Korean" and "American" identities. Thus, religion has supplanted ethnicity as the primary focus for identity and sense of the self. But according to Kim, this does not mean that ethnic identity ceases to be important. He found that members of the churches felt more comfortable relating to other Korean Americans with whom they shared similar experiences. Furthermore, a shared Christian identity became the basis for growing closer to other Korean Americans in the churches and ultimately coming to further embrace a Korean American identity. Kim's case study reveals that particularistic and universalistic impulses in second-generation Korean American ministries can interact in complex ways.

Kelly Chong's (1996) study of second-generation ministries in two Chicago-area churches presents a contrast to the previous one. Chong found a strong symbolic linkage between Korean and Christian identities. In the minds of the church members, being a good Christian was synonymous with accepting traditional Korean cultural values. As a former member of one of the churches argued, "The more you believe in God, the more Korean you tend to be" (19). However, Chong also describes a minority of church members who objected to the strong Korean cultural emphasis in the churches. Many in this group felt that the cultural aspects of the church hindered them from being "true" Christians. Chong's study gives valuable insight into the second-generation Korean American ministries that are close to the particularistic pole and shows that even in these ministries there is always tension with the universalistic aspects of Christianity.

Field Site and Methods

The site for this case study is Glory Korean Presbyterian Church (GKPC), located in a suburban town in the New York metropolitan area. Like many Korean Presbyterian churches, GKPC rents space from a non-Korean Presbyterian (PCUSA) church. GKPC holds two services in the afternoon—a

Korean-language service involving about 150 adults per week, and an English-language service aimed at second-generation young adults with about 70 people attending each week.

The English congregation was started by leaders in the church who saw the need to minister to second-generation Korean American young adults who are more comfortable worshiping in English than Korean. The church hired Joe Kim, a seminary student who had been involved with the church as an undergraduate, to serve as *Jundosah*[4] and to preside over the English congregation. English services began in 1992 with about 35 young adults, mostly undergraduates from a nearby public university who were active in the campus's Korean Christian Fellowship (KCF). As word of the congregation spread among KCF members and other Koreans on campus, attendance rose to its current levels.

Like most second-generation Korean ministries, the GKPC English congregation models its worship after that of evangelical parachurch organizations like InterVarsity or Campus Crusade for Christ. Songs by Vineyard and other evangelical publishers are played on acoustic guitars, synthesizer, and drums while the lyrics are displayed via overhead projector. The order of service, however, roughly follows Presbyterian convention.

Data for this study was gathered using participant observation at the English congregation services and small group meetings over a two-year period and through interviews with fifteen congregation members.

The Desire for Ethnic Fellowship

It is important to recognize that for members of the GKPC English congregation, attendance at a Korean church is something they have freely chosen from among other available alternatives. Unlike many in the first generation, those in the Korean American second generation face no language barrier preventing their participation in a non-Korean church. Similarly, while those in the first generation have few alternatives to the Korean church as a source of ethnic fellowship (Hurh and Kim 1984, 1990), second-generation members on college campuses can choose to participate in Korean or Asian American student associations in lieu of attending a Korean church.

Perhaps reflecting the conscious decision of its members to attend a Korean-specific church, the congregation displays its Koreanness in a variety of ways. While the congregation usually sings in English, a small choir that

---

4. *Jundosah* translates literally as "evangelist" and refers to a nonordained pastor usually serving youth.

performs during the offertory frequently sings with verses alternating between English and Korean. The *Jundosah's* sermons frequently contain references to the congregation's Korean American background, as well as occasional Korean phrases that go untranslated. Perhaps the most striking way in which the congregation displays its Korean identity is through a distinctly Korean form of prayer. During certain times of prayer in the services, members of the congregation will all pray individually, speaking out loud, their voices in something of a loud whisper and intensely emotional.[5] A swirl of intermingling voices fills the room for several minutes until the worship leader brings the service back to order with some closing words. If the use of Vineyard songs and "contemporary Christian"-style arrangements signals a degree of acculturation to the norms of American evangelicalism, the English congregation's service still remains unmistakably Korean.

In the course of interviews with members of the English congregation, I asked respondents why they had decided to join GKPC. Some had specifically sought out a Korean church. Others came at the invitation of friends, remaining after they found that they liked the church. But for the vast majority of both groups, the opportunity for fellowship with other Korean Americans was an important reason for their continued involvement.

One theme that came up repeatedly in interviews was that being in a Korean fellowship put members in touch with people who had similar backgrounds—people they could relate to better than non-Koreans. For example, one woman I talked with shared that she had gone to a non-Korean church during her freshman year. While she enjoyed the church, she found that she missed having fellowship with other Koreans: "There are a lot of benefits to going to a Korean fellowship because it gives you ... I guess the same way my parents felt, like that comfort and bonding and being able to relate with other people who have similar struggles. In that sense, it's kind of an added bonus, knowing that other people are going through the same challenges as you."

For some individuals, the Korean church (along with the Korean campus ministry) provides a refuge from the white-dominated larger society. One woman shared why she sought out fellowship with other Koreans: "I wanted to become part of a Korean [fellowship] because I really didn't like my suburban town with all the Caucasian people, and I really wanted to get away. . . . I was the only Korean in my [high school] grade, and I really wanted to meet some Korean people so I could relate better."

---

5. The *Jundosah* told me that he believes this form of prayer can be traced back to the tradition of Korean revivals. He noted that the second-generation approach was slightly "toned down" compared with that of their parents.

Another reason people gave for wanting to attend a Korean church is that they had been going to Korean churches all of their lives and were used to them. The Korean church was "home" for these individuals, and they were not ready to venture outside of its boundaries. The familiarity of the Korean church seemed to be particularly important to students during their first year, when some found the transition to young adult life overwhelming. One man shared that during his freshman year, "I was so confused, because you're exposed to all these different kinds of people and culture, and there are no parents or any guidance to lead you." For him a circle of Korean Christian friends functioned as a surrogate family while he adjusted to life away from home.

In sum, the majority of church members expressed a desire for fellow-ship with other Korean Americans and considered the opportunity for such fellowship to be one of the principal advantages of attending GKPC. But along with this particularistic tendency to gather with their coethnics, these individuals displayed another tendency: to see their Korean identity as explicitly less important than their identity as "Christians."

Christians Before Koreans

During one of his sermons, the *Jundosah* declared forcefully to the English congregation, "I am proud to be a Korean American, but I am first and fore-most a child of God." This belief that Korean identity, while important, must be explicitly subordinated to a "Christian"[6] identity was a theme that fre-quently arose in the discourse of these second-generation Korean Christians.

To learn about their views on the relationship between their Korean and Christian identities, I asked the congregation members whether they thought Korean and Christian values were mostly compatible or incompatible. While people generally found areas of compatibility between the value systems, particularly regarding respect for the family, many that I talked with pointed out ways in which Korean Christians, in following Korean values, deviate from Christian ideals.

One woman objected to Korean culture's emphasis on success, which she saw as leading to un-Christian behavior in the churches: "The Korean culture really harbors on success. If your child goes to Harvard—I know a

6. It is noteworthy that denominational identities, such as Presbyterian, were almost never mentioned by members of the congregation. It seems that for these individuals the denomination does not play a sig-nificant "ethnic" function like that described by Greeley (1972) in the case of earlier European immigrants.

lady whose kids go to Harvard, Yale, and Brown, and she brags about them all the time! And she's a Christian. She's an avid churchgoer. That's one thing wrong with Korean people—they love to brag. And Christians need to be humble." Another church member was troubled by the Korean tendency to give uncritical respect to people in positions of authority: "Sometimes you have a pastor who is not biblical, who is clearly wrong, but the congregation is hesitant to say anything 'because he's a pastor' or 'because he's up there and I'm down here.' And that can be a problem.... I also don't like the fact that the elders are esteemed so much that they have a higher say than what the Bible says. When an elder says something, that's just like God said something. I don't agree with that." For both of these individuals, the Korean church was in error when it placed Korean values above Christian ones. Both believed that it is Christian identity, not Korean identity, that should be the primary guide in the Korean church.

The subordination of Korean identity to Christian identity was also evident in individuals' views on marriage. As many theorists have argued (Herberg 1955; Gordon 1964; Kibria 1995), marriage patterns are a significant indicator of ethnic boundaries, with the loosening of these boundaries normally resulting in an increased number of interethnic marriages. Who members of the English congregation include in their pool of acceptable marriage partners therefore tells us a lot about how they understand their individual identities.

Perhaps not surprisingly, most of the people I talked with said that they would prefer to marry another Korean. They mentioned a variety of reasons for this, including parental approval/disapproval and being able to relate better to someone with a similar background. But most of them insisted that while marrying another Korean was important, marrying another Christian was essential. As one woman put it: "It is very important [that my spouse be Christian], more important than being Korean. I think if I ultimately married a non-Korean by fate, it would be okay. There must be a good reason why I would marry a non-Korean for all the trouble it would cause. But with a non-Christian, it could never be turned around." Another member of the congregation expressed a similar sentiment: "I came to the conclusion that as long as my future spouse is a believer and she walks with God, I don't care what color she is. If God tells me she's my woman, I'll marry her. (Laughs.) But I would prefer to marry a Korean. That would help me a lot because, first of all, I would be able to eat with her the kind of food I like. And we would have a lot in common based on culture. But that doesn't have to be." Both of these individuals considered Korean spouses to be preferable,

for reasons that could be described as utilitarian—being able to relate better, sharing a common culture. In contrast, marrying a Christian was something intrinsically important that reflected a "deeper" identity as a Christian.

Implicit in the emphasis on "Christian" identity is a sense of connected-
ness to a community of believers that transcends ethnic divisions. This
sentiment is not surprising considering that, unlike members of the first
generation, second-generation Korean Americans are likely to have primary
group relations with people from different ethnic backgrounds. A consequence of these broad social networks—and the mandate of an evangelical
theology—is that most members of the GKPC English congregation make
an effort to share the gospel with both Korean and non-Korean acquain-
tances. All people, regardless of race, are seen as potential brothers and sisters in Christ. As we might expect, the universalism inherent in evangelical
Christianity has profound implications for how second-generation Korean
Americans view the future of their church.

The Question of Boundary

Thus far we have seen that members of the GKPC English congregation
desire fellowship with other second-generation Korean Americans and that
the opportunity for this type of fellowship is one of the principal reasons
individuals remain with the ministry. At the same time, members of the congregation consider their Korean identities significant but subordinate to their
"Christian" identities. This latter tendency leads to a universalism that transcends ethnic boundaries. The tension between these opposing impulses
leads to one of the major unresolved questions for the congregation: Should
the congregation exist solely for Korean Americans, or should it seek to minister to all people regardless of race?

The dilemma facing the GKPC English congregation is much like that
facing other Asian American evangelical ministries aimed at the second generation. In a recent article on Asian American evangelical college students,
Rudy Busto notes that a sampling of Web sites from Asian American campus ministries "reveals mission statements targeting Asian American students
for outreach and membership, while simultaneously affirming a non-race
specific evangelical identity" (1996, 138).

The English congregation's Sunday bulletin states their mission thus: "To
reach the 1.5 and 2nd generation Korean American college students and
working young adults who are unchurched, disciple them to Christ-like

maturity, and equip them for their service in the church and mission to the whole world, in order to glorify God's name."While this mission statement targets Korean Americans only, the *Jundosah* has said that he hopes the congregation will evolve into a multicultural ministry "as the Spirit leads."

Asking members of the congregation whether they agree or disagree with the *Jundosah's* vision for the future, I found broad support for the idea of multicultural ministry. Here, the responses reflected the universalism inherent in evangelical Christianity. One woman's response was typical: "I think [multicultural] ministry is right. I don't think people should just say 'it's Korean' or 'it's this' because we're all the same. We just look different on the outside. But we all have the same desires, we all have the same wants, we all have the same needs. . . . We could all understand each other and say, 'Hey, we're all God's children.'" One man who supported the move to a multicultural ministry expressed concern that the Korean-specific nature of the congregation interfered with evangelism to people of other races: "[The church] is just so Korean that even if you try to evangelize and try to bring people to church, it's really awkward. I mean, American people won't feel comfortable in an all-Korean church. Even during the sermon there are Korean jokes being passed along. So I think it's a barrier to evangelism, to Christianity. And I think it's a sin!"

Further questioning of the respondents, however, revealed some ambivalence, or at least the admission that the shift to a multicultural ministry would not be without costs. The cost most often mentioned was the loss of ethnic fellowship. Several people admitted that they would miss the comfort of having fellowship with other Korean Americans and the familiarity of the Korean church that they had been a part of all their lives. One of the English congregation deacons reflected on some of the difficulties she envisioned: "I think it will be a culture shock for a [non-Korean] coming in, and also for the Korean Americans who are used to seeing just Korean Americans all around. I think it will take time. It will take a lot of work ... because one of the reasons they are at a Korean church is so that they would feel comfortable in a Korean environment. But it's something that should happen."

A pattern I observed in a few interviews was a series of contradictory responses on questions related to ethnic fellowship and multicultural ministry. That is, respondents would first state their unequivocal support for multicultural ministry, then later reaffirm their desire to be part of a church focusing on Korean Americans. Perhaps this reveals that their views on the subject have yet to be fully worked out. At least one respondent realized her contradictory statements and apologized for giving "double takes" on the issue.

The English congregation has plenty of time to sort out its collective feelings about multicultural ministry. At present, there is no real effort being made to incorporate non-Koreans into the fellowship. Nor is it clear why any non-Koreans would want to come to this congregation when they have plenty of other options.[7] This is not to say that it is impossible for the congregation to move beyond a Korean-specific ministry if they so desire. But at present it is not clear that the majority of the congregation is willing to make the sacrifices necessary to bring this change about.

Conclusion

This case study illustrates the difficulty facing some second-generation Korean American ministries as they attempt to reconcile the conflicting tendencies toward particularism and universalism. Members of the GKPC English congregation desire fellowship with others who share their Korean backgrounds. At the same time, they find an ethnically exclusive ministry difficult to reconcile with an evangelical theology that proclaims that "all are one in Christ." The question of who should be included in the congregation—Koreans only or people of all races—has yet to be resolved.

As long as Korean Americans remain marginalized by their status as racial minorities, it is probable that this tension between particularism and universalism will continue to have an impact on the churches of the second and subsequent Korean American generations. And as Lincoln and Mamiya (1990) argue for the African American churches, we should not expect this tension to head toward any kind of Hegelian synthesis. Rather, we should expect Korean American churches to shift between polarities in time and space.

To speculate further about the future of the second-generation Korean American church, it is possible that we will see three different trajectories emerge in response to the tension described above. Some congregations may choose to minister exclusively to Korean Americans, perhaps formulating an appropriate theological justification[8] for this course of action. Other congregations may pursue multicultural ministry by actively reaching out to

7. I never observed more than two regular participants in the congregation who were non-Koreans. Both of these were friends of members of the congregation.

8. This theological justification could involve a belief that Korean American churches are superior (theologically and/or morally) to other American churches, as was found in the congregations in Chong's (1996) study. Alternatively, a Korean-specific congregation could maintain the belief that there is a division of labor among Christian ministries, with each ministry given a specific mission (field) from God. I have encountered at least one Asian American campus ministry taking this approach.

non-Koreans. This move could be fraught with difficulties, not least of which would be maintaining relations with a first-generation congregation that might not approve of opening the church to "outsiders."[9] Still other congregations may live with an ambiguous vision, focusing on the needs of Korean Americans while theoretically welcoming people of all races.

As Joe Kim from GKPC shared with me, second-generation church leaders have no blueprints to follow. In the final analysis, the future of the second-generation Korean American church remains open for them and their congregations to determine.

9. At present very few second-generation congregations exist independently from churches operated by the first generation. Since one of the latent functions of the Korean immigrant church is to provide a microcosm of Korean society (Hurh and Kim 1990), the development of multicultural ministries could face considerable opposition in some churches.

References

Busto, Rudy V. 1996. "The Gospel According to the Model Minority? Hazarding an Interpretation of Asian American Evangelical College Students." *Amerasia Journal* 22 (1): 133–47.

Chong, Kelly H. 1996. "Religion, Ethnicity, Authority: Evangelical Protestantism and the Construction of Ethnic Identity and Boundary Among Second Generation Korean-Americans." Paper presented at the Annual Meeting of the American Sociological Association, New York, N.Y., August.

Gordon, Milton. 1964. *Assimilation in American Life*. New York: Oxford University Press.

Greeley, Andrew M. 1972. *The Denominational Society: A Sociological Approach to Religion in America*. Glenview, Ill.: Scott, Foresman.

Herberg, Will. 1955. *Protestant, Catholic, Jew*. Garden City, N.Y.: Doubleday.

Huhr, Won Moo, and Kwang Chung Kim. 1984. *Korean Immigrants in America*. Cranbury, N.J.: Associated University Press.

——. 1990. "Religious Participation of Korean Immigrants in the United States." *Journal for the Scientific Study of Religion* 29 (1): 19–34.

Kibria, Nazli. 1995. "The Construction of 'Asian American': Reflections on Intermarriage and Ethnic Identity Among Second Generation Chinese and Korean Americans." Paper presented at the Annual Meeting of the American Sociological Association, Washington D.C., August.

Kim, David Kyuman. 1993. "Becoming: Korean Americans, Faith, and Identity—Observations on an Emerging Culture." Master's thesis, Harvard Divinity School.

Kim, Illsoo 1981. *New Urban Immigrants: The Korean Community in New York*. Princeton: Princeton University Press.

Lincoln, C. Eric, and Lawrence Mamiya. 1990. *The Black Church in the African American Experience*. Durham: Duke University Press.

Min, Pyong Gap. 1995. "Korean Americans." In *Asian Americans: Contemporary Trends and Issues*, ed. Pyong Gap Min, 199–231. Thousand Oaks, Calif.: Sage.

Williams, Raymond Brady. 1988. *Religions of Immigrants from India and Pakistan: New Thread in the American Tapestry*. Cambridge (U.K.) Cambridge University Press.

11

The Intersection of Religion, Race, Ethnicity, and Gender in the Identity Formation of Korean American Evangelical Women

Soyoung Park

THROUGHOUT U.S. HISTORY RELIGION has played an important role for immigrants, who use their religious traditions in the process of formulating their self-identity in a new social world (Williams 1988, 293). Religion functions as "a powerful scheme for secularizing the elements of identity and preserving them through the identity crises that are endemic to emigration" (278). It is one of the effective ways of helping immigrants construct and maintain their ethnic identity (Sheth 1995, 185).

The religious disestablishment and pluralism of the United States allows this integration of religion and ethnicity (Greeley 1971:117). Denominations often play ethnic or quasi-ethnic roles by providing their members with a sense of self-definition and social location (108). For example, there are Irish Catholics, Greek Orthodox, Dutch Reformed, and so on. Also, based on their experiences of slavery and racism, African Americans have established their own denominations and churches, such as the African Methodist Episcopal Church. Following this logic, ethnicity and race in the United States are often the skeletons of religion, providing the supporting frameworks, "the bare outlines" or "main features," of religion (Marty 1972, 9).

Korean immigrants are not an exception to this historical continuity. They establish their own ethnic churches and denominations in the United States, such as Korean Presbyterian Churches in America (KPCA), or their own ethnic ecclesiastical structures within American denominations, such as "Han-Mi," Korean American presbyteries in the Presbyterian Church in the U.S.A. (PCUSA). Similarly, their children also set up their own ethnic churches and parachurch organizations.

Within this milieu, the religious identity of Korean American evangelical women is largely shaped by their socialization in conservative Korean ethnic churches and contemporary American evangelicalism, focusing on a born-again conversion. As long as they confess their sins and accept Jesus as their personal savior and adhere to a strict evangelical morality, they achieve their religious identity as evangelical Christians.

Concerning their identity as Korean Americans, it is important to consider both race and ethnicity. According to the *Harvard Encyclopedia of American Ethnic Groups, ethnicity* is an inclusive term and is determined by common origins such as religion, language, and nation and by common biological characteristics (Petersen 1980, 235). Nevertheless, ethnicity is mostly used as distinct from race in the United States. Whereas *race* is usually applied to physical and biological differences and thus to nonwhites, *ethnicity* is predominantly used for Americans of European ancestry (235–36). Hence, ethnicity alone does not address the experiences of racial minorities such as African Americans, nonwhite Latin Americans, Native Americans, and Asian Americans (Omi and Winant 1994, 16). This study employs race and ethnicity to refer to the experiences of Korean American evangelical women derived from their Asian physicality and their Korean cultural heritage, respectively, although the distinction is not always easy to maintain.

Because Korean American evangelical women were born to Korean immigrants in the United States, they *acquire* their ethnic identity as Korean Americans. In this regard, their racial and ethnic identity is an individual sense of historical continuity with the past (De Vos 1975, 17). On the other hand, it is "emergent," created and sustained in relation to the larger U.S. society and to other racial and ethnic groups in the United States. That is, it is "a means of sociocultural adaptation," a "social" and "relational" construct in the United States (Morawska 1990, 214; Kivisto 1993, 99; Roosens 1989, 19; Yancey, Ericksen, and Juliani 1976, 392). Accordingly, the racial and ethnic identity of second-generation Koreans cannot be understood without considering their social contexts (Yancey, Ericksen, and Juliani 1976, 393; Yinger 1985, 162). One of the social contexts, as we shall see, is their place in the U.S. racial order, which complicates the formation of their identity.

Furthermore, the religious, racial, and ethnic components of their identity also interplay with their gender. Coupled with their evangelical views and stances on women, their contact with the larger U.S. society and with their own ethnic communities shapes their gender identity. As the term "Korean American evangelical women" denotes four threads of identity—Korean American (race and ethnicity), evangelical (religion), and women (gender), as briefly outlined above, this study explores the intersection between religion, race, ethnicity, and gender in the formation of their identity.

Method and Data

For this research, I studied the Korean Christian Fellowship (KCF), an ethnic evangelical parachurch organization of Korean Americans on college campuses. It is present at City College of New York (CCNY), New York University (NYU), Cooper Union, School of Visual Arts (SVA), Parsons, Hunter College, St. John's University, Rutgers University, Boston University, SUNY at Stony Brook, and so on. Each KCF is an independent club that is basically organized and operated by a group of Korean American students and a volunteer pastor or a seminarian without any affiliation with a local church, denomination, or higher governing body.

More specifically, I focused my research on the Korean Christian Fellowship at "Downtown University" (DU KCF) in a major metropolitan city in the Northeast region.[1] Having celebrated its seventeenth anniversary in April 1997, the DU KCF consisted of officers, pastoral staff, alumni staff, and small groups, with forty to forty-five students regularly in attendance. While conducting interviews with the DU KCF members, I also observed and participated in their weekly meetings, retreats, and revivals for about one year from 1996 to 1997. For the sake of comparison and breadth, in addition to other evangelical organizations such as the Asian American Christian Fellowship (AACF) and Multi-Ethnic Fellowship (MEF), the chapters of the InterVarsity Christian Fellowship (IVCF), I visited other ethnic groups on campus such as the Korean Campus Crusade for Christ (KCCC), the Korean ethnic chapter of Campus Crusade for Christ, and the Korean Students' Association (KSA), a nonreligious ethnic organization. I also interacted with volunteer pastors, officers, and regular members from KCFs at other schools.

---

1. The names of the city, university, informants, and interviewees have been changed. I have used Korean names and Americanized names in a manner parallel to the informants' real names. The interviews were conducted in English.

Evangelical Christianity, Race, and Ethnicity: Christian or Korean

Korean vs. Non-Korean

One of main theological tenets of evangelical Christianity is a born-again conversion experience. Since all human beings "fall short of the glory of God" (Romans 3:23), they have to confess that Jesus Christ died for their sins and ask him to forgive them for all their sins (Hunter 1983, 64; Warner 1988, 51). This emphasis on born-again experience assigns group identity, whether racial or ethnic, to secondary importance (Busto 1996, 138). As Grace explains, "I am Christian first ... Korean American second."[2] That is, gaining salvation takes precedence over being a Korean American. This personal, individualistic approach to their Christian confession leads Korean American evangelical women to develop "ontological individualism" and thus "stand alone before God" in separation from their social identity as Korean Americans (Roof 1993, 105).

As Korean American evangelical women interact with a variety of groups in their daily lives, however, they cannot always hold their religious identity higher than their racial and ethnic identity. However convincingly they claim that their religion is the most integral part of their identity—as Myung Joo claims, "[B]asically, it [my identity] comes down to Christianity"—they do not go to just any evangelical organization on campus, but mostly to the Korean Christian group.

Since members of campus parachurch organizations share a common evangelical subculture, they could ideally attend any fellowship without much difficulty. Whether they sit at the meetings of the KCF, the KCCC, or the AACF, they sing the same gospel songs and listen to similar messages. Whereas Korean American evangelicals attend the KCF or the KCCC, however, Chinese American evangelicals join the AACF, formerly the Chinese Christian Fellowship (CCF). Similarly, as contemporary evangelicalism puts emphasis on "witnessing for Christ" (Hunter 1983, 79), they often speak about reaching out to non-Christians and evangelizing them as their Christian duty. In reality, however, reaching out to a wider community rarely takes place, since they exclusively interact with their own coethnic evangelicals. As the special speaker for the annual retreat of the DU KCF, Keith Kim, claimed, "Koreans are too caught up with their own ethnicity."

In addition to their common cultural background as Korean Americans

2. Due to their commonality as Korean Americans and evangelical Christians, this study can also be applicable to the experiences of Korean American evangelical men. Hence, in illustrating the intersection of religion, race, ethnicity, and gender, I refer to my male interviewees as well as female.

in the United States, the status and experiences of Korean American evangelical women as a racial and ethnic minority are the main reasons behind their exclusive involvement with the KCF (Lee and Edmonston 1994, 102–3). Their Korean American identity indicates their socialization in the two worlds of the United States and Korea, from both of which they often feel alienated and marginalized. Due to their insufficient socialization in Korean culture, history, and language, Korean American evangelicals do not always understand what constitutes the Korean part of their identity. In this respect they are much like other children of immigrants, such as Indian Americans (Kurien 1998, 53) and Iranian Jews (Feher 1998, 81); that is, to the first generation they are not Korean enough. At the KCF, however, they enjoy common ethnic culture as an Americanized generation in the absence of their predecessors. For special occasions, such as the Christmas Banquet and the Anniversary Celebration, they cater and savor Korean food. They also have fun imitating their parents who speak English with a heavy Korean accent.

At the same time, at the KCF they can avoid any unpleasant experiences due to their race. Their Asian physicality means that they are not American enough to the eye of some Americans who are "still unaccustomed to thinking of Asians as part of the national landscape of humanity" and view them as foreigners or "sojourners" (E. Kim 1997, 70; Sung 1967, 267). For example, when they stopped by a gas station in a predominantly white rural area on the way back from their spring retreat, they remarked that the owner of the gas station acted as if he had never seen Asians before. They also express their objection to being called "Orientals," which denies them their specific identity as Korean Americans in the United States.

Korean Americans cannot simply be Christians in the larger society. Thus, there is a tension between their "pure" and "spiritual" identity as evangelical Christians, and their "cultural," "social," and "political" identity as Korean Americans. Hence, Korean American evangelicals find ways to explain why their seemingly universal religious confession mainly applies within their own racial and ethnic group. Above all, they claim that they feel "comfortable" in the presence of coethnics at the KCF, where they enjoy mutual support and acceptance. Explaining his lack of effort to evangelize the general population, one Korean American evangelical student admitted, "Koreanness is my limit, reaching out to other non-Koreans. . . . This is not easy. I don't socially fit in."

Furthermore, Korean Americans find a way to interpret their race and ethnicity through their evangelical Christianity. As Harry, the president of the KCF explained, "I think God created Koreans, so we should take pride in Korean cultures." Thus, their racial and ethnic identity claims its place as

God's creation in their evangelical confession. Moreover, for them it is precisely *because* of their Korean identity that they can reach out to other Korean Americans and witness to them more effectively and easily than to people of other races and ethnicities. They claim that there are still many Korean Americans who have not yet found Jesus Christ as their personal Savior and that a Korean identity links them together.

Their Korean identity also gains a special importance as to a world mission. The pastors and seminarians at Unity '97, an annual retreat of the KCFs in the Northeast, claimed that God has a special purpose for Korean Americans in evangelizing the non-Christian population in the world. God brought them to the United States, where they learn English and obtain American citizenship, in order that they can easily go to any country and win people over to Jesus Christ. They will be like the apostle Paul, who took advantage of his Roman citizenship. In a more local sense, the KCFs and their pastoral leaders frequently talk about their vision of evangelizing the entire campus, although reaching out to a wider community rarely takes place, as mentioned earlier.

In acting on their ideas, Korean American evangelicals create a Korean American version of evangelical Christianity that contributes to constructing and maintaining the boundaries of their ethnic identity (Swierenga 1991, 182; Rutledge 1985, 65). Their religious identity as evangelical Christians is used as a means of expressing their experiences as Korean Americans, as Claire admits: "If you are a Christian and a Korean, it might bind you closer to them. If you are a Christian, Korean, and American, that will truly help me sync with them a lot more. I really ... see that because that's kind of [person] I am."

Their experiences as Korean Americans are different from those of other racial and ethnic groups, even if they are also evangelicals. As a result, they "Korean Americanize" the "colorless" evangelical Christianity and thus bridge the gap between their experiences as Korean Americans and evangelical Christians. This example of religioethnic group identification occurs because Korean American evangelical women share a common ancestry and sociocultural experiences based on their race and ethnicity (Dashefsky 1972, 242–43).

First Generation vs. Second Generation

For the community of immigrants, religion becomes "a significant arena of negotiation" between first-generation immigrants and their children (Williams 1988, 287). As Chong (1998, 281) claims, some Korean Americans leave their ethnic churches, not out of rejection of Christianity but because of Korean cultural aspects of their churches such as the strict division of roles between men and women. They try to detach themselves from first-generation Korean communities without abandoning their religious faith (Lee, Chu, and Park 1993, 247). Thus, the foundation of the identity of second-generation Korean evangelicals becomes no longer Koreanness but evangelical Christianity (Chai 1998).

Within Korean ethnic churches, the liturgical style of second-generation Korean Christians often becomes one of the avenues through which they express the generational and cultural conflict with their parents (McGuire 1997, 62). Korean ethnic churches have separate worship services for different age groups, such as the nursery school, kindergarten, elementary students, a youth group (middle and high school students), and a young adult group (college students and singles). Among these groups, the youth group is a benchmark where second-generation Koreans are separated from their first-generation parents and develop their own subculture within their ethnic church.

The strict separation of the parents and their youth leads them to develop different religious and liturgical experiences. On the one hand, since second-generation Koreans do not regularly attend Korean-language services, they simply feel "disconnected" and "bored" at the adult worship service. On the other hand, the adults cannot worship with their children due to their lack of English language. When they come to the English-speaking services, they also feel out of place.

It is not only the language barrier that separates parents from their children but also the entirely different worship styles that coexist between the two groups, as shown in many Korean ethnic congregations (Chai 1998, 310). By and large, the settings in which the parents and their youth worship are different. While Korean-language services include the recitation of the Apostles' Creed, the Psalter reading, pastoral prayers, and traditional hymns accompanied by organ and piano, English-language services are mainly composed of two parts: the time of singing contemporary gospel songs accompanied by guitar, keyboard, and drum, and the delivery of a sermon.

For many Korean American youth, the lengthy format of the adult worship service appears to be superficial and less edifying than their fervent, emotion-filled, gospel-singing worship service. For example, one Korean American evangelical student describes the contrast between first-generation worship—that is, "formal" and "hypocritical"—and second-generation worship—that is, "true" and "spiritual." Judy also states this perspective well:

"They [second-generation Koreans] don't like hymns at all. They think hymns are really boring. They think, since parents sing hymns, they think it's so boring. They are like that." By dissociating themselves from the worship style of their parents, the youth try to distance themselves from Korean culture and language and thus construct their own autonomous culture and identity as second-generation Korean evangelicals.

Especially during adolescence, when they try to develop their autonomous identity in separation from their parents, they try to distance themselves from Korean identity as an attempt to conform to the larger society. To prove that they are "real Americans," they often try to become "whiter than white" (Lee, Chu, and Park 1993, 241). Judy explains this: "Second generations and 1.5 generations who speak more English . . . when they are in teenage years, they think Korean values are low."

Korean American evangelicals also protest against first-generation Koreans who emphasize Koreanness over Americanness. Their parents often tell them, "Speak Korean. Don't speak English all the time. You are a Korean. You have to know Korean." Furthermore, their parents remind them of their racial identity as Koreans by claiming that they cannot change how they look. As one Korean American evangelical woman describes, her parents tell her, "Look at yourself in the mirror. You are a Korean, not an American." As Korean American evangelical women choose their own brand of evangelical Christianity over their Korean American identity, therefore, they create an identity apart from first-generation Koreans and free from the confines of their race and ethnicity.

Social vs. Christian

The strong emphasis on a born-again experience and strict personal morality leads Korean American evangelicals to be apart from "social" and "secular" Korean Americans, who are usually affiliated with the Korean Students' Association (KSA), a nonreligious ethnic organization on campus. They distance themselves from those Korean Americans who are lenient about drinking, smoking, "clubbing," and partying and who are thus detrimental to their evangelical moral stance. Although ethnicity and race are still fundamental concerns for their organizational affiliation, they set themselves apart from nonevangelical Korean Americans whose activities appear to be antagonistic to their religious confession. In doing so, they consider social and secular ethnic students to be "the other," and thus the subjects of their evangelism.

In response, nonevangelical Korean Americans often feel that Korean

American Christian club members stigmatize them as only a partying and drinking crowd. Christina, the president of the KSA, upon finding out that KCF and KCCC members told new students not to go to the KSA, comments "How dare *they* criticize *us*." According to her, since they did not attend all the meetings and events held by the KSA, they were not eligible to make that judgment. In sum, KSA members consider their coethnic evangelicals as exclusive "separatists."

Another fundamental difference between Korean American evangelicals and nonevangelicals lies in fact that while the primary interest of the former is to pursue their religious ideals, that of the latter is to promote social interaction among Korean Americans and to learn about Korean ethnic culture. In contrast to the mission statement of the KCF, which is composed of evangelical doctrinal tenets, the freshman orientation flyer of the KSA articulates this purpose: "The Korean Students' Association has been established as the premiere Korean cultural club at DU. Simply stated, it creates a social atmosphere among DU students. [The] Korean Students' Association welcomes all individuals who are interested in learning more about Korean culture." In other words, while Korean American evangelicals socialize and form a family through their common confession of Jesus as Lord and Savior, their nonevangelical coethnics foster interaction through Korean cultural events and social events.

To illustrate this noticeable difference, while evangelicals played contemporary evangelical songs and presented gospel singing in sign language in their freshman orientation, the nonevangelicals played Korean popular songs and had their dance team present hip-hop dances. Their skits were also markedly different from each other. Whereas the skit of the KCF focused on Paul's image of the church as one body with different parts, the KSA presented a skit on finding dates and true love. Whereas the KSA holds Korean Culture Night every year where its members learn and demonstrate Korean dances, martial arts, and music, the KCF holds an annual revival where its participants sing gospel songs, pray, and listen to a sermon.

As John Y. Fenton (1988, 232) postulates, Asian Indian Christians lose touch with their ethnic culture more quickly than do those of other traditions because culture is deemphasized. Similarly, Korean American evangelicals will lose contact with Korean ethnic culture more quickly than their nonevangelical counterparts because they focus on their religion rather than on their ethnic cultural heritage. In this way, evangelical Christianity contributes to the formation of an intra-ethnic identity among Korean Americans.

Gender and Race: Woman or Korean

The experiences with gender relationships of Korean American evangelical women can be first detected from Korean ethnic churches and families, where social relationships and roles are based on the Confucian principle of seniority and the strict division between the sexes (Shon and Ja 1982, 209). In the case of Korean ethnic churches, since important leadership positions are mainly reserved for men it is not easy to see women pastors or elders. Whereas Korean men are located at the center of the church and behind the pulpit, their female counterparts are found in the pews and in the kitchen (J. Kim 1996, 96). It is not surprising that they often find first-generation Korean pastors and elders to be "distant," formal, and intimidating.

Furthermore, Korean immigrants from middle-class backgrounds in Korea experience severe downward mobility in their occupational adjustment in the United States and have limited opportunities for achieving social status in the mainstream society; thus the earning of ecclesiastical status enhances their mental health (Hurh and Kim 1990, 26–27). This is more applicable to Korean men than to Korean women, whose mental health is more directly related to having friends at their church than to holding titles, partly because they cannot have them, and thus they have lower expectations. The achievement of Korean men's church-related titles and positions often comes at the expense of Korean women's rights and privileges. Therefore, the male-centered structure of Korean ethnic churches and the strict division of roles between men and women can be oppressive to many Korean American evangelical women.

At home, Korean American evangelical women also encounter gender inequality. Even though the larger society has witnessed the gradual increase of autonomy and liberation for women, that is not the case for many working Korean women. For example, they carry out most domestic chores such as cooking, washing, and cleaning. When both a husband and a wife are employed outside the home, the wife continues to work after she comes home. In spite of their oppression, however, Korean American women are expected to renounce their interests and concerns about their equal rights in order to remain loyal to their ethnic group as a minority in the United States. In this sense they are a "double minority," suffering from sexism in their own community and racism in the larger society (Lee 1993, 202).

By contrast, Korean American evangelical women enjoy greater gender equality and leadership opportunities in their own religious organizations than in Korean ethnic churches. In fact, several female students describe the gender relationships in KCF to be equal. Women have been elected to leadership positions such as president, vice president, secretary, and treasurer. They also serve the KCF as small-group leaders.

In general, the KCF as a community of second-generation Koreans is more egalitarian than the communities of first-generation Koreans. Compared to the hierarchical and patriarchal culture of Korean ethnic churches, the leadership of pastors and seminarians at the KCF is peripheral, limited to their respective weekly speaking roles. Besides, the KCF is a student-centered and student-run organization where the members can develop a democratic and mutually accountable relationship with each other. As Hyo Jin, an alumni staff, describes: "Many people think that ministers are just pastors and youth pastors. But the best minister we can have is student . . . students ministering to one another." In the process, they also gain a greater sense of responsibility and unity.

The KCF as a second-generation Korean community, however, does not exhibit equal gender relationships in every instance. The pastors and seminarians who preach at the weekly meeting are predominantly male. The special speakers who are invited to speak at revivals and retreats are also exclusively male. During my research, I did not encounter any female guest speakers. This reflects the lack of women's leadership in Korean immigrant churches and Korean ethnic communities. By the same token, it demonstrates that Korean Americans seem more accustomed to seeing men than women as their religious leaders. As Claire, the only female pastoral staff of the DU KCF complains, KCF officers tend to turn to her at the last minute, after they fail to schedule male pastoral staff members or male guest speakers to speak at the regular meeting. Often disappointed and angry, she says that they take her for granted rather than seeing her as their spiritual leader as they would another man.

Furthermore, whether at DU or at other schools, the praise leader is usually a man. Praise is the time of gospel singing accompanied by musical instruments and followed by a sermon. While leading praise by singing and playing the guitar, the praise leader often suggests that the members might have neglected praying to God and reading the Holy Bible during the week, and that they need to renew their faith and their commitment as Christians. He also shares devotional and inspirational remarks. At times the remarks can become specific, containing words and phrases such as "sexual immorality," "temptation," "worldly," "purifying hearts and minds," and so on. Listening to them, Korean American evangelicals are expected to reflect on their lives and abandon "worldliness" in any form and adhere to "strict codes of personal morality" (Balmer 1989, 4). Since praise is an integral part of the regular meeting of many evangelical organizations, its leaders become very important, reinforcing and disseminating the evangelical doctrines and morality. These observations attest to the double-minority status of Korean American evangelical women, who face sexism from their own ethnic community and racism from the larger society as their mothers do.

During my research, I was also intrigued to notice that it was Korean American evangelical women who raised questions about the Confucian principle of seniority. For example, Judy says, "It's funny. I mean, these people cannot speak Korean, yet they adopt this seniority." According to another female member, it is acceptable that the seniors guide the juniors in a right direction and help them adjust to school life, as long as they do so "moderately." She argues that the underclass students do not want to always be treated as underlings, but as grown-ups. Tiffany claims that she tries to treat the first-year students "equally," not merely based upon age difference. While women were aware of the seniority principle's possible abuse and expressed their concern, their male counterparts took it for granted and adopted it to bond with younger members. This reflects the observation that Korean and Korean American men tend to be more traditional than Korean or Korean American women or than many American-born white men (Min 1995, 220).

Correspondingly, the gender socialization of Korean American evangelical women goes beyond their own ethnic boundaries, exposing them to women's studies in college and equal rights movements, which have made space for a variety of opportunities for women, as well as to various women role models in the larger U.S. society. This exposure can make them more sensitive to the practice of seniority than are Korean American men. In other words, Korean American women tend to look to the larger society, whose gender relationships are more favorable to them. On the contrary, their male counterparts show a tendency toward adhering to the traditional gender roles in their own ethnic communities, which benefit them more than women. Thus, although Korean American women and men have race and ethnicity in common, they are different in shaping their gender identity.

Evangelical Christianity and Gender: "Big" or "Little Bit" Feminist

As do evangelicals generally, Korean American evangelicals set their boundaries against radical feminism. For example, saying, "I am a little bit feminist," Judy differentiates herself from "big feminists," or radical feminists in the larger U.S. society. As I witnessed in one of the women's Bible study sessions, their goal was to become first "godly," born-again Christian women, not thinkers critical of patriarchy and sexism in society. At the same time, while distancing themselves from the feminists of the larger society, they do not seem to be exposed to the critical analysis of women's roles and places within evangelical feminist women in the larger U.S. society.

Similarly, God is always addressed using masculine pronouns in prayers, praise songs, and sermons. In my informal talk with two men, I changed their reference to the gender of God from "King" to "Queen." They immediately responded to me, saying, "Don't even go there." Since the Bible is always literally interpreted as the inspired Word of God, the practice of inclusive language is unacceptable to Korean American evangelicals, whether men or women.

Since feminism is often intertwined with liberalism, the women's uneasiness with feminism also reflects their ideological boundaries against liberalism. They are very careful in employing the term "liberal" to describe the characteristics of their club. As one alumnus claims: "KCF is liberal. I am not talking about a theology, but I am talking about activity-wise. . . . Basically, we decide what we are going to do, and we do it." To give another example, when referring to one seminarian as "liberal," one KCF member paused and then added, "Maybe more open-minded than liberal. It might be a better description." He seemed to be aware of the negativity attached to the term "liberal" within evangelical circles.

In recruiting a pastor or a seminarian for the KCF, these boundaries are equally applicable. Claire explains that the officers and pastoral staff are careful in choosing biblical and evangelical speakers, making sure to avoid "someone radical who might come up [with] a kind of concept that they [KCF members] might not understand. . . . They might take it in a wrong way." Although, as shown earlier, she complains that her female gender prevents her from assuming equal leadership of the KCF with male pastoral staff, she uses her role as a pastoral staff person to keep the KCF's evangelical identity intact. Although Korean American evangelical women demonstrate a more critical attitude toward gender relationships than their male counterparts, they are constrained by their evangelical boundaries against feminist and liberalism and share their common religious identity as evangelical Christians with them and with first-generation Korean Christians.

Summary

Based on these observations, depending on whether Korean American evangelical women relate to the larger U.S. society or to their own ethnic groups, religion intersects with race and ethnicity differently. In a society consisting of a variety of racial and ethnic groups, their race becomes a main principle in shaping their identity. The larger U.S. society considers their visible racial identity, not their religious identity, as the primary component of their identity. By contrast, since race is a common factor in Korean American groups, religion becomes dominant in the formation of their identity in separation from first-generation Korean Christians and nonevangelical Korean Americans. At the same time, since Korean American evangelicals focus more on their religion than on their ethnic culture, they formulate an identity different from that of nonevangelical Korean Americans or of first-generation Koreans who are interested in Korean ethnic culture rather than in religion per se. In terms of the interaction between religion, race, and ethnicity, Korean American evangelical women and men share common experiences both in their own communities and in the larger society.

As to gender relationships, however, Korean American evangelical women are different from their male counterparts. They are more liberal about gender relationships than Korean American evangelical men, being critical of the Confucian practice of seniority within their own ethnic organization. And yet evangelical theology leads them to share a common bond with their male counterparts while distancing them from the feminist women of the larger U.S. society.

Religion, race, ethnicity, and gender intersect differently depending on social relationships in the lives of Korean American evangelical women. Their relationship to the members of the larger U.S. society, to first-generation Koreans, and to other Korean Americans creates a web of social networks in which they construct and negotiate their identity as Korean Americans, evangelical Christians, and women.

References

Balmer, Randall. 1989. *Mine Eyes Have Seen the Glory: A Journey into the Evangelical Subculture in America*. New York: Oxford University Press.

Busto, Rudy V. 1996. "The Gospel According to the Model Minority? Asian American Evangelical College Students." *Amerasia* 22 (1): 133–47.

Chai, Karen J. 1998. "Competing for the Second Generation: English-Language Ministry at a Korean Protestant Church." In *Gatherings in Diaspora: Religious Communities and the New Immigration*, ed. R. Stephen Warner and Judith Wittner, 295–331. Philadelphia: Temple University Press.

Chong, Kelly H. 1998. "What It Means to Be

Christian: The Role of Religion in the Construction of Ethnic Identity and Boundary among Second-Generation Korean Americans." *Sociology of Religion* 39(3): 259–86.

Dashefsky, Arnold. 1972. "And the Search Goes On: The Meaning of Religio-Ethnic Identity and Identification." *Sociological Analysis* 33:239–45.

De Vos, George. 1975. "Ethnic Pluralism: Conflict and Accommodation." In *Ethnic Identity: Cultural Communities and Change*, ed. George De Vos and Lola Romanucci-Ross, 5–41. Palo Alto. Calif.: Mayfield Publishing Company.

Feher, Shoshanah. 1998. "From the Rivers of

Babylon to the Valleys of Los Angeles: The Exodus and Adaptation of Iranian Jews." In *Gatherings in Diaspora*, ed. R. Stephen Warner and Judith G. Wittner, 71–94. Philadelphia: Temple University.

Fenton, John Y. 1988. *Transplanting Religious Traditions: Asian Indians in America*. New York: Praeger.

Greeley, Andrew M. 1971. *Why Can't They Be Like Us? America's White Ethnic Groups*. New York: E. P. Dutton.

Hunter, James D. 1983. *American Evangelicalism: Conservative Religion and the Quandary of Modernity*. New Brunswick: Rutgers University Press.

Hurh, Won Moo, and Kwang Chung Kim. 1990. "Religious Participation of Korean Immigrants in the United States." *Journal for the Scientific Study of Religion* 29 (1): 19–34.

Kim, Jung Ha. 1996. "The Labor of Compassion: Voices of 'Churched' Korean American Women." *Amerasia* 22 (1): 93–105.

Kim, E. H. 1997. "Korean Americans in U.S. Race Relations: Some Considerations." *Amerasia* 23:69–78.

Kivisto, P. 1993. "Religion and the New Immigrants." In *A Future for Religion? New Paradigms for Social Analysis*, ed. William H. Swatos Jr., 92–108. Newbury Park, Calif.: Sage.

Kurien, Prema. 1998. "Becoming American by Becoming Hindu: Indian Americans Take Their Place at the Multicultural Table." In *Gatherings in Diaspora*, ed. R. Stephen Warner and Judith G. Wittner, 37–70. Philadelphia: Temple University.

Lee, Inn Sook. 1993. "Korean American Women and Ethnic Identity." *Korean American Ministry: A Resource Book*, ed. Sang Hyun Lee and John V. Moore, 192–214. Louisville, Ky.: General Assembly Council—Presbyterian Church (U.S.A.).

Lee, Sang Hyun, Ron Chu, and Marion Park. 1993. "Second Generation Ministry: Models of Mission." In *Korean American Ministry: A Resource Book*, ed. Sang Hyun Lee and John V. Moore, 233–55. Louisville, Ky.: General Assembly Council-Presbyterian Church (U.S.A.).

Lee, Sharon M., and Barry Edmonston. 1944. "The Socioeconomic Status and Integration of Asian Immigrants." In *Immigration and Ethnicity*, ed. Barry Edmonston and Jeffrey S. Passel, 101–32. Washington, D.C.: Urban Institute Press.

Marty, Martin E. 1972. "Ethnicity: The Skeleton of Religion in America." *Church History* 41 (March): 5–21.

McGuire, Meredith B. 1997. *Religion: The Social Context*. Belmont, Calif.; Albany, N.Y.; and Bonn: Wadsworth Publishing Company.

Min, Pyong Gap. 1995. "Korean Americans." In *Asian Americans: Contemporary Trends and Issues*, ed. Pyong Gap Min, 199–231. Thousand Oaks, Calif.: Sage.

Morawska, Ewa. 1990. "The Sociology and Historiography of Immigration." In *Immigration Reconsidered: History, Sociology, and Politics*, ed. Virginia Yans-McLaughlin, 187–238. New York: Oxford University Press.

Omi, M., and H. Winant. 1994. *Racial Formation in the United States from the 1960s to the 1990s*. New York: Routledge.

Petersen, W. 1980. "Concepts of Ethnicity." In *The Harvard Encyclopedia of American Ethnic Groups*, ed. Stephan Thernstrom, 234–42. Cambridge: Harvard University Press.

Roof, Wade Clark. 1993. *A Generation of Seekers: The Spiritual Journeys of the Baby Boom Generation*. New York: HarperCollins.

Roosens, Eugeen E. 1989. *Creating Ethnicity: The Process of Ethnogenesis*. Newbury Park, Calif.; London; and New Delhi: Sage Publications.

Rutledge, Paul. 1985. *The Role of Religion in Ethnic Self-Identity: A Vietnamese Community*. Lanham: University Press of America.

Sheth, Manju. 1995. "Asian Indian Americans." In *Asian Americans: Contemporary Trends and Issues*, ed. Pyong Gap Min, 169–98. Thousand Oaks, Calif.: Sage.

Shon, Steven P., and Davis Y. Ja. 1982. "Asian Families." In *Ethnicity and Family Therapy*, ed. Monica McGoldrick, John K. Pearce, and Joseph Giordano, 208–28. New York: Guilford Press.

Sung, Betty L. 1967. *The Story of the Chinese in America*. New York: Collier Books.

Swierenga, Robert P. 1991. "Religion and Immigration Behavior: The Dutch Experience." In *Belief and Behavior: Essays in the New Religious History*, ed. Philip R. Vandermeer and Robert P. Swierenga, 164–88. New Brunswick: Rutgers University Press.

Warner, R. Stephen. 1988. *New Wine in Old Wineskins: Evangelicals and Liberals in a Small-Town Church*. Berkeley, Los Angeles, and London: University of California Press.

Williams, Raymond B. 1988. *Religions of Immigrants from India and Pakistan: New Threads in the American Tapestry*. Cambridge (U.K.): Cambridge University Press.

Yancey, William L., Eugene P. Ericksen, and Richard N. Juliani. 1976. "Emergent Ethnicity: A Review and Reformulations." *American Sociological Review* 41 (3): 391–403.

Yinger, J. Milton. 1985. "Ethnicity." *Annual Review of Sociology* 2:151–80.

Part *IV*

BUDDHISMS IN
NORTH AMERICA

12

The Growth of Korean Buddhism in the United States, with Special Reference to Southern California

Eui-Young Yu

SINCE THE IMMIGRATION ACT OF 1965 removed the severe restrictions on Asian immigrants, the Korean population in the United States has experienced an accelerated growth. The number of Koreans in the United States increased from about 70,000 in 1970 to more than one million in 1999. About one-third of all Koreans in the United States live in California, concentrated especially in Southern California. As of 1999, approximately 300,000 Koreans reside in Los Angeles and Orange counties.

There are approximately 650 Christian churches, 20 Buddhist temples, and 150 Korean secondary associations. Thirty-two newspapers, three television stations, and two 24-hour radio stations serve Koreans in Southern California.[1] These organizations provide a basic network for the dispersed immigrants to interact with each other and form an associational community.[2] They conduct cultural and artistic activities, maintain strong ethnic ties, and adhere to their linguistic and cultural traditions through these organizations.

Religious institutions play an especially important role in the Korean

---

1. Figures given here are the author's estimates as of 2000, based on information from various community sources.

2. Illsoo Kim, *New Urban Immigrants: The Korean Community in New York* (Princeton: Princeton University Press, 1981).

community. A number of surveys conducted in Los Angeles, New York, and Chicago reveal that about 70 percent of Koreans are affiliated with Christian churches.[3] While the proportion of Buddhists is not clearly determined, a survey conducted in the Los Angeles Korean community in 1981 showed that 5.3 percent of the respondents identified themselves as such.[4] Do Ahn Sunim, a leading monk in the Los Angeles Buddhist community, estimates, however, that about 15 percent of Koreans in Southern California are Buddhists.

Korean churches in America, whether Christian or Buddhist, not only respond to the spiritual needs of the community but also perform a variety of secular functions. Churches are the focal point of social interaction for the majority of the immigrants and the center of their community life. Korean values and traditions are reinforced through church activities. Most large-size churches maintain Korean language and culture programs; worship and other church programs are conducted mainly in Korean. Buddhist temples, although small in number and membership compared to Christian churches, maintain similar functions and activities.

There are three distinct paths by which Korean Buddhism is being rooted in American soil. One is through the work of individual Zen teachers. They work on individual bases, and their main targets are Westerners. Such activities began in 1964 when Seo Kyongbo Sunim came to visit America and started giving dharma talks to small groups of people in the New York area. A few years later, in 1972, Seung Sahn Sunim began organized Zen activities in Providence, Rhode Island. Several other Zen masters have been particularly active in spreading Korean Buddhism to American, Canadian, and European audiences.

Another method of spreading Buddhism has been through the activities of temples located in cities where Koreans are concentrated. Since the first Korean temple appeared in Carmel, California, in 1972, the number has since grown to sixty-seven temples with about 25,000 active members.[5] The Won Kak Sa temple (Abbot: Bop An) in New York draws approximately 300 worshipers (a little over one-tenth of the 2,500 registered members) to its Sunday *pophoe* (worship service).[6] Dae Won Sa in Honolulu also has 2,500

3. Won Moo Hurh and Kwang Chung Kim, *Korean Immigrants in America* (Rutherford: Fairleigh Dickinson University Press, 1984); Bok Lim C. Kim, *The Korean-American Child at School and at Home* (Urbana, Ill., 1980); Eui-Young Yu et al., eds., *Koreans in Los Angeles: Prospects and Promises* (Los Angeles: Koryo Research Institute and Center for Korean American and Korean Studies, California State University, 1982).

4. The survey covered 301 Korean households randomly selected from telephone directories of Los Angeles and Orange Counties. The author was a codirector of the survey.

5. According to Abbot Do Ahn Sunim of the Kwan Um Sah temple in Los Angeles.

6. Telephone interview with Park Sung Bae, March 1988.

registered members.[7] The average attendance at Sunday *pophoe* at the Kwan Um Sa temple in Los Angeles is about 150. The temple has 670 registered members. In Los Angeles, there are fifteen temples that conduct their services in Korean and mainly serve the needs of first-generation Korean immigrants.

The third path has been through research and teaching by scholars specializing in Korean Buddhism. These scholars are making contributions by writing books in English and teaching courses on Korean Buddhism in American universities. Several Ph.D.'s have been awarded to scholars specializing in Korean Buddhism.[8]

Korean Zen Teachers

Several Korean monks have actively engaged in promoting Korean *Son* (Zen, or meditation) Buddhism in North America. Due to their efforts, the number of Zen centers (as well as the number of American and Canadian followers) has increased greatly in recent years. Their activities are all on an individual basis, and there has been no coordinated effort between them. Although they all stress meditation, their approaches and emphases vary significantly.

The Korean monk who started Zen teaching in America was **Seo Kyungbo Sunim,** who visited Columbia University in 1964 and stayed in the country for six years. He moved from one city to another giving talks on Korean Buddhism. "I employed a unique method of using the rented house as a temple site. So whenever I moved to a new place, I was able to meet more people and teach Buddha's message to the American audience," he recalls.[9] Returning to Korea, he served as dean of the Buddhist College at Dong Kuk University.

Since 1973 he has made frequent visits to America, delivering dharma talks to both Korean and American audiences. He has also held numerous calligraphy exhibitions. He is president of the Il-Bung Zen Buddhist Association, which coordinates activities of his affiliated groups. His American disciples number approximately forty. His selected poems and dharma talks have been translated and published in the book *Zen Mind Buddha Mind*.[10]

7. Interview with Jinwol Sunim, November 11, 1987.

8. They are Seo Kyungbo Sunim (Temple University), Professor Park Sung Bae (University of California Berkeley), Professor Robert Buswell (University of California Berkeley), and Bop An Sunim (New York University).

9. Interview with Joong Ang Libo, May 5, 1984.

10. Seo Kyung Bo Sunim, *Zen Mind Buddha Mind* (Seoul: Hoam Choolpan Sa, 1985).

A disciple of Seo Kyungbo Sunim, **Kosung Sunim** came to America in 1969 and has been active in the East Coast cities. Later, he established the Bulkuk Sa (now Hankook Sa) temple in the Washington, D.C., area. In 1976 he established the Seneca Zen Center and American Zen College on a large property in Germantown, Maryland, serving both the American and Korean followers.[11]

Master Kusan of Songgwang Sa made his first visit to the United States in order to inaugurate the Sambo Sa temple in Carmel, California, in 1972. Some of the American audiences he met on the trip returned with him to Korea to receive a traditional Korean Zen training. Later he established the Bul-il International Meditation Center to coordinate the training activities of foreign followers interested in the practice of Korean Zen. Since then scores of his foreign followers have undergone Zen training in Songgwang Sa. In 1976 *Nine Mountains,* a collection of Master Kusan's Zen teachings, was published in Seoul.[12] In 1980 he inaugurated the Korea Sa temple in Los Angeles as the first foreign branch temple of Songgwang Sa. The temple mainly serves Koreans in Los Angeles. He also delivered many lectures and speeches at universities and community gatherings. In 1983 he toured the United States and Europe, delivering lectures and establishing the Bulsung Sa temple in Geneva. Another book by Kusan Sunim, *The Way of Korean Zen,* was published in New York and Tokyo in 1985.[13]

Samu Sunim (one of the two dharma disciples of Solbong Sunim) came to the United States in 1967 and established the Zen Lotus Society in New York in 1968. Later that year he moved to Montreal. In 1972 he moved to Toronto, and after a three-year solo retreat in his basement apartment, he began to teach Zen. The current membership in the Toronto temple is about 170 (mostly Americans). Children's *pophoe* is conducted once a month.[14]

In 1981 Samu Sunim started a temple in Ann Arbor, Michigan.[15] The director of the Ann Arbor temple is Sudha Sunim, a Canadian who has been a Zen teacher for ten years. Two additional Zen workers reside at the temple, which is a four-story building including the basement. The living room is used as a meditation hall, and there is no Buddha hall in the temple.[16] The membership of the Ann Arbor temple is about seventy (all Americans). Sunday *pophoe* is attended by twenty to sixty members on the average. About

11. Sam-Woo Kim, *Zen Buddhism in North America* (Toronto: Zen Lotus Society, 1986), 18.

12. Ibid., 21.

13. Kusan Sunim, *The Way of Korean Zen,* trans. Martine Fages, ed. Stephen Batchelor (New York: Weatherhill, 1985).

14. Telephone interview with Samu Sunim, March 1988.

15. Sam-Woo Kim, *Zen Buddhism in North America,* 26–28.

16. Interview with Sudha Sunim, March 1988.

twenty Korean students from the University of Michigan go to temple on Sundays and conduct their own *pophoe* (in Korean) when Samu Sunim is there. The children's *pophoe* is conducted in English with an attendance of eight to ten. The daily meditation sessions are attended by ten to twelve persons on the average. According to Sudha Sunim, Samu Sunim emphasizes the development of American Buddhism rather than focusing on ethnic Buddhism, and the groups under Samu Sunim's leadership are called the North American Buddhist Order.

In 1984 Samu Sunim visited Mexico, and in the following year El Centro Zen Loto de Mexico was born in Mexico City. The Mexican temple is directed by Doyun Sunim (Edith La Brely). Two additional Zen groups have recently been established in Mexico under the leadership of Samu Sunim, one in Moralia and another in Cuernavaca.

Samu Sunim serves as president of the Zen Lotus Society, which functions as the umbrella organization for eight meditation groups under his leadership: Zen Buddhist temple in Toronto, Zen Buddhist temple in Ann Arbor, meditation groups in London (Ontario) and Ottawa, El Centro Zen Loto de Mexico, and two other meditation groups in Mexico.[17]

The Buddhist Institute of Canada, which was established by Samu Sunim in Toronto, coordinates a series of lecture and training sessions throughout the year. So far six people have completed dharma teacher training programs at the institute, and eighteen people are currently undergoing the training. The training program at the institute lasts between three to five years and consists of 300-day meditation, study, and practice sessions each year. Instructors are mostly affiliated with McGill University, the University of Toronto, and the University of Michigan, according to Samu Sunim. The Ann Arbor temple sponsors Summer Lectures that are attended mostly by Americans. The instructors are poets, writers, and professors, many of who are affiliated with the University of Michigan.[18]

In order to channel meditation to social action, Samu Sunim established the Buddhists Concerned for Social Justice and World Peace in 1987. He has actively voiced his concerns about various issues related to social justice, democratization, and world peace. He travels extensively and stays in Mexico for one month a year on the average.

Since 1981 the Zen Lotus Society has published a quarterly journal, *Spring Wind-Buddhist Cultural Forum*. The society published a booklet, *Zen Buddhism in North America* in 1986. *The Zen Lotus Society Handbook* (1986) includes a

---

17. Sam-Woo Kim, *Zen Buddhism in North America,* 28; telephone interview with Samu Sunim, March 1988.

18. Sam-Woo Kim, *Zen Buddhism in North America,* 29.

detailed autobiographic sketch of Samu Sunim and describes activities of the affiliated temples and groups.

Myobong (formerly Daesoo) Sunim is the dharma disciple of Hyeam Sunim (the last surviving dharma disciple of the great Zen master Man'gong Sunim) and carries on the work of his teacher at the Neungin Sunwon temple (Hoso Son Academy: Western Son Academy) in Irvine, California. He first came to the United States in 1972. Feeling that this way of teaching *Son* (Zen) was not going well, he went back to Korea and received Zen training under Hyeam Sunim at the Soodok Sa temple. He returned to the United States and established the Neuning Sunwon temple in Mission Viejo in 1980. When he parted ways with another monk at the temple in 1982, one of his disciples invited him to open a temple in Huntington Beach. The temple moved to rented quarters again in Irvine in 1984.

Myobong Sunim feels that his emphasis on *Whadoo* (Kong-an: dharma dialogue) has gained momentum since 1984. He emphasizes the importance of dialogue on an individual basis. So far ten of his disciples have become monks or nuns adopting his methods of Son (Zen). About twenty additional persons are regular members undergoing training at the Zen groups he has established in California and Texas. Myobong Sunim travels frequently to lead Korean Son (Zen) sessions for these groups. He is currently working on a translation of IljoTankyong.

Myobong Sunim feels that the individual encounter through dialogue *(Whadoo)* is the best approach to Zen. He regrets that most of the Korean monks and nuns working in the Korean community are not practicing Zen because they have to struggle to make a living. He feels strongly that in order for Korean Buddhism to take a firm hold in American soil, this situation must change. Myobong Sunim translated and published a bilingual (Korean and English) text on master Hyeam's Son teaching in 1986.[19]

Simwol Sunim (Julie Moigaard: Myobong Sunim's first American disciple) is the Abbot of Neungin Sunwon. Its daily programs are coordinated by Yongjo Sunim and an Ecuadorian nun who became Myobong Sunim's disciple in 1986 and later a nun. Daewoo Sunim (Ken King) is another regular member of the Sunwon. Daily meditation sessions are held at 10:30 A.M. and 6:00 P.M. Three people are staying in the Sunwon. They make a living and contribute to paying the rent by delivering papers in the early morning hours. The Sunday *pophoe* (they call it the "retreat") consists of meditation, chanting, dharma talk, and feasting with a vegetarian diet. Approximately

19. Hyeam Sunim, ed., *Gateway to Son* (Ch'an), trans. Myobong Sunim (Irvine, Calif.: Hoso Son Academy, 1986).

thirty people regularly attend the retreat. The attendance increases when Myobong Sunim is present, according to Yongjo Sunim.

Seung Sahn Haeng Won Sunim (his foreign disciples call him Soen Sa Nim) has been the most active monk proselytizing Korean Zen Buddhism in North America and Europe. His emphasis on "doing-together" meditation is gaining a wide acceptance among Westerners. With his pleasant personality and strong leadership, he is building a strong network to promote Zen Buddhism worldwide.

Seung Sahn Sunim came to America in 1972 at the invitation of Yu Young Soo, a friend and Dong Kuk University alumnus. He started Zen teaching in Kingston, Massachusetts, to a group of college students whom professor Jong Sun Kim brought. The number of followers grew, and he soon moved to Providence, Rhode Island. On October 10, 1972, he established the first Providence Zen Center and the KBC (Korean Buddhist Chogye Order) Hong Poep Won in Providence. This organization oversaw Buddhist groups under his direction. Chung Jung Dahr Sunim joined him briefly in Providence. At Brown University he met Dr. Leo Pruden, who came to his aid and provided the translation for the dharma talks.

By 1975 three other Zen centers were established in New York, Cambridge, and New Haven, all under his leadership. By 1979 five more Zen centers had formed under his direction. By 1982 approximately one thousand students were receiving meditation training in ten Zen centers established by him in the United States and Canada. The Head Temple (Providence Zen Center) in rural Cumberland grew into a respected residential training center, and intensive meditation retreats (90-day *Kyol ches*) were initiated.[20]

In August 1983 Seung Sahn Sunim founded the new Kwan Um Zen school in order to accommodate the western Bodhisattva monks, who are married, and dharma teachers, who are lay believers. The membership of the Kwan Um Zen School as of 1986 totaled 285, the main body of which consisted of dharma teachers.[21] The school coordinates activities of the forty-five Zen centers and groups established under his leadership. Jacob Perl is the abbot, and Richard Streitfeld is the director. The school publishes the monthly newsletter and the quarterly journal *Primary Point,* which has become an important means for spreading the Seung Sahn's teaching worldwide.

In 1984 the Diamond Hill Zen Monastery was established at the Head Temple complex in Cumberland for the traditional monks who would remain celibate and follow the Korean style of training. As of 1986 there

20. Dianna Clark, ed., *Only Doing It for Sixty Years* (Cumberland, R.I.: Kwan Um Zen School, 1987), 31.
21. Sam-Woo Kim, *Zen Buddhism in North America,* 21–26.

were eight monks and one nun of the school who were leading the lifestyle of the traditional monks of the Korean Chogye Order.[22]

According to Seung Sahn Sunim, forty-five Kwan Um Zen centers and affiliated groups have been established throughout the world: thirteen in the United States, two in Canada, ten in western Europe, fifteen in Poland, two in Brazil, and three in Korea. Seung Sahn Sunim says that approximately 2,500 Americans and 1,500 Europeans have received O-Kye (the Five Precepts) through these establishments. In addition, more than 50,000 people have become interested in Buddhism, although they have not yet received O-Kye. According to Seung Sahn Sunim, approximately 250 Americans, 60 Poles, and 20 Europeans have become Ilban Popsa (Dharma Teachers). Thirty of these are designated as Seondo Popsa, who counsel and teach Ilban Popsa. At the top of the lay leadership is Jido Popsa (Master Dharma Teacher), who acts as Seung Sahn Sunim's deputy in his absence. Seung Sahn Sunim has given authorization to teach and lead retreats to eight (seven Americans and one Pole) of his Jido Popsa. They travel to different Zen centers of the Kwan Um Zen School to conduct the Yong-maeng Jongjin (intensive meditation retreat) for three to seven days and to lead Kido (a chanting retreat called "energy path").[23]

The Dharma Sah Zen Center in Los Angeles was established in January 1976 by Seung Sahn Sunim. The center is presently located at Cloverdale Avenue, a quiet residential neighborhood in West Los Angeles. Lincoln Rhodes came from the KBC Hongpop Won in Providence to establish the Zen center. He was affiliated with MIT when he met Seung Sahn Sunim at the Cambridge Zen Center in 1974. He established a Zen center in New York City under the guidance of Seung Sahn Sunim in 1975.

Lincoln Rhodes is optimistic about the future of Korean Zen in America because many people are tired of the materialistic orientation of society and are seeking spiritual enlightenment, which Korean Zen offers. According to Rhodes, some Americans are interested in meditation to sleep well, others to obtain good health, and still others to find and understand themselves. He is not sure about reincarnation or about the world of Nirvana after death. His main concern is how to live in the present world, according to his interview with a *Hankook Ilbo* reporter (April 30, 1976).

The daily schedule at the center starts with a 5:30 A.M. meditation; then comes 108 bows at 6:00 A.M., followed by 30-minute chanting (scripture recital) at 6:30 A.M. The morning meditation sessions are attended by three resident disciples and an additional three or four people from the outside.

22. Ibid., 26.
23. Ibid.

Kong-an sessions (intensive interviews with master dharma teachers) are held on Wednesdays. There are twelve regular members participating in Wednesday sessions. Altogether, about twenty people (including irregular members) attend the Wednesday sessions. Their activities include meditation, testimonial, chanting, and dharma talks. Most of the people attending the meditation sessions are Americans.[24]

Intensive meditation sessions (Youg-maeng Jongjin) are held from time to time in Seung Sahn's meditation centers. This is a three- or seven-day retreat involving thirteen hours of formal meditation practice a day. Although the emphasis is on sitting meditation, the programs include bowing, sitting, chanting, eating, and working. Interviews with the Master Dharma Teacher or with Seung Sahn Sunim are conducted during the retreat.[25] Seung Sahn Sunim visited Poland in 1978 and established the first Chogye Zen Center in that country. In the opening ceremony sixteen people received the O-Kye, according to the report in *Hankook Ilbo* (May 19, 1978).

Seung Sahn Sunim's Korean style of teaching Zen is earthly, syncretic, and vigorous, according to Samu Sunim, a Korean Zen teacher based in Toronto and Ann Arbor. Some describe Seung Sahn Sunim's method as an assimilated form suitable to the American setting, combining both Korean and Japanese ways of meditation.

Seung Sahn Sunim's disciples include some Koreans, but a great majority of his followers are Westerners. Altogether, eleven Koreans (including two second-generation Koreans) now hold the title of Popsa, according to Seung Sahn Sunim.

Six books have been published in English bearing Seung Sahn Sunim's name: *Only Doing It for Sixty Years; Dropping Ashes on the Buddha; Only Don't Know; Bone of Space; Ten Gate;* and *Compass of Zen Teaching.*

Research and Teaching Korean Buddhism in America

An important route by which Korean Buddhism is being transmitted to America is by way of research and teaching in universities and colleges. Several scholars are making significant contributions in this respect and are slowly building a solid theoretical foundation of Korean Buddhism in America.

Park Sung Bae, who has a Ph.D. in Buddhist Studies from University of California Berkeley (1979), is a professor and director of the Korean Studies

24. Interview with Ronald Ross, March 1988.
25. Seung Sahn, *Only Don't Know* (San Francisco: Four Seasons Foundation, 1982), 192.

Programs at the University of New York at Stony Brook. He teaches courses on Buddhism, Religious Traditions in Korea and Japan, and Introduction to Korean Culture. He has incorporated Korean Buddhism (its history; the theories of Won Hyo, Jinul, Sosan, and Han Yong Woon; Buddhist arts; and Son Schools) in these courses. He also directs a graduate seminar, Reading on Korean Buddhism. His book, *Buddhist Faith and Sudden Enlightenment* (SUNY Press, 1983), has been popular as a textbook in many universities. He co-authored with Lewis Lancaster at University of California Berkeley the book *Descriptive Catalogue to Korean Canon* (University of California Press, 1979).

In addition to these scholarly activities, Professor Park has been actively involved in promoting Buddhism in Korean communities on the West and East Coasts. He has delivered hundreds of lectures and talks on Korean Buddhism to Korean community groups since he arrived in the United States in 1969. He has been a leading member of the Won Kak Sa temple in New York. For several years, he led the general *pophoe* at the temple every second Sunday of the month.

Robert Buswell, also a Ph.D. in Buddhist Studies from the University of California Berkeley, is one of Kusan Sunim's foreign disciples who has become a productive Buddhist scholar. So far U.C. Berkeley has produced two Ph.D.'s in Buddhist studies with topics on Korean Buddhism. Robert Buswell is presently a professor at the University of California Los Angeles. At UCLA he has developed and taught courses on Korean Buddhism, an upper division lectures class on Korean Buddhism, and a graduate seminar on Readings on Korean Buddhism. These are probably the first and only courses on Korean Buddhism ever offered as a regular curriculum in American universities. Cho Seung Taek is a Ph.D. candidate in Korean Buddhism working under his supervision.[26] Professor Buswell's *The Korean Approach to Zen: The Collected Works of Chinul* was published in 1983 by the University of Hawaii Press. The book is the most important work to appear in English on Korean Zen Buddhism.[27]

Professor **Kim Kusan** is another Korean who has taught Korean Buddhism in an American university. He taught a course on Korean Buddhism to American and Third World students at the University of Oriental Studies in Los Angeles from 1981 to 1983, when the school was closed due to internal strife.[28] Since the early 1980s professor Kim has been a regular lecturer on Indian philosophy and Korean Buddhism at Buddhist lecture series sponsored by the Kwan Um Sa temple.

26. Telephone interview with Professor Robert Buswell, March 1988.
27. Sam-Woo Kim, *Zen Buddhism in North America,* 21.
28. Interview with Professor Kim Kusan, March 1988.

Buddhist Temples in the Los Angeles Korean Community

The appearance of Buddhist temples in Los Angeles coincides with the growth of Koreatown in the early 1970s. Korean immigrants were arriving in Koreatown in large numbers, and for the first time monks were able to visit the United States in significant numbers. Soon afterward Buddhist groups began to establish temples.

The first Korean Buddhist temple established in Los Angeles was Dahl Ma Sa, which opened on February 1, 1973. Out of this temple have eventually sprung some fifteen temples serving the Korean community in Los Angeles.

While activities of Zen centers targeting Westerners are focusing on sitting meditation, ethnic temples are largely centered around Sunday *pophoe*; scripture studies; ceremonies; chanting; and cultural, social, and fellowship activities. In contrast to the American emphasis on meditation, Korean

Table 12.1. Korean temples and Zen centers in the Los Angeles area, 1988

Name	Year started	Abbot	Order	Pophoe
Korean temples				
Sam Bo Sa[1]	1972	Mrs. Han Sang Lee	Cho Gye	yes
Won Bul Kyo	1972	Rev. Suh Se In	Won Bul Kyo	yes
Dahl Ma Sa	1973	Rev. Jung Do	Cho Gye	yes
Kwan Um Sa	1974	Rev. Do Ahn	Cho Gye	yes
Soo Doh Sa	1976	Rev. Kae jeung	Cho Gye	yes
Jung Hye Sa[2]	1980	Rev. Jung Dhar	Cho Gye	yes
Korea Sa	1980	Rev. Hyun Ho	Cho Gye	yes
Ban Ya Sa	1981	Rev. Pyong Il	Cho Gye	
Bo Moon Sa	1981	Rev. In Kwon	Bo Moon	yes
Hae In Sa	1981	Mrs. Mu Jin Dung	Cho Gye	no
Bop Hwa Hong Tong Won	1981	Rev. Won Kyung	Bop Hwa	yes
Bop Ryun Sa[3]	1985	Rev. Sul Song	Tae Go	no
Moon Soo Chung Sa	1985	Rev. Kyung Duk	Cho Gye	yes
Bop Wang Sa[4]	1986	Rev. Hyun Il	Cho Gye	yes
Dae Sung Sa	1987	Rev. Kwon Pob In	Cho Gye	yes
Bo Kwang Won	1988	Rev. Park Jong Mae	Cho Gye	yes
Yun hwa Sa	1988	Rev. Myung Soo	Cho Gye	yes
Zen centers				
Dharma Sa	1976	Rev. Seung Sahn	Kwan Um Zen school	
Hoso Son Academy	1980	Rev. Myo-bong	Cho Gye	

1: in Carmel City
2–4: in Orange County

practice is much more devotional and religious. Sunday *pophoe* attendance at Kwan Um Sa and Dahl Ma Sa temples averages more than one hundred adults. The attendance at Pyong Hwa Sa, Soo Doh Sa, Korea Sa, Jung Hye Sa, Pop Wang Sa, and Won Bul Kyo temples numbers between fifty and one hundred. Because of the Korean Buddhist tradition of not requiring members to attend Sunday services regularly, the *pophoe* attendance averages only about one-fifth of the registered members. Regular attendants tend to be mostly officers and their families. General members attend the *pophoe* only occasionally, and others attend on special occasions only. Some members never attend. On special occasions such as Buddha's birthday, therefore, several hundred worshipers flock to their respective temples.

The membership of Los Angeles temples has increased rapidly in recent years, and some former Buddhists who were attending Christian churches are now returning to Buddhist temples. For example, about 30 percent of the current membership in the Kwan Sa temple are former attendants of Christian churches, according to Do Ahn Sunim. About 20 percent of the members of temples at Pyong Hwa Sa are former Christians, according to Abbot Sung Do Sunim. The membership of Pyong Hwa Sa increased from 60 families in 1985 to 200 families at the end of 1987. Kwan Um Sa's membership was increasing by 150 families a year recently and now it has reached 670 families.

Until the 1970s all the temples in Los Angeles were using an apartment or single dwelling originally designed for residential use. The situation changed drastically when Dahl Ma Sa completed a spacious Korean-style *popdang* (worship hall) (1986) and Kwan Um Sa purchased a large temple formerly used as a Jewish synagogue (1986). Dahl Ma Sa's Korean-style *popdang* is conspicuous in the middle of Koreatown at the intersection of Olympic Boulevard and Wilton Avenue. Many local and national Buddhist events take place in the various meeting halls of the Kwan Um Sa temple, which occupies 37,000 square feet of floor space. Korea Sa, a Los Angeles branch of Song Kwang Sa, recently purchased a three-building complex (two two-story and one single-story building) at Ingraham Street. On the other hand, most other temples still use apartment buildings and experience problems related to zoning regulations.

Since 1974 Kun Sunim and other Buddhist scholars from Korea have given dharma talks and lectures at Korean temples.[29] These talks and lectures provide unique opportunities for Southern California Koreans, both believers

29. They included Seung Sahn Sunim, Kwsan Sunim, Seo Kyungbo Sunim, Yun Koam Sunim, Pop Jung Sunim, Sohn Kyong san Sunim, Chung Kwan Ung Sunim, Moo Jin Janf Sunim, Park wan Il Kosa, Lee Nung Ka Dae Seonsa, and Professor Park Sung Bae.

and nonbelievers, to hear the great monks of Korea. Sometimes several hundred Koreans flock to hear such talks. Bop Jung Sunim's appearance at the Hankook Ilbo auditorium on January 21, 1988, for example, drew a crowd of nearly five hundred.

Buddhist cultural festivals, lotus lantern festivals, musical events, and dharma painting and calligraphy exhibitions take place in parks, theaters, and galleries of Koreatown at frequent intervals throughout the year. The international Buddhist cultural festival held in early 1988 at the Wilshire Ebel Theater drew several hundred people. The festival was sponsored by Kwan Um Sa, and six different national Buddhist groups took part, presenting their traditional music and dance. Buddhist study seminars are regularly held at Kwan Um Sa. A locally based Buddhist newspaper, *Mijoo Bulkyo,* is also published, although at irregular intervals. Articles and news items related to Buddhist programs and activities frequently appear in local community newspapers.

Several temples maintain Korean language and cultural programs and provide many types of social services, such as family counseling and senior citizen support. Sunday school programs for children are being attempted at Dahl Ma Sa, Kwan Um Sa, and Pyong Hwa Sa. The Federation of Young Buddhists meets regularly for *pophoe* and scripture study. Sunims contribute dharma essays to local Korean newspapers and have been active in voicing concerns about social justice and democratization in Korea.

The abbot of Kwan Um Sa, Do Ahn, has been the leading monk in the Buddhist community of Los Angeles. He frequently contributes dharma essays to local Korean newspapers and magazines and publishes a Buddhist journal, *Bul Kyo Si Bo* (The Buddhist Times). He was instrumental in raising funds to purchase the $800,000 former Jewish synagogue and convert it into a spacious temple that has promoted Buddhist culture in the community by sponsoring Buddhist music, dance, and art festivals in the theaters and galleries of Koreatown since the early 1980s.

Do Ahn Sunim was elected cochair of the American Buddhist Congress at its first convention hosted by the temple in November 1987. Other cochairs elected were the Rev. Karl Springer Ratanasara, of Colorado, and the venerable Havan-pola Ratanasara, a Sri Lankan monk living in Los Angeles. The convention represented some fifty Buddhist groups in the United States.

Abbot Do Ahn attributes the rapid growth of Koran Buddhist temples to the general increase in the size of the Korean population in Los Angeles and also to the modernization of activities at the temples. The abbot notes church membership service and family counseling programs, including marriage and youth counseling, hospital visits, and arrangement for social security benefits. The church's van provides transportation for the elderly members. The temple operates with an annual budget of $120,000, most of which is expended for the temple's programs. The abbot lives in the temple and does not receive a salary.

Under Abbot Do Ahn's leadership, Kwan Um Sa has sponsored a regular lecture series on Korean Buddhism starting in May 1980. The series is held once or twice a year, each one lasting for one to three months. The 1980 series, which lasted three weeks, featured professor Park Sung Bae (Buddhist scholar), Lee Nung Ka Dae Seonsa (dharma master), and Dr. Ha Tai Kim (Methodist minister and scholar). The 1988 series lasted for three months with lectures given every Friday, Saturday, and Sunday for three hours each day. Shin Popta Sunim, Moo Jin Jang Sunim, and Professor Kim Kusan were regular lecturers, and guest lecturers included Popjung Sunim, Professor Park Sung Bae, Professor Lee Young Moo, and Chung Kwan Ung Seon Sa Nim. The curriculum dealt with Buddha's life, the history of Korean Buddhism, Indian philosophy, early Buddhism, the thought of Won Hyo and Jinool, Buddhist theories, and Kye Yool.

The Sunday *pophoe* in Korean temples is very informal compared to Christian church services. People move in and out at ease throughout the service. The service normally consists of hour-long chanting by priests, several Buddhist hymns, scripture recital, yombul (prayer), and a sermon. *Daejoong Kongyang* (fellowship lunch) follows the Sunday service in many temples. Most of the temples lack serious meditation programs, although a few are struggling to establish them.

Challenges and Promises

Korean Buddhism is slowly but firmly taking root in American soil. Through the works of Zen masters, Buddhist scholars, and monks working in the Korean community, the central message of Buddhism imbedded in Korean thought and culture—harmony, nonaggression, compassion, and benevolence to all beings—is gradually being transplanted to this new land. The number of Zen centers and temples spreading this message has increased to an impressive level, and a growing number of Americans and Koreans are accepting this message.

There are, however, many problems and challenges that the Korean Buddhist body in America faces. The most serious challenge lies in the creation of an effective organizational structure that can plan, coordinate, regulate, and improve Buddhist programs and activities. At the present time, most of the Korean Buddhist activities in the United States are conducted on an individual basis. Some individuals have shown remarkable strength in building their congregations, but there is no organizational network coordinating the works of Zen masters, monks in ethnic temples, and scholars. Many of the temples claim to be affiliated with the Korean Buddhist Chogye order, but there is no formal connection between individual temples and the order in Korea. Consequently, practices, behaviors, and lay members are not being evaluated or regulated.

Another challenge lies with the developing of a legitimate credential system for monks and lay leaders working in the Korean community. There is no agency or organization regulating the standard of conduct or the qualification of monks. Almost anybody can claim to be a monk and establish a temple. As a result, some of those claiming to be monks do not have any formal training. In fact, there are some establishments in Los Angeles that practice something quite different from Buddhism.

There is also a need to provide monks the opportunity to adjust to the new situation in America. A majority of Koreans in the Unites States are college graduates, and unless the monks' education level is at least on a par with them, it will be difficult to deal with the general public. Much of the conflict between priests and lay leaders in Korean temples is at least partly due to this discrepancy. Furthermore, most of the monks serving Korean community temples do not speak English adequately and cannot relate to the English-speaking younger generations.

Still other problems are related to the level of commitment of some of the monks working in the Korean community. Most of them came to the United States for purposes other than administering temples. Therefore, when they encounter problems, many simply leave the temple instead of trying to find a constructive solution. About fifty monks have left the priesthood after receiving the *youngjookwon* (permanent residency), according to an abbot of a Korean temple. In Los Angeles alone, there are about ten such former monks.

In addition, there is a need to reach second-generation Koreans and train some of them as monks or lay leaders; but training facilities are totally lacking. Developing an effective training program for lay leadership (like Seung Sahn Sunim's Zen center) may be a practical alternative for this problem. Second-generation Koreans growing up in the United States would probably be more interested in meditation than in the religious orientation of their parents, and future programs designed to reach the younger generation should incorporate meditation training.

Traditionally, the development and operation of programs at Buddhist temples is entirely left to the priests, and lay participation has generally been limited. The rise and decline of a temple is attributable for the most part to the monk's individual activity. This tradition of temple operation tends to discourage many able lay people from actively involving themselves in church programs. Therefore, the modernization of the organizational structure of individual temples remains another big challenge.

Financial difficulties often force monks to engage in menial labor, particularly in the beginning of temple establishment. Consequently, their images have been negatively affected. Sometimes monks are not decently treated by lay leaders. Under these circumstances, able monks are discouraged from coming to serve the Korean community. According to an abbot, there are not many incentives for able monks to immigrate to the United States to work in the Korean community.

13

Turning the
Wheel of Dharma in the West

Korean Sŏn Buddhism in North America

Samu Sunim (Kim, Sam-Woo)

THE FIRST KOREAN BUDDHIST CLERGY who traveled to the West were Paek Sŏng'uk (1897–1981) and Kim Pŏmnin (1899–1964). Paek Sŏng'uk traveled to Paris in 1920. In 1922 he went to Germany and studied Western philosophy. After receiving a doctorate in 1925, he returned to Korea. Kim Pŏmnin traveled to Paris in 1921. There he studied philosophy at the University of Paris. After graduating in 1926, he returned to Korea. Both Paek Sŏng'uk and Kim Pŏmnin were student monks. After their return to Korea, they became active in the young people's Buddhist movement. Through the 1930s up to 1945, Kim Pŏmnin was involved in Korea's independence movement and was imprisoned twice by the Japanese, while Paek Sŏng'uk devoted himself to Buddhist studies, his meditation practice, and training students. Following Korea's Liberation in 1945, Paek Sŏng'uk and Kim Pŏmnin actively participated in rebuilding the nation and contributed to the modernization of Korean Buddhism, particularly in the field of education.

The first Korean Buddhist priest who took up residence for the purpose of the propagation of Korean Buddhism in the West was Tough Chinho (To, Chinho, 1889–1986?).[1] In July 1930 Tough Chinho attended the first

---

1. Margaret K. Pai mentions meeting "the Venerable ninety-year-old Tough Chin Ho" in the 1980s without indicating the year. See Margaret K. Pai, *The Dreams of Two Yi-Min* (Honolulu: University of Hawaii Press, 1989), xii.

Pan-Pacific Conference for Buddhist Young People as a representative of Korean Buddhist young people. The conference was held in Honolulu, Hawaii, and organized by the Japanese Buddhists. In August of the following year, Tough Chinho returned to Honolulu to found the Koryŏ Sŏn-sa (Korean Sŏn Temple). This Koryŏ Sŏn-sa must have been the first Korean temple in the West. Unfortunately we do not know what activities were carried on at Koryŏ Sŏn-sa, nor do we know how long the temple lasted.

On July 5, 1978, Professor Yŏng-ho Ch'oe of the Department of History, University of Hawaii, had a long conversation with Mr. Tough (Chin-ho Do).

> When he arrived Hawaii in 1931 to assume the task of Buddhist missionary, the political situation of the Korean community in Hawaii was going through a bitter turmoil. He accepted ... the editorship of the *T'aep'yŏng-yang Chubo* upon repeated prodding from different people, on the condition that he would have the final authority on the contents and the editorial policy. Not satisfied with the acrimonious attacks exchanged by the organs of opposing organizations, he hoped to tone down the editorial and news contents of the *Chubo*. The subscription and advertisement fees were not sufficient to defray the cost of publishing the *Chubo,* and it was supported by the Dong Ji Hoi financially. When he worked for the newspaper, he was not paid. Since he came as a Buddhist missionary, he was not allowed to have gainful employment and had to depend on good-will support from his friends, such as Kim Sang-ho, who had a rooming house in downtown, and others.
>
> In January 1932, he was accused by Kim Chin-ho and Hyŏn Sun of having been sent here by the Japanese Government-General to spy on the Koreans, and some 800 people gathered at a Chinese restaurant to discuss the status of Mr. Do. Informed of this accusation, the Immigration and Naturalization Service called on him to investigate, in which he explained his innocence to the satisfaction of the Immigration and Naturalization Service. At one time he taught the Korean language and history at the Korean Christian Church in which he explained Buddhism in Korean history, and many criticized him for spreading Buddhism.[2]

Tough Chinho stayed on in Honolulu and eventually became an American citizen. From the late 1930s to the early 1940s he was involved in the overseas Korean independence movement as an active member of Tongji-hoe (the Comrade Society) of Hawaii, a political organization started by Dr. Syngman

---

2. Two pages of typewritten notes of professor Yŏng-ho Ch'oe dated July 5, 1978. I am indebted to Professor Ch'oe for this and other information on Tough Chinho.

Rhee. In 1946 Tough Chinho visited South Korea as one of the Hawaiian members of United Korean Committee in America and stayed for one year.

It was no coincidence that these three Korean Buddhist pioneers who traveled to the West separately were friends who worked together in Korea for national independence and Buddhist reforms. For instance, as active members of Chosŏn Pulgyo Ch'ŏngnyŏnhoe (Korean Buddhist Young People's Association), Tough Chinho, Paek Sŏng'uk, and Kim Pŏmnin played important roles in organizing the historic Chosŏn Pulgyo Sŏn'gyo Yangjong Sŭngryŏ Taehoe (Conference of Korean Buddhist monks representing both meditation and doctrinal schools), which was held in January 1929.[3]

In May 1930, Kim Pŏmnin, Tough Chinho, and other monks formed the Man Party, a secret anti-Japanese society, with the famous nationalist monk and author of *The Treatise on Revitalization of Korean Buddhism,* Han Yong'un (1878–1944), who was the real leader of the group, although he was never openly recognized as such.[4] All three priests received higher education abroad and pursued socially engaged Buddhism for the threefold purpose of promoting a youth Buddhist movement, Buddhist reform, and national independence. Their exposure to secular and liberal education abroad helped raise their social consciousness and awakening, which in turn led them to social activism.

However, the Buddhist activities of these three pioneers in the West suffered from the political situation in Korea. Korea was under Japanese colonial rule, so Koreans either had to endure the humiliation of carrying Japanese passports as Japanese citizens in order to travel abroad, or they had to go into exile. After graduating from the Buddhist college, Paek Sŏng'uk went to Shanghai in 1919 to assist the Korean Provisional Government there. Later he continued on to Paris to study. Tough Chinho had to convince other participants of the Pan-Pacific Buddhist Conference that he was representing Korean Buddhism as a Korean and not as a Japanese citizen.[5] This is just one example of how the independence of their motherland always preoccupied their minds.

However, Tough Chinho had other difficulties as well. He had to learn to get along with the Korean Christians who formed the majority of the Korean community in Hawaii. They were not sympathetic to Buddhism. Some of them became suspicious of his presence among them, partly because he was educated in Japan and initially came to Hawaii to attend a Buddhist conference

3. See Kwangsik Kim, *Han'guk Kŭndae Pulgyo-sa Yŏn'gu* (Seoul: Minjoksa, 1996), 315ff.

4. Ibid., 274ff. Also see Chŏng, Kwangho, *Kŭndae Hanil Pulgyo Kwan'gyesa Yŏn'gu* (Inch'ŏn: Inha Taehakkyo Ch'ulp'anbu, 1994), 146ff.

5. Kwangsik Kim, *Han'guk Kŭndae Pulgyo-sa Yŏn'gu,* 244ff.

organized by the Japanese Buddhists. The irony was that his fellow Buddhists on the island were all Japanese, most of whom supported and/or collaborated with Japanese imperialism. Many Korean Buddhist leaders and intellectuals felt that they were betrayed by the Japanese, who owed Korea for the Buddhist culture and advanced technology of their past. It seems that Tough Chinho chose to work with the Korean Christians in Hawaii for the Korean independence movement.

After Tough Chinho, it took more than three decades before another Korean Buddhist priest was able to make it to the West. In the intervening years, Liberation, political division of the country into Communist North and Capitalist South, American occupation in the South from 1945 to 1948, the Korean War from 1950 to 1953, the authoritarian rule of the Syngman Rhee regime, the April the 1960 Student Revolution, the Military Coup in 1961, and the *Minjung* Movement, all in the South, followed each other at a breathtaking pace.

Sŏn Buddhism in Korea

The nonethnic Korean Sŏn Buddhist movement in the West owes its beginning largely to the courageous efforts of three masters: Ven. Dr. Seo, Kyung-Bo; Kusan Sunim; and Zen master Seung Sahn. All three are from the Korean Buddhist Chogye Order, which represents traditional Korean Buddhism. It is important to know something about traditional Korean Buddhist thought and practice in order to understand the teachings and activities of these three masters. In the following section I will introduce three earlier monks who made critical contributions to the shaping of native Korean Buddhist thought and practice.

Wŏnhyo (617–686) was a great scholarly monk. But he was also a great popularizer of Buddhism. He lived close to common, ordinary people, often unrestrained. As a scholar he faced the daunting task of not only comprehending the vast array of varied Mahayana scriptures brought by Korean monks returning from China but also reconciling and harmonizing the diverse and contradictory teachings they represented.

Aside from his scholarly interests, Wŏnhyo must have been concerned with the possibility that the diverse and contradictory teachings of the different scriptures might confuse the minds of believers and that sectarian disputes could arise among the adherents of the different schools of teachings. After all, the country was small and could ill afford any serious dissension that would fuel national disunity. Wŏnhyo read widely and expounded on more than eighty texts. In interpreting them, he recognized their intrinsic nature of equality and unity and minimized their differences. The methods he used to achieve this were *hoit'ong,* or total understanding, and *wŏnyung,* or perfect interfusion. Over the centuries the spirit of *hoit'ong* as a means of achieving harmony and unity has been one of the main characteristics of Korean Buddhism. For this reason, Korean Buddhism has been often known as *t'ong pulgyo,* which means interdenominational or ecumenical Buddhism. For his work, Wŏnhyo is seen as the father of *t'ong pulgyo.*

However, Wŏnhyo was more than a thinker. He was also a "mad monk" who practiced "perfect interfusion" and "nonobstruction." He composed a song of "unlimited action" and sang and danced for people. He always urged the people to return to their "One Mind." He compared the One Mind to the great ocean mind, where all the waters return in order to enjoy peace, equality, emancipation, and unity.

The story of his awakening to this One Mind is well known. In 661 Wŏnhyo and his good friend Ŭisang (625–702) set out to travel to China in order to pursue the advanced study of Buddhism there. After days of traveling on foot, they retired one evening near a roadside grave mound. In the middle of a summer night, Wŏnhyo woke up with a burning thirst and was groping for water in the dark when he felt something in the shape of a gourd. He drank from it deeply. Refreshed, he went back to sleep. Waking up the next morning, he discovered that the vessel he drank from so sweetly was a human skull. Wŏnhyo became violently ill and threw up several times. Then he wondered if he had one mind or two different minds. The last night's experience was so sweet. Now when he knew what he had drunk—bloody rainwater—it made him sick. Suddenly his wisdom eye opened, and Wŏnhyo awakened to the great unknowing One Mind.

He saw no need to continue his journey to China, so he bade Ŭisang farewell. It was a heartbreaking experience for Ŭisang, but the two dharma companions parted. Ŭisang traveled alone to China. When Wŏnhyo returned home, people noticed a change in the scholarly monk's conduct and behavior. Wŏnhyo spent more time playing with the children on the streets and hanging out in the marketplace. In one of his trips to the downtown section of the capital city (now Kyŏngju), he met Taean (Priest Great Peace). This monk was so named because he always made people happy with shouts of peace and happiness and great chuckles. Wŏnhyo learned *minjung pulgyo* (the way of people's Buddhism) from Taean and served him as his student.

Wŏnhyo followed the ways of commoners and slept with women, drank wine, and played music. Now, as a fallen monk, he called himself "a lowly layman." With deep humility and reverence, the lowly layman "would enter

232 | Korean Americans and Their Religions

taverns and brothels"[6] in order to share Buddhism with society's underbelly. However, his Buddhism did not exclude high Buddhism, because he continued to write commentaries on the sutras and was invited by the court to give lectures. Basically, he was free and happy to "do as he pleased according to the occasion, without schedule or restriction."[7] Whether it was sacred or profane, the ultimate or conventional path, for Wŏnhyo everything served as a nondual gate of liberation and the practice of "perfect interfusion and non-obstruction."

People who admired him addressed him as Great Master Wŏnhyo, while people who had contempt for him just called him lowly "layfart." But Wŏnhyo taught them all the dance of nonobstruction so they could become free from the two basic hindrances. The movement of the dance consisted of raising the left foot with a bent knee and stretching out one's right sleeve into the sky in order to exorcise attachment to one's self, and raising right foot with bent knee and stretching out one's left sleeve into the sky in order to drive away one's delusion of assuming thoughts and feelings are real. For his efforts to harmonize and reconcile differences and to establish peace and harmony, Wŏnhyo was honored posthumously as the "National Teacher Who Harmonizes Disputes."

Like Wŏnhyo, who never had a formal teacher or traveled to China, Chinul (1158–1210) was a self-trained, homegrown master. Chinul had three Awakenings, all while he was reading scriptures. One of the scriptures he read was *Avatamsaka Sutra* (Flower Adornment Scripture). Chinul was a Sŏn monk. He practiced meditation eagerly but had no formal teacher, so he relied on Sŏn literature and sutras to guide his practice. Chinul was concerned with the tension and split between Sŏn practice and doctrinal schools that had been building up in the *sangha* (community) during the eleventh and twelfth centuries. Therefore, using his own understanding of the scriptures, he incorporated doctrinal teachings into Sŏn practice and promoted the basic unity of Sŏn and doctrinal teachings. His role was to promote interdenominational Buddhism from the standpoint of Sŏn—that is, that "Sŏn is the mind of Buddha and sutra the words of Buddha."

Unlike Wŏnhyo, Chinul pursued a monastic life. He lamented the worldly life of the Buddhist clergy of his time and formed a Community for the Cultivation of Samādhi (Meditation) and Prajñā (Wisdom) with his like-minded friends. At a retreat center called Susŏn-sa, which he established at the present-day Songgwang-sa for the purpose of cultivation of meditation and

6. Peter H. Lee, *Sourcebook of Korean Civilization*, vol. 1, *From Early Times to the Sixteenth Century* (New York: Columbia University Press, 1993), 140.
7. Ibid.

wisdom, Chinul introduced pure rules for the training of monks and urged the student monks to read the scriptures as well as do meditation practice and manual work. The establishment of Samādhi-Prajñā Community served as a reform movement and inspired retreat community movements for more than two centuries.

Chinul is also known for his systemization of Korean Sŏn training and for revitalizing the Chogye Order during the mid-Koryŏ dynasty (918–1392). His theory of Sŏn Enlightenment is based on a premise of *sudden awakening* and *gradual cultivation*. According to Chinul, sudden awakening means clearly understanding that "one's own mind is the true Buddha." This is called understanding awakening. To practice meditation without understanding awakening is not a true practice and "will only add to their tribulation,"[8] he warned. As for the period of gradual cultivation following an initial sudden awakening, Chinul wanted to provide a comprehensive and practical guide to meditation practice that would work for students of all different capacities, regardless of traditions. For instance, a student could use awareness of his meditation in order to transform himself in everyday life, or a student could stay focused on the awareness of the innate nature of his Buddhahood, becoming at one with all situations. Finally, the adroit student would know that true cultivation is no other than realization awakening.

Chinul came up with the three primary and two supplementary practice gates in order to support his teaching of sudden awakening and gradual cultivation. The three main gates are balanced Cultivation of Samādhi and Prajñā, Faith and Understanding according to the complete and sudden teachings, and Hwadu (koan) Investigation. Each is based on the three awakenings he had while reading the Platform Sutra, the Exposition of the Avatamsaka Sutra, and the Records of Ta-hui. Two supplementary gates include the gate of No-Mind that coincides with the Way, and the gate of Chanting the Buddha's Name. Within the range of these five practice gates, from the Pure Land–style of chanting to the teachings of Hwaŏm (Avatamsaka) school to the direct pointing hwadu Sŏn, any student could find a suitable path and follow the dharma regimen of sudden awakening/gradual cultivation to the realization of his Buddhahood.

All schools and traditions benefited from Chinul's inclusive program and method of awakening. In the case of Hwaŏm and other doctrinal schools, Chinul's incorporation of their teachings strengthened their stand and made it more viable. Perhaps more than anything else, Chinul's accomplishment

---

8. Robert E. Buswell Jr., ed. and trans., *The Korean Approach to Zen: The Collected Works of Chinul* (Honolulu: University of Hawaii Press, 1983), p. 141, "Secrets of Cultivating the Mind."

was that he could accommodate all the traditions and put students through a flexible training program without compromising authentic practice. The thought and practice of Chinul's Sŏn was unique in the history of Ch'an and Zen, where patriarchs and dharma lineage ruled in the exclusive manner and the wordless tradition that took place outside of any scriptures prevailed. The legacy of his syncretic vision and ecumenical Buddhism greatly influenced Korean Buddhism. Today he is regarded as a founder of native Korean Sŏn Buddhism.

In 1564, following Chinul's work, Hyujŏng (1520–1604) wrote *Sŏn'ga Kugam,* or *The Handbook for Sŏn Students,* which advocates *sagyo ipsŏn* (abandoning doctrine and entering into Sŏn). Student monks were encouraged to acquire a basic doctrinal knowledge and to gain an understanding of the training process geared toward attaining Enlightenment. In his handbook, Hyujŏng says, "Therefore, students should first understand clearly through the study of true teachings that the meanings of immutability and adaptability are, respectively, the nature and appearance of one's own mind and that the ways of sudden awakening and gradual cultivation are the beginning and end of one's practice. Afterward, the student should abandon *kyo* doctrine and enter Sŏn practice with one thought constantly present in his mind. Only then will he gain something without fail. This is called the living road out of samsāra [cycle of birth-and-death]."[9]

In the same book, Hyujŏng comments on the above, saying,

This does not apply to men of great capacity and wisdom but to people of middling and inferior capacity who would not be able to jump and skip the steps. The intention of *kyo* is that there is a sequence in the teachings of immutability and adaptability, and those of sudden awakening and gradual cultivation. The purpose of Sŏn is to show that immutability and adaptability, nature and appearance, and essence and function, are all concurrent in one thought.... Therefore, the adepts, relying on Dharma free from words and pointing directly at one thought, see into their own nature and attain Buddhahood. This is the meaning of abandoning *kyo* [teaching].[10]

It is clear from the above quotations that *sagyo ipsŏn,* or the Sŏn teaching promoted by Hyujŏng, included *kyo* teachings, but *kyo* teachings played only a secondary role in entering the way of Sŏn. In other words, Sŏn was superior to *kyo.* One important point to note here is that Hyujŏng classifies

9. *Sŏn'ga Kugam* (Seoul: Yonghwa Sŏnwŏn, 1984), 45ff.
10. Ibid., 46.

Chinul's sudden awakening/gradual cultivation as *kyo* teaching. With that classification, Hyujŏng skillfully replaced Chinul's sudden awakening/gradual cultivation with his own teachings of *sagyo ipsŏn*. *Sagyo* and *ipsŏn* are compared to the boat that has crossed the river and the landing on the other shore. People of great strength and superior capacity would be able to swim across the river, but people lacking in great faith and true heart, as well as those caught up in theoretical understanding, would need a boat (*kyo* teachings) to take them across to the other shore. Once they have crossed the river, they must land. In order to land (*ipsŏn*), they must abandon the boat (*sagyo*).

Hyujŏng's spirit of *sagyo ipsŏn* was firmly established in the monastic educational system by his disciples via a curriculum called *sajip* (four collections), which consists of four textbooks, one of which is *Excerpts from the Dharma Collections and Special Practice Record* by Chinul. As such, *sagyo ipsŏn* has had lasting influence on Korean Buddhism.

Korean Sŏn Buddhism in the West

Ven. Dr. Seo, Kyung–Bo (1914–1996)

The first Korean monk to visit the West in the postwar period was Ven. Dr. Seo, Kyung-Bo,[11] who taught at the Buddhist College of Seoul's Dongguk University and served as abbot of the well-known Pulguk-sa Temple in 1962. In 1964 he visited the United States as a visiting scholar at Columbia University, the University of Washington, and the University of Hawaii. He returned in 1966 to enroll in a Ph.D. program at Temple University in Philadelphia.[12] In 1969 he received a Ph.D. from Temple University for his *A Study of Korean Zen Buddhism Approached Through the Chodangjip*. It was during this period that Dr. Seo, Kyung-Bo started teaching Korean Sŏn to a small group of Americans in Philadelphia. In his *A Life Story of Ven. Dr. Seo, Kyung-Bo,* Dr. Seo relates his experience in America and his reasons for "making up his mind to devote himself to propagate Korean Zen Buddhism in America." He was very much impressed with the great interest in Zen and Buddhism among young Americans. However, he deeply regretted that "most of the Koreans in America believed in Christ because there were few [Buddhist] priests to lead them to Buddhism. Generally, they [Koreans]

---

11. Throughout this chapter, titles and honorifics used by the person in question are followed.

12. In his "Miguk-e issŏsŏ Han'guk Pulgyo-ŭi Changnae," Grant S. Lee says, "In 1964 when I was taking a Ph.D. course at Temple University in Philadelphia the following year Seo, Kyung-Bo Sunim of Chogye Order arrived from Korea to do Ph.D. course. I had heard that he taught Sŏn meditation to some people at his apartment. This was the occasion when Korean Buddhism took the first step in the U.S" (in Kwak T'aehan et al., *Chaemi Hanin Sahoe* [Seoul: Yangyŏnggak, 1991], 240).

thought it good for their business interests to believe in Christ."[13] He met many Americans who wanted to know more of Korean Buddhism but did not have any information.

In May 1969 Dr. Seo's Korean disciple Rev. Shin, Il-Kwon (later Gosung) arrived in the United States at the invitation of his teacher. In 1970 they established the World Zen Center on ninety acres of land near Newport, Virginia, which was donated by the family of Col. and Mrs. Thell H. Fisher. The inspiration for the World Zen Center was "a scholar, Zen Master and Bishop in the Cho Ke Jong of Korean Buddhism, the Ven. Dr. Kyung-Bo Seo, whose energy and bright laughter light up the whole mountain, leading his students towards self-realization through the wordless teachings of his daily life."[14] In its first winter ten people sat eight hours a day in a hundred-day winter retreat.

By 1970 Dr. Seo had seven American disciples. However, he never took up residence in the United States. After completing his Ph.D. program at Temple University, he returned to Korea and was invited to serve as the academic dean of the Buddhist College at Dongguk University. Although he was based in Korea, he frequently traveled abroad, visiting the United States almost every summer until he passed away.[15]

The teaching style of Ven. Dr. Seo, Kyung-Bo was both spontaneous and impromptu. For instance, in the late 1960s when Murshid met the Korean Master Rev. Seo, Kyung-Bo, "there was immediate recognition. He accepted Seo as 'My present Zen Master' and upon request submitted a Gatha to him. Seo ordained him immediately as a Zen-shi and gave him the name HeKwang."[16] Don Gilbert "began his career as a Zen teacher. He became a member of the World Society for Zen Academy.... In 1972 he met the Korean Zen Master Il Bung Seo, Kyung-Bo in California. He began to study with Master Seo, and was empowered as his dharma successor in the United States."[17]

In the mid-50s Robert Maitland became interested in Asian Religions.... His prevailing interest however was the practice of meditation.... In 1970

---

13. *A Life Story of Ven. Dr. Seo, Kyung Bo* (Seoul: Ilbung Samjangwön, 1981), 208.

14. World Zen Center Brochure, June 26, 1970.

15. A letter from Edward Wilkinson dated July 4, 1974, reads, "Dr. Seo is expected to arrive in San Francisco on July 17 (1974) and stay here about three weeks, and travel to the other cities for three weeks. He will return to Korea around September 1."

16. Letter from Wali Ali to Royall Tyler dated January 29, 1973.

17. "Search for the Bone of Enlightenment," review article of *The Upside Down Circle* by Zen master Don Gilbert (Nevada City, Calif.: Blue Dolphin Publishing, 1988), in the *Vajradhatu Sun* (August/September, 1989): 19.

he formalized what he had learned and upon request began classes in meditation in Huntsville, Alabama, at the Free University of Alabama.... In 1972 he wrote to the Hui Neng Zen Temple at Easton, Pennsylvania, requesting admission for Zen training.... Shortly thereafter Master Hearn visited Huntsville where he lectured on the "Origins of Zen" and the "Training of the Zen Monk." Mr. Maitland visited Hui Neng Temple for a week's meditation training during August.... During the course of the next year, a group of meditators formed in Huntsville. Eight of them visited Hui Neng Zen Temple along with Mr. Maitland in August 1973, where they received Buddhist names and meditation training from the Ven. Korean Zen master Il-Bung Seo, Kyung-Bo.... Disciple Maitland was then called to San Francisco during August 1974 where he was ordained a Dharma Master (lay Zen Minister) and authorized to start a Zen center in Huntsville with the understanding that Master Seo would come to the U.S. from Korea for permanent residence and that support would be received from Master Seo's descendents, Masters Sŏng Ryong Hearn and Tae Hui Gilbert. In San Francisco, a Holy Name ceremony was held by Master Seo and eight more Huntsville students were named in absentia. Upon his return, Maitland proposed the formation of a Zen Center in Huntsville in the line of Dharma Father Seo. From the monthly donations of students and friends, a house at 307 8th Street, Huntsville, AL., was rented in October of 1974 and the Il-Bung Zen Center was founded.[18]

By 1975 five Zen centers, or Sŏn Wŏn, run by Dr. Seo's instant Zen disciples had sprung up around the country. Aside from the World Zen Center, there were the Hui Neng Zen Temple in Easton, Pennsylvania; Il-bung Sŏn Wŏn in San Francisco, established in November 1974 by Rev. Donald Gilbert and Rev. Ed Wilkinson; Cho Ge Sŏn Wŏn in Santa Fe, New Mexico, run by Gary Brown; and Il-Bung Zen Center in Huntsville, Alabama. Most of his American disciples had previous Zen training in the Japanese tradition, except Robert Maitland (whose Korean Buddhist name was Tae Chi) and Edward Wilkinson (whose Korean Buddhist name was Ilsan), who became interested in Buddhism while serving as a Peace Corps teacher in Korea from 1966 to 1968.

Ven. Dr. Seo's Sŏn (Zen) teachings included silent sitting, *tanjun* breathing, walking meditation, Sŏn question-and-answer in writing, and eye-to-eye "confrontation." He stressed three things for his disciples, "A Zen Master, a Zen Temple, and friends." Although he showed interest in propagating the

18. Robert Maitland, *Essentials of Meditation,* Lakemont, Ga.: CSA Press, 1975, 138–39.

Korean Sŏn of Chinul and Hyujŏng,[19] there is not much evidence that he actually tried to teach their Korean Sŏn to his disciples. His poor English and restricted visiting time must have prevented him from doing so. Instead, he resorted to simple and easy teachings such as abdominal breathing, walking meditation, or just laughing.[20] His two American dharma successors, Sŏng Ryong Hearn and Tae Hui Don Gilbert (1909–), and Murshid Wali Ali and Robert Maitland (1922–), who received almost instant recognition and ordination from Ven. Dr. Seo, were all mature, well-read in Buddhism and Eastern philosophy, and spiritually developed.[21]

19. Dr. Seo wrote one book on Hyujŏng in Korean, *Sŏsan Taesa* (Seoul: Poryon'gak, 1972); and an English translation of Chinul's Chinsim Chiksŏl, "Master Bojo's Zen Teachings," *Maitreya* (Berkeley, Calif.: Shambhala Publications, 1970), 12–14.

20. Dr. Seo occasionally engaged himself in Sŏn question-and-answer with his American students. The following are his own response and responses from his two Dharma successors to the question, "What is Zen?"

> Willows are green and flowers are red.
> Flowers are red and yet not red,
> Willows are green and yet not Green,
> Now again, willows are green, flowers are red.

> There is nothing so close as the teaching of "Suchness."
> A grain of sand contains all land and sea.
> When we have found the Truth,
> Mountain is mountain, water is water,
> Willows are green, flowers are red,
> One is all, all in all, I am Universe, Buddha is I.
>
> Ven. Dr. Kyung-Bo Seo, Korean Zen Master

> 'Every sound
> penetrates silence;
> Silence penetrates
> every sound ...'
>
> Rev. Sŏng Ryong Hearn

> On writing-on speaking
> Use a pen with no
> Point
> for paper use the
> Sky
> Remember speech is
> but a warm breeze
> Rustling dry leaves
> as it passes by
>
> Rev. Gilbert

Sŏ Paksa-wa Pulgyo Kyori Mundap (Taegu: Chöksön-sa, 1974), 319–22.

21. I met Wali Ali in San Francisco in the summer of 1967 and Sŏng-Ryong Hearn in Los Angeles in the 1980s. I did not see any sign of the traditional Zen masterly style of detachment and aloofness from them. They were warm, friendly, and humble; and I was impressed with their spiritual cultivation. Sŏng-Ryong Hearn, born in England, was the grandnephew of the famous Japanologist Lafcadio Hearn.

As the two titles he loved to use, Zen Master and Tripitaka Master, indicate, it seems that he tried to represent both Sŏn practice and *kyo* doctrinal teachings as much as possible without favoring one over the other. Now he added Sŏn poetry and Sŏn calligraphy to his propagation and social activities. This artistic side of his was picked up by one of his American disciples. Don Gilbert founded Blue Dragon Zen Academy after being inspired by his Korean teacher's Sŏn calligraphy and humor and produced two books of comic strips and Sŏn commentary, *Jellyfish Bones: The Humor of Zen* (1980) and *The Upside Down Circle: Zen Laughter* (1988). They are about a dog, Unk, and his search for Enlightenment. Praising *Jellyfish Bones,* Dr. Seo writes,

> Master Ta Hui's book is a fresh approach to Zen. He does not adhere to tradition nor does he deny it. The work seems light and humorous, but his pen is a Zen sword and it is very sharp indeed. Humor is an integral part of Zen and here it is employed with consummate skill. Those that have studied under Master Ta Hui know him for his gentle humanism. They know too that he can, in one flash of incisive wit, burst conceptual bubbles in a cascade of laughter. In his book be aware of the little dog with his bone. He is often depicted as saying, "This bone is delicious." This is a most important clue. This book then is a finger pointed at the moon. If the reader can stop staring at the finger and look at the moon, the moon will be revealed smiling back at the looker. When the little ego is recognized for what it is, then the Buddha will romp and play, filling the world with unimpeded laughter. Master Ta Hui's book may just be the instrument that will help bring this about.[22]

Sometime between 1971 and 1976 the World Zen Center must have dissolved, and the main training center for Dr. Seo's disciples in America moved to Hui Neng Zen Temple in Easton, Pennsylvania, where Dr. Seo's Korean disciple Shin, Gosung (Shin, Il-Kwon) resided before he moved to New York State. Around this time the World Society for Zen Academy was created, perhaps in lieu of the World Zen Center, and Dr. Seo served as president. It appears that Dr. Seo's activities with his American disciples peaked toward the end of 1970s. The World Zen Center and the World Society for Zen Academy suffered from both a lack of a sustained teaching relationship with the teacher and a lack of organization. In the early 1980s most of the groups of the World Society for Zen Academy, if not all, ended their activities and

22. Back jacket of Zen master Don Gilbert's *Jellyfish Bones: The Humor of Zen* (Oakland, Calif.: Blue Dragon Press, 1980).

folded or merged with the Zen Meditation Center of Washington run by Shin, Gosung, who was also setting up the American Zen College on a ten-acre property in Germantown, Maryland. Perhaps it would be more accurate to say that Dr. Seo's shift in focus contributed to the demise of the World Society for Zen Academy.

In 1975 Dr. Seo created Il Bung Sŏnjong-hoe or Il Bung Zen Buddhist Association with a view to consolidating all of his activities in Korea and abroad. The World Society for Zen Academy was one of the organizations created to support his multifaceted activities under the Il Bung Zen Buddhist Association. His popular and favorite activities included holding Sŏn calligraphy art shows, receiving people who wanted to see him, collecting letters of commendation and plaques of thanks, and assuming perfunctory positions of distinction. He was a prolific writer, and as of 1993 he had authored more than five hundred books. Apparently he loved honorary doctoral degrees and by 1993 had collected sixty-seven of them.[23]

In 1994 when Dr. Seo was asked in the middle of a radio interview in New York about his quest for titles, he said, "It is not because I seek fame. I am a Korean and a Buddhist. Korea and Buddhism need to be better known and they deserve publicity. If I can make a small contribution, if I can go in the Guinness Book of Records, both my country and Buddhism will benefit from that."[24] There are many in the Korean Buddhist world who would disagree with him. Part of the reason is that traditionally Buddhists are used to the values of renunciation, seclusion, and ego attrition; and what Ven. Dr. Seo did was almost completely the opposite. It is very possible that Dr. Seo was practicing nonrenunciation and self-advertising as values for modern-day Buddhism.

In September 1988 Ven. Dr. Seo split from the Chogye Order and established his own religious order, Il Bung Sŏn'gyo-jong or Il Bung Order for Sŏn and kyo (doctrine) named after his style, Il Bung. In 1989 Dr. Seo became the first dharma king of Korea for the secretariat of world dharma-raja. In 1991 he obtained approval from several Buddhist organizations in the United States, the Soviet Union, and Myanmar to serve as the first world dharma-raja. The office of world dharma-raja or dharma king, and the position of

---

23. When it was learned that Dr. Seo wrote so many books and received so many honorary degrees, Korean newspapers reported that a listing in the *Guinness Book of World Records* was almost a certainty. However, according to the 1996 edition, Dr. Seo was neither listed as the most prolific author nor as one who was awarded the greatest number of honorary degrees. The world record for the greatest number of honorary degrees is held by Rev. Father Theodore M. Hesburgh, former president of the University of Notre Dame, Indiana, who has received 130.

24. Information supplied by Ms. Kim Chawon, who runs a Korean radio Buddhist program in New York City.

world dharma-raja, were supposed to be the Buddhist equivalents of the Vatican or the papal government and pope.

The Ven. Dr. Seo must have felt that world Buddhism suffered from the lack of a central hierarchy. At the World Fellowship of Buddhists conferences, he constantly raised the issue of the great need for world Buddhist leadership in order for Buddhism to cope with changing world situations. However, to most inward-looking Buddhist elders this was a strange and novel idea. Undaunted, Dr. Seo forged ahead and established a secretariat for the office of the world dharma-raja and then campaigned for the position. It is true that his incongruous behavior turned off many serious Buddhists. But he was popular with his lay followers, who admired him for his courage and accomplishments. It is too early to assess his achievements and failures.

Kusan Sunim (1909–1983)

Kusan Sunim was the first traditional-style Korean Sŏn master who visited America. After his teacher Hyobong Sunim (1888–1966) passed away, he moved to Songgwang-sa in 1967. It was here that Kusan Sunim was first ordained as a monk under his teacher Hyobong in 1937. In May of 1969, Kusan Sunim was installed as a Sŏn master of Chogye Ch'ongnim of Songgwang-sa. In the spring of 1970, Kusan Sunim completed the renovation of an old Susŏn-sa building as a Sŏn meditation center.

Kusan Sunim arrived in the United States on the last day of 1972 at the invitation of layman Tŏksan (Han-Sang Lee) to attend the ceremony of the completion of the dharma hall of Sambo-sa Temple. Sambo-sa, the first traditional-style Korean temple in the United States, was built by layman Tŏksan and his wife in Carmel Valley, California. After the ceremony on January 28, 1973, Kusan Sunim delivered his first formal dharma talk in America. The master "struck his staff three times, and said, 'Throughout the length and breadth of the world, people in all societies say 'I, I.' But actually what is this 'I?' Clearly, all men need to realize this 'True-I.' When you can truthfully say, 'With one stroke I can knock down the Empire State Building; in one gulp I can swallow the entire Pacific Ocean,' then and only then will you have realized it."[25] After the ceremony, Kusan visited the New York area and the West Coast. In March he returned to Korea with his first foreign disciple, Hyŏn Jo, a seventeen-year-old American boy. Later that year he started Bul-il International Meditation Center at Songgwang-sa in order to

---

25. Rick Fields, *How the Swans Came to the Lake* (Boston: Shambhala Publications, 1992), 352.

accommodate the growing number of Westerners interested in the practice of Korean Zen. The first of its kind in the history of Korean Buddhism, the center was the brainchild of Kusan Sunim's vision and opened an opportunity for the globalization of Korean Buddhism.

In 1976 the foreign *sangha* (community) of the International Meditation Center translated his teachings into English and published them in a book form, *Nine Mountains: Dharma Lectures of the Korean Meditation Master Kusan. Nine Mountains* (literal meaning of Kusan) was distributed gratis as a dharma gift. By 1982 four editions had been printed.

By 1976 the foreign *sangha* had grown large enough to require its own compound separate from the Korean monks. Toward the end of 1979, Kusan Sunim made his second visit to America, accompanied by his two Western female disciples, Suil and Söngil, who served as his translators. During this trip Kusan Sunim dedicated Koryŏ-sa (Korea Temple) in Los Angeles as the first overseas branch of Songgwang-sa and held a Bodhisattva precepts-taking ceremony therein. He also led a week-long meditation retreat at Sambo-sa. While visiting the East Coast he was invited to the Zen Arts Center in Woodstock, New York, and to Princeton University to give dharma talks.

Pŏpch'ŏn Stephen Batchelor, who arrived at Songgwang-sa in 1981, describes his first encounter with Kusan Sunim: "Accompanied by a translator, I entered the Zen master's room.... He was a tiny, radiant man of about seventy.... He smiled with much kindness.... He listened with patient bemusement as I nervously explained why I had come to Korea and expressed my wish to study with him. He confidently told me just to look into the nature of my mind and ask myself 'What is it?'"[26]

At the formal opening of the three-month summer retreat right after Pŏpch'ŏn's arrival,

> Kusan Sunim pounded his heavy wooden staff on the platform and asked, "Is your original face brilliantly clear to you?" No one said a word. He insisted, "If you have the Dharma-eye, say something!" Again there was silence. He gave a loud shout, "HAK!" and said, "When the eye on the boulder opens, then you will understand." He read a verse he had composed:

> In the beginning awakening shines perfectly.
> Now the circle of illumination is scattered with broken tiles
> Which people claim are precious gems.
> Flowers bob softly on the river as they float beneath the bridge.

---

26. Stephen Batchelor, *The Faith to Doubt: Glimpses of Buddhist Uncertainty* (Berkeley, Calif.: Parallax Press, 1990), 21.

He turned to his audience with an impish smile and casually asked what kind of teaching these swallows could be giving. After another perplexed silence, he replied for us, "Brrr, skwok, skwok, brrr …" There then followed a more intelligible account of Zen practice, "The Dharma taught by the Buddhas and patriarchs is medicine prescribed according to the kind of disease. What would be the use of medicine if there were no disease to fight? The darkness of the mind is due to your delusive thoughts and emotions alone. When you find yourselves in good or bad circumstances, you neglect your true mind and surrender to the power of conditions. To be swayed by circumstance and to indulge in rash, ill-considered actions causes the mind to be diseased. For the great truth to appear, stop all this now. Throw it away! To awaken your mind, press your face against the wall and ask with all your strength, 'What is it?'"

The retreat began in earnest the following morning at two. And this insane routine—thirteen hours of meditation ending at ten at night—was to continue for eighty-nine more days. Fifty minutes seated on a cushion followed by ten minutes walking briskly around the hall, each session measured by the tedious ticking of an ancient clock and the shocking cracks of a wooden clapper: such were the new parameters of my temporal world, interrupted only for food (as above) and insufficient sleep. The first two weeks were the worst. After that knees and mind become resigned and, imperceptibly, the routine switches from an outrageous exception to the very norm against which all else is understood.[27]

In the late spring of 1982, Kusan Sunim visited America and Europe. In Europe he traveled to Switzerland and Denmark to teach. In Geneva he dedicated Bulsung-sa temple, the second overseas branch of Songgwang-sa with the help of his disciple Hyehaeng. In early fall of the same year, Kusan Sunim dedicated another temple, Daegak-sa (Temple of Great Enlightenment), the third overseas branch of Songgwang-sa in Carmel Valley, California, for his first Western disciple, Hyŏn Jo.

In the new year of 1983, Kusan Sunim reminded himself of his teacher Hyobong Sunim's injunction to restore previous fame to Songgwang-sa as the Sangha-Jewel Temple by training prominent and distinguished disciples. So he made a vow to launch the second spiritual movement for building the Community of Samādhi and Prajñā according to the legacy of Chinul. In March he appointed an abbot to carry out this historic task. On the anniversary of Master Chinul's death in May, the national support organization

27. Ibid., 22–23.

Bulil-hoe met to discuss Kusan Sunim's proposal and to develop a master plan for the eighth development project of Songgwang-sa. In early October Kusan Sunim came down with an illness and suffered a series of strokes. On December 16, 1983, he passed away at his residence in a meditation posture supported by his disciples. The time was 6:20 P.M., on Friday.

Pŏpch'ŏn captures the moment of the Parinirvana of Kusan Sunim in his "When the Light in Your Eyes Falls to the Ground":

> At six that evening we ... were preparing to sit until nine. But at twenty past six they rang the main bell. . . . With each successive note I realized with a mounting certainty that Kusan Sunim had died. One by one we stood up from our cushions and paced around the hall. It was as if the pressure of the bell was too unsettling to be contained in stillness: the echoes of each stroke spread into my belly and limbs and forced me to move. The monastery was roused. . . . The bell was still ringing when the nine of us assembled in the courtyard in front of the hall. We had put on our formal gowns and robes and stood in a group waiting to go up to his room. . . . We walked in single file through the tile-covered gate and up the path to his room. A single lamp flickered across the sad and bewildered faces of the monks. . . . We lined up and bowed in unison. Then Yongjin (Kusan Sunim's attendant) . . . beckoned us to come and see the body behind the screen. . . . I peered behind the screen. Fully robed, his slumped body was seated clumsily on a chair. . . . His face. . . . It was as though the light had gone out of his eyes.[28]

In October after he became ill, Kusan Sunim prepared his Parinirvana (deathbed) verse:

> The autumn leaves covering the mountain are redder than flowers in spring.
> Everything in the universe fully reveals the great power.
> Life is void and death is also void.
> Absorbed in the Buddha's ocean-seal Samadhi, I depart with a smile.[29]

Although he quoted from Chinul's teachings from time to time in his dharma talks, Kusan Sunim's Sŏn teaching was *hwadu Sŏn,* or the shortcut path. His main *hwadu* for his Western students was "What is this?" Following his dharma talk at the Zen Arts Center in Woodstock, New York, in 1980, Kusan Sunim was asked, "How can I raise a great doubt?" He answered,

28. Ibid., 89 and 91.
29. Stephen Batchelor, ed., and Martine Fages, trans., *The Way of Korean Zen* (New York: Weatherhill, 1985), 50.

Our mind is present when we are talking and listening, but because we have forgotten the mind and live for the body, our minds have become dark. Mind, self, soul, I, and spirit are all names. So before the name, what is this? Question, "WHAT IS THIS? WHAT IS THIS?" this will make a doubt arise. When sentient beings awake, they become Buddhas, and when Buddhas sleep, they become sentient beings. We are all originally Buddhas. So you have to believe that the reason you are living the life of a sentient being is that your mind has become deluded. Practice to awaken the mind, question before the word, "WHAT IS THIS?" To a question, "What is the original mind?" he counter-questions, "What is asking?" To the answer "Mind" he replies, "If you have the mind, why are you asking me? You should know Buddhism is a very simple thing. A person is a combination of a body and a mind. If you have a body and no mind, you're dead. And if you have a mind and no body, you're a ghost. When a person has both a body and a mind and only knows his body, we call him a sentient being. Sentient beings mean all creatures.... When we practice and awaken the mind, we know both the body and the mind; then we are complete people. We are the Buddhas."[30]

The purpose of *hwadu* questioning, "What is this?" (that is, what is this before everything?) is to develop the power of concentration (*king samādhi*) or a single mind. To develop a single mind is to remove all of our defilements. To remove all of our defilements is to awaken to the original mind. To awaken to the original mind is to discover that we have been Buddhas from the beginning. To the confused and deluded, it is simple but incomprehensibly hard. To the awakened mind it is simple, clear, and easy.

In the late fall of 1982, I visited South Korea and paid a visit to Sŏngch'ŏl Sunim at Paengnyŏn-am (White Lotus Hermitage) in Haein-sa Monastery and Kusan Sunim at Samil-am (Three-Day Hermitage) in Songgwang-sa Monastery. At the time, Sŏngch'ŏl Sunim and Kusan Sunim were two giant towering figures representing Korean Sŏn Buddhism. However, they differed in their views on attaining Enlightenment. Sŏngch'ŏl Sunim maintained *tono tonsu* (sudden awakening sudden cultivation) or "radical subitism," while Kusan Sunim seemed to support *tono chŏmsu* (sudden awakening gradual cultivation) or "moderate subitism." For instance, Sŏngch'ŏl Sunim maintained that *kyŏnsŏng* (seeing into your true nature) is identical to *sŏngbul* (attaining your Buddhahood). In other words, you are a Buddha if you clearly see into your true nature. When I met Kusan Sunim, I asked for his views. "If so, has Sŏngch'ŏl become a Buddha?" he retorted. He disagreed with Sŏngch'ŏl

30. *Lectures by Venerable Ku San,* Carmel Valley, California, n.d., 3–4.

Sunim and pointed out that kyŏnsŏng and sŏngbul are different. Was Kusan Sunim following the line of Chinul's Korean Sŏn in this? I do not know.

In the eleven years following the establishment of the International Meditation Zen Center at Songgwang-sa, Kusan Sunim ordained forty-six foreign disciples from the United States, Canada, Australia, New Zealand, and Europe, both male and female. Among them were Anna Proctor (Suil), Martine Fages (Sŏngil, now Martine Batchelor), Renaud Neubaur (Hyehaeng), Stacey Krause (Hamwŏl), Larry Martin (Hyŏnsŏng), Kim Quennalt (Hyŏn Jo), Audrey Kitson (Jagwang), Robert E. Buswell Jr. (Hyemyŏng), Gerald Eule (Hyegak), Henrik H. Sorensen, and Deborah Caine (Chi Kwang).

In the Korean-mountain monastic community, old ways and conservatism prevailed, and negative reaction to outsiders was still strong in the 1970s. It was revolutionary and unprecedented that Kusan Sunim invited Western men and women and ordained them as disciples for training. Robert E. Buswell Jr., who spent five years (1974–1979) training at the International Meditation Zen Center, recalls: "His monastery [Songgwang-sa] was at the time the only one in Korea that allowed foreigners to participate in the traditional Buddhist training. While I could travel freely among Korean monasteries during the vacation seasons of spring and autumn, I was never able to spend a retreat season elsewhere."[31]

Under the circumstances, Kusan Sunim had to make extra effort to protect his foreign *sangha*. Buswell continues: "Westerners seeking to study Buddhism in Korea had no stronger proponent than Kusan, and I personally would never have been able to practice for so many years with the Korean monks in the main meditation hall at Songgwang-sa without his constant backing. Korean monks from other monasteries who came to practice at Songgwang-sa were often suspicious of foreigners' motivations in meditating; Kusan did everything possible to assuage their concerns about my presence among them."[32]

During his career, Kusan Sunim made three visits to the West and dedicated three temples, two in the United States and one in Geneva, Switzerland. The temple in Geneva closed in 1985. The temple in Carmel Valley, California, stopped functioning not long after it opened. Koryŏ-sa in Los Angeles is still operating for local Korean Buddhists but is not what it was envisioned for Americans. The International Meditation Center in Songgwang-sa that Kusan Sunim had hoped to develop as the world center for the study and training of Korean Sŏn now exists more in name than in reality. In 1985

31. Robert E. Buswell Jr., *The Zen Monastic Experience: Buddhist Practice in Contemporary Korea* (Princeton: Princeton University Press, 1992), 19–20.

32. Ibid., xii.

when Jagwang left the center, Chi Kwang was the only Westerner remaining.[33] Many of them were brokenhearted when Kusan Sunim passed away. In addition to the death of Kusan Sunim, lack of direction from the new leadership contributed to the departure of the Western sangha. Out of forty-six Western monks and nuns ordained and trained at the center, only three or four function as Buddhist teachers now. Have they all failed Kusan Sunim's wishes?

Robert E. Buswell Jr., Stephen Batchelor, Henrik H. Sorensen, and Martine Batchelor all have written about their teacher Kusan Sunim, Korean Buddhism, Songgwang-sa, and Korean nuns; and they have been active in their academic research and dharma teaching. Among them, Robert E. Buswell Jr. stands out for his contribution to introducing Korean Sŏn Buddhism to the academic and Buddhist world and Zen practitioners. He has written three books and numerous articles on Korean Buddhism. *The Korean Approach to Zen: The Collected Works of Chinul* (University of Hawaii Press, 1983), which he started with Kusan Sunim's encouragement and help while still in training at the Center of Songgwang-sa, was the first major work on Korean Buddhism. It helped to remove the general ignorance about Buddhism of Korea. In 1989 Princeton University Press published his *The Formation of Ch'an Ideology in China and Korea: The Vajrasamadhi-Sutra, A Buddhist Apocryphon,* which explores Wŏnhyo's syncretic vision and reevaluation of East Asian traditional Buddhism. In 1992 Princeton University Press published *The Zen Monastic Experience: Buddhist Practice in Contemporary Korea.* The book is dedicated to Kusan Sunim and the monks of Songgwang-sa. As an honest first-hand account of Korean monastic life and practice, this book is an outstanding documentary that removes the myth surrounding a Zen monk's life.

All this may seem a far cry from what Kusan Sunim may have expected of his Western disciples. Perhaps some of his Western disciples decided to repay their indebtedness somewhat differently to the "true man of Zen" who cared for them so much.

Zen Master Seung Sahn (1927–)

Zen Master Seung Sahn, or Soen Sa Nim as he is addressed by his American students, arrived in the United States in May 1972 from Tokyo, where he had been teaching the dharma to Korean residents in Japan. Haengwŏn Sunim, as he was known to the Buddhists in South Korea, held important

33. Telephone conversation with Jagwang, August 17, 1999.

positions in both administrative and legislative sections of the Korean Bud-dhist Chogye Order (KBC) before he ventured overseas. With full backing from the power circles in the Chogye Order, he visited Japan in 1964 and established the first overseas KBC, Hong Poep Wŏn (Korean Buddhist Chogye Order Dharma Propagation Center), in Tokyo in 1966. In 1969 he established KBC Hong Poep Wŏn in Hong Kong.

Soen Sa Nim was the first official Buddhist missionary representing the Korean Buddhist Chogye Order abroad. As the youngest of the three pio-neers and one who actually took up residency in America and was able to communicate in Konglish (broken Korean-style English often without verbs) with a flourish of gestures, he had a distinct advantage over Dr. Seo, Kyung-Bo, and Kusan Sunim in doing dharma work in the West. In addition, his wonderful chanting voice and vibrant dharma spirit helped and inspired many people.

In October 1972 Soen Sa Nim opened the Providence Zen Center in Rhode Island for his American students, his first Zen center in the United States. In 1974 the Cambridge Zen Center was started. In 1975 the New Haven Zen Center, near Yale University, and the New York Zen Center opened. In January 1976 he and his American disciple Lincoln Rhodes went to Los Angeles to begin a Zen center there. By 1977, five years after his arrival in the United States, he had started and helped to start eight Zen centers, and had conducted many precept ceremonies. The first one was held on November 8, 1972. He approved two master dharma teachers to teach kong-an study and retreats, and many dharma teachers. In 1976 his first English book, *Dropping Ashes on the Buddha,* edited by Stephen Mitchell, was published. It was a dharma blitzkrieg! He stormed into New Age America with an empty mind (no money, no English) and great enthusiasm.

The year 1978 was an important one for his growing Zen center move-ment. The Providence Zen Center, which had started in his apartment on Doyle Avenue in 1972 and then moved to 48 Hope Street in 1974, now acquired a 50-acre property in Cumberland, Rhode Island. This new Pro-vidence Zen Center in Cumberland became the headquarters for Seung Sahn's movement in the United States and abroad. In 1978 he made his first trip to Europe. His visit to Poland was a great success. His dharma rela-tionship with Poland over the following years blossomed into four full Zen centers and ten affiliated groups. Numerous Polish Zen students later vis-ited Soen Sa Nim's Zen centers in the United States and South Korea for study and practice.

Since 1982 was the tenth anniversary of Soen Sa Nim's mission in the West, he wanted to do something big and meaningful to celebrate the occasion. So he had his disciples organize a "Great Masters World Peace Assembly" to formally mark the tenth anniversary of the "Korean Buddhism Chogye Order Hong Poep Won." Soen Sa Nim invited Pope John Paul II, the Dalai Lama, and Söngch'ŏl Sunim, the Supreme Patriarch of Korean Chogye Order, as well as other religious leaders. Each declined to attend. According to Mu Sang, a Jewish American Zen monk and Soen Sa Nim's secretary during the three-day event September 17–19, 1982, Soen Sa Nim "wanted the Pope, the Dalai Lama and the Pope of Korean Buddhism all to come here to Cumberland for this ceremony, have a hot meal together, take off their clothes, have a hot bath, get dry, get dressed, say thank you very much and leave. It would have been a demonstration of how we are of different cultures, races, religions, but that—underneath our clothes—we all have human minds. We are all one. It's so simple, everyone would probably have been blown out by it."[34]

Bodhisattva Monks

The event of KBC Hong Poep Wön still managed to attract five hundred people. A large contingent of delegates to the World Peace Assembly came from South Korean Chogye Order. They consisted of the head of the administrative section of the Chogye Order and abbots of head monasteries. Many were Soen Sa Nim's old friends. They were all impressed with his dharma work in America. Everything went smoothly except for one incident. Some of the Korean delegates noticed that many of Soen Sa Nim's ordained American disciples did not quite look like traditional-style monks, even though they were dressed in *changsam* and *kasa,* a monk's formal dress and robe. Many had hair, and some were holding their own children. Upon inquiry they were told that these American monks were Bodhisattva monks, that is to say, married priests. Furthermore, when they learned that Soen Sa Nim had a plan to found a new school of Buddhism to replace KBC Hong Poep Wön, they were hurt and upset.

The issue of married Buddhist clergy is an emotional one for Chogye Order monks.[35] Obviously the new realities of Buddhism in America had no relation to South Korea's Chogye Order's recent past. Soen Sa Nim was just trying to cope with the realities of Buddhism in America. Young people in America are more inclined to ministry Buddhism than to monastic

34. *Providence Sunday Journal,* September 19, 1982, C-16.
35. See Sam-Woo Kim, *Zen Buddhism in North America* (Toronto: Zen Lotus Society, 1986), 23–26.

Buddhism. Even when they are interested in leading a monastic life for sustained cultivation, most are not prepared to spend the rest of their life as a celibate monk. They prefer a middle ground where they can combine their commitment to Buddhist practice with their secular life. Soen Sa Nim was responding to these realities. As one of his disciples put it, Americans needed a "wider approach" to Buddhism than the traditional narrow approach.

Kwan Um School of Zen

In August 1983 the Kwan Um School of Zen was established as an umbrella organization in order to meet the growing demand of the many Zen center duties and to "facilitate teaching schedules and communications among the many centers and groups."[36] KBC Hong Poep Wön had outgrown its useful purpose. "The first annual School Congress was also initiated at that time, providing opportunities for people from all the centers and groups to gather, hold teaching workshops, and share ideas for making their practices stronger and their Zen Centers function better. The first School Council Meeting was also held with representatives from all the Zen Centers. The decision-making process became much more democratic."[37]

In 1984 the school started the publication of *Primary Point,* a quarterly newspaper, in order to spread Soen Sa Nim's teaching worldwide, carry the school news, and announce the retreats and special programs of the different centers. "In the summer of 1984, the Diamond Hill Zen Monastery was dedicated in a formal ceremony on the site at the Providence Zen Center. . . . the Monastery was established for the 'traditional-style monks' who would remain celibate and follow the Korean style of training. . . . The first Kyol Che (ninety-day intensive meditation retreat) at the new monastery was held from December 1984 through March 1985."[38] In the same year, Soen Sa Nim established Seoul International Zen Center at Hwa Gae Sa, the temple in Seoul where his relationship with the temple began in 1958.

Although Soen Sa Nim made important departures from the Chogye Order style of Buddhism by creating a new form of Bodhisattva monks (married male and female) and founding a new school of Buddhism, he always maintained a strong connection with the Chogye Order and made sure that the Korean Buddhist world was informed of his activities. It was not an easy task to bring together traditional Korean-style Buddhism and the New Age

36. Zen Master Seung Sahn, *Ten Gates* (Cumberland, R.I.: Primary Point Press, 1982), 122.
37. Diana Clark, ed., *Only Doing It for Sixty Years* (Cumberland, R.I.: Kwan Um Zen School, 1987), 34.
38. Sam-Woo Kim, *Zen Buddhism in North America,* 25.

American-style Buddhism and make it work. Soen Sa Nim had to perform many balancing acts and dance skillfully in order to smooth out the difficulties and obstacles he faced. The Diamond Hill Zen Monastery in America and the Seoul International Zen Center had as their purpose serving as linkups for the Korean Chogye Order and the Kwan Um School of Zen as well as for traditional-style monks and nontraditional temporary or Bodhisattva monks. With this in mind, the Seoul International Zen Center has been organizing international ninety-day Kyol Che in the summer and the winter, first at Su Dok Sah and then at Shin Won Sa since 1990 for those who can sit the full ninety days; and Hwa Gae Sa for those who can sit a minimum of one week. In 1994 a new modern building of the Seoul International Zen Center was dedicated on the site of Hwa Gae Sa. Since 1983 Soen Sa Nim has been presented in the Kwan Um Zen School literature and publications as "the first Korean Zen Master to live and teach in the West" and "the 78th patriarch in the Korean Chogye Order" who "became a Zen Master at the age of 22."[39]

International Traveler and Funky Zen Master

"Something like a comet rushing in from the unknown universe and engaging all the little asteroids for a few moments, and then rushing out again into the vast reaches of empty space."[40] This remark by Robert Aitken-roshi of the Diamond Sangha in Honolulu, Hawaii, pretty much sums up the lightning speed with which Soen Sa Nim travels around. One of his disciples who traveled in South Korea with him once commented to me: "A busload of us would pull up at famous temples. Some of us are still in line to enter the Buddha hall for three bows while others would come out the other door to return to the bus."

In the early years the whirlwind trips and sightseeing of this energetic and "funky Zen Master" were confined to the East Coast, the West Coast, and Canada. Then in 1978 he made his first trip to Europe. From this trip the "Polish connection" was established, and many wonderful dharma fruits were produced from Polish dharma trees. In 1980 Soen Sa Nim undertook a journey around the world with his students. They visited Korea, Japan, Hong Kong, Thailand, Nepal, India, and Europe. The highlight of this journey was a pilgrimage to the sacred places of Buddhism in India. In 1985 he visited

39. *Primary Point* 2, no. 2 (May 1985): 11; *Ten Gates*, 121.
40. "Do you see this? An Appreciation for Tubby Teacher," *Only Doing It for Sixty Years* (Cumberland, R.I.: Kwan Um Zen School, 1987), 49.

China with twenty people. In 1986 he visited Russia. He was the first South Korean monk to visit the communist countries of Poland, China, and Russia. These trips are his first visits to different countries in the world to "spread apple seeds" and do not include his annual whirlwind teaching tours to the many centers and groups of the Kwan Um Zen School worldwide. Following his first visit to Europe and Poland in the spring of 1978, he returned in 1980. Since then he has visited Europe once every year. With the establishment of the Kwan Um School of Zen of Eastern Europe at the Warsaw Zen Center in 1984 and with the Centre Zen de Paris starting in 1985, Soen Sa Nim began visiting Europe three or four times annually.

Since 1992 for health reasons Soen Sa Nim has operated out of Hwa Gae Sa, his Korean home base, and visits countries in Asia in addition to his annual dharma trips to the United States and Europe. According to a report in *Dharma Light,* "Despite repeated threats of retirement, Dae Soen Sa Nim shows no sign of slowing down. On the contrary, his schedule gets busier by the month. Since leaving here in February, he has been teaching in Korea, as well as travelling to Hong Kong, China, Singapore, Malaysia, and Australia, where new Zen groups have been forming. Following his stay in Los Angeles, he will continue to the East coast, officiating at a Transmission Ceremony and his birthday celebration at the Providence Zen Center on August 1. The next weekend, Dae Soen Sa Nim will attend the opening ceremony for the newly built temple at Furnace Mountain in Kentucky."[41]

The Teachings of Master Seung Sahn

Soen Sa Nim's teachings are three-dimensional. The first is doctrinal teaching (*kyo*) and the second is meditation (Sŏn), both of which he inherited from Korean Buddhism. To this he added his own third dimension, teaching by correspondence, or Postcard Zen. Since he was always on the move, his students contacted him by letters or telephone calls when they had questions or sought advice. He would always answer their letters, signing with his initials, SS. These teaching letters and the letters to him were collected and then distributed periodically to the Zen centers. The reading of these letters formed an important part of morning and evening practice.

From early on, Soen Sa Nim devised a Buddhist catechism for his students called the *Compass of Zen Teaching* (ca. 1976). *Compass of Zen Teaching* was his

41. "Traveling Zen Master," *Dharma Light* (Newsletter of Dharma Zen Center in Los Angeles, Summer 1994.

version of *sagyo ipsŏn* and represented his doctrinal view of Buddhism. In 1982 Providence Zen Center published *Only Don't Know: The Teaching Letters of Zen Master Seung Sahn*. Along with *Compass of Zen Teaching,* Soen Sa Nim came up with *Your Mind Meal* (1979), which consisted of ten Kong-ans called "Gate." Over the years his teachings have expanded. The two-page *Your Mind Meal* has turned into two books of Kong-an collections: *The Whole World Is a Single Flower: 365 Kong-ans for Everyday Life* (Boston: Charles E. Tuttle Company, 1992) and *Ten Gates: The Kong-an Teaching of Zen Master Seung Sahn* (Cumberland, R.I.: Primary Point Press, 1987), while the 39-page *Compass of Zen Teaching* has expanded into a 394-page book, *The Compass of Zen* (Boston: Shambhala, 1997). *The Compass of Zen, The Whole World Is a Single Flower, Ten Gates,* and *Only Don't Know* form the three-dimensional nucleus of his teachings. Add to these his famous slogan practice, "Only don't know," "Only go straight," "Just do it," and "Don't make anything," and so forth.

Soen Sa Nim comes from the Kyŏnghŏ (1849–1912) and Man'gong (1871–1946) line of Korean Sŏn. The *sagyo ipsŏn* of Kyŏnghŏ, who revitalized Korean Sŏn in the late nineteenth century, is well known. Kyŏnghŏ was a sutra teacher. When he finally realized that his knowledge of doctrinal teachings was no help to people dying of cholera, he abandoned it for hwadu Sŏn. Soen Sa Nim's experiment of Korean Sŏn with his American students proved over and over again that they know and think and worry a lot. So he began to promote "don't know" practice. Being a highly versatile and engaging teacher, he would always have proper prescriptions ready in his dharma shop with, "Clear mind, don't know" mantra, doing prostrations, including kido chanting or some kind of one-hundred-day practice, all to attain a "don't know" mind. It would not be wise to risk examining his Kong-an system here. But his cure-all "don't know mind" would sum up his teaching style.

"A don't know mind is a before-thinking mind. Before-thinking is clear like space. Clear like space is clear like a mirror."[42] This "don't know" comes from Chinul's *Susim-gyŏl* (Secrets on Cultivating the Mind), where it says, "Only if you know that you don't know, this is seeing into your nature."[43] Seeing into your nature is *kyŏnsŏng* (J. kensho). Soen Sa Nim's *sagyo* (abandoning *kyo* doctrinal teachings) has been to help his students *abandon* a discriminating mind by practicing "don't know" so they can enter into Sŏn,

---

42. *Only Don't Know: The Teaching Letters of Zen Master Seung Sahn* (San Francisco: Four Seasons Foundation, 1982), vii.

43. *Pojo Pŏbŏ,* Sangwŏn-sa, 1937, 16. 但知不會 是即見性 which Robert E. Buswell Jr. translates as, "Simply by knowing that there is no other way to understand, you are seeing the nature." (See his "Secrets on Cultivating the Mind" in *The Korean Approach to Zen: The Collected Works of Chinul,* 145. But Soen Sa Nim used 但知不知 instead of 但知不會.

which is the practice of waking up to realize their true nature. He teaches his students "Action Zen" as everyday Zen practice and advocates "Just do it," "Only go straight," and "Moment to moment great love."[44]

He has been a great proponent of "together actions," traveling all over the world and urging his students to live together for "together actions," that is, dharma practice and fellowship. His charisma, dynamic personality, and disarming attitude have touched many people. During his twenty-seven years of dharma service, Soen Sa Nim has ordained and produced many disciples. At present, there are twenty-three monks (seventeen male and six female) and nine Bodhisattva teachers (formerly Bodhisattva monks) and eight Zen masters who received dharma transmission, eighteen Jido Poepsa (Guiding Dharma teachers, formerly Master Dharma teachers), and one hundred and twenty-five dharma teachers. Today there are three Kwan Um Zen School headquarters in the world, with a Kwan Um Zen School in Providence serving as world headquarters.[45] In the United States there are about thirty centers and groups that are affiliated with the Kwan Um Zen School.

Reactions to Master Seung Sahn

In spite of his selfless devotion and great achievements, Soen Sa Nim has not been free from criticism. One criticism involves his penchant or missionary zeal for quantitative achievement at the expense of quality. "A number of Zen centers have appeared and disappeared in Seung Sahn's firmament with great rapidity.... He is most interested in gaining a large number of students, even if they turn out to be short-term catches. This striving for numbers for numbers' sake has left a parallel impression that Seung Sahn has been remarkably unconcerned with the spiritual training of those who might come into contact with the groups within his organizations."[46] This is harsh criticism coming from a former student of Soen Sa Nim's. Although

---

44. "Zen Master Seung Sahn is a born teacher, an astonishingly adept and fertile inventor of skillful means. In the early days, just after he came to America, he would change his slogan every few months. One month it was 'Only go straight,' which he would repeat so often that it seemed to be the theme song of the whole universe, even in the depths of our dreams. Then, two months later, it was 'Just do it' (this was long before some hotshot at Nike came up with the phrase). Then it was 'Don't check other people's minds.' You get the idea." "Foreword" by Stephen Mitchell in *The Compass of Zen* (Boston: Shambhala, 1997).

45. I am indebted to J. W. Harrington of the Kwan Um School office for the information.

46. See "Korean Buddhism in America: A New Style of Zen" by Mu Soeng (Prakash Shrivastava) in *The Faces of Buddhism in America,* ed. Charles S. Prebish and Kenneth K. Tanaka (Berkeley: University of California Press, 1998), 124–25.

somewhat exaggerated, there is a truth in the critique. I may note, however, that Soen Sa Nim's carefree attitude and generosity must have contributed to this impression. Many people have been helped by Soen Sa Nim, some greatly, including the author of the critique quoted above. Sometimes Soen Sa Nim has tried to help too many people, with the result that an "easy come, easy go" style of his Zen centers may have created confusion in the minds of serious students. I remember his once telling me when I questioned him on his nondiscriminatory open-door policy, "Even though people have just been inside the temple and experienced peace and quiet by looking at Buddha statue, they have been helped and a Dharma seed planted." I have heard this before, growing up in the temples of Korea, but obviously I have not lived the teachings. It is comforting to know that even "short-term catches" can be helped and perhaps awakened. Hasn't this been a Mahayana approach all along?

Another criticism of his style is about his making instant-Zen teachers. "Lay students are permitted to wear the traditional Korean monk's robes. Until quite recently, almost as a matter of routine, a person who had been around for a few months was made a 'Dharma teacher' and was given a monk's robes to wear. At times it has seemed more like a sop to the practitioner's ego and to the need for identity confirmation through a uniform than an authentication of the person's immersion in practice."[47] Furthermore, the author Mu Soeng (Prakash Shrivastava) describes Soen Sa Nim as "an evangelist in the service of Korean Buddhism" and Kwan Um Zen School as "a tribe of individual nomads trying to fit into a mold of clan loyalty and group identity."[48] Apart from the truth or nontruth of this description, it has to be said that there are many mature and wonderful people in the Kwan Um Zen School, and there is no lack of sincere effort on the part of its leadership.

Since 1987 when he celebrated his sixtieth birthday, a special occasion for Koreans, Soen Sa Nim has progressively spent less time at Providence Zen Center, his American residence, and Kwan Um Zen School headquarters. Soen Sa Nim has had health problems for many years. In July of 1977 he went into the hospital to have his irregular heartbeat monitored and to begin using insulin to control an advanced case of diabetes.[49] In the last five years he had to be hospitalized for heart problems more than ten times. In April of 1999 he had to be rushed to the hospital the following morning after he

47. Ibid., 123.
48. Ibid, 123 and 125.
49. *Only Don't Know*, 3, footnote.

delivered a dharma talk at Union Theological Seminary in New York City. His dharma power, vital spirit, and tireless efforts are simply amazing. Bodhidharma from Korea, as he was sometimes called, will continue to travel for the sake of the Way of Buddha until his body wears out.

Conclusion

Following the forward movement of Korean culture and riding on the new wave of immigration, the three pioneers of Korean Buddhism arrived in America at the right time. In the 1960s and 1970s young people of the counterculture and the flower generation who were "turning East" started practicing meditation and looking for gurus. Zen and Buddhism became a "freewheeling enterprise" between Enlightenment seekers and Zen masters or New Age gurus. The three masters from Korea were not familiar with Western culture in general, nor did they speak the language properly. They arrived already advanced in age and came from a country that was not particularly known for its flourishing Buddhist tradition. Therefore, if anything, they were at a great disadvantage in their dharma work. What compensated for their disadvantage was the Korean character of Buddhism, flexibility and adaptability. They inherited the spiritual tradition of Wŏnhyo's *hoit'ong*, reconciliation and integration, or syncretic Buddhism, Chinul's fundamental unity of doctrine and meditation, and Hyujŏng's *sagyo ipsŏn* (abandonment of doctrine and entrance into Sŏn).

Understandably, they differed with each other in their application of syncretic Buddhism in their dealings with the new environment. In the dynamic equilibrium of doctrine (*kyo*) and meditation (Sŏn) that has persisted throughout the history of Korean Buddhism, Ven. Dr. Seo, Kyung-Bo and Kusan Sunim stood at almost opposite ends. Although Ven. Dr. Seo, Kyung-Bo acted as a Zen master toward his Western students, he occupied himself most of the time in literary, academic, and secular pursuits. By contrast, Kusan Sunim was a Zen master with traditional and monastic background who showed no interest in the scriptures. But both suffered from the nonresidential and visiting nature of their teachings in America. I have not heard of any of Dr. Seo, Kyung-Bo's direct American disciples functioning as Buddhist teachers. However, his teaching tradition in America survives at two Korean temples run by his Korean disciples, Han'guk-sa (Korean Temple) or Zen College in Germantown, Maryland, and Paegnim-sa on Mt. Vernon in New York State.

Being the youngest and a full-time resident, Soen Sa Nim was poised best for the dharma work. And in style and character he proved to best represent the syncretic Buddhism of Korea in America so far. The diverse activities of his modified Korean Buddhism in America included interreligious gatherings, Buddhist-Christian retreats, and the making of Christian Kong-ans. Yes, such activities are the work of his genius and a product of his eclectic mind. But they are also the extension of the legacy of syncretic vision of Wŏnhyo, Chinul, and Hyujŏng brought to America by Soen Sa Nim. A proper investigation of the experimentation of Soen Sa Nim's Korean Buddhism in America would shed much light on the future direction of Korean Buddhism in America. However, it is not within the scope of this chapter. Suffice it to say for now that one can learn much, both positive and negative, from his enculturation experience of Korean Buddhism in America.

The three pioneers introduced Korean Buddhism to the West and paved the way for their followers. Perhaps unawares they also brought with them Korean traditional culture and values along with Buddhist culture. Paegnimsa Temple on Mt. Vernon in New York State and Buddhist Pagoda at Diamond Hill Monastery in Providence were built in the traditional Korean-style architecture.

Soen Sa Nim built a Korean-style temple in Los Angeles for his Korean followers. His American disciple, Master Dae Gak (Robert Genthner), built a traditional temple at Furnace Mountain in Kentucky in 1994 following the traditional geomantic (wind-and-water) principles in order to create a great harmony of location of the temple with the land. Another American disciple of his, Muryang Sunim (Erik Berall), has been building since 1994 a Korean-style temple, T'aego-sa monastery and Mountain Spirit Center, on 318 acres of canyon area at the southern tip of a Sierra mountain in California. Muryang Sunim says that an important work takes more than one lifetime to complete. He is not in a rush. He keeps building the monastery every day on a remote mountain.

The three Korean Sŏn masters were also responsible for inviting traditional master carpenters, wood-carvers, tanch'ŏng painters, and sculptors who provided their services at Korean temples in the different U.S. cities. Since 1990 Kusan Sunim's former disciple, Professor Robert E. Buswell Jr., has been serving as editor-in-chief for the quarterly magazine *Korean Culture,* published by Korean Cultural Service in Los Angeles. Ven. Dr. Seo, Kyung-Bo; Kusan Sunim; and Soen Sa Nim were instrumental not only for the transmission of dharma from Korea to the West but also for the transmission of traditional Korean culture, thereby contributing to the globalization of Korean culture as well as Korean Buddhism.

Glossary of Sino-Korean Characters

Sŏn 禪

Kyo 敎

Sagyo ipsŏn 捨敎入禪

Hwadu (interchangeable with Kong-an in meaning) 話頭

Tono tonsu 頓悟頓修

Tono chŏmsu 頓悟漸修

Kyŏnsŏng (J. kensho) 見性

Sŏngbul 成佛

Kong-an (J. koan; interchangeable with hwadu in meaning) 公案

Susim-gyŏl 修心訣

14

Won Buddhism in the United States

Bok In Kim

BOTH WON BUDDHISM AND HARE KRISHNA entered the United States after Asian origins. Both arrived on Western shores about the same time. What can Won Buddhism[1] learn from the International Society of Krishna Consciousness (hereafter ISKCON)[2] in order to comprehend the complexities of the process of acculturation? By examining the success and failure of ISKCON, I would like to present some suggestions to the Won Buddhist mission in the United States.

1. Won Buddhism: *Won* means "circle" in Korean, a symbol of Buddha's cosmic body, the enlightened nature of all sentient beings, and the noumenal nature of all beings in the universe; Buddhism means a religion of Enlightenment. Won Buddhism thus teaches how to be enlightened to the truth that the whole universe is none other than the manifestation of Buddha's cosmic body, the enlightened nature of all sentient beings, and the noumenal nature of all beings in the universe. Won Buddhism was founded by Sot'ae-san (1891–1943) upon his great enlightenment to this truth in 1916 in Korea. The religion was founded with the goals of delivering all sentient beings suffering in the bitter seas of life and curing the world of illness. The way of deliverance lies in Correct Enlightenment and Right Conduct; the way to cure the world is Awareness and Recompense of Beneficence. The object of religious worship is the Fourfold Beneficence (Heaven and Earth, Parents, Brethren, Law) to which one owes one's life. The religious practice aims at the moral perfection with respect to the three aspects of one's Buddha nature: calmness (*samadhi*), wisdom (*prajna*), and morality (*sila*). The unitary circular form (*Irwonsang*) is enshrined as the symbol of the object of religious faith and the standard of religious practice. The two main objectives of Won Buddhism thus aim at helping one be enlightened to one's original nature and delivered from the tormenting seas of life, and realizing a paradise by being aware of one's indebtedness to and recompensing the fourfold beneficence.

2. Burke E. Rochford, *Hare Krishna in America* (New Brunswick: Rutgers University Press, 1985), 209.

Before comparing ISKCON and Won Buddhism, however, I would like to describe Won Buddhism in terms of its belief as well as its distinctions from other Buddhist schools. Understanding Won Buddhism in the context of the historical Buddhist stream would be beneficial to the readers of the West for their comprehension of comparison between ISKCON and Won Buddhism.

Won ("circle" in Korean") symbolizes Buddha's cosmic body, the enlightened nature of all sentient beings, and the noumenal nature of all beings in the universe. According to Sot'aesan, Park Chung Bin (1891–1943), the founder of Won Buddhism, the fundamental truths of Buddhist teachings are that (1) all things are either being born nor dying, and (2) all things are causally interrelated.[3] Won Buddhist belief in truth is not different from other Buddhist schools' belief. Thus, Sot'aesan taught his teaching, named Chongjon (Correct teaching), based on the fundamental truths of Buddhism.

However, the Won Buddhist movement has been shown to have departed from traditional Buddhism in many ways. Won Buddhism is the only school of Buddhism in Korea that is not categorized as a sect or school of Buddhism. It relies on its own canon of scripture, the teachings of Sot'aesan. It has a unique community of temples and clergy. And it has shifted the focus of its worship away the figure of the human Buddha to the Truth Buddha. Still, Won Buddhism is defined as new or reformed Buddhism on the basis of Sot'aesan's creative interpretations of the three jewels: Buddha, Dharma, and Sangha.[4]

Though the historical study of the mission of Buddhist schools in the United States is interesting, this chapter focuses on Won Buddhist mission in the United States in relation to ISKCON's mission. ISKCON's giant footprint in the U.S. mission is so distinctive that it is worthwhile to compare it with that of Won Buddhism. In terms of size alone, there cannot be much comparison between them, even though their introduction to the United States appeared around the same time. The founder of ISKCON, S'rila Prabhupada (1896–1977)—originally named Bhaktivedanta Swami—arrived in New York in 1965 and founded the first Hare Krishna temple in New York in 1966. By the time Won Buddhism was introduced to the United States in 1972, seven years later, ISKCON had established sixty-eight centers in the United States and abroad. The Won Buddhist mission in the United States twenty-five years later had not reached what ISKCON had in the first seven

---

3. *The Scripture of Won Buddhism*, trans. Pal-khn Chon (Iri, Korea: Won Buddhist Publishing, 1988), 378.
4. Bok In Kim, "Sot'aesan and the Reformation of Korean Buddhism," *Korean Studies* 19 (1995): 59.

years of its mission.[5] The present number of non-Korean members in the Won Buddhist mission in the United States is fewer than ISKCON's 200 converts during its first two years.[6]

Though ISKCON appealed to the American population right away and made fast progress during its first decade (1965–74), it began to face its decline after the first decade. The speed of its decline was very fast; in fact, it was almost equal to its growth. In the beginning ISKCON did not start with the characteristics of an Indian ethnic religion, although the Hare Krishna movement originated in India as a sect of devotionalism around the fifteenth century. ISKCON appealed to the American population as an alternative religion and philosophy that rejected institutionalized religions and traditional cultural forms.

The era during which ISKCON had its strongest public appeal can be characterized as a countercultural age—a time that was antiwar and anti-institutional. Thus, ISKCON's success has a lesson to teach. After the first decade of advance and acceptance derived from its countercultural context, ISKCON had to adapt itself to the culture since it could not change the whole culture by its ideology nor could it survive independently as an anti-cultural movement. During its most recent adaptation process, ISKCON has tried to create "the image of themselves as an ethnic church (of Hinduism)" and "the image of bearer of Vedic culture." Thus the mission has followed a process that started with the characteristics of universality and shifted into those of ethnicity.

The Won Buddhist experience in the United States is the reverse of ISKCON's. When Won Buddhism was introduced to the United States in 1972, its movement was strictly confined to the Korean community in Los Angeles.[7] A year later in 1973, a Won Buddhist mission started in the Chicago Korean community. In 1974 Won Buddhism was introduced to the New York Korean community. Thus, the Won Buddhist mission started as an ethnic church in the United States; only later did Won Buddhist teaching

---

5. There are six Won Buddhist temples on the East Coast of the United States, nine on the West Coast, and one in the Midwest. Each temple—except Miami and Manhattan temples, the majority of whose members are non-Korean—has its regular Dharma meeting on Sunday. The Dharma meetings have fewer than one hundred adult members in attendance except at special gatherings such as the founder's enlightenment day or the Buddha's birthday.

6. In 1997 three Won Buddhist temples in the United States have regular English-speaking services for non-Koreans and second-generation Koreans. Each temple's regular attendance is fewer than thirty people. See Burke E. Rochford, "Hare Krishna in America: Growth, Decline, and Accommodation," in *America's Alternative Religions*, ed. Timothy Miller (Albany: State University of New York Press, 1995), 217.

7. At the first meeting of Los Angeles Won Buddhist Temple (October 8, 1972) thirteen members were in attendance. All of them were Koreans.

began to focus on its characteristics of universality that can be applied to the American public.

The greatest obstacle in reaching out to Americans has been the language barrier. Almost fifteen years after its arrival on American soil, there was not much change in its function as an ethnic church. Won Buddhist services in English did not start until the mid-1980s, first in Miami and later in Won Buddhist temples in Philadelphia, San Diego, Manhattan, and San Francisco. Among these temples, Won Buddhism of Miami and Manhattan have English-only congregations—part of the congregation is second-generation Korean immigrants. Though fifteen other temples in the United States have only informal contact with English-speaking audiences, their eagerness and effort to go beyond being merely an ethnic church represents the general spirit of Won Buddhist mission in the United States. Won Buddhism's mission, restricted at the start to an ethnically related context, has tried to make a shift to an emphasis on its universal nature.

Thus, the Hare Krishna mission and the Won Buddhist mission have had distinctively different patterns. In this chapter I will examine two aspects of ISKCON—its internal structure and its external evaluation—comparing them with the Won Buddhist movement in the United States. However, it is too early to make an external evaluation of the Won Buddhist mission, since Won Buddhism has not at this point had much exposure to non-Koreans. However, Won Buddhism can examine what the Hare Krishna mission faced when exposed to a non-Indian culture and can ask why ISKCON faced such an evaluation.

Internal Structure

ISKCON's essential teachings and values have come from its founder, Prabhupada, who teaches Krishna Consciousness only and emphasizes the value of extreme antimaterialism. When we examine the root of ISKCON, Chaitanya Mahaprabhu (1486–?), the founder of the Krishna movement in India, was not challenged by any scientific revolution or materialism. Based on the founder's teaching, Prabhupada's missionary project in the United States was to reject the material world as Maya (delusion) and to rely on the protection of Krishna.[8]

---

8. Stillson J. Judha, *Hare Krishna and the Counterculture* (New York: John Wiley & Sons, 1974), 156. There were levels of devotees—householder, unmarried devotee, and *Sannyasi*. *Sannyasi* is the one who renounces all relationship with material world because the service to *Krishna* is spiritual and transcends the materiality of the illusory world.

Unlike Chaitanya, Sot'aesan (1891–1943), the founder of the Won Buddhist movement, was clearly aware of the problem of modernity—that is, the advanced material civilization of the present and the future. To solve the problem of modernity, Sot'aesan talked about the necessity of the re-creation of spirit, which can respond positively to the influence of Western material civilization. It is thus important to elaborate Sot'aesan's positive perspective on material civilization and his vision of spirituality in the future, for it is very different from ISKCON's negative perspective on material civilization.

Though he has a positive perspective on material civilization, Sot'aesan realizes that there are human problems derived from scientific development, namely materialism. He points out contemporary suffering due to material civilization, saying that "nowadays, because of the rise of materialism, people are becoming more covetous ... the world will never have peace without overcoming covetousness."[9] As Siddharta Gautama declared twenty-five hundred years ago, human suffering can be defined as "deriving from covetous or greedy human nature." Especially in the modern era, human suffering is related to materialism. That is, people become more desirous for material things, easily ignoring moral or spiritual values in order to pursue more material luxuries. These people then lose spiritual strength and finally fall into a life of slavery to materialism. Sot'aesan is clearly aware that material civilization is the cause of various human sufferings.

However, Sot'aesan also realizes that material civilization is an essential element[10] in creating a truly civilized world, though it needs to be integrated with spiritual civilization. Thus, his response is not to reject matter in order to recover spirituality, as ISKCON teaches. Rather Sot'aesan teaches the recreation of spirit, namely the radical improvement of spiritual civilization to cope with the scientific revolution or radical improvement of material civilization.[11] His teaching talks about concrete methods to accomplish this recreation of spirit in order not to fall into a life of slavery to materialism. His vision for the future is that there will be a truly civilized world, where spiritual civilization is equally as developed as material civilization and where both civilizations—material and spiritual—are well integrated. Sot'aesan sees a positive value for matter, in contrast to ISKCON's negative evaluation and antimaterialism. Material civilization is an essential element in creating

9. *The Scripture of Won Buddhism,* trans. Pal Khn Chon (Iksan, Korea: Won Buddhist Publishing, 1970), 170.

10. Bok In Kim, "Re-creation of Spirit in Response to Western Material Civilization," *Seoul Journal of Korean Studies* 7 (1994): 109.

11. Ibid., 104.

a truly developed civilization. Without one or the other, human civilization can be considered partial or crippled. Won Buddhist teaching talks about the balance and harmony between matter and spirit without total rejection or surrender of one to the other.

People in the ISKCON community, in contrast, share an extreme anti-materialism and find security through communal life in the local temple or on farms.[12] Though there was a 1972 directive that married devotees should live outside the temple,[13] their communal life gives security and bonding to people who join in the movement. In their community all follow a uniform style of life—shaving their hair, wearing orange robes, drawing a mark on their foreheads, and chanting the Hare Krishna mantra.

The Won Buddhist mission in Korea eighty years ago started with communal life under the guidance of Sot'aesan, the founder. In the beginning stage of the Won Buddhist community, there was no clear distinction between priests and laity. Now, about eighty years later, communal life in Won Buddhism is mainly limited to female priests who lead a celibate life. Male priests and their families live in their private houses like the laity in general. When Won Buddhism was introduced to the United States in 1972 (Won Buddhist year 57), the concept or model of communal life did not exist even in Korea. Thus, the Won Buddhist mission in the United States has never tried any communal center since the beginning of its mission here. One or two priests reside at the temple and perform the missionary role for each temple. Since the priests do not live with their family in the temple, according to the Won Buddhist tradition, celibate priests tend to work for the missionary field in Won Buddhist temples in Korea. This tendency became stronger in the United States, and all temples in the United States except two are run by female priests. Though there are experimental plans for recovering communal life in the Won Buddhist community, those plans are not yet in practice even in Korea.

The Won Buddhist mission in the United States, therefore, did not start with communal life as ISKCON did. Since communal life was not the original setting in Won Buddhism in the United States, the Won Buddhist mission has not shown a distinctive style like ISKON's robe, hairstyle, or makeup. Even in Korea there is no special form of identity for Won Buddhists except the female priests' attire. Though a Won Buddhist member's

---

12. According to the data of 1985 ISKCON mission of the United States there were forty-two centers, eleven farms, and nine restaurants recorded. See lists of ISKCON centers recorded in Satsvarupa Dasa Goswami, *Prabhupada* (Los Angeles: Bhaktivedanta Book Trust, 1985), 408–12.

13. Judah, *Hare Krishna and the Counterculture*, 180.

identity is established by dharma name—a tradition that started in an early year of Won Buddhist history—that identity obviously is not apparent to others in the same degree as is the distinctive appearance of ISKCON's members.

In the early years of Won Buddhism when disciples lived in a communal setting, sitting meditation and chanting were daily practices shared in the Won Buddhist community. Besides these two practices, there were two regular meetings a week—one at night during weekdays and one on Sunday morning. The basic principle of a communal life in the Won Buddhist community was that each member had to work for his living. Since the Won Buddhist community started with a self-sufficient way of living without relying on external sources such as almsgiving or donation, members were given work to provide expenses for their living.

Though married disciples and celibate disciples lived together in one boundary, there was a clear distinction in terms of financial management. Since disciples, married or celibate, were asked to devote themselves to the order, the families of the married disciples were supported by their spouses. In principle, women are allowed to be priests while being married. However, there have not been any women priests with spouses and families since the time of the founder. So the spouses referred to above are women only. When Won Buddhism in the United States seriously considers the condition of its priests, the rule that requires women to be celibate needs to be reconsidered.

As we see, the Won Buddhist community allowed economic self-sufficiency from the beginning and even required the spouses of the married disciples to manage their private lives. Now the Won Buddhist community in Korea faces the problem that spouses of married priests have difficulty handling their economic condition by themselves. In other words, many families need a husband's income to survive. Such a condition was not expected in the early period of the order. These economic situations led to a break in the setting of the communal life of the early period. Since the numbers of married priests are growing, their spouses cannot manage their financial condition just staying in the boundary of community. Slowly, wives of the married priests started to move from the communal life, and husbands became commuters just like regular workers. So now the Won Buddhist communal life in Korea is composed of female priests and a few celibate male priests who reside in the headquarters. If female priests are allowed to have family and move from the community, there will not be any communal setting such as existed in the early period of Won Buddhism. Thus, it is not clear what kind of communal life Won Buddhists can create if the American Won Buddhist

Headquarters is to be similar to the Won Buddhist Headquarters in Korea—in terms of size and scale—and is set up in the near future.

The reason I consider the particular form of the Won Buddhist community so seriously is that the success and failure of the ISKCON's mission is closely related to its communal life. Communal life was a great source in appealing to people who felt a need for security and bonding. People who joined in that communal life shared the value of antimaterialism and could happily flee from the competitive society, the main direction of which is materialism.[14] Though an individual in the ISKCON community could escape from any competition or pressure they had previously experienced in society, the ISKCON community itself needed to survive in the competitive world, that is, the materially oriented world. Thus, the ISKCON society later—because of its need for financial resources in order to maintain communal life—had to spend great energy and concern with money making.[15] That is, the communal form of life, lacking sufficient funds or skills to maintain itself, can be considered one of the major causes of the failure of ISKCON's mission in the United States. If we seek a further cause, members of ISKCON, whose fundamental value is antimaterialism, are not ready to deal with the material world of U.S. culture. Thus, we can easily draw the conclusion that the ISKCON society, as a collection of those members, would expect economic hardship from its beginning.

External Evaluation

ISKCON's internal structure in the 1960s and 1970s was fitting to the anticultural groups of that time, including the Hippies and other countercultural communities. Through its teaching and value system and its practice of communal life, the ISKCON movement made very rapid progress during the first decade—1965–74.[16] The first decade was the period during which ISKCON was introduced to a new culture with the characteristics of being "counter" or "anti." After the first decade of its mission, ISKCON, with its alternate ideology and philosophy, needed to respond to external evaluation

14. Larry Shinn and David G. Bromley, *Krishna Consciousness in the West* (Lewisburg, Pa.: Bucknell University Press, 1989), 227. ISKCON offers an antimaterialistic lifestyle in which individuals no longer crave material goods and are no longer motivated by competition for success.

15. Rochford, "Hare Krishna in America," 217. After the period of growth during which its major source of income was selling books—over thirteen million dollars on selling hardback books between 1974 and 1978—ISKCON found it difficult to secure the economic resources necessary to sustain its communities.

16. Shinn and Bromley, *Krishna Consciousness in the West*, 92.

with its ideology and philosophy since it was neither powerful enough to change the society as whole nor self-sufficient enough not to be influenced by society.

As mentioned before, ISKCON's philosophy of antimaterialism functioned as a source of refuge so that people could flee from competitive society into the ISKCON community. There was a positive evaluation by the public in its early mission. However, later ISKCON as a community received negative and harsh response from the public, whose chief encounters with ISKCON occurred in its continual attempts at raising money by selling books or other products. Though ISKCON's goal after the first decade was to adapt itself to society, its mission focused on a wrong way, causing its public definition "as a threatening movement."[17] Mainly, its money-making mechanism was criticized by the public. Later, the public criticized even its religious practice of chanting mantra, portraying it as "a mind-manipulating technique that dulls the senses, destroys the rational faculties, [and] actually causes physical damage."[18]

According to sociologists, new religious movements start with the characteristics of sect—rejection of the conventional rules or values of the society. Those movements appeal to people because of their shock value, their appeal to the spirit of anti. Later, those movements need to adapt themselves to the general scheme of the society. Strictly speaking, the Hare Krishna movement is not a new religious movement like various Christian sects of twentieth century. The Hare Krishna movement originated in the fifteenth century, and its renewal movement occurred due to the spiritual teachings of Swami Bhaktivedanta, Prabhupada in the late nineteenth century. When Prabhupada's mission started in the United States, the Indian heritage of Prabhupada's mission was not asked or cared about much. ISKCON's mission in the United States in the beginning appealed to American audiences as an alternative to their established religion and value system. That is, without asking about its deep heritage, it was introduced more as a sect simply because it was new to the West. Later, ISKCON felt a familiar necessity, the process of adaptation. Its movement needed to transform from the stage of a sect to the status of denomination or church.[19]

ISKCON's theoretical foundation, an antimaterialistic and anticultural ideology and value system, was a great challenge to the general public. Its

17. Rochford, *Hare Krishna in America,* 217.

18. Shinn, *Krishna Consciousness in the West,* 93.

19. Rochford, *Hare Krishna in America,* 216. A sect rejects the value of prevailing society, while a church (or a denomination) accepts community norms and values. Thus, the tendency for sects to develop into denomination has been presented as an inevitable linear progression.

exotic style of dress, hairstyle, makeup, and practice planted the impression that its members were very different. Their communal lifestyle was contrary to American individualism. Though their ideology, practice, or communal life was acknowledged only as different in the beginning, those differences became seen as threatening through the process of ISKCON's recruitment or its way of raising money. The movement quickly became labeled a cult. ISKCON was represented as "social marginal" or a form of "social marginality" in a scholarly sense, "pagan and heretical" in the Christian sense, and "destructive mind control" in anticultist sense.[20] Especially from anticultists, it received severe hostility, being defined as "an example of a pagan, unchristian cult ... where deception and indoctrination keep members under the strict control of a despotic ruler who masquerades as a guru."[21]

ISKCON thus underwent difficulties of adaptation because of negative evaluation from the general public. Now, however, ISKCON portrays itself as a traditional Indian religious group, while creating an image of itself as "bearer of Vedic culture."[22] ISKCON is a denomination within Hinduism, the world's oldest religion; thus, it is claimed as "an ethnic church."[23] It is true that the Indian American community has generally considered the Hare Krishna movement as orthodox and attended Krishna temples in the absence of an Indian temple. By emphasizing ethnicity, ISKCON tries to overcome the external evaluation made of it as a cult movement. However, ISKCON's mission seems retrogressive when it starts to confine itself within the category of an ethnic church or denomination of Hinduism after thirty years of mission in the United States. Through this confinement, ISKCON's spirit of universality shrinks and becomes localized. Again, sooner or later its mission will need a strategy on how to overcome its ethnicity in order to adapt itself to the United States, a foreign culture.

Practical Concerns of Won Buddhist Mission in United States

Examination of ISKCON's mission in the United States raises two issues about the Won Buddhist mission in the United States. As was addressed in the beginning, the Won Buddhist mission in the United States started with the Korean ethnic community and now tries to overcome the boundary of

20. Shinn and Bromley, *Krishna Consciousness in the West,* 96.
21. Ibid., 225.
22. Ibid., 95.
23. Ibid.

ethnicity. The Won Buddhist mission in the United States is expected to focus more on the English-speaking community, within which the second-generation of Korean Americans are included, than on the Korean ethnic group, namely the first generation of Korean immigrants.

What kind of problems can Won Buddhism of the United States antici-pate during the process of overcoming the ethnic boundary? In order to discuss this question, I will examine two data of 1998—attendance rate and donation ratio between the two groups, Korean members and English mem-bers of the Won Buddhist Temple in Philadelphia.

The numbers of the Korean group are twice those of the English-speaking group. The striking contrast is not just different size of membership but atten-dance rate. More than 90 percent of Korean members keep over 50 percent of attendance. That is, unless they move to another state or to Korea, they continuously come to the temple. On the other hand, only about 20 percent of English-speaking members keep over 50 percent of attendance. Though there are many visitors at the English-speaking meetings, many of them hardly visit the temple a second time. The attitude of their first visit also is very different. The Korean people visit the temple with quite a determina-tion to join the temple later. The English-speaking group, who have been ex-posed to many Buddhist temples, consider the Won Buddhist Temple as one of the optional choices; thus it is hard for them to make up their minds on Won Buddhist practice the first time.

The financial management of the temple is taken care of mainly by Korean members. The English-speaking group's cash donation is about 1 percent. Though English-speaking members—almost 50 percent—participate in var-ious community work as volunteers based on their skills or specialties, they do not practice primary responsibility for the temple's finance. Can the shift of missionary focus—Korean ethnic community to the English-speaking community—actually happen? How long does the Won Buddhist mission in the United States take in order to overcome the ethnic boundary and take root in the United States?

Won Buddhist teaching—as a new Buddhism and a new religion—is dif-ferent from the Hare Krishna movement, which has been defined as a sec-tarian denomination within Hinduism. Won Buddhism has denied its status as a Buddhist sect in all-Korean context since its foundation. The Won Bud-dhist unique use of the symbol *Irwonsang* (a unitary form of a circle)[24] creates

24. *Irwon* refers to unitary circle representing Dharmakaya Buddha. The figure of *Irwon* (O or *Irwon-sang*) is enshrined in the Won Buddhist temple instead of Buddha's images, namely *Nirmanakaya* Buddha. Sot'aesan defines *Irwon* as the source of *Eun* (grace or beneficence), explaining the fundamental structure of beings in the world as *Eun* because all beings are related and mutually indebted. *Irwon* manifests itself

the image of a new religious community rather than a Buddhist sectarian community. Thus, the Won Buddhist temple in the United States does not function much as an alternative of the Buddhist temple for the Korean American community, unlike members of the Indian American community who attend Krishna temples in the absence of an Indian temple in their own community. That is, Won Buddhism has been more a new religion in Korea, as it is in the United States.

Unlike Korean Buddhists' response to Won Buddhism, the symbol of *Irwonsang* enshrined in the Won Buddhist temple does not give any unfamiliar impression to the general public of the United States. In a sense, the symbol of *Irwonsang* fits better the Western mentality,[25] whose mind-set has been against any type of idolatry, and thus has been troubled with the image or statue of Buddha. Since people in the United States start to learn Buddhism through books or lectures, they do not have any fixed idea of what a Buddhist temple is supposed to be. Thus, the Won Buddhist temple functions well as a nonsectarian Buddhist temple to the public in the United States.

However, the image of Won Buddhism as a new religion—which is the attractive point to the Korean community—cannot be ignored easily, because the Won Buddhist temples rely heavily on the Korean community. At the same time, if it loses the connection with Buddhism, Won Buddhism might face external evaluation similar to what ISKCON encountered—an image as a cult movement. Later, Won Buddhism might undergo a similar effort to relate itself to the heritage of Buddhism, if not an ethnic Korean Buddhism. Though Won Buddhism might not meet Hare Krishna's kind of danger in the future, it seems worthwhile to speculate how the Won Buddhist mission in the United States will create its image, whether as a new religion, a new Buddhism, or both in a skillful manner.

---

as *Saeun* (Grace of Heaven and Earth, Grace of Parents, Grace of Brethren, Grace of Law), Sot'aesan's four categories of *Eun*.

25. *Irwonsang,* the perfect circle, is the central image in the Won Buddhist religion. Like the Jewish Star and the Christian Cross, *Irwonsang* is a symbol of the essential truth.

References

Bainbridge, W. Sims, and Rodney Stark. 1985. *The Future of Religion*. Berkeley and Los Angeles: University of California Press.

Goswami, Satsvarupa Dasa. 1983. *Prabhupada*. Los Angeles: The Bhaktivedanta Book Trust.

Judah, J. Stillson. 1974. *Hare Krishna and the Counterculture*. New York: John Wiley & Sons.

Kim, Bok In. 1994. "Re-creation of Spirit in Response to Western Material Civilization—Sot'aesan's Perspective." *Seoul Journal of Korean Studies* 7:99–109.

Rochford Jr., E. Burke. 1985. *Hare Krishna in America*. New Brunswick: Rutgers University.

———. 1995. "Hare Krishna in America: Growth, Decline, and Accommodation." In *America's Alternative Religions*, ed. Timothy Miller, 215–21. Albany: State University of New York Press.

Shinn, Larry, and David G. Bromley, eds. 1989. *Krishna Consciousness in the West*. Lewisburg, Pa.: Bucknell University Press.

The Scripture of Won Buddhism. Trans. Pal Khn Chon. Iksan, Korea: Won Buddhist Publishing, 1970.

15

Intra-Ethnic Religious Diversity

Korean Buddhists and Protestants in Greater Boston

Karen J. Chai

IT IS ELEVEN O'CLOCK SUNDAY MORNING, and Korean families and young adults from around the Boston area are gathered in the suburb of Lakeview[1] for the weekly worship service and fellowship. Fancy cars—Mercedes, BMW, Lexus—are intermingled with Fords, GMs, Hondas, and Toyotas in the parking lot. Children run about the grounds, squeezing in last-minute play before their Sunday lessons. In the kitchen a group of women puts the final touches on the lunch that is to be served after the service. Members sit, ancient scriptures in front of them, facing the altar that is the focal point of the worship hall. Above the altar is a large golden icon, set against the backdrop of brightly colored religious murals, shiny finished wood, and plush burgundy velvet. Candles and various offerings are set in brass vessels at the altar. The clergy, wearing their ceremonial robes and stoles, are ready to lead members in the religious rituals.

Thirty minutes later another group of Koreans gathers for worship about fifteen miles away in the affluent suburb of Paxton. Children scurry off to Sunday school, and dozens of cars fill the large parking lot, even spilling over

---

1. Although the study was indeed based in the Boston metropolitan area, the names of the religious communities, the specific locations, and the names of their clergy and members have been changed.

onto the street and the lot of a neighboring school. A group of women works in the kitchen, and the cleric puts on his ceremonial robe and stole. Members sing spiritual songs while awaiting the commencement of worship service, facing the focal point of this sanctuary—also a large golden icon set against the backdrop of burgundy velvet, framed by white and gold carved wood. Candles and flowers are set at this altar, along with several brass offering plates that will be distributed later during the service.

These Sunday morning attendees have gathered for worship and fellowship, seeking deeper meaning to their lives as well as the comfort of interacting with fellow Korean ethnics. Among them are students, professionals, and small business owners who have driven long distances on this Sunday morning for the worship services—both conducted in Korean. Not only do these two groups of attendees share the same cultural heritage, but they live in the same towns, work in the same occupations, and even belong to some of the same associations—such as the Korean American Association of New England or the New England chapter of the Seoul National University Alumni Association. Their children study the American educational curriculum at many of the same schools, and they may learn the Korean language at the same Korean School of New England held on Saturdays at one of Paxton's public junior high schools. Although members of both groups share background characteristics and fall into the same monolithic "ethnic Korean" category, their Sunday activities draw a sharp distinction: the first group is gathered at a Buddhist temple, and the second group at a Protestant church.

The Buddhists sit in incense-infused silence, cross-legged and shoeless on individual burgundy cushions on the gray-carpeted floor, facing a four-foot sitting golden Buddha. Overhead, rows and rows of colorful paper lotus lanterns adorn the ceiling, each affixed with a white slip of paper that bears family names, addresses, and dates of birth.[2] Meanwhile, the Protestants sit in wooden pews, singing Korean translations of traditional Protestant hymns and facing a five-foot golden cross. The Buddhists begin with a forty-minute series of sutra chants transliterated from Chinese and Sanskrit,[3] bowing to

2. Each year, Boh Won Sa volunteers assemble these lanterns over the two months leading up to the Buddha's Birthday celebration, usually in early May. During the celebration, Buddhists wishing to "make merit" for their families buy the lanterns at a booth at the front of the temple (Buswell 1992, 43). Some temples have a set price for the lanterns, but Boh Won Sa does not. As one member put it, they pay "according to the amount of faith they have in the Buddha" (translated from Korean).

3. Some sutras originally written in Sanskrit were later translated into Chinese, with portions left untranslated and simply transliterated. Korean Buddhists chant the Korean pronunciations of these Chinese characters. Other sutras, however, were left in the original Sanskrit and were entirely transliterated. According to a monk at the temple described in this chapter, the sutras were not translated in their entirety due to the lack of equivalent vocabulary or the belief that there was a profound meaning hidden in the sounds of the original language.

the Buddha and prostrating themselves dozens of times. Three monks lead the chants, each with a shaven head, wearing the traditional gray robes and brown stoles, or *kasa,* of Korean *Chogye*[4] order Buddhist monks. The chants are followed by meditation, a dharma talk, announcements, and closing chants. The Protestant worship service begins with an organ prelude and a call to worship. The range of motion required from this congregation is either standing—for hymns, responsive scripture readings, and the benediction—or sitting comfortably in the pews. The pastor, wearing his traditional black Protestant robe and stole, bases his sermon on Bible passages that have been translated into Korean from Hebrew and Greek.

A number of scholars have documented the importance of ethnic Christian churches for Korean immigrants in the United States (Hurh and Kim 1984, 1990; Min 1992; Kim 1987). They have noted that as the most important institutions in Korean immigrant society, churches serve multiple functions for their members—religious and secular. Unlike other Korean groups such as alumni associations, professional associations, and informal social networks, churches are open to all Koreans, regardless of gender, age, or socioeconomic background. The ethnic church also provides immigrants with weekly opportunities to see friends as well as to meet new Koreans. Hurh and Kim (1984, 135) characterize the ethnic church as a "microcosm" of both the informal and formal aspects of the Korean society that the immigrants left behind. Churches can also serve as "substitute ethnic neighborhoods" for those who are residentially assimilated (Kim 1987, 233).

With the historical importance and numerical dominance of the Christian church for Koreans in the United States, religious variation within the Korean ethnic group has largely been ignored by scholars. Since 1972, however, an estimated eighty-nine Korean Buddhist temples have been established in the United States, many of them begun within the last decade (Kim and Yu 1996, 95). Korean economic development, a growing American interest in Asian religions, continued immigration from Korea, and perhaps disillusionment with Christianity have contributed to the establishment of these Buddhist temples. Yu (1988, Chapter 12 in this volume) identifies three paths through which Korean Buddhism is taking root in the United States: (1) through the work of individual Zen teachers, whose efforts are mainly directed toward Westerners; (2) through research and teaching by scholars specializing in Korean Buddhism; and (3) through the activities of temples attended by Korean immigrants. Although the Korean Buddhist temples tend

---

4. Boh Won Sa follows the Chogye order, a conservative monastic order of Zen practitioners noted for their vows of celibacy. Although there are more than twenty Korean Buddhist orders, over 60 percent of the Buddhist temples in Korea are of the Chogye order.

to be overshadowed by the more than three thousand Korean Christian churches in the United States, their growing numbers indicate that temples are presenting an alternative setting where immigrants can regularly mingle with fellow Koreans.

Those who had not been Christian in Korea can now be affiliated with a religious and social community extending many of the same benefits as church membership without having to convert to Christianity. These new organizations have entered the religious economy, offering a form of religious affiliation that is arguably more "authentically Korean," with less emphasis on recruitment and conversion. In Chapter 9, I presented a case study of one Korean Protestant church in the Boston area, focusing on generational transition and the establishment of its English Worship Service. In this chapter, I will present a case study of Boh Won Sa, a Korean Buddhist temple also in the Boston area, and compare it with Paxton Korean Church (PKC) on the basis of three broad dimensions of organizational life as classified by Ammerman et al. (1997): resources, structures of authority, and cultures. Although Boh Won Sa and PKC serve many of the same functions for their members, they are remarkably different along these three dimensions.[5] These differences, if they persist, indicate that the two groups may be on divergent trajectories.

My findings are based on data obtained through: (1) interviews with members and leaders; (2) participant observations conducted concurrently at both sites for over one year; and (3) a short written survey, in Korean, distributed to members of both groups after their respective worship services. I supplemented this information by reviewing temple and church archives and visiting other churches and temples outside New England. I conducted the interviews and participant observations in both English and Korean, depending on the interviewee's English ability and the activities being observed.[6] Translations from Korean, denoted by an asterisk (*), are my own.

Introduction to Boh Won Sa Korean Buddhist Temple

Founded in 1992, the temple is tucked away on a residential street in the quiet suburb of Lakeview, Massachusetts. A large wooden sign with gold lettering announces in both Korean and English that this is a Buddhist temple,

---

5. Because Chapter 9 contains much description and analysis of Paxton Korean Church, I will devote more space in this chapter to Boh Won Sa Korean Buddhist Temple.

6. For more about my ethnographic research methods, see Chai (1998, 296, 324).

but the temple complex consists of two light-gray buildings that could easily be mistaken for American homes. The two-story main building is actually composed of two adjacent buildings that have been joined together. What was once a private home now serves as living quarters for monks as well as for temple guests. The lay women prepare much of the communal Sunday lunch in its residential kitchen. A former business office and day care center has been transformed into a building that includes a second-floor dharma hall (*bup dang*) and a large meeting/dining hall. Behind the main building, a three-story annex houses a library, a conference room, additional living quarters, and another altar. Outside the annex sits the abbot's gold-trimmed Lexus.

Although Boh Won Sa was established primarily with funds from private donors in Korea, its annual budget of over $125,000 currently comes from member contributions. There are 131 Korean and 7 interracial families listed in Boh Won Sa's membership directory. The number of Boh Won Sa Sunday attendees varies widely, however, ranging from just a handful to over one hundred on special occasions. After the two-hour Sunday service, attendees pile their cushions neatly by the door, put on their shoes, and chat while waiting in line for the free lunch buffet. Lunch, paid for and prepared in rotation by members of the temple, typically includes steamed rice, soup, and about seven Korean vegetable dishes. Fruit and other foods that had been placed at the altar are also served. Boh Won Sa is an eclectic mixture of things Korean, American, ancient, and unmistakably modern.

Introduction to Paxton Korean Church

Founded in 1974, Paxton Korean Church is the largest Korean Protestant church in New England.[7] Two hundred Korean immigrants and students gather each week at 11:30 A.M. for the Korean Worship Service, and an additional 250 people—second-generation Korean Americans and about twenty-five non-Koreans—gather at 1:45 P.M. for the English Worship Service. Both services also run simultaneous Sunday school programs for a total of 150 children. Although it rented various church facilities in its first fifteen years, PKC currently enjoys joint ownership of the Paxton church facilities with the predominantly white Community Church of Paxton.

The Paxton Korean Church facilities are built around a simply designed,

---

7. For a more detailed introduction to Paxton Korean Church, see Chapter 9 in this volume and Chai (1998, 302–6).

modestly adorned two-story New England sanctuary that can comfortably fit about 400 people. An American flag hangs alongside a South Korean flag in the front left corner of the sanctuary. Rows of white-trimmed wooden pews hold English and Korean Bibles and hymnals. Directly underneath the sanctuary and balcony is a large basement fellowship hall and adjacent institutional kitchen. In addition to the typical coffee and donuts, PKC recently began serving lunch after the Korean Worship Service. Unlike the more elaborate lunch at Boh Won Sa, PKC's fare is typically a large bowl of beef-based soup mixed with steamed rice. Korean ministry women prepare this meal in rotation in the church kitchen, and there is a charge of one dollar per person.

Structures of Authority

Boh Won Sa is currently run by three monks: the 57-year-old Venerable Chong Woo, the 34-year-old Ki Mu, and the 33-year-old Ji Wol. Temple members address them as *Sunim,* which literally means "monk" in Korean. When members greet the monks, they press their hands flat together in front of their chests and bow politely; the monks reciprocate in the same prayer-like manner (*hap chang*). The abbot, Chong Woo Sunim, was the prior at Korea's largest temple before coming to the United States. He is a well-respected meditation specialist, and he is popular for his warm personality and his extensive experience. As one member says, "My mother [in Korea] says I am very lucky to be able to have close contact with such a high-ranking monk. If we were in Korea, we wouldn't even be able to come into contact with someone such as Chong Woo Sunim."* The two younger monks are students at local universities: Ki Mu Sunim is pursuing a master's degree in philosophy, and the intern Ji Wol Sunim is taking courses in English as a second language.

All three monks were trained in Korea, and they are accountable to the Chogye order. Temples in Korea founded with Chogye order funds would be directly under the control of the order, but Boh Won Sa is more independent because it was founded with private donations. Boh Won Sa's affiliation with the order in Korea is rather loose, with complete financial autonomy and its own board of trustees in compliance with American requirements for nonprofit organizations. The Chogye leadership in Korea would be called upon only in cases in which a monk is accused of misconduct, or if the temple were seeking an additional monk or nun. The order would then send an individual to fill the position, but it does not mandate where and how long clerics in the United States can serve. This stands in contrast to the control that PKC's denomination has over where its pastors serve and for how long.

Whereas some Buddhist temples in the United States have large boards of trustees, Boh Won Sa has only four members—the two senior monks, a male lay leader, and a female lay leader. Ethnic churches and temples are notorious for the prevalence of schisms (Numrich 1996; Shin and Park 1988), and Korean Buddhist temples are no exception. The reason for the small size of the board, Ki Mu Sunim explains, is to prevent power struggles and factions among lay members and the monks, problems that have plagued other temples (e.g., Kim and Yu 1996, 92–93). Boh Won Sa's board, however, holds no formal meetings, which indicates that it exists primarily on paper, with most decisions made informally or by the abbot himself. As a Chicago-area Korean monk told me, "Buddhist structure is not layperson-oriented [as in Protestantism]. All functions are done by monks." Because lay members are generally accustomed to leaving official temple matters to the clergy, "the rise and decline of a temple is attributable for the most part to the monk's individual ability" (Yu 1988, 91). Nevertheless, lay participation in temple matters is greater in the United States than in Korea, and it is likely to increase over time. In fact, there is much more lay leadership at some larger temples, including Kwan Eum Sa in Los Angeles. According to its abbot, Doh-An Kim, "In Korea, the abbot is responsible for managing the temple finances, but here [Kwan Eum Sa] the board of trustees takes charge" (Kim and Yu 1996, 93).

Boh Won Sa's loose affiliation with the Chogye order and its informal administration is echoed by its loose association with other Korean Buddhist temples in the United States. Although monks from East Coast temples occasionally gather in New York for causes such as North Korean famine relief, there is no official organization of temples. Temples are affiliated with one another to the extent that they all serve predominantly Korean immigrant memberships and their monks were trained in the Chogye order. Monks from Korea and the United States also stay at various Korean immigrant temples in the course of their travels, giving dharma talks and socializing with their fellow Buddhists along the way.

Decentralization is also reflected in the fact that temples catering to immigrants remain completely separate from those catering to the wider American population. "Home-grown" or "new" Buddhists—the group of predominantly white Americans drawn to Buddhism—practice what is considered a "distinctively 'American' Buddhism," quite independent of practices at Korean ethnic Buddhist temples (Eck and Pierce 1998, 12).[8] For example, Zen master Seung Sahn has established a network of meditation groups and Kwan Um Zen centers whose members are predominantly white. Although Boh Won Sa monks know of Seung Sahn Sunim's work and his nearby Zen center, they do not consider Boh Won Sa and the Zen center to be comparable institutions. Not only is "immigrant" Buddhism separate from "American" Buddhism, but American Buddhism itself takes many forms according to the training and disposition of the various Buddhist teachers. As Mu Soeng (1998, 123) notes, "A case has been made that the culture of Kwan Um Zen School is hardly anything more than an expression of Seung Sahn's personality as it has been shaped by the Confucian-Buddhist amalgam in Korea during the last thousand years."

Despite the dichotomy that exists between American and immigrant Buddhism, some American Buddhists bridge the gap by leaving their Zen centers and establishing what Numrich (1996) calls a "parallel congregation" within an ethnic temple.[9] At Boh Won Sa, a parallel congregation of six non-Koreans holds a meditation session in English on Saturday afternoons. Although one of the temple monks occasionally joins them, they are usually led by one of their peers—a white man who holds a degree in Buddhist Studies. Some of these non-Koreans are, in fact, former members of the local predominantly white Zen center. According to Chong Woo Sunim, "They [the non-Koreans] came to Boh Won Sa, because they said that they wanted to learn genuine Buddhist practice from genuine Korean Buddhists."

Thus, the decentralized nature of Korean Buddhism in the United States means that practices, power relations, teachings, and other characteristics of the temples are somewhat "congregation"-specific.[10] For instance, Abbot Doh-An Kim of Los Angeles states, "We have adopted many worship features from Christian churches: we use an organ and sing Buddhist hymns. We pass the offering plate and deliver *solpop* [sermons]" (Kim and Yu 1996, 94). It seems that his temple has embarked on a deliberate campaign to

8. Other terms suggested by scholars to refer to the Buddhism of native-born Americans organized around Asian teachers include "missionary Buddhism," "Euro-American Buddhism," "Western Buddhism," and "white Buddhism." Although each of these terms is somewhat problematic, Fields (1998, 197) chooses "white Buddhism" in order to highlight the fact that "the so-called missionary or Euro-American Buddhism, in all its bewildering variety, is largely white and middle-class."

9. Numrich's (1996, 63) study of Theravada Buddhism uncovered an ethnic parallelism at the local level, where "ethnic-Asians and non-Asian converts follow separate forms of Theravada Buddhism under a single temple roof and at the direction of a shared monastic leadership."

10. Although Buddhism is not a traditionally congregation-based religion, Warner (1993, 1067) writes, "Congregational patterns seem to be emerging among non-Christian religious groups." I use the term "congregation" loosely in order to emphasize the fact that the temples are very much locally controlled.

compete directly with local Korean Christian churches. He has formalized a Sunday school program for children, begun speaking from a Christian-style pulpit, and started a choir, complete with Christian-style choir robes. This is reminiscent of the adaptations made by Japanese American Buddhists decades ago, using terms derived from Christianity such as "Buddhist churches," "Sunday schools," and "Young Men's Buddhist Association" (Kashima 1977).[11] Boh Won Sa, however, has made few changes in an effort to compete with or imitate Christian churches. Its clergy and lay members are well aware of their minority status, but they are not making a concerted effort to change in the ways that other temples have.

As for PKC, it is led by Reverend Kim, but there are numerous committees of lay leaders that take care of official church business. For example, lay leaders have titles such as "deacon," "exhorting steward," and "elder" (in ascending status). These terms are "back translations" of titles introduced to churches in Korea by American Protestant missionaries, which were subsequently brought back to the United States by immigrants. The many lay leaders work in committees such as the finance committee and the building committee. Although these lay leader titles are not used in non-Korean congregations in the denomination, PKC's Korean and English ministries both continue the convention of bestowing the titles on lay members after nomination, training, and congregational approval of candidates.

Both PKC and Boh Won Sa are examples of "de facto congregationalism" as conceptualized by Warner (1993, 1994). However, these congregations exist within different organizational structures and are therefore subject to different types and degrees of hierarchy. PKC is ultimately subject to the rules and authority of its denomination. It contributes a percentage of its annual budget to the denomination's New England conference, and it follows the denomination's *Book of Discipline* with some allowances made for ethnic churches. In practice, the denomination may give PKC leaders a large degree of flexibility in its church operations, but PKC must still report to denominational headquarters. In contrast, the Chogye order in Korea has a certain degree of transnational authority over Boh Won Sa monks, but it functions more like a professional licensing board: it certifies members who have completed the requisite training, but it has no control over the way in which the professionals subsequently run their "private practices." Thus, Boh Won Sa is more congregational than PKC, because it neither answers

---

11. I do not claim that these types of activities and subgroups are exclusively Christian. In fact, there is evidence of a historical precedent for Sunday schools, choirs, and youth groups among Buddhists in Korea and in Japan. Here, I focus not on the origin of these activities, but on the motivations for establishing and adopting them in the United States.

directly to a higher organization nor makes regular financial payments to support the higher organization.

Resources

In this section, I will compare the resources that are available to Boh Won Sa with those available to PKC in terms of money, building facilities, human resources, and the organizational support offered by larger religious bodies and movements. Boh Won Sa and PKC can tap into some of the same resources that stem from their location in greater Boston, such as the concentration of colleges and universities that draw Korean and Korean American students. PKC, however, has a greater amount of resources at its disposal because of its longer history, the prominence of Christianity among Koreans, and its ties to a larger American Christian community, including the American evangelical movement.

PKC's monetary resources and operating budget are much greater than that of Boh Won Sa, perhaps due in part to the degree of emphasis placed on members' responsibility to give financially. At PKC's Korean Worship Service, the issue of giving is brought up nearly every week in the context of Reverend Kim's sermon or in an announcement of various fundraisers for specific purposes—such as purchasing a new van or repaving the church parking lot. There is also a time of offering at each service, and leaders as well as committed members are encouraged to tithe, or give one-tenth of their income, to the church. Offering time is followed by a reading of various thanksgiving offerings that have been placed in the offering plates in special envelopes. Reverend Kim reads the statements on the envelopes, which range from "Thank you, Lord, that our son has been accepted to M.I.T. By the Lee family,"* and "We present this in honor of our grandson's birthday. By the Parks,"* to simply, "Anonymous."* After reading messages on the special envelopes, Reverend Kim says a short prayer on behalf of the congregation, focusing on those who have made a thanksgiving offering. The following week, various figures appear on the back of the Sunday church bulletin: (1) the total attendance; (2) the total amount of offering collected the previous week; (3) the amount of that offering that was presented as a tithe, followed by the names of those who tithed; (4) the amount presented as fulfillment of an annual pledge, followed by names; and (5) the amount that was presented as thanksgiving offering, followed by names. While this practice is not uncommon in Korean Protestant churches, it has drawn criticism from those who feel that it places too much public emphasis on money.

Although the English ministry leaders do not raise the issue of money as often, leaders and committed members are also expected to tithe. Offering is collected during the English Worship Service as well as at Friday night Bible study. The English ministry bulletin states, beneath the attendance figure, the total amount of offering collected the previous week. In keeping with a seeker-sensitive orientation, however, the offering time is marked with an asterisk in the bulletin, informing first-time visitors that they should not feel obligated to contribute. Spring is the most important fundraising time of the year, as members who plan to go on summer missions trips send out request letters and organize fundraisers such as auctions, bake sales, and bike-a-thons.

Whereas most of the PKC funds are drawn from the offering collection, Boh Won Sa relies on a type of fee-for-service system. For example, funds are raised when members buy the lotus lanterns or when monks perform funeral and ancestral rites. Instead of an offering time during the Sunday service, there is a wooden box to the right of the Buddha altar into which members can periodically place money. Because offering is not actively solicited, even some well-meaning members do not regularly contribute. One woman admits, "I used to be good about putting money in the [offering] box, but now I'm not so diligent. I forget. You also have to put it in when people aren't looking, and it's awkward to wait until everyone goes downstairs."* Often members will just locate a need in the temple—for a piano or a new piece of equipment—and then make a lump-sum donation in the form of the actual item. According to Ki Mu Sunim, it has been difficult to teach the non-Korean members this tradition because they "just do not have the instinct"* to identify areas of need and make donations. He adds that support also comes from the parents of students from Korea who come to visit their children in Boston.

The way in which members conceive of and utilize the building facilities is also quite different in the two religious communities. Although built in a Western style, the temple, with its Buddha figures, Buddhist texts, and other religious artifacts—all imported from Korea—is reminiscent of Korea. In a sense, it is a Korean "oasis," serving as a reminder of Korea—a place to meet other Koreans as well as to honor one's cultural and ancestral heritage. Because the monks reside in the temple complex, the temple is also a home. When members gather at the temple, they often share a meal prepared in the residential kitchen. The temple is open at all times for visitors, who even sleep over if they are participating in special prayer events or if they are taking time to meditate. It is at once a literal and figurative home and a community center.

In contrast, Paxton Korean Church facilities are thoroughly American, with the only Korean artifacts being Korean-language materials, the Korean flag, and Korean food in the refrigerator. Because the church facilities were built by and are shared with a predominantly white congregation, PKC members are quite conscientious about keeping the facilities clean and pleasant in the eyes of Community Church of Paxton members. Although members regularly cook Korean food in the large kitchen, they clean up thoroughly, putting away all telltale Korean items so that Community Church members will feel comfortable using the same kitchen later on.

Not only do they have non-Korean "roommates," but PKC members also share their building with secular groups during the week. For example, some Paxton rooms are rented out during the week for aerobics classes and Boy Scout troop meetings. An independent preschool occupies the first floor of the church on weekdays, limiting access to the facilities by church members. In contrast, Boh Won Sa members can linger at the temple and watch movies, sing karaoke, play cards, read, or simply chat with one another. Although Reverend Kim can typically be found in his church office seven days a week, no one actually lives in the church facilities, so PKC is not a physical "home" and community center in the sense of Boh Won Sa. The PKC facilities are even less significant for the English ministry, because the pastors do not work in their offices every day, preferring to meet with members on campus visits or to communicate with members through e-mail.

One drawback that both PKC and Boh Won Sa facilities have in common is their lack of accessibility by public transportation. Although both locations are convenient for suburban residents with cars, those without cars—often college students—must find alternative means of transportation. PKC's English ministry realized early on that their growth potential was severely limited by transportation issues. In order to maintain the size of its college ministry, it pays hundreds of dollars each weekend to hire a bus service to transport members from various campuses on Fridays and Sundays. College students who would like to visit Boh Won Sa, however, must secure a ride from a temple member. This can be difficult, because many Boh Won Sa members attend temple services erratically. Thus, the lack of convenient transportation can act as a barrier to entry for newcomers who do not have cars, further limiting the potential appeal of Boh Won Sa to Boston-area college students. It is no surprise that there are no college students who attend Boh Won Sa regularly.

As for human resources, both groups draw from the same pool of Boston immigrants, students, and visiting scholars, and professionals from Korea.

What Boh Won Sa lacks compared to PKC, however, is an active second-generation Korean American membership, let alone a second-generation emergent clergy. The young adults who regularly attend Boh Won Sa are foreign students from Korea or those who spent their formative years in Korea. Although some second-generation Korean American young adults do attend Boh Won Sa on special holidays, they attend only with their parents and extended families. To them, temple attendance is a family ritual, not an expression of their personal faith.

Because they have limited Korean-language abilities, these second-generation visitors neither participate fully in the services nor interact with other attendees. While young adults who regularly attend Boh Won Sa socialize in the lunch line and eat together at a designated young adults' table, he second-generation visitors sit with their families. Still, these second-generation young adult visitors represent only a fraction of all of the second-generation Korean American young adults whose parents are listed as members of the temple. The parents may attend temple services a few times a year, but some young adult children have never attended Boh Won Sa at all. The only second-generation Korean Americans who attend Boh Won Sa regularly are the handful of elementary-school-age children who accompany their parents. Even at larger Korean temples such as one in New York, there may be a group of high school and college age attendees, but very few of them are second-generation Korean Americans. The second generation is unlikely to attend temple regularly beyond their childhood years because of two main reasons: the temples lack English-language programming, and regular temple attendance is neither required nor strongly urged.

A Chicago-area monk told me that he expects second- and third-generation Korean Americans to rediscover Buddhism much the same way that more white Americans are gaining interest: "They will realize that it is a sound philosophy and a good way of life. They will return on the basis of reason." If second-generation Korean Americans are interested in Buddhism, however, they may be more likely to attend one of the American Buddhist centers in the area. To some extent, this has happened in the case of Jim, a 23-year-old Korean American professional in New York City. Jim was not raised in any religious tradition, but he was introduced to Buddhist meditation as an undergraduate in Boston by a white Zen teacher from a local American Zen center. He has since taken the Five Precepts and considers himself a practicing Buddhist. Nevertheless, he is involved in the American version of Korean Buddhism, not the Korean Buddhism as practiced by members of immigrant temples. Furthermore, he did not specifically seek out Korean Buddhism; rather, he acknowledges that it was only by "chance" that he came to learn a Korean form of Buddhism.

In the future, immigrant temples such as Boh Won Sa can potentially join with the American Buddhist centers, thereby drawing from the staffing resources and growing popularity of American Buddhism. Just as PKC's English ministry draws from the resources offered by the American evangelical movement and nearby Gordon-Conwell Theological Seminary, Boh Won Sa could potentially draw from local Zen centers and hire English-speaking clergy who have access to a wide network of American Buddhist resources. Nevertheless, Boh Won Sa's future trajectory will mostly likely be determined by the patterns of migration from Korea as well as by how much effort monks and lay members make to cater to English speakers.

Even if Boh Won Sa does tap into American Buddhist resources, it may not be at Boh Won Sa's initiative, but rather at the initiative of American Buddhists. For example, curious observers have visited Boh Won Sa so many times that members are unfazed by the occasional non-Korean visitor at Sunday services. Although they do not approach visitors with the same evangelical zeal as the Korean Protestants, a few members will engage them in conversation over lunch and answer questions. In fact, on my first visit to the temple, I mentioned to the abbot that I had heard of the temple through Harvard Professor Diana Eck. This in and of itself is notable, since I, a Korean American student in Boston for over ten years, had never heard of a Buddhist temple in the area until I was told of it by a white professor. Not only does it reflect the Christian bias in my own Korean American networks, but it also indicates the lack of emphasis placed on recruitment of Korean American students by the temple. In response to my statement, the abbot remarked, "It seems that all of Harvard Divinity School has visited this temple at some point!"* In contrast, PKC and other Korean Protestant churches often advertise their events through newspaper advertisements and posters around campus.

In effect, PKC and Boh Won Sa draw from their Boston resources in different ways. Much of the difference can be attributed to the fact that PKC was established twenty-five years ago and has benefited from the evangelical zeal of a critical mass of Korean American Christians. Boh Won Sa, on the other hand, is not evangelical, and it was established less than ten years ago. Boh Won Sa members and clergy currently acknowledge their "underdog" status in Korean American religion, but they do not feel compelled to increase their numbers or to expand their programming. For the time being, they are content to maintain the status quo, confident in the wisdom of their Buddhist perspective and their faithfulness to ancestral traditions.

Culture

At first glance, members of Boh Won Sa and PKC are similar in that they for the most part share Korean culture and heritage. However, these two groups differ in the nature of their activities, their worldviews, and the way in which they see themselves vis-à-vis American and Korean American society.

Food is a focal point of both communities' fellowship. Around the lunch table members socialize and get to know one another. Whereas the large number of people makes PKC's lunch time more rushed, lunch at Boh Won Sa is a leisurely affair for most. Because the monks do not have their own families, temple members act as extended families for the monks. Children often sit on the monks' laps, whereupon the monks give them candy. At special events the temple's karaoke machine is brought into the dining hall, and the monks and members take turns singing Korean pop songs and classics. This stands in contrast to the more formal interaction that Reverend Kim has with PKC congregants.

Dress at Boh Won Sa is markedly more casual than at PKC. This could be attributed to a number of factors, but it is most likely due to practical considerations. Because of the need to sit on the floor for two hours and perform multiple bows that require full prostration, it would be impractical to wear formal constrictive clothing to Boh Won Sa. While immigrant women at PKC typically wear skirts and dresses, the women at Boh Won Sa usually wear pants—even very baggy, pajama-like pants. Because of the relatively small number of attendees, a high proportion must "pitch in"—help with cooking, serving, and cleaning—so it would be impractical to dress in fancy clothing. It is not unusual to see mothers wearing jeans and fathers in canvas jackets and polo shirts. In contrast, PKC Korean Worship Service attendees are usually attired in dresses and suits. At the church, members keep their shoes on and sit in comfortable wooden pews. While a group of women must cook for the whole congregation, most women on any given Sunday do not, so they can dress in finer clothing. English Worship Service participants have adopted a more casual look within the past year, following the lead of larger new-style evangelical churches. On any given Sunday, some English Worship Service attendees will be wearing dressy clothing, while others will be in jeans.

Another difference between Boh Won Sa and PKC lies in the range of their programming and activities. Beyond the Sunday services, Boh Won Sa currently does not offer regular meetings or instructional classes for its Korean members. At one point, Ki Mu Sunim did lead a Sunday study group for the young adults, but the group disbanded when members' schedules, including Ki Mu Sunim's, got busy. When I asked a young adult if there were any special activities held by the temple young adults, she replied apologetically, "We all gather here at the temple and say that we're Buddhist, but really, we like to go out together, and we eat plenty of meat and drink plenty of alcohol!"* Indeed, young adult members often recount their weekend activities, which usually involve gathering at a restaurant or at someone's house, playing cards or going to a karaoke club, and having drinks. During one Sunday lunch, for example, an attendee jokingly said, "Oh, we stayed up playing cards and drinking last night, and that is why so many people aren't here today."* Although Boh Won Sa young adults are called on periodically to help make rice cakes or lanterns for special events, they are required neither to make a regular commitment nor to adhere to an ascetic lifestyle.

Boh Won Sa's programming for the second generation is limited to informal Sunday instruction in Korean. As stated earlier, the only second-generation Korean Americans who are a regular presence are young children who accompany their parents to the temple. One volunteer teaches the children some Buddhist songs, explains some Buddhist ideas, and leads them in Korean origami or in practicing writing Korean. This stands in contrast to the highly structured Sunday school curriculum run in English by second-generation Korean Americans (members of the English Worship Service) at PKC. Although the lack of second-generation involvement is an issue of concern to those at Korean Buddhist temples in the United States, a critical mass of second-generation Korean American young adults has yet to emerge.

One of the most significant differences between the PKC and Boh Won Sa is in how members conceive of and maintain identity boundaries; in other words, how they determine who is Buddhist and who is Christian. Taking the Three Refuges Vow[12] and the Five Precepts[13] (Prebish 1988, 675) can be considered the most basic criteria for identification as a Buddhist. In the United States, however, ethnic Koreans are generally accepted as Buddhists by virtue of their cultural heritage, whereas American converts are expected to go through a more formal initiation.[14] While Buddhist tradition is accepting and accommodating of other cultural practices, such diffuse boundaries make it difficult to discern exactly who is a Buddhist. Similarly, because

12. "I go to the Buddha for Refuge, I go to the Dharma for Refuge, I go to the Sangha [Buddhist community] for Refuge."

13. The Five Precepts are lay vows to refrain from lying, killing, stealing, taking intoxicants, and engaging in sexual misconduct.

14. According to Hurh (1998), more people in Korea profess to be Buddhist (27.6 percent) than Christian (24.3 percent). Whereas Christian groups in Korea maintain a "fairly clear-cut distinction between believers and nonbelievers," Seekins (1992, 127–28) notes that there is no exact or exclusive criterion by which Buddhists or Confucians can be identified.

many Korean immigrants at least initially attend a Christian church for the social services that it provides, not all church members consider themselves Christian.

Some immigrants choose to attend a church but still see themselves as Buddhists. For example, Illsoo Kim (1987, 233) recounts the words of a Korean engineer in New Jersey: "On Sunday, I do not want my children watching TV all day long. At least one day a week, I want them to inter-mingle with other Koreans and learn something about Korea. This is the reason why my family and I attend [Protestant] church even though I am a Buddhist. My offerings are nothing but the payment for the services my fam-ily has received from the church." Somewhere along the spectrum between "committed" Buddhists and "committed" Christians, there are Korean Amer-icans who have a sense of religious duality. Like the man quoted above, they may attend a Christian church for the social benefits but still consider them-selves to be Buddhist. Likewise, they may consider themselves Christian but explore Buddhism as a part of their cultural heritage or as a philosophical tradition.

Sometimes, this duality results from a couples' attempt to accommodate differences in interfaith marriages. For example, in the course of my research, I saw one couple attending both PKC and Boh Won Sa. Neither partner is an active temple or church member, but the husband, who is Christian, explained to me that he occasionally brings his wife to Boh Won Sa because she is Buddhist. Another man told me that he and his wife had at one point attended PKC because his wife comes from a devout Protestant family. Although they stopped going after a little while, he recalls, "Reverend Kim called me for a year to try to get me to go to his church." Because he him-self came from a Buddhist family in Korea, the man later decided to learn more about Buddhism and is now one of the most active members at Boh Won Sa. His wife and children, however, do not attend with him; nor do they attend a church.

When I asked Reverend Kim about his contact with members or leaders of Boh Won Sa, he replied, "Before there was a Buddhist temple or a Catholic church, the Catholics and the Buddhists used to come to PKC, so I know a lot of them. Then when they built the temple and started a Catholic church, they went to those places."* Reverend Kim's reply indicates that he is also aware of this duality among some Korean immigrants.

During the announcement time at Boh Won Sa one week, a new couple stated that they had immigrated from Korea just a few weeks ago. Because they were staying with Protestant relatives, the woman said they had felt obligated to attend a Korean church with their hosts. All the while, this woman maintained a makeshift Buddhist altar at home and longed for the opportunity to attend a temple. She and her husband finally heard of Boh Won Sa through a chance encounter with an acquaintance from New York. The couple expressed their happiness at having found a Buddhist community. If there had been no temple in the area, however, they would have continued attending the Christian church.

In the case of some earlier immigrants, having a Korean Buddhist temple in their area when they first arrived in the United States may have prevented them from becoming Christians. One Korean churchgoer states, "If there had been a Buddhist temple in our area when we first immigrated, we would definitely have gone there instead of to a church. We probably would never have converted to Christianity."* His wife recalls "praying to Buddha"* before undergoing medical treatment, and having no interest in Christianity. Even though their families had been Buddhist for many generations, they had identified with Buddhism only in a cultural sense and actually had known very little about the religion itself. Once they started attending church regularly, Christianity became their new religion, and they learned Christian doctrine and traditions in Bible studies and church activities. This couple did not maintain their Buddhist identity but rather chose to convert to Christianity. They now see their conversion as an adoption of modern Western values and culture.

Among current temple members that I spoke with, many had attended church at some point in their lives. One had even been baptized a Catholic, and one Boh Won Sa member attends PKC when his Christian relatives visit Boston. According to an active temple member, "There is not a single Korean who hasn't been to church!"* Indeed, many talk about how they had attended a church with their friends or relatives, one woman even having sung in a church choir for a year. This woman asserts, however, that during the time that she had attended church, she had never really believed the doctrine, so she had never been a true Christian.

Another member says that as a college student (from Korea), she had attended PKC's English Worship Service but had found it too large and impersonal. Although she was raised in a Christian family in Korea, she likes Buddhism and feels that she has found her niche at Boh Won Sa. She finds a better cultural fit, due to the temple's Korean orientation. She also likes the fact that members do not proselytize. They take pride in remaining authentically Korean rather than acquiescing to the trend of Christian Westernization followed by many of their peers. Temple members are striving to be faithful to their ancestral religious heritage, resisting the all-too-easy trend of conversion to Christianity. Some are even disaffected former churchgoers, rediscovering the wisdom of Buddhist thought.

Despite the religious duality exhibited by some Korean Americans, both PKC and Boh Won Sa have a core of committed members who have a strong sense of their single religious identity. Consequently, there is a strong minority consciousness at Boh Won Sa. The minority consciousness exists on three levels: as members of a racial and ethnic minority, as members of a religious minority, and most of all, as members of a religious minority within the Korean immigrant community. For example, one longtime Massachusetts resident told me that he had been very upset by the fact that meetings of the Korean American Society of New England have traditionally been opened in a prayer by a Protestant minister. As a Buddhist, he saw this tradition as a "violation of his civil rights" and had even considered filing a lawsuit. He was pleased with the recent decision on the part of the organization to stop this practice out of respect for members who are not Christian.

Every dharma talk at Boh Won Sa contains a statement about how Buddhists are different from Christians, sometimes urging participants to be as fervently committed as Christians, at other times pointing out a flaw in the Christian worldview. One week the Dalai Lama's visit to Boston prompted the abbot to talk about Christianity: "Christians will tell you that there is a heaven and a hell. If you are not a Christian, you will go to hell. Our people [Koreans] of our country [Korea] have not been Christian for that long. Christianity hasn't been around for a very long time. That means that from the Christian perspective, all previous Koreans who had not been introduced to Christianity went to hell. We must not judge people like that and condemn them. The Dalai Lama's message is that of not judging others."*

Virtually every temple member can recount a story of how they were hurt, offended, or annoyed by the overzealous recruiting efforts of Korean Christians. Boh Won Sa members talk about how they were told that they were going to hell or asked, "How can you *still* be going to a Buddhist temple, all the way over here in America?"* They feel that they are labeled "backward" and "stubborn" for holding onto the Buddhist faith and resisting conversion to Christianity, when conversion is so prevalent and offers membership in a larger extended network of Korean Americans. Several of the young women noted that while they had no problem with possibly marrying someone from a Christian background, they find that Christians tend to resist dating someone who is a practicing Buddhist.

Julie, a college student, grew up attending a Korean Buddhist temple in California but has neither sought out nor heard of a temple since moving to

Boston. She says that her friends from the Asian American Christian Fellowship are always trying to convert her. For example, one of her friends gave her a C. S. Lewis book for her birthday. She also sees the people from the Asian American Christian Fellowship "herding the freshmen together and baking them cookies, taking them to retreats." Since she is on the e-mail list for the group (she has attended a few Bible studies as well as church services), she receives e-mail messages saying things such as, "We had forty-four seekers and twenty-two converts at last week's large group meeting!" She is turned off by the "overzealous proselytizing aspect" of the group. Julie has a sympathizer and commiserator in a white Episcopalian friend, and they both agree that to them religion is more of a "family tradition, not a conversion experience." When I asked Julie what she thinks will happen to her home temple once her parents' generation dies out, she speculated that it will "probably disappear." Although she does not represent all second-generation Korean American Buddhists, she sees "virtually no interest" among her peers in "keeping their Buddhist commitment alive."

At the same time that they are keenly aware of their minority status within the Korean immigrant community, Buddhists display a subtle pride in remaining true to their ancestral traditions, resisting the trend toward religious assimilation, and being a peaceful and open-minded people. One member of the temple who left Korea at age ten says: "Because so much of what we do at the temple is a mixture of Buddhism and Korean culture, I was able to maintain a lot of my Korean speaking ability and my knowledge of Korean culture. If I had gone to a [Korean] church instead of the temple, I really don't think I would have remembered as much."* Boh Won Sa members also talk of the wisdom of Buddhist philosophy and point to the fact that many non-Asians are discovering that wisdom and practicing Buddhism as well. To them, this is further evidence that the Buddhist way is a more enlightened and sound path than Christianity.

Conclusion

This chapter has been an initial attempt to draw attention to the religious variation within the Korean immigrant community that has long been ignored by most scholars. However, because this chapter is largely descriptive, it is likely to have raised more questions than it has answered; there is much research still to be done.

In many ways, Boh Won Sa and PKC are very similar, serving comparable functions in the lives of their members. In some cases, Korean immigrants maintain a duality in their religious lives, attending services at a temple or at a church while asserting a different religious identity. In the words of one Boh Won Sa member, "Buddhists are very accepting and open-minded. You are free to come [to the temple], but you are also free to go [to another religious community]."* Nevertheless, there is a strong core of members at PKC and at Boh Won Sa who see themselves and members of the other group in stark contrast.

Boh Won Sa members have a strong sense of minority consciousness—with respect to American society, but more so with respect to the predominantly Christian Korean immigrant community. With respect to American society, the Buddhists are keenly aware of the different orientation they have by virtue of their Korean heritage, language, culture, and race. They also know that they are different in their adherence to a religion largely unknown to most Americans. At the same time, they recognize the growing popularity of American Buddhism and are used to having the occasional white visitor at the temple services. With respect to the Korean immigrant community, they know that they are overwhelmingly outnumbered by their Protestant counterparts, and they often note differences between themselves and the Protestants. Boh Won Sa members and clergy respond to needs as they arise, not seeking large growth or a high profile; they are content with their quiet piety and their unobtrusive manner.

One of the most significant differences between PKC and Boh Won Sa is the fact that Boh Won Sa has no second-generation young adults. Whereas young children accompany their parents to temple, older children do not. Some parents do not believe that their children must practice Buddhism; others believe that their children are very much Buddhist, even though their adult children rarely visit any temples. Furthermore, Boh Won Sa does not make an effort to recruit second-generation Korean Americans, so their young adult membership is limited to those who spent their formative years in Korea. In contrast, a critical mass of Korean American Christians and resources drawn from the evangelical movement have enabled PKC to successfully target the second generation.

Both PKC and Boh Won Sa face numerous challenges ahead. As PKC addresses differences between first-generation and second-generation leadership, Boh Won Sa must consider who will be the heirs to their temple. If it joins forces with American Buddhism, Boh Won Sa may eventually become an American Buddhist temple, dominated not by Korean monks and immigrants but by native-born American converts. As long as migration from Korea continues, however, the temple is likely to remain a place for the successive waves of immigrants and students from Korea. The most pressing challenge for Boh Won Sa is in incorporating more active members, especially second-generation Korean Americans. In order to attract and retain new members who can ensure organizational survival for years to come, both PKC and Boh Won Sa must utilize their resources efficiently and develop relevant programs and a strong organizational culture within an effective structure of authority.

References

Ammerman, Nancy. 1997. *Congregations and Community*. New Brunswick: Rutgers University Press.

Buswell, Robert Jr. 1992. *The Zen Monastic Experience: Buddhist Practice in Contemporary Korea*. Princeton: Princeton University Press.

Chai, Karen. 1998. "Competing for the Second Generation: English-Language Ministry at a Korean Protestant Church." In *Gatherings in Diaspora: Religious Communities and the New Immigration*, ed. R. Stephen Warner and Judith Wittner, 295–331. Philadelphia: Temple University Press.

Eck, Diana L., and Elinor J. Pierce. 1998. *World Religions in Boston: A Guide to Communities and Resources*. Cambridge: The Pluralism Project, Harvard University.

Fields, Rick. 1998. "Divided Dharma: White Buddhists, Ethnic Buddhists, and Racism." In *The Faces of Buddhism in America*, ed. Charles S. Prebish and Kenneth K. Tanaka, 196–206. Berkeley and Los Angeles: University of California Press.

Hurh, Won Moo. 1998. *The Korean Americans*. Westport, Conn.: Greenwood Press.

Hurh, Won Moo, and Kwang Chung Kim. 1984. *Korean Immigrants in America: A Structural Analysis of Ethnic Confinement and Adhesive Adaptation*. Madison, N.J.: Fairleigh Dickinson University Press.

———. 1990. "Religious Participation of Korean Immigrants in the U.S." *Journal for the Scientific Study of Religion* 29 (March): 19–34.

Kashima, Tetsuden. 1977. *Buddhism in America: The Social Organization of an Ethnic Religious Institution*. Westport, Conn.: Greenwood Press.

Kim, Elaine, and Eui-Young Yu. 1996. *East to America: Korean American Life Stories*. New York: New Press.

Kim, Illsoo 1987. "The Koreans: Small Business in an Urban Frontier." In *New Immigrants in New York*, ed. Nancy Foner, 219–42. New York: Columbia University Press.

Min, Pyong Gap. 1992. "The Structure and Social Functions of Korean Immigrant Churches in the U.S." *International Migration Review* 26 (4): 1370–94.

Numrich, Paul. 1996. *Old Wisdom in the New World: Americanization in Two Immigrant Theravada Buddhist Temples*. Knoxville: University of Tennessee Press.

Prebish, Charles S. 1988. "Buddhism." In *Encyclopedia of the American Religious Experience: Studies of Traditions and Movements*, ed. Charles H. Lippy and Peter W. Williams, 2:669–82. New York: Charles Scribner's Sons.

Shin, Eui Hang, and Hyung Park. 1988. "An Analysis of Causes of Schisms in Ethnic Churches: The Case of Korean-American Churches." *Sociological Analysis* 49 (Fall): 234–48.

Seekins, Donald. 1992. "The Society and Its Environment." In *South Korea: A Country Study*, ed. Andrea Matles Savada and William Shaw, 67–134. Washington, D.C.: Federal Research Division, Library of Congress.

Soeng, Mu. 1998. "Korean Buddhism in America." In *The Faces of Buddhism in America*, ed. Charles S. Prebish and Kenneth K. Tanaka, 118–28. Berkeley and Los Angeles: University of California Press.

Warner, R. Stephen. 1993. "Work in Progress Toward a New Paradigm for the Sociological Study of Religion in the U.S." *American Journal of Sociology* 98 (March): 1044–93.

———. 1994. "The Place of the Congregation in the American Religious Configuration." In *American Congregations*, ed. James Wind and James Lewis, 54–99. Chicago: University of Chicago Press.

Yu, Eui-Young. 1988. "The Growth of Korean Buddhism in the United States, with Special Reference to Southern California." *Pacific World: Journal of the Institute of Buddhist Studies*, n.s., 4:82–93.

Notes on Contributors

ANTONY W. ALUMKAL was born in Wilmington, Delaware, in 1969. He received a B.A. degree from the University of California at Berkeley in 1991 and a Ph.D. from Princeton University in 2000, both in sociology. He is Assistant Professor of Sociology of Religion at Iliff School of Theology in Denver, having previously taught at the University of Pennsylvania.

PETER T. CHA was born in Pusan, Korea, in 1959 and immigrated to the United States in 1972. He received his B.A. degree (in sociology) from the University of Chicago in 1982 and his M.Div. degree from Trinity Evangelical Divinity School (Deerfield, Ill.) in 1986. He was founding pastor of Parkwood Community Church (Glen Ellyn, Ill.) and is currently a Ph.D. candidate at Northwestern University and a faculty member at Trinity Evangelical Divinity School.

KAREN J. CHAI was born in 1968 in Seoul, Korea, and immigrated to the United States with her parents in 1973. She received her undergraduate education at Wellesley College (B.A., 1990) and her Ph.D. in sociology from Harvard University (2000). She has been a research fellow with the New Ethnic and Immigrant Congregations Project and the project on The Immigrant Second Generation in Metropolitan New York. She is coinvestigator, with Michael Emerson and George Yancey, of the Multiracial Congregations and Their Peoples Project, funded by the Lilly Endowment.

ROBERT D. GOETTE was born in Camden, South Carolina, in 1954. From 1960 to 1972 he went to school in Korea, where his parents were missionaries. He received his B.S. degree (in mathematics) from Valdosta State College in 1976, his M.Div. from Southwestern Baptist Theological Seminary in 1981, and his Th.M. from the Asian Center for Theological Studies in Seoul, Korea, in 1985. He is an ordained Baptist minister and was founding pastor of Grace Baptist Church in Glenview, Illinois. He is currently director of the Chicagoland English-speaking Asian American Church Planting Project.

MAE P. HONG has degrees in social work (M.A., 1996) from the University of Chicago and journalism (B.S., 1991) from Northwestern University and is Manager of Public Policy and Research for the Illinois Facilities Fund, a not-for-profit community development organization. She has been a member of churches pastored by Peter Cha and Robert Goette.

BOK IN KIM was born in Korea in 1954 and earned her B.A. and M.A. degrees in Buddhist Studies at Won Kwang University before coming to the United States to study at Temple University, where she earned her Ph.D. (in religious studies) in 1989. She has taught at Won Kwang University, Temple University, and Gettysburg College and is currently priest of the Won Buddhist Temple of Philadelphia.

KWANG CHUNG KIM was born in Seoul, Korea, in 1937. He received his undergraduate education at Yonsei University (B.A., 1961) and his Ph.D. from Indiana University in 1973. He has taught at Western Illinois University, where he is Professor of Sociology, since 1969. He has been awarded numerous research grants from the National Institute of Mental Health and other agencies and is author (and coauthor, with Won Moo Hurh) of many articles, chapters, research reports, and books on Korean Americans, including *Korean Immigrants in America* (1984). Most recently, he edited *Koreans in the Hood: Conflict With African Americans* (1999).

SHIN KIM earned her B.A. in English Literature at Yonsei University and is currently a Ph.D. candidate in the School of Social Service Administration at the University of Chicago, where she is also an Adjunct Professor. She is coeditor, with Ho-Youn Kwon, of *The Emerging Generation of Korean Americans* (1993).

TONG-HE KOH was born in Korea and earned her B.A. (English literature) and M.A. (psychology) degrees at Ewha Women's University in Seoul before coming to the United States to study at Boston University, where she received her Ph.D. in psychology in 1960. She has served on the research and teaching staffs of the University of Illinois at Chicago and is active in community organizations in Chicago, where she has been an independent clinical psychologist since 1978.

HO-YOUN KWON was born in Kyunggi-do, Korea, in 1938 and received his B.A. in sociology from Seoul National University in 1961. His graduate work was done in the United States at the University of Hawaii and Utah State University, where he received his Ph.D. in 1982. He is active in Korean and Korean American community affairs and is Associate Professor of Sociology and Executive Director of the Center for Korean Studies at North Park University. He is coeditor, with Shin Kim, of *The Emerging Generation of Korean-Americans* (1993).

SANG HYUN LEE was born in Korea in 1938 and immigrated to the United States in 1955, earning her B.A. at Wooster College in 1960, her S.T.B. at Harvard Divinity School in 1963, and her Ph.D. in theology at Harvard University in 1972. He taught at Hope College from 1970 to 1980 and since then has taught at Princeton Theological Seminary, where he is K. C. Han Professor of Systematic Theology. He is author of *The Philosophical Theology of Jonathan Edwards* (1988) and is at work on a book on Asian American theology.

SOYOUNG PARK was born in Sun-san, Korea, in 1965 and received her undergraduate education in English literature both in Korea (at Keimyung University in Taegu) and in the United States (at Long Island University), graduating in 1988. She holds an M.Div. degree from New York Theological Seminary (1993) and received her Ph.D. in sociology from Drew University in 2000. She has served as youth pastor of Presbyterian churches in New York and New Jersey and is currently an Adjunct Professor at New Brunswick Theological Seminary.

SAMU SUNIM was born in Korea in 1941. Orphaned during the Korean War, he entered a Buddhist monastery in 1956 and later completed his Zen training under Master Solbong Sunim at Pomo-Sa Monastery, in Pusan, Korea. He came to North America in 1967 and along with his students has built Buddhist centers in Toronto, Ann Arbor, and Chicago. He is Founder and President of the Buddhist Society of Compassionate Wisdom (formerly the Zen Lotus Society), publisher of the journal *Buddhism at the Crossroads,* and Master of the Zen Buddhist Temple of Chicago, Illinois.

R. STEPHEN WARNER was born in 1941 in Oakland, California. He was both an undergraduate and a graduate student at the University of California at Berkeley, where he earned his Ph.D. in 1972. A past president of the Association for the Sociology of Religion, he is Professor of Sociology at the University of Illinois at Chicago, where he was director of the New Ethnic and Immigrant Congregations Project (1992–97). He is author of *New Wine in Old Wineskins* (1988) and coeditor, with Judith G. Wittner, of *Gatherings in Diaspora: Religious Communities and the New Immigration* (1998).

EUI-YOUNG YU, born in Seoul, Korea, in 1937, earned his B.A. degree in sociology at Seoul National University in 1961 and his Ph.D. in demography at the University of Pennsylvania in 1969. He is Professor of Sociology and Director of the Center for Korean American and Korean Studies at California State University, Los Angeles, where he has taught since 1968. He is author or editor of numerous articles, research reports, and books on Korean Americans, including, with Elaine H. Kim, *East to America: Korean American Life Stories* (1996). He is a frequent contributor to news media on Korean American issues.

Index

AACF. *See* Asian-American Christian Fellowship
Acts (book of the Bible), 115, 116, 117–21, 122
African American Presbyterians, 77, 78–79, 93; church participation of, 82; eldership among, 83, 84; neighborhood churches attended by, 80; and sanctity of heterosexual marriage, 87; sizes of churches attended by, 80; stability of membership among, 81; theological orientation of, 85, 86, 87; volunteer time and finances outside communities of, 83
Afro-Caribbeans, 41
Aitken-roshi, Robert, 251
Allport, G. W., and J. M. Ross, 97
Alumkal, Antony W., 17, 46, 47, 48, 172
American Buddhist Congress, 35, 223
American Zen Buddhists, 45
American Zen College, 214, 240
Ammerman, Nancy, 177
Appenzeller, Henry G., 7
Asian American Association, 176
Asian American Christian Fellowship (AACF), 195, 196, 292
Asian American churches: and Confucianism, 67; and home, 64–68; liberation through ethnicity in, 66; non-race-specific evangelical identity of, 188; relations with other people and churches, 68; and second-generation Asian Americans, 66; transformation of, into bilingual second-generation churches, 127–28 and Fig. 7.2, 129–35, 139; and women, 67
Asian Americans: and Christian pilgrimage, 63; ethnic identity formation by, 152–55; and in-betweeness, 58–59, 60, 66; interethnic difference in psychopathy among, 102; and marginality, 55–57, 58–59, 61–62, 65, 68; mental disorders among, 102; second-generation, 66
Asian Indians, 31
assimilation, 47, 59, 182,
Atkinson, D., G. Morten, and D. Sue, 153, 154
attachment theory, 97

Bachelard, Gaston, 67
Bacon, Jean, 168

Bartels, William K., 35
Batchelor, Martine, 246, 247
Batchelor, Pŏpch'ŏn Stephen, 242–43, 244, 247
BCC. *See* Buddhist Churches of Canada
Berall, Erik, 257
Bhaktivedanta Swami, 260, 267
Bickel, C., 100
Blue Dragon Zen Academy, 239
Bodhisattva monks, 249–51, 254
Boh Won Sa Korean Buddhist temple, 276–77; and American Buddhism, 293; Buddha's Birthday celebration at, 274 n. 2; challenges faced by, 293–94; and the Chogye order, 275, 275 n. 4, 278, 279, 281; culture at, 287–92; identity boundaries maintained in, 288–92; minority consciousness at, 291, 293; non-Koreans in, 280, 286, 293; resources available to, 277, 282, 283–86; and second-generation Korean Americans, 285, 293–94; service at, 273, 274, 274 n. 3, 275; structures of authority in, 278–82
Bone of Space (Seung Sahn Sunim), 219
Bop Jung Sunim, 223
Brown, Gary, 237
Buddhism, 175 (*see also* Theravada Buddhism; Won Buddhism); fundamental truths of, 260; immigrants in congregations of, 19; interdenominational, 231, 232, 234; in Korea, 5, 6, 7, 18; missionary task of, 18; parallel congregations of, 19; in United States, 5, 18, 19
Buddhist Centers, 27
Buddhist Churches of Canada (BCC), 33–34
Buddhist Faith and Sudden Enlightenment (Park Sung Bae), 220
Buddhists: immigrant, 27; Japanese American, 281; and race and ethnicity, 3
Buddhist temples, 212–13, 221 and Table 12.1, 222–24
Bulil-hoe, 244
Bul-il International Meditation Center, 214, 241
Bul Kyo Si Bo, 223
Busto, Rudy, 171, 172, 188
Buswell, Robert E., Jr. (Hyemyŏng), 246, 247, 257

Caine, Deborah (Chi Kwang), 246, 247
California, 9, 211
Cambridge Zen Center, 218, 248
Campus Crusade for Christ, 184, 195
Catholic Church, 29, 33, 72
Caucasian Presbyterians, 93; church participation
    of, 82; eldership among, 83, 83 n. 14, 84;
    neighborhood churches attended by, 80; and
    sanctity of heterosexual marriage, 87; sizes
    of churches attended by, 80; stability of
    membership among, 81; theological orienta-
    tion of, 85, 86, 87; volunteer time and
    finances outside communities of, 83
Center for Korean Studies of North Park Univer-
    sity, 19–20, 22–23
Cha, Peter, 13, 46, 126, 158
Chai, Karen: analytical models used by, 17; and
    Korean American Catholicism, 22; men-
    tioned, 15, 18, 21, 46, 47, 48
Chaitanya Mahaprabhu, 262, 263
China, 5, 6, 7, 22
Chinese American Christianity, 15
Chinese American churches, 128
Chinese Americans, 65, 102, 196
Chinese Christian Fellowship (CCF), 196
Chinese Exclusion Act, 8
Chinul, 232–34, 243, 244, 256, 257
Chogye Order. *See* Korean Buddhist Chogye
    Order (KBC)
Cho Ge Sŏn Wŏn, 237
Chogye Zen Center, 219
Chong, Kelly, 43, 46, 157, 172, 183, 190 n. 8,
    198–99
Chong Woo Sunim, 278, 280
Cho Seung Taek, 220
Choson dynasty, 6–7
Choson Pulgyo Cho'ongnyonhoe / Korean
    Buddhist Young People's Association, 229
Christianity: ethnic identity strengthened by, 47;
    evangelical, 196; in Korea, 6, 7–8, 11, 18;
    and Korean immigrants, 15, 30, 47, 275; and
    pilgrimage, 63; symbols in, 60
Chung Jung Dahr Sunim, 217
Chung Kwan Ung Seon Sa Nim, 224
Chung Kwan Ung Sunim, 222 n. 29
church: defined, 267 n. 19; as household of God,
    64–68
church churches: black, 181, 190; established by
    first-generation Korean immigrants (*see* immi-
    grant churches); established by second-
    generation Korean immigrants (*see* second-
    generation churches); ethnic-specific, 115,
    181–82; European American, 138–39; immi-
    grant (*see* immigrant churches); Japanese

American, 128; multiethnic, 138; theories of
    strength and success of, 163–64, 176–78
church participation, 72
clergy, 96; Korean American, 33; role of, 94,
    99–101
cognitive therapy, 101, 105–6
Community Church of Paxton, 160, 161, 163
Compass of Zen Teaching (Seung Sahn Sunim), 219,
    252–53
Confucianism: and Asian American youth, 47;
    Catholicism opposed by, 6–7; combined with
    evangelism in second-generation churches,
    48; in immigrant churches, 202; influence on
    family relations, 8, 46; in Korea, 6, 7, 8, 22;
    principle of seniority, 204, 206; and women,
    15, 43, 67
conservatives, 85, 86
Corinthians (book of the Bible), 120
Cornelius, 118, 119
culture: as bridge to cross-generation gaps and
    other cultures, 121–22; and depression, 102;
    differences between Korean and American,
    122–23, 183, 186–87, 189; and mental
    health, 96, 101–4; and the practice of faith,
    120

Dae Gak, 257
Daesoo Sunim, 216
Dae Won Sa, 212–13
Daewoo Sunim, 216
Dahl Ma Sa, 221, 222, 223
Dalai Lama, 249, 291
denomination: and African Americans, 193;
    defined, 267 n. 19
depression: and culture, 102; and religious belief,
    97, 98
Descriptive Catalogue to Korean Canon (Park and
    Lancaster), 220
Dharma Light, 252
Dharma Sah Zen Center, 218–19
Diamond Hill Zen Monastery, 217–18, 250, 251
Do Ahn Sunim, 212, 222, 223–24
Doh-An Kim, 279, 280, 281, 282, 284, 287, 289
Dolan, Jay, 29
Doyun Sunim, 215
Dropping Ashes on the Buddha (Seung Sahn Sunim),
    219, 248
DU KCF. *See* Korean Christian Fellowship at
    "Downtown University"
Durkheim, Emile, 100

Eck, Diana, 286
El Centro Zen Loto de Mexico, 215
Elliott, John H., 65, 65 n. 23

ethnicity: defined, 194; liberation through, 66; and racial differentiation, 16; and religion, 3, 196–98, 200–201
ethnic roles, 74
Eule, Gerald (Hyegak), 246
European Americans, 102
evangelical Christianity: and college, 195, 200–201; and feminism, 204–5; and gender, 204–5; and race and ethnicity, 196–98, 200–201
evangelicalism, 165, 165 n. 9, 171
evangelical morality, 200–201
Evergreen Baptist Churches of Southern California, 138

Fages, Martine (Söngil), 246
faith culture. See culture
feminism, 204–5, 206; and evangelical Christianity, 204–5
Fenton, John Y., 201
Fields, Rick, 280 n. 8
Filipino Americans, 102
Filipinos, 22, 31, 39
Finney, Henry, 5
Fisher, Colonel and Mrs. Thell H., 236
Formation of Ch'an Ideology in China and Korea (Buswell), 247
Freud, Sigmund, 100

Galatians (book of the Bible), 118
Geerts, Clifford, 100
gender: differentiation in Korean American community, 38–39, 42; and evangelical Christianity, 204–5
generation: differentiation in Korean American community, 14, 38–39, 42
Gennep, Arnold van, 58
Genthner, Robert, 257
Gentiles, 117, 118–19
Germans, 31
GI brides, 9
Gilbert, Tae Hui Don, 236, 237, 238, 239
GKPC. See Glory Korean Presbyterian Church
Glory Korean Presbyterian Church (GKPC), 183–84; Christian identity before Korean at, 186 n. 6, 186–88; English service in, 184; Korean identity displayed by, 184–85, 185 n. 5, 190; and multicultural ministry, 188–90, 190 n. 7; reasons for attending, 185–86, 188
God, loving and angry, 92
Goette, Robert, 5, 15, 17, 21, 48–49
Gordon-Conwell Theological Seminary, 48, 161, 170, 171, 286

Grace Baptist Church, Glenview, Ill., 136
Greek Orthodox, 29, 33
Greeley, Andrew M., 186 n. 6

Haddad, Yvonne, 27
Haengwön Sun. See Seung Sahn Haeng Won Sunim
Han'guk-sa, 256
Handlin, Oscar, 27, 27 n. 4
Han Yong'un, 229
Hare Krishna movement, 259, 262, 267, 268, 269
Harvard Encyclopedia of American Ethnic Groups, 194
Ha Tai Kim, 224
Hatch, Nathan, 33
Havan-pola Ratanasara, 223
Hawaii, 8–9, 31, 228, 229
Hearn, Lafcadio, 238 n. 21
Hearn, Söng Ryong, 237, 238, 238 n. 21
Hebraic Jewish Christians, 115, 116, 117–21, 122
HeKwang, 236
Hellenistic Jewish Christians, 115, 116–21, 122
Herberg, Will, 26–27, 32, 46
Hindus, 27–28, 80
Hispanic American Presbyterians, 77, 77 n. 8, 77 n. 9, 78–79, 93; church participation of, 82; eldership among, 83, 84; neighborhood churches attended by, 80; and sanctity of heterosexual marriage, 87; sizes of churches attended by, 80; stability of membership among, 81; theological orientation of, 85, 86, 87; volunteer time and financial contributions outside communities of, 83
Hispanic Americans, 29, 30, 32, 33
Hiot'ong, 231, 256
home, 57, 64–69
Hong, Mae, 5
Hui Neng Zen Temple, 237, 239
Hurh, Won Moo, 10, 288 n. 14
Hurh, Won Moo, and Kwang Chung Kim, 22, 26 n. 3, 27, 37, 72, 95; "additive" model of religion, 28
Hwadu Son, 233, 244, 253
Hyeam Sunim, 216
Hyobong Sunim, 241, 243
Hyön Jo, 241, 243
Hyön Sun, 228
Hyujöng, 234–35, 256, 257

identity, 45–47, 152–56
Il Bung Order for Sön, 240
Il Bung Seo, Kyung-Bo, 236, 237
Il-bung Sön Wön, 237
Il-Bung Zen Buddhist Association, 213, 240

Il-Bung Zen Center, 237
Illsoo Kim, 289
Ilsan, 237
immigrant churches, 193–94; affected by reduction in immigrants, 76 n. 5 and n. 6, 77; conference on, 25 n. 1, 25–26; de facto congregationalism of, 44; eldership in, 83, 83 n. 13;
English-language worship groups in, 48–49;
ethnic role of, 18, 75–76, 121; evangelism in,
44; functions of, 32, 44, 65, 72, 75–76,
88–90, 92, 93, 95–96, 157, 182, 212; future
of, 17; homogeneity of, 31; intrachurch
conflict regarding officers' elections in, 37;
language spoken in, 32–33, 121, 126, 127;
male-centered and hierarchical power structure of, 14–15, 36, 202; and ministry,
121–22; as model, 43–44, 45; numbers of,
141; particularism in, 182; Presbyterian (see
immigrant churches, Korean Presbyterian);
and reduction in immigrants, 76; relationship
with second-generation churches, 15, 17,
76, 191 n. 9; schism in, 33; and second-
generation Korean Americans, 47–49, 141–
44, 155–56, 157, 158, 199; size of, 32, 32 n.
11, 33, 44; social functions of, 17, 32, 88–90,
92, 93, 95–96; and strictness, 163–64,
176–78; supported by American churches,
18; transformation of, into bilingual second-
generation churches, 127–28 and Fig. 7.2,
129–35, 139; viewed by Korean Americans,
36–37; worship styles at, 36, 37, 199–200;
youth ministry in, 130–31, 131 n. 11, 132
immigrant churches, Korean Presbyterian: attendance in, 82, 87; commitment of members
to, 82–83, 87, 89, 90–91, 93; eldership in,
83, 83 n. 13, 84–85, 87, 91, 93; evangelical
orientation of, 85–86, 86 n. 16, 87, 91–92,
93; membership instability in, 81–82, 87,
89, 93; proximity of, 79–80, 87; and sanctity
of heterosexual marriage, 87; sizes of,
80–81, 87
immigrants: Chinese, 31; diversity of, in U.S.,
71; Dutch door, 31, 31 n. 9; European, 10,
17, 59, 62, 186 n. 6; importance of religion
to, 4, 26–28, 40, 71, 193, 275; Korean (see
Korean Americans); and legal residence, 74 n.
3; negotiation of identities among, 45–46;
Pakistani, 181–82, 182 n. 2
immigration: European, 10; illegal, 74; Korean
(see immigration, Korean); laws, 10–11, 71,
95, 211; and occupation, 10–11
immigration, Korean: decline in, 17, 38, 39, 74,
75, 76, 88, 92; and the development of
churches, 9 n. 1, 9–10; pattern of, 8–11, 12
(Table 1.1), 34 n. 12; reverse, 74

Immigration and Naturalization Service, 40, 228
inclusive organizations, 89
India, 27, 39, 40
Indian Americans, 168, 197
Indian Orthodox Christians, 45
Indians, 46, 181–82, 182 n. 2
in-group commitment, 82, 83
interdenominational Buddhism. See Buddhism
International Meditation Center, 241–42, 246
International Meditation Zen Center, 246
International Society of Krishna Consciousness
(ISKCON), 259; and communal life, 264,
264 n. 12, 266, 268; decline in, 261, 266,
266 n. 15; and ethnicity, 268; external
evaluation of, 266–68, 270; and identity, 264,
265, 268; material world rejected by, 262,
263, 264, 266, 266 n. 14, 267; in the U.S.,
260–61, 267
InterVarsity Christian Fellowship (IVCF), 195
Iran, 40
Iranian Jews, 197
ISKCON. See International Society of Krishna
Consciousness

Japan, 5, 7, 22; and Korea, 6, 7, 9, 229
Japanese American Christianity, 15
Japanese Americans, 46, 65, 102
Japanese Canadian Buddhists, 33–34; shortage of
clergy among, 33
Japanese Canadians, 17
Jellyfish Bones: The Humor of Zen (Gilbert), 239
Jesus, 117, 120
Jewish Christians, Hebraic and Hellenistic,
115–17; cultural tensions between, 117–20;
lessons for Korean church, 120–22
Jews, 31–32; Ashkenazic, 26
Ji Wol, 278
John Paul II, 249
Jong Sun Kim, 217
Jundosah, 184, 184 n. 4, 185, 185 n. 5, 186

KCF. See Korean Christian Fellowship
Kim, Ai Ra, 14, 43
Kim, Bok-In, 45
Kim, Chan-Hie, 28
Kim, David, 183
Kim, David Kyuman, 172
Kim, Die Young, 158
Kim, Joe, 184, 191
Kim, Jung Ha, 14
Kim, Kwang Chung, 14, 20, 26 n. 3, 27, 28,
37, 43
Kim, Shin, 14, 43
Kim Chin-ho, 228
Kim Kusan, 220, 224

Kim Pömnin, 227, 229
Kim Sang-ho, 228
Ki Mu Sunim, 278, 279, 283, 287–88
King, Ken, 216
Kirkpatrick, L. E., 97–98
Kitano, H., and R. Daniels, 152
Kitson, Audrey (Jagwang), 246, 247
Koh, Tong-He, 15
Korea (see also North Korea; South Korea); Buddhism in, 5, 18, 40; Christianity in, 6–7, 18, 89; division of, 7, 75 n. 4, 230; economy in, 88; evangelism in, 30; International Monetary Fund (IMF) crisis in, 74; and Japan, 6, 7, 9, 229; modernization of, 6, 7, 8; racial differentiation in, 16; treaty with U.S. in 1882, 7
Korean American identity, 194;
Korean American Presbyterians, 28, 77, 78–79, 93 (see also immigrant churches, Korean Presbyterian)
Korean Americans (see also men, Korean American; women, Korean American); adjustment patterns of, 12–13; ages of, 11, 12, 38, 81, 92; American-born (see second-generation Korean Americans); Buddhists among (see Korean Buddhism); Catholics among, 21–22; children of (see second-generation Korean Americans); and Christian identity, 15, 17, 18, 39, 71–72, 88–89, 95, 194, 211–12 (see also Korean Christians); church participation of, 46, 65, 65 n. 22, 72–74, 75, 82, 87, 92–93, 95–96; class background of, 73, 75; conference on religion of, 19–20; and economic opportunity, 13, 31, 75; and education, 30, 39, 173–74; English speaking, 125, 125 n. 1; and gender-role expectations, 91; homogeneity of, 31; importance of religion to, 13, 38, 46, 95, 157; indifference to out-groups of, 83; in-group commitment of, 42, 83, 89, 93; jeopardy faced by, 88, 91; language barriers experienced by, 39–40; limited interarea mobility of, 81, 81 n. 12; marginal (see second-generation Korean Americans); as model minority, 41; and national identification, 46; occupations of, 30, 31, 39–40; population of, 12 and Table 1.1, 125, 211; racial differentiation experienced by, 16; racial/ethnic identity of, 17; and religious duality, 289, 292–93; residential pattern of, 80; and the second generation, 14, 43, 75, 115–16, 168–69; sociocultural resources of Korea utilized by, 13
Korean Approach to Zen (Buswell), 220, 247
Korean Buddhism (see also Sön Buddhism); American, 181–89, 279–80, 280 n. 8, 285, 288, 288 n. 14; Bodhisattva (married) monks in,

249–50, 254; challenges in U.S. faced by, 224–26; decentralized nature of, 280, 280 n. 10, 281, 281 n. 11; missionary task of, 18–19; research and teaching of, 213, 219–20; spread to the West of, 227–30, 256, 275; teachers of, in U.S., 212, 213–19; in the U.S., 3, 5, 18, 212–13, 275–76
Korean Buddhist Chogye Order (KBC), 230, 233, 240, 248, 249, 250, 251
Korean Buddhist Chogye Order Hong Poep Won, 217, 218, 225, 248
Korean Campus Crusade for Christ (KCCC), 184, 195, 196, 201
Korean Christian Fellowship (KCF), 184, 195, 196, 197, 198, 200–201; gender relations in, 202–3; and liberalism, 205
Korean Christian Fellowship at "Downtown University" (DU KCF), 195, 196, 203
Korean Christians: and biculturalism, 37–38; Catholics among, 21–22; church participation of, 32; numbers of, 3; recent converts among, 32; and reformation of American Christianity, 5; reverse missionaries among, 45
Korean Culture (magazine), 257
Korean ethnic church, 193–94, 189–200
Korean immigrants. See Korean Americans
Korean Methodist Church of San Francisco, 9
Korean Methodists, 28
Korean migration. See immigration, Korean
Korean Presbyterian Church, 9, 28
Korean Presbyterian Churches in American (KPCA), 194
Korean Protestantism, 44
Korean Sön Buddhism, 235–49
Korean Students Association (KSA), 174–76, 184, 200–201
Korean War, 9, 230
Koreatown, 63–64, 75, 221
Koryo dynasty, 6
Koryö-sa, 242, 246
Koryö Sön-sa, 228
Kosung Sunim, 214
Kraft, Charles H., 118 n. 2
Krause, Stacey (Hamwöl), 246
Krishna Consciousness, 45
KSA. See Korean Students Associations
Kun Sunim, 222
Kusan Sunim, 214, 220, 230, 241–47, 248, 256, 257
Kwan Eum Sa, 279
Kwan Um Sa, 44, 222, 223, 224
Kwan Um School of Zen, 217, 218, 250–51, 252, 254, 255, 280
Kwon, Ho-Youn, 19–20, 22–23
Kwsan Sunim, 222 n. 29

Kyo, 234, 235, 239, 240, 252, 253, 256
Kyönghö, 253
Kyung-Bo, 230, 248, 256, 257

La Brely, Edith, 215
Lancaster, Lewis, 220
Lee, Grant S., 235 n. 12
Lee, Helen, 158
Lee, Sang Hyun, 10, 20 n. 4, 26 n. 2, 26 n. 3,
    35, 48; on the importance of Korean Ameri-
    cans holding church offices, 36–37; Korean
    Christians viewed as pilgrims by, 5; and
    Korean Presbyterians, 28; and marginality of
    American Christians, 45
Lee Nung Ka Dae Seonsa, 222 n. 29, 224
Lee Young Moo, 224
liminality, 57–60
Lincoln, C. Eric, and Lawrence Mamiya, 181,
    181 n. 1, 182, 190
Linton, Stephen, 157 n. 1
Los Angeles uprising, 63
Lummis, Adair, 27

Maitland, Robert, 236–37, 238
male elders, 83, 84
Man'gong Sunim, 216
Man Party, 229
marginality, 55–59, 61–64, 65, 68
marriage, 87, 187
Martin, Larry (Hyönsöng), 246
Masters, K. S., and A. E. Bergin, 97
Maton, K. I., 100
Mayan Indians, 39
Meaning of Revelation, The (Niebuhr), 63
men, Korean American: church positions held by,
    37, 40, 44, 45, 202; eldership held by, 84,
    87, 91, 93; and gender identity, 204; in
    immigrant churches, 14
mental health: and culture, 101–4; as foreign to
    Korean Americans, 96; and religion, 96–98,
    110–11
mental health professionals: and cultural diversity,
    101, 104–10; and religion, 98–99, 103
MID. See Minority Identity Development
Minjung pulgyo, 231
Minority Identity Development (MID), 153–54,
    155
missionaries, 4
Mitchell, Stephen, 248
Miyamoto, Joann, 55–56, 57
Moigaard, Julie, 216
Moo Jin Janf Sunim, 222 n. 29, 224
Moon, Sun Myung, 21
Morinis, Alan, 61 n. 14
Mullins, Mark, 33

multiculturalism, 122
Multi-Ethnic Fellowship (MEF), 195
Muryang Sunim, 257
Mu Sang, 249
Muslims, 27, 40, 80
Mu Soeng (Prakash Shrivastava), 255, 280
Myobong Sunim, 216, 217

National Origins Act of 1924, 71
Neubaur, Renaud (Hyehaeng), 246
Neungin Sunwon temple, 216–17
Niebuhr, H. Richard, 63, 118 n. 2
Niebuhr, Richard R., 61 n. 14
Nine Mountains (Kusan Sunim), 214, 242
nonobstruction, 231, 232
North Korea, 74–75, 75 n. 4
Norwegian Lutherans, 26
Numrich, Paul, 280, 280 n. 9

One Mind, 231
Only Doing It for Sixty Years (Seung Sahn Sunim),
    219
Only Don't Know (Seung Sahn Sunim), 219, 253
out-group indifference, 82, 83

Paegnim-sa, 256, 257
Paek Söng'uk, 227, 229
Pai, Margaret K., 227 n. 1
Pai, Young, 35, 37
Pakistan, 27
Palestinians, 46
pan-Asianism, 41
Pan-Pacific Buddhist Conference, 228, 229
Pargament, K. I., 97
Park, Robert E., 57
Park, Soyoung, 17, 21
Park Chung Bin, 260
Park Chung Hee, 10, 11
Park Sung Bae, 219–20, 222 n. 29, 224
Park wan Il Kosa, 222 n. 29
Partin, H. B., 61 n. 14
Paul, Saint, the apostle, 117, 118–20, 121, 122,
    139, 198
Paxton Korean Church (PKC), 158–59, 276,
    277–78; adaptation at, 164–66; boundaries
    defended by, 164–66, 288–92; challenges
    faced by, 293–94; culture at, 166–67,
    287–92; distinction between churchgoing and
    secular Korean Americans in, 174–76; dis-
    tinctions between Christian and non-Christian
    at, 170–71; distinctions between Korean and
    non-Korean in, 171–74; distinctions between
    second and first generations at, 168–69; dis-
    tinctiveness and success at, 176, 177, 178;
    English Worship Service in, 162, 162 n. 8,

163, 166, 170, 172, 178; and evangelism, 286, 293; facilities of, 284; resources available to, 282–83, 284–85, 286; schism at, 178–79; second-generation Korean American ministry at, 159, 159 n. 4, 160, 161 n. 72, 162, 162 n. 8, 163, 164–65, 166–68, 170–71, 178–79; service at, 273–74, 275; strictness at, 163–64, 165, 166; structures of authority in, 279, 281

people group, 127, 127 n. 5

perfect interfusion, 231, 232

Perl, Jacob, 217

Peter, 118, 119

phenomenological approach, 101

Philippines, 39

pilgrimage, 4–5, 57, 61–64, 68–69; defined, 61 n. 14

PKC. *See* Paxton Korean Church

Polish Catholics, 26

Pop Jung Sunim, 222 n. 29, 224

possession, 103

Prabhupada, 260, 262, 267

Presbyterian Church, 28, 77 n. 7, 183–84

Presbyterian Panel (PP), 77–78

Primary Point, 217, 250

Proctor, Anna (Suil), 246

Protestantism: associational character of, 32; evangelical, 29; Hispanic conversion to, 29, 29 n. 6, 30; influence on family relations, 8; in Korea, 7, 8; and Korean Americans, 72

Providence Zen Center, 217, 248, 250, 252, 253, 255

Pruden, Leo, 217

psychologists: and cultural diversity, 101, 104–10; and religion, 98–99, 103; role of, 93. *See also* psychotherapy

psychology, 96, 98; transpersonal, 106–8

psychotherapy: and religion, 100; transpersonal, 102

Pyong Hwa Sa, 223

Quennalt, Kim (Hyŏn Jo), 246

race, 3, 16, 182, 188, 189; defined, 194

Racial Ethnic Presbyterian Panel (REPP), 77 n. 7, 77–78

racism, 41, 59, 102

religion: diversity of, in U.S., 25; and immigrant identity formation, 193; importance to immigrants of, 4, 26–28, 71, 193; intrinsic and extrinsic orientations in, 92, 97, 104; and Korean Americans, 19–20, 25–26, 95; and mental health, 96–99, 103, 110–11; negotiated between first- and second-generation immigrants, 198; phenomenological approach to, 104–5; and sociological issues, 23; and

stress, 99–101; transformed through migration, 4, 5, 28–29, 40

religion and mental health, 91

reverse migration, 74

Rhodes, Lincoln, 218–19, 248

Roman Catholic Church, 29, 33, 72

Russia, 5, 7, 22

sagyo ipson, 234, 235, 253, 256

salvation, 86, 91, 95, 118, 119, 196,

Samadhi-prajña Community, 232, 233, 243

Sambo-sa Temple, 241

Samu Sunim, 6, 18–19, 214–16, 219

Sano, Roy, 66

Saran, Parmatma, 27–28

second-generation churches: challenges facing, 35–38, 136–37; and Confucianism, 48; ethnic composition of, 16; evangelism in, 48; gender equality in, 16; language spoken in, 35–36, 44, 48; as primary Korean ethnic churches in future, 17; raison d'être of, 16; relationship with immigrant churches of, 15–16, 17, 191 n. 9; worship styles at, 199–200

second-generation Korean Americans: 1.5 generation of, 15, 22, 143 n. 1, 159 n. 4, 182 n. 3; acculturation of, 12, 13, 35, 121–22; adolescent experiences in immigrant church, 146–49, 199–200; ages of, 11; alienated, 121, 126 and Fig. 7.1, 127; assimilation desired in elementary years by, 13, 16–17, 144–45; and Buddhism, 225, 285; career opportunities for, 42; Christians among (*see also* Korean American Christians), 15, 17, 46; church participation of, 35–36, 76, 131, 131 n. 10, 157, 157 n. 1, 158, 184; church preferences of, 132–33, 134 (Table 7.1); commonalities of, 17; defined, 143 n. 1; early childhood experiences in immigrant churches, 144–45; and education, 173–74; as emerging people group, 127; ethnic heritage recognized by, 13, 16–17, 36, 147–48, 152–55, 183; filial piety reinforced by conservative Christian ideology of, 43; and gender, 46; growth and increasing visibility of, 38; and identity, 17, 36, 46, 147–48, 152–55, 168, 172, 183, 200; and the immigrant church, 47–49, 76, 121, 145, 148–49, 199–200; influence of home-country and host-country values and structures on, 13, 42–43; marginalization of, 126 and Fig. 7.1, 127, 134–35, 136, 138, 172, 182; and ministry, 121–22, 136–39, 182; negotiation btween particularism and universalism by, 182–83, 190, 190 n. 8, 191; nonevangelical, 200–201; relationships with non-co-nationals,

42; relations with parents, 14, 75, 115–16, 168–69, 199; young adult experiences in immigrant churches, 151–52, 199–200

Second Great Awakening, 33

sect: defined, 267, 267 n. 19

Seo Kyungbo Sunim, 214, 248, 256; books written by, 213, 235, 238 n. 19, 239, 240 n. 23; Korean Buddhism spread in U.S. by, 212, 213, 222 n. 29, 230, 235 n. 12, 235–41, 236 n. 15, 238 n. 20, 257

Seoul International Zen Center, 250, 251

Seung Sahn Haeng Won Sunim, 222 n. 29, 225, 230, 280; and American Bodhisattva monks, 249–50; books written by, 219, 248, 252–53; criticism of, 254–55; Korean Buddhism spread in U.S. by, 212, 217–19, 222 n. 29, 230, 247–56; teachings of, 252–54, 254 n. 44

Seventh Day Adventist Church, 45

shamanism, 8, 22

Shibley, Mark, 176

Shin, Il-Kwon (later Gosung), 236, 239, 240

Shin Popta Sunim, 224

Shintoism, 7

Siddharta Gautama, 263

"silent exodus," 141, 155

Simwol Sunim, 216

Smith, Christian, 163–64

Smith, Timothy L., 25 n. 1

socially engaged Buddhism, 229

Soen Sa Nim. *See* Seung Sahn Haeng Won Sunim

Soen Sa Nun. *See* Seung Sahn Haeng Won Sunim

Sohn Kyong san Sunim, 222 n. 29

Solbong Sunim, 214

Sŏn Buddhism: in Korea, 230–35; in the West, 235–49

Song, Minho, 158

Songgwang-sa, 243, 244

Sŏngil, 242

Sorensen, Henrik H., 246, 247

Sot'aesan, 259 n. 1, 260, 263, 264, 269–70 n. 24

Soucek, J. B., 61 n. 14

South Central Los Angeles racial uprising, 63–64, 75

South Korea, 6, 10, 21, 74, 75 n. 4

Springer Ratanasara, Karl, 223

Spring Wind–Buddhist Cultural Forum (Zen Lotus Society), 215

St. Andrew Kim, 22

Stonequist, Everett, 57, 58

Streitfeld, Richard, 217

sudden awakening / gradual cultivation 233, 234, 235, 245

sudden awakening / sudden cultivation, 245

Sudha Sunim, 214, 215

Suil, 242

Sung Do Sunim, 222

Suson-sa, 232, 241

Syngman Rhee, 228–29, 230

Taean, 233

Tae Chi, 237

Takaki, Ron, 59

Taoism, 60

Tao Te Ching, 60

Ten Gates (Seung Sahn Sunim), 219, 253

Theravada Buddhism, 27, 280 n. 9

Tŏksan (Han-Sang Lee), 241

t'ong, pulgyo, 231

Torah, 116

Tough Chinho, 227, 227 n. 1, 228–30

transpersonal psychotherapy, 106–8

Treatise on Revitalization of Korean Buddhism (Han Yong'un), 229

Turner, Victor, 58, 64

"twinkie" identity, 144, 148

U.S. Census, 11, 40

Uisang, 231

Underwood, Horace G., 7

Unification Church, 21

United Methodist Church, 28

United States: Buddhism in, 5, 18, 19; and Korea, 7–8; Koreans lumped together with other Asians in, 16; racial formation in, 16, 17; religious diversity in, 25

Upside Down Circle: Zen Laughter (Gilbert), 239

Vietnam, 40

Wali Ali, 238, 238 n. 21

Warner, R. Stephen, 20, 21, 71, 280 n. 10, 281

Wat Dhammaram, 35

Way of Korean Zen, The (Kusan Sunim), 214

Weber, Max, 32

Whole World Is a Single Flower (Soen Sa Nim), 253

Wilkinson, Edward, 236 n. 15, 237

Williams, D. R., 100

Williams, Raymond, 27, 28–29, 181–82, 182 n. 2

Wilson, John F., 25 n. 1

women, Asian American, 67

women, Korean American, 9 (*see also* women, Korean American evangelical); and Christianity, 43; and clergy careers, 33; and Confucianism, 43; eldership held by, 84, 84 n. 15, 87, 91; in Hispanic Protestant churches, 30; in immigrant churches, 14–15; influence of home-country and host-country values and structures on, 42–43; sexism experienced by, 202, 204; single, 42

women, Korean American evangelical: compared

to nonevangelicals, 200–201; and evangelizing non-Christians, 197–98; and feminism, 204–5, 206; first-generation versus second-generation, 198–200; gender relations of, 202–4, 205, 206; identity formation of, 194–98, 205–6

Won Buddhism: circle symbol in, 259 n. 1, 269, 269–70 n. 24, 270, 270 n. 25; and communal life, 264, 265–66; and ethnicity, 261, 261 n. 6, 262, 268–69; founding of, 259 n. 1; goals of, 259 n. 1; and identity, 264–65; and material civilization, 263–64; missionary task of, 18–19, 45; sectarian status denied by, 260, 269–70; and traditional Buddhism, 260, 270; in the U.S., 45, 260–62, 261 nn.5, 7, 269, 270

Wŏnhyo, 230–32, 256, 257

Won Kak Sa temple, 212

World Fellowship of Buddhists, 241

World Society for Zen Academy, 236, 239–40

World Zen Center, 236, 237, 239

Yang, 92

Yi dynasty, 6–7

Yŏng-ho Ch'oe, 228

Yongjin, 244

Yongjo Sunim, 216, 217

Young Nak Presbyterian Church, 36, 37, 48

Young People's Buddhist Movement, 227

Your Mind Meal (Soen Sa Nim), 253

Yu, Eui-Young, 18, 21, 44

Yuen, Peter, 128, 128 n. 6

Yun Koam Sunim, 222 n. 29

Yu Young Soo, 217

Zen Arts Center, 242, 244

Zen Buddhism in North America (Zen Lotus Society), 215

Zen College, 256

Zen Lotus Society, 214, 215

Zen Lotus Society Handbook, The (Zen Lotus Society), 215–16

Zen Meditation Center, 240

Zen Mind Buddha Mind (Seo Kyungbo Sunim), 213

Zen Monastic Experience (Buswell), 247

Zen teachers, 212, 213–19